SEXISM
IN AMERICA

ALIVE, WELL, AND
RUINING
OUR FUTURE

Barbara J. Berg, Ph.D.

Lawrence Hill Books

Library of Congress Cataloging-in-Publication Data

Berg, Barbara J.
  Sexism in America : alive, well, and ruining our future / Barbara J. Berg. —
1st ed.
    p. cm.
  Includes bibliographical references and index.
  ISBN 978-1-55652-776-0 (hardcover)
1. Sexism—United States. 2. Sex discrimination against women—United
States. 3. Sex role—United States. 4. Women—United States. 5. Men—
United States—Psychology. I. Title.

  HQ1237.5.U6B47 2009
  305.420973—dc22

                            2009011473

Interior design: Pamela Juárez

Published by Lawrence Hill Books
An imprint of Chicago Review Press, Incorporated
814 North Franklin Street
Chicago, Illinois 60610
ISBN 978-1-55652-776-0
Printed in the United States of America
5 4 3 2 1

In loving memory of my mother, an early feminist who fought the good fight and taught me never to give up.

And for my husband, who has helped me to fulfill my mother's dreams.

There is no insurmountable solitude. All paths lead to the same goal: to convey to others what we are. And we must pass through solitude and difficulty, isolation and silence, in order to reach forth to the enchanted place where we can dance our clumsy dance and sing our sorrowful song—but in this dance or in this song there are fulfilled the most ancient rites of our conscience in the awareness of being human and of believing in a common destiny.

—Pablo Neruda, *Towards the Splendid City,*
Nobel Lecture, 1971

CONTENTS

ACKNOWLEDGMENTS

I am fortunate to have received ongoing encouragement and support while writing this book. Deborah and Ralph Blumenthal, Jane and John Brickman, Miriam Forman-Brunell, Nina and Peter Cobb, Susan Heath, Rosalind and Bob Konigsberg, Susan Maier, Susan Pollock, Amanda Rolat, Patty Wineapple, and Gerri Woods have all offered cogent, critical insights to the manuscript in its different stages. Their generosity of time and spirit and their unfailing interest and abiding friendships have enhanced my work and kept me going through the inevitable rough spots.

I am also indebted to Lynn La Pierre, who was always at the ready to read and discuss my writing, and whose help in developing my online survey was invaluable. Lynne Hirsh did a wonderful job of designing my Web site, making it possible for me to reach hundreds of women across the country. Kari Etter and Laura Harrington graciously assisted with my many emergency computer problems and saved my manuscript on numerous occasions.

My editors at Chicago Review Press, Sue Betz and Lisa Reardon, have been steadfast allies in this project. I'm deeply appreciative of their commitment to the topic as well as their sage counsel and hard work.

Deborah Schneider, my literary agent, is truly in a class by herself. She is that rare being—uncommonly intelligent, deeply dedicated to her writers, remarkable in her understanding of how and where a manuscript will flourish, and unstinting in her efforts to make it happen. *Sexism in America* originated over the course of several conversations in her office. Her passionate response to the subject matter and her professional expertise transformed our wonderful talks into this book. And while I don't want her to be overrun with authors, she epitomizes the best in the business. I am grateful as well to Cathy Gleason, Britt Carlson, and Victoria Marini of the Gelfman Schneider Agency for their ongoing, enthusiastic assistance.

Thank you also to all the women and school-age girls who took time out of their hectic schedules to answer my survey and then pass it on to their friends, relatives, and colleagues. Your stories have motivated and enriched this endeavor. I have integrated them throughout the book, changing the names of those who requested I do so. Any book as comprehensive as this one has many roots (and many intellectual debts). My thinking has been shaped by students in my history and medical school classes and by the women I've met through various organizations and associations who have touched my life.

My entire family has been magnificent throughout this entire process. The younger generation, especially, has formed the go-to group for reality checks about what's up and "in" with the twenty- and thirtysomething set. My children and their spouses—Alison and Michael Dalewitz, Andrew Schlanger, and Laura and Alexis Maged—have been a constant source of love and enthusiasm. Always available to talk and always interested in my progress, their unflagging belief in my ability to "meet my deadline" made me believe it also, even when time and energy argued otherwise.

Finally, my husband, Arnold Schlanger, has listened to, read, and discussed every aspect of my book. I could not and would not write without him. He is an eternal optimist and my partner in everything. My gratitude extends beyond what I can adequately convey. It is ineffable and everlasting.

My great sadness is that my mother—an educator, social activist, and inspiration—did not live to see *Sexism in America* published. Her death during the final stages of its revision was for all of us an immeasurable loss. I humbly hope that this book, in some small way, honors and pays tribute to her life.

INTRODUCTION

INEQUALITY—THE NEW NORMAL

"**A**live and well?" my dentist asks. "After Hillary almost got the Democratic nomination, and Sarah Palin had the number-two spot on the Republican ticket, how can you say sexism is alive and well?" I wonder if he'd say Barack Obama's presidency has obliterated racial discrimination in America, but before I can ask, he says, "Besides, with so much wrong in this country, why are you worrying about women?"

He lifts a dental mirror and curette from the tray. Since I have a policy never to argue with someone about to put sharp instruments in my mouth, I don't respond as I want to. But my dentist, thoughtful and progressive though he is, has just proven my point. Women are *part* of this country—51 percent of it. And the problems facing us as a nation fall mightily upon them.

Hillary Clinton's candidacy did show women's potential even as it encouraged the Republicans' misguided attempt to woo her supporters with the VP nomination of Sarah Palin. Yet neither candidate, although worlds apart in experience, knowledge, and commitment to women's rights, managed to escape the cage of gender politics—a cage fortified by retrograde media coverage.

Senator Clinton, presenting herself as the most qualified presidential contender, who just happened to have an X chromosome, encountered fierce resistance from a press determined to peg her as a "feminazi." And when the strategy of selecting Governor Palin—intended to buoy up a faltering McCain campaign—sank beneath the weight of its own cynical miscalculations, Palin too became drenched in a tsunami of criticism with a distinctly antifemale hue. "Arm candy," "ditz," "shopaholic," "diva"—charges torpedoed from in- and outside the Beltway. With incredible speed, Palin descended from it girl to mean girl to—in the wake of Team McCain's mudslinging fest—gossip girl.

However much the 2008 election ushered in the stunning historic breach of the racial divide, it also dredged up—and reinforced—chronically familiar ways of demeaning women. The issue of sexism in America, a nonstarter for decades, suddenly flashed before our eyes. A hot topic one week, it cooled considerably the next. But the animosity revealed during the campaigns was only a small outcropping from the solid bedrock of misogyny.

A new and particularly virulent form of sexism is taking root throughout the country. I couldn't expect my dentist to know about it. In truth, I didn't realize its commanding power until I began writing this book a full two years before Clinton launched her campaign—a project I started because of another woman also trying to break into an all-male arena.

"FOR GOD'S SAKE! Why don't they leave her alone?" my friend Roz blurted out. We had just joined a few young women who'd gathered around the television in my son Andrew's apartment to watch Katie Couric on CBS while waiting for the other guests to arrive.

It was October 31, Andrew's birthday. Ever since he was a baby we've thrown him Halloween-themed birthday parties. Over the years they've become an honored tradition, even though Andrew is out of college and now hosts the parties himself. We no longer bob for apples or go trick-or-treating, but we still dress up in costumes, munch from bowls of candy corn, and use my husband Arnie's intricately carved pumpkins for decoration. Best of all, Andrew's Halloween birthday parties remain a gathering of relatives, longtime family friends, classmates, and colleagues—ours as well as our children's. In short, an eclectic mix of backgrounds and ages, somehow always managing to work.

"I liked Katie's 'Hi everyone' and eager smile," Roz continued. "She was really refreshing. Now she's all manned up."

"But that's what they wanted," Lisa, one of Andrew's friends, put in. "There were so many negative vibes about her girlishness. Didn't someone, Dan Rather, I think, accuse the network of going 'tarty' with her?"

"I hate it when men say things like that," my niece, Nancy, said. "Most of the female associates at my firm wear the dark-suit uniform, but there's one who's a little less conservative. She's not over the top by any means, but the guys call her the Law Whore."

"Speaking of whore," my daughter Alison said, quickly glancing at the others' outfits—either homemade or of the traditional black cat or witch variety—"wasn't this year's selection of costumes awful? That's why I decided to go as a Mets fan. It was either this"—she pointed to her team jersey—"or Miss Sexy Sergeant, the Promiscuous Pirate, or some version of it. Everything in the stores looked like leftovers from a *Playboy* photo shoot. I don't ever remember it being like this."

"If you think it's bad for us, it's even worse for little girls," Danielle, another friend, said. "I couldn't find anything in the stores for Hannah that didn't make her look like a six-year-old slut. And it's not just the costumes; it's toys, dolls—everything. Even though I swore I'd never allow it, Hannah is now the proud 'mother' of two Bratz dolls."

Danielle glanced around. "What? You don't know about Bratz?" A few of us didn't. "They're so seductive they could be strippers. Compared to them, Barbie looks like your wholesome next-door neighbor. Hannah's friends don't even play with Barbie anymore—too babyish! They all have Bratz. I was one of the holdout moms, but Hannah got a Yasmin Bratz and a Baby Bratz for her birthday—it made me nuts. And the mothers who gave them to her are really great, they're intelligent. Why aren't they bothered that their daughters are playing with dolls that look like pole dancers?"

"Well, pole dancing is very new wave," Lisa said. I didn't really know her and couldn't tell if she was trying to be funny. "It's just the way our culture is. Look at TV," she continued. "Maybe I shouldn't admit this, but I'm absolutely addicted to *Beauty and the Geek*. One part of me is comparing myself to the contestants. Am I as thin? How did Andrea get her hair that way? But another part hates it when the girls say they use their looks to get what they want. And they're encouraged to act like such idiots. The other night when Drew, who's a major geek, talked about Excel, the girls giggled and mouthed, 'What's that?' The show pushes the same old stereotypes about women. We can't be both smart and pretty, so, of course, it's better to be a bimbo than brainy if we want to be happy."

"I guess that's why so many of my friends are getting boob jobs and tummy tucks," our daughter Laura, from Arnie's first marriage, chimed in. "You remember Vickie?" I nodded. "Well, she had everything fixed. And I mean *everything*."

"She did?" Ali and I gasped in unison. Vickie was Laura's friend from middle school. "I always thought she looked fine," I said. Laura agreed. "But I think she was feeling like, with the kids' schedules driving her nuts and Mark working all the time, she wanted to do something for herself."

For a minute or so no one said anything. Then a woman named Stephanie, a friend of my niece's, spoke. "I can totally relate to your friend," she said to Laura in a voice barely rising above a whisper. "I can't remember the last time I did anything just for myself. Don't get me wrong; I love my kids, and it was my decision to stop work. But Jack outearned me by a lot, there was no decent child care available, and I wasn't in love with the different nannies we had. When we were in the city, we managed, but when we moved to Connecticut the thought of commuting to my office and juggling the boys' schedules and all the after-school stuff was overwhelming."

She paused and glanced around, I think to make sure her husband was out of earshot, then started speaking again in a voice full of emotion. "Once I stayed home, Jack started doing less and less. . . . He doesn't have a clue how insane my days are, how I never have a moment to myself. When I try to point this out to him, it's like I'm background noise; he's not paying any attention. Sometimes when I'm going to pick up one of the kids at karate or something, and I hear a song on the radio that reminds me of when I was younger, I just start to cry. This is so not what I expected."

"Amen to that," said one of Andrew's neighbors, a woman in her thirties. "When I landed my job at Morgan Stanley I couldn't believe how lucky I was. Now I'm not so sure. I started the same year as a few guys in my Dartmouth graduating class. And believe me, I'm already seeing the difference between their careers and mine. Two have been promoted to managing director, and their compensations are off the charts. And the thing is, I just got married; I don't even have kids yet. And already I'm hearing comments from these guys like 'When are we going to see a baby bump?' All of a sudden, I'm not taken as seriously. I feel that women get penalized just for having a working womb. I never say anything about it because I don't want them to think I'm not a team player. I keep thinking I should have gone into another field, but my friends at different jobs are having the same experiences. At least I know I'm on the cutting edge," she said with a forced laugh.

I LISTENED TO these women with an accumulating sense of sadness. What accounted for the undercurrent of malaise so evident in their stories? Evident even though they tried to lighten the dark edges with humor. Evident even though they were all economically comfortable, freed from worries about affordable housing and child care. Here were these women—all beneficiaries of decades of feminism and assumed to enjoy unlimited possibilities for fulfillment and happiness—sounding like members of a 1970s consciousness-raising group. The terminology was different. Words like *objectified* or *second-class citizen* never made their way into the night's conversation as they surely would have back then. But the vulnerability, the sense of powerlessness, and the deep awareness of being treated and even *feeling* that you were somehow a lesser person—that was all there. And it troubled me.

I couldn't stop thinking about it. Not for days, even weeks, after. Why were these women, with so much going for them, slipping into roles rather than deciding upon them? Were these women a skewed sample? Or were they representative of the general population? I didn't know. And if it hadn't been for a paper I had to write, I might not have found out.

Earlier that month, the Horace Mann School in New York had invited me back to address the Women's Issues Club, an organization I'd founded when I was a teacher and dean there over a decade ago. I'd accepted immediately. Few subjects could have been more interesting to me than my planned topic, "The Advances Made by the Women's Movement." I looked forward to talking with these forward-striding students and helping them to imagine meaningful futures, unfettered by rigid gender roles.

Now I felt a nagging uncertainty. That evening at Andrew's party, combined with some reading I'd been doing, had thrown some pretty significant red flags onto the level playing field women have supposedly achieved. And the more I unearthed, the more confusing it became. My discoveries put me sharply at odds with the current prevailing wisdom. Books, news outlets, and popular culture all insist we are living in a glorious, wished-for *post*feminist era. But I was beginning to sense a disconnect between what society tells us about ourselves and what we understand, at our deepest levels, to be so. The last lines of a poem by Muriel Rukeyser came into my head:

> *What would happen if one woman told the truth about her life? The world would split open.*

WHAT *IS* THE truth about women's lives in the new millennium?

I called on experts in a variety of fields, groups of former students, colleagues, young mothers, friends, women I'd interviewed years back for a book I wrote on balancing work and motherhood—women of different ages, backgrounds, experiences, and starting points.

Here's a small sample of what I heard:

When Alexi, a lawyer in New Jersey who'd given birth to twins, returned to work after her maternity leave was up, she thought she was doing the right thing. Instead, the partners said, "I can't believe you're back so soon" and "How could you leave your babies so young?"

"They made me feel as though I was doing something unnatural by coming back to work. It was awful," Alexi told me. "And I became aware of a difference in the way I was being treated. Then I looked around and saw something I'd never noticed before: all the partners are men, except one, and she's not married."

On a different front, thirty-year-old Julia told me, "I still can't believe this happened at one of the biggest hospitals in Chicago. Even though my obstetrician told me that the fetus wasn't growing, the heartbeat was slow, and we were headed for serious trouble, he refused to do an abortion." Not one doctor in the entire practice—eight in all—would do it. Their answer, according to Julia, was "Wait until you miscarry naturally." But the doomed pregnancy took its toll on Julia, her husband, and their three-year-old daughter. With Planned Parenthood booked for six weeks, as a last resort Julia ended up at a dirty, overcrowded abortion clinic, "a horrible, horrible experience," she said.

And on yet another, Evelyn, a home-health aide who couldn't afford private hospital care, described how doctors in an emergency room casually dismissed her seven-year-old daughter's coughing and labored breathing as a "bad cold." Evelyn urged further testing, but they simply sent the pair home. Three days later, when her daughter's temperature spiked to 106 followed by a convulsion, the ER doctors finally ordered a chest X-ray and discovered the pneumonia Evelyn had worried about from the start.

I spoke to thirteen- and fourteen-year-old girls at the best private schools who had to give the boys blow jobs before they were allowed to join lunchtime sports events, incidents of sexual harassment at a top California law school left unaddressed because the female students were afraid to jeopardize their positions, cadets at our service academies so casually viewing pornography online that they didn't even attempt to hide it when faculty walked over.

A health care expert told me about cuts in the budget of the FDA Office of Women's Health that were so extreme they threatened to halt all the office's activities and programs for the rest of the fiscal year. An executive recruiter enumerated the loss of female-held jobs in math, computer science, and engineering as well as in the Fortune 500 companies. The head of a public relations firm confided her concern about the lack of positive role models for girls, leading them to "emulate the antics of the Brit Pack, whose lives seem to be so much more powerful than their own." A college professor friend detailed what the rollbacks in Title IX will mean to her students. A journalist noted how many female bylines are disappearing from our mainstream press.

I learned about Angie, by all accounts a competent and doting young mother, whose ex-husband and new wife were awarded custody of her three-year-old son because Angie was temporarily out of work. I spoke to Jeannie, who left her MBA program because her boyfriend wanted her to become a teacher. There was Jessica, brutally raped in the ladies' room of a New York club and nearly talked out of bringing charges against her assailant by a demeaning and harassing law enforcement team. And Kathy, who would have continued working on Wall Street if she'd had daughters so she'd be a strong role model to them, but with two sons, didn't think it mattered.

And then this, from a former student in my women's history course who has remained close to my family:

> Two months ago I went to speak to one of the partners about a brief I'd written. We were just getting started when he said, "You know, Emily, with legs like yours, you don't have to worry about writing a decent brief." I said, "I'm going to pretend I didn't hear that," and he continued like nothing had happened.

But whenever the partner saw Emily after that, he'd make some little sexual remark. "It made me really uncomfortable," she said. "I mean, this kind of thing isn't acceptable in the workplace anymore. Right?

Emily approached the executive director of the firm, who advised her, "Don't take everything so seriously. The guy's only kidding with you. If you want to stay here you better get used to it. It's a man's world."

"End of story," Emily said, her voice drooping with resignation. "Now I keep hoping I didn't hurt my career."

I simply shook my head, too stunned to say anything. But I couldn't escape feeling that I'd let her down.

LISTENING CLOSELY, I detected a definable thread running through these women's stories—a bending, an acquiescence to situations and conditions seemed shaped to accommodate needs and interests at variance with their own. I became aware of a palpable lack of agency, of validation, a lack of real control over everyday existence reaching across boundaries of geography, class, race, and age. It was as if we were being marginalized in our own stories. What Simone de Beauvoir, writing in an earlier era, famously called the experience of being "the other."

I knew it was becoming commonplace to think of American women, particularly those of the middle class, as suffering from a "too muchness," a glut of options and choices. But I began to question that interpretation. "Choice" is a knotty concept, and, excepting its relevance to reproductive rights, it doesn't necessarily equate with freedom and empowerment. True, we can now "choose" to drive ourselves nuts over getting our children into the best preschools, to go under the plastic surgeon's knife three times a year, to keep working for a boss who refuses to grant well-deserved promotions, to take our chances without health insurance, to get up on a bar and dance topless. But we should all be encouraged to take a hard look at the conditions influencing these choices, to examine what pressures women feel and what limitations are imposed by intractable social and economic institutions, unfriendly business communities, and unresponsive government.

Far from hearing about a "too muchness" in women's lives, I perceived, in fact, a sense of *too little*. Women confessed to feelings of loss, to a generalized insecurity about their futures, to something very wrong at the core of their existence. These emotions weren't expressed as complaints or grievances. Most women accepted the difficulties they encountered. They saw them as individual issues, even as their own fault—as life.

But as I outlined my notes and put the separate pieces together, a far broader picture began to emerge. Larger than the gender pay gap, the "mommy wars," the glass ceiling, or the child penalty. Larger than all these problems women, through the years, have identified and tackled. What I was seeing was endemic and profound, and it sliced through the jaundiced platitudes of postfeminism to reveal a complicated and painful look at the reality of American society today.

I discovered renewed sexism in our national policies and our jobs; on college campuses, the Internet, and major television shows; and in our most intimate relations—an unequivocal resurgence of sexism in this country so potent, so complexly and broadly expressed, so much a product of the twenty-first century, it should be called nothing less than the sexism of mass destruction. Yet astonishingly, the nation is in a collective state of denial over this deepening misogyny and these growing gender inequities. It's as if we'd rather believe that the emperor really has new clothes than confront the naked truth.

A dangerous and startling trend is short-circuiting the inheritance of feminism in every aspect of women's lives. Roles are being redefined both *for* us and *with* us. Measured by every standard, women's independence and self-determination are being eroded. The world of equal rights and treatment that so many of us struggled for, the one I believed and hoped we were still working to achieve, is slowly but most definitely coming apart.

I'm not talking about a repressive Republic of Gilead somewhere in our future, but a danger at our very doorsteps.

How HAVE WE gotten to this point? What has become of the movement dedicated to winning respect for all women—the most significant social revolution of the twentieth century? When did we start to lose our voice? Our sense of authenticity? Our autonomy?

When did inequality start to feel normal again?

Being trained as a historian, I tend to seek understanding in the past. My mind started pedaling back through all the terrible and traumatic experiences our nation has weathered—times of vast uncertainty, sharp pain, and collective grief, when the moorings upon which we'd anchored our lives seemed to be slipping from under us and made us rethink and sometimes reconfigure deeply held notions of gender, sexuality, fairness, sacrifice, responsibility. Without a doubt, we are living through one such time.

I wondered, How much have our anxieties in the wake of 9/11 and in the face of the continuing threat of terrorism made us yearn for the security of traditional roles? To what extent have the war in Iraq and the subsequent masculinization of American politics and culture affected women's position in society? In what ways have the devastating pincers of financial uncertainty narrowed opportunities to escape gender stereotypes?

I thought about how thirty years of conservative influence—the millionaire-backed, prominently placed right-wing think tanks and their media machines—might have impacted our policies and ideas. How the climate of absolutes—good versus evil, us versus them—and the either/or mentality of our nation have shaped our perceptions about gender roles and how we lead our lives, making us believe there's only *one* way to be a good mother, wife, human being. I wondered whether we've become distracted from the real issues uniting women by the media-manipulated "cat fights." Whether we've become so immersed in the ethos of individualism that we've forgotten one another, and so obsessed with celebrity culture we've lost sight of ourselves.

As I looked back over my list of questions, I realized there'd be no simple explanation, no one cause, but an array of multifaceted and overlapping factors, what one of my dissertation advisers, the late Arthur Schlesinger Jr., called "the chronic obscurity of events." Still, when a talented lawyer, a young woman who is like another daughter to me, is told and accepts that "it's a man's world," I knew it was time to start finding answers.

I DEVISED AN online survey and sent it to women I know living all over the country, asking them to fill it out and also to forward it to their relatives, friends, and colleagues across the nation and abroad. Upward of three hundred respondents of various ages and backgrounds wrote detailed answers to the five-page questionnaire; most wanted to have follow-up conversations. And I interviewed an additional two hundred other women. Their stories—honest, humorous, often sad, but always heartfelt—shaped and informed this book. Specifically, they directed me to the starting point. So many women confessed uncertainty about the rights women have and how they'd been secured I realized I had to begin in the 1950s—that ultraconformist era impelling defiantly courageous women to look beyond the sharp inequities, the weary banalities, to imagine shimmering possibilities of a new womanhood.

1

THE AWAKENING OF AMERICAN WOMEN

The room is dark, the music is dramatic. Suddenly, on the screen a brick two-story house comes into view. The camera settles on this shot, imparting a sense of gravity and importance. We watch—as we are meant to—with the awe usually bestowed on one of the seven wonders of the world, but this is just a man's home.

Then the words appear: *Father Knows Best*. And there's a collective groan from my women's history class.

"They really believed that garbage?" someone mutters in the back of the room.

The answer is a resounding yes.

The World of Our Fathers

Television sitcoms of the 1950s reinforced the golden age of masculinity. Whether used to mete out punishment or to resolve a dilemma, the father's patient and all-encompassing authority reigned supreme. His wisdom was Solomonic, his judgment unquestioned. He presided over a world placid as pudding. Toddler hissy fits, mouthing-off teens, and frazzled wives had no place in TV land, with its subliminally consistent messages of order and tradition.

My class is quiet now as the show unfolds. We're introduced to the Anderson family: Jim (Robert Young), his wife Margaret (Jane Wyatt),

1

and their children. Bud is the oldest, followed by two daughters with the unpromising nicknames Princess and Kitten.

A daring producer might have called this episode "Margaret Gets a Life—*Not!*" In it, we get a glimpse of restiveness lurking beneath the bodice of the wifely shirtwaist. Margaret, feeling incompetent because she's the only family member never to receive an award for anything, takes the daring step of entering a women's fishing contest. With help from a pro, she discovers—to her utter amazement—she's a natural. As the day of the competition approaches, Margaret's confidence soars. Victory is in reach. But rushing up the stairs to tell this to a neighbor, she trips and sprains her wrist, deep-sixing any hope of a trophy.

A hand shoots up in the classroom. "Do you think she fell because she was afraid of success?"

"Maybe she was being punished for her self-assurance," another student suggests.

We debate these alternatives without coming to a conclusion. But either way, we agree on one thing: Margaret's sense of self will always be "the one that got away." Margaret's family, while sympathetic to her disappointment, minimizes the loss. Why is it so important to learn how to fish?

In the final scene, they give her the award they think she deserves: a frying pan engraved with the words "World's Greatest Mother." The gift establishes her rightful, really her *only*, role.

Sitcoms like *Father Knows Best*, *The Adventures of Ozzie and Harriet*, *Leave It to Beaver*, and *The Donna Reed Show* are the perfect vehicles to show my students the social hierarchies of the idealized postwar family. However much individual episodes might have differed, they offered the same cookie-cutter characters: the benign breadwinning patriarch, a dutiful mom living in material suburban bliss, and a couple of kids whose missteps always found easy resolution within twenty-two minutes of airtime.

Even watching with my class so many years after these shows ended their spectacular runs, it's easy to understand their popularity. The cult of domesticity may have been light-years away from the reality of how most Americans lived, but it satisfied both private longings and political ideology.

DURING WORLD WAR II, some six million women were recruited into the labor force. Sixty percent were married, and the majority had young children. "There's not a job a woman cannot do," our government said, launching the propaganda effort to enlist women into the workforce. With her iconic bandana and rolled-up sleeves, Rosie was not only a riveter, she welded, cut lath, loaded shells, and handled acetylene torches like the strongest of men.

Uncertain at first, women found they liked their work, basking in the income, friendships, sense of self-worth, and newfound independence. When polled, a staggering 80 percent of these wartime workers said they wanted to stay on the job even after the men returned. As economist Caroline Bird noted in her 1971 book, *Born Female*, "Girls who started working during World War II never learned that some jobs belonged to men and others to women." But they were going to get that lesson soon enough.

Within two months of VJ Day, eight hundred thousand workers, most of them women, lost their jobs in the aircraft industry—a number matched by layoffs in the electrical and automotive industries. Major companies such as Detroit Edison and IBM restored the prewar policy of refusing to hire married women. *New York Times* reporter Lucy Greenbaum, noting these changes, declared "the courtship of women workers" at an end.

With postwar inflation high and memories of the Great Depression's soup lines fresh, experts worried that the economy couldn't support both the returning GI and the newly energized woman. "The war worker cannot be cast off like an old glove," protested labor expert Theresa Wolfson. But cast off they were. By the end of 1946, millions of women had been fired from heavy industry. And women, told one week they could operate cranes, were advised the next to go back to the kitchen and make jam.

The redomestication of the American woman became the driving purpose of prime-time television. Night after night predictable minidramas normalized woman's role as drudge-in-chief. That sitcom characters June Cleaver, Harriet Nelson, and Donna Reed scrubbed floors, chopped onions, and sorted through dirty laundry while implausibly dressed in pearls and high heels imparted a deliberate sense of glamour to their chores. But television women remained all dressed up with nowhere to go—hermetically sealed inside their houses like leftovers pushed into Tupperware and dumped in the deep freeze.

Over the decade, television's popularity surpassed movies and other forms of entertainment. In 1950, 4.4 million families had purchased televisions; ten years later 50 million sets had been sold. For advertisers, television proved to be immensely valuable. As Ella Taylor points out in *Prime Time Families*, it was a "home appliance used to sell other appliances," helping to secure consumerism as the centerpiece of the American dream. By promoting upwardly mobile individuals who had plenty of leisure time, television transitioned women from Depression-bred austerity into a new acceptance of spending.

Each 1950s sitcom episode integrated a subtle sales pitch, from the demure Harriet Nelson taking a salad out of her gleaming Hotpoint refrigerator to the riotous Lucy Ricardo ceaselessly coaxing Ricky into buying something for her or the house. Millions of American women were nightly sold a particular version of the perfect family and the possessions necessary to sustain it.

As women flocked to shopping centers loading up on toasters, washing machines, and ovens, they unwittingly aided our propaganda war with the Russians. In what has come to be called the kitchen debate of 1959, then–vice president Richard Nixon boasted to Soviet premier Nikita Khrushchev about the variety of appliances available to consumers, all "so our housewives have a choice," Nixon said. Proof positive, he believed, of capitalism's superiority over communism.

Throughout the 1950s the cold war menace loomed large. The Soviets were ostensibly a civilization opposed to everything our nation believed in—God, family, free enterprise—and actively plotting our destruction. Each news story sent our anxiety levels soaring. Senator Joseph McCarthy's frenzied reports of spies lurking in our midst seemed authenticated by the conviction of Ethel and Julius Rosenberg, charged with smuggling our atomic secrets to the Soviets. Russia's launching of Sputnik, the first satellite into outer space, and Red China's role in North Korea's invasion of South Korea underscored America's vulnerability. We were engaged in a deadly game of brinkmanship, edging ever closer to nuclear annihilation.

The Federal Civil Defense Administration (FCDA), the 1950s version of today's Department of Homeland Security, fueled terrors of a sneak attack. The screech of air-raid sirens blasted midday test warnings. Spotters rushed to rooftops to stand guard. Along our highways, billboards blazed with images of the searing flash, the mushroom cloud. At any moment, evil could blast from the skies. It wasn't a matter of *if*, but *when*. And Americans needed to be prepared.

Television and movie theaters carried cartoons of the ubiquitous Bert the Turtle—think Barney in today's world—pitching the "duck and cover" campaign. At the command of their teachers a generation of schoolchildren scooted under their desks, trying to imitate a turtle holed up in its shell.

"A clean building seldom burns," declared a CD Alert manual in 1951, ludicrously charging housewives with the task of scrubbing their homes to avoid a nuclear inferno. Our civil defense strategy rested on an unfathomable premise: Americans could prevail in an atomic war. And the key to survival could be found—where else?—in the individual family, divided along traditional gender roles. With women busily scouring and stocking up on emergency supplies, husbands were urged to build home bomb shelters where they and their loved ones could sit out the devastation.

Basements, backyards, garages—all these made for perfect fallout shelters, or grandma's pantries, as they were called, the name meant to evoke a comforting homespun image. Popular magazines used upbeat messages to coax their readers into accepting the family shelter as a part of everyday existence. *Time* magazine in 1959 had this advice: "When you're not using it for an emergency, it can be a perfect playroom for your kids!" And in the same year *Life* told its readers: "Fallout can be fun," featuring a couple who spent their two-week honeymoon in a steel and concrete room twelve feet underground.

While relatively few families actually constructed subterranean hideaways, what the *New York Times* called "shelteritis" loomed large in our collective consciousness. Homes became endowed with transcendent attributes; they were safe harbors, domestic shrines, possessing ineffable powers to nurture and protect. A bulwark against the ever-present threat of wholesale carnage, the idealized home seemed within easy reach of many Americans. The federal GI Bill, granting war veterans educational benefits, job assistance, generous housing loans, and highway construction jobs, hastened our retreat to the sheltering hearth. Sequestered and isolated, the family became invested with a religious aura.

When *Father Knows Best*'s Jim Anderson wins his town's award as a model father, he daydreams of meeting St. Peter, who lauds Jim's status as head of his household, community leader, and scrupulous businessman. Such celestial sanction bolstered the prevailing ideology—men ruled, in both the domestic and political spheres.

Throughout the 1950s, masculine prowess was equated with an impenetrable America. The times called for supersized masculinity, the kind of tough men who populated Mickey Spillane's fiercely anti-Communist, bestselling thrillers—heroes who relished nothing more than murdering unarmed Commies.

Women's function was somewhat different. The only part they were expected to play in keeping the country strong was to maintain the hegemony of their men. And they did this best by being docile and compliant, by making the home a place of serenity, of calm—by living the fantasy they nightly saw on their television screens.

Being a caregiver was a time-honored role, dating back to the Bible. This was what women were *meant* to do. In the aftermath of war, countless women threw themselves back into full-time nurturing and enjoyed it. But what about those who didn't? What about those having trouble fitting their recently realized autonomy into the confines of extreme domesticity? They were held to the script by authoritative, expert voices.

How Are You Going to Keep Her Down on the Ranch (-Style House)?

"An independent woman is a contradiction in terms," said authors Marynia Farnham and Ferdinand Lundberg. Their 1947 bestselling book, The Modern Woman: The Lost Sex, decreed motherhood to be woman's duty, civic responsibility, and true fulfillment. That Marynia Farnham herself enjoyed a successful career didn't seem to blunt her argument or widespread appeal. Women who challenged traditional roles put the nation's security at risk—a view given widespread support by an assorted array of professionals. Female fiends gleefully destroying nationhood and manhood crowded the pages of the prolific author Philip Wylie's books. Gaining international fame for his concept of momism, Wylie popularized the wholesale condemnation of women, but especially mothers, an overbearing lot, he said, raising ineffectual sons too weak to defend America.

The fearful label *emasculating* was stamped on outspoken, successful, or even knowledgeable women, effectively constraining female ambition. In this heyday of Freudian psychology, everyone knew the fate of "castrating" women. They ended up bitter and alone: old maids. By the end of the 1940s the term *ball breaker*, once used by our military to describe a grueling job, became the epithet of choice for a woman who sapped the masculinity from a man.

"I remember clearly being told, and more than once, that I should never win a tennis match against a boy, even though I was an ace player," a woman now in her eighties told me. "There was a long list of don'ts. Like don't ever let a boy know you're smart, and certainly not that you're smarter than he is."

"For the American girl, books and babies don't mix," admonished *Newsweek* magazine in 1946, while eminent psychiatrist Dr. Eustace Chesser, author of *How to Make Success Out of Your Marriage*, chided, "Certainly the happiest women have never found the secret of their happiness in books or lectures." Rather than trying to compete with men—a misguided endeavor doomed to failure anyway—women should stick to their own sphere and make that their life's work.

"Back then it was the two Bs," Gloria Gruber, a woman I interviewed, said, remembering her years as a young suburban housewife in Arlington, Virginia. "Having babies and buying. That's what we talked about, what we were told to do. The more of both, the better!" Lundberg and Farnham underscored this maternal imperative in their book by urging the federal government to award prizes to women for the birth of every child beyond the first.

As never before in our history, women were marrying at younger ages than their mothers. After one hundred years of decline, the birthrate soared in 1956 to a twentieth-century high. The number of women with three children doubled, those with four tripled, sparking the postwar baby boom. College girls proclaimed interest in only one degree—an MRS. In class they daydreamed—not of sex, not even of fairy tale weddings, but of setting the dinner table in a cozy ranch-style home, telling their children to wash up as their husbands came smiling through the door. Recalling her own fantasies, songwriter and singer Carly Simon said, "I was going to live in the kitchen and serve little pouffy mousses with demitasses to my husband."

The postwar consensus rested on the efficacy of the upwardly mobile suburban family to ensure the well-being of its members along with the entire nation. But the mythmakers of the 1950s got it wrong. A comfortable lifestyle remained beyond the reach of much of this country.

By the mid-1950s, some forty to fifty million people, 25 percent of our population, were living below the poverty level. Before Medicaid or any housing or food programs, the tobacco farmers of Appalachia, the African Americans laboring under institutionalized, legal, and vicious segregation, and the Mexican Americans just moving to our cities lived out their days in grinding desperation. This was the "other America" Michael Harrington wrote about in a 1962 book by that name. And its plight would soon "shake the windows and rattle the doors" of the richest country in the world.

And even for those living out the middle-class dream, the headlong rush into marriage and maternity didn't always deliver as advertised. All the Sears catalogs and the do-it-yourself home repair kits couldn't keep the bricks from falling off the hearth.

"It was that third B," Gloria Gruber remembered, "the one we *didn't* talk about: boredom. The terrible, unrelieved boredom of our lives."

The typical day for millions of American women was consumed by housekeeping and child care. Authorities urged making housework more creative and personal and, as a result, more time-consuming. In his 1950 book, *Educating Our Daughters*, Mills College president Lynn White told women to stop wasting their energies on studying abstract science and philosophy and study instead the "theory and preparation of a basque paella, of a well-marinated shish-kebab, lamb kidney sautéed in sherry, an authoritative curry."

Studies coming out of marketing expert Dr. Ernest Dichter's Institute for Motivational Research counseled advertising companies to combat the repetitive, wearisome nature of household chores by initiating a campaign to "make housework a matter of knowledge and skill." You didn't just dump your clothing into the washing machine, you put each item in separately. And as for that all-purpose cleaner? Replace it with one especially for floors, another for countertops, a third for Venetian blinds.

In their efforts to become professional homemakers, 1950s women baked cupcakes from scratch, sewed their own decorations on ready-made clothing, and washed, starched, ironed, and mended—logging in a staggering 99.6 hours of housework per week. They spent far more time, in fact, than their mothers' generation, which *lacked* the new time-saving appliances, had spent on household chores.

But ironically, women weren't looking to save time. When asked by Dr. Dichter's staff to choose among imaginary methods of cleaning, ranging from one process so automatic it was part of the heating system to another one they would have to operate and push, they overwhelmingly chose the latter. As for the easier method, one woman remarked, "Well, what would happen to my exercise, my feelings of accomplishment, and what would I do with my mornings?"

Women I interviewed answered that question by recalling a frenzy of activities. "Oh, I did all the volunteer work imaginable. The museum, the garden club, the hospital, but it doesn't give you much self-esteem. It didn't matter how much I enjoyed the children. I had to do something to get out of that world I was in," one woman said of her childrearing days in Ohio, while another ticked off her twenty-some odd hours a week spent behind the steering wheel going back and forth to the supermarket, her children's schools, and their various after-school activities.

Underneath the busy dailiness of women's lives pooled a deep well of frustration and sorrow. Helen Perlman of New York went back to work as a designer for a Manhattan textile company after her own children were grown. "I stayed home with my daughter because that's what I was supposed to do, but when my daughter was about ten years old I realized that I was walking around crying all the time," she told me. And Betty Schlein, who ultimately became active in politics, recalled her unhappiness with what she called the "classic route"—college, marriage, staying home with the kids. "I wanted to put my head in the oven every day."

Some women did attempt suicide; others courted it with alcoholism and self-medication with drugs such as Valium. They escaped into daytime television and long afternoon naps. Depression rates climbed, but women who consulted psychiatrists were told, "Go home and have more babies."

Describing the postwar era in her book *Occupation: Housewife*, sociologist Helena Lopata said, "This is one of the few times in recorded history that the mother-child unit has been so isolated from adult assistance." In our present self-revelatory day, with so many available ways of telling our stories, it's hard to imagine the conspiracy of silence surrounding the 1950s housewife. One woman, now a great-grandmother, remembering her own despondency as a young mother, said, "You didn't admit these feelings, not even to your best friend."

Shameful, embarrassed, somehow twisted—that's how many women felt. Told they had everything they could possibly ever want or need, their discontentment festered into guilt and confusion. As one woman who left college at nineteen said, "All I ever wanted to do was to get married and have four children. I love the kids and Bob and my home. There's no problem you can put a name to. But I'm desperate."

It was this desperation that Betty Friedan identified in her groundbreaking 1963 book, *The Feminine Mystique*—a scathing indictment of the domestic ideal. "I needed a name for whatever it was that kept us from using our rights, that made us feel guilty about anything we did, *not* as our husband's wives, our children's mothers, but as people ourselves," Friedan reflected a decade later in the *New York Times*.

It was her hope that "women, once they broke through the feminine mystique and took themselves seriously as people, would see their place on a false pedestal, even their glorification as sexual objects, for the putdown it was."

Friedan, who'd given up her career as a journalist to stay home with her children, urged women to break out of their confining roles and "go back to school, pursue careers and revive the vision of female independence that had been alive before World War II."

The book became an instant bestseller, a sensation. Finally someone was looking past the glossy photographs in *Life*, the happy families on the TV screen, to expose the tedious, undervalued, unfulfilled reality of women's lives. Friedan's words resonated with women across the nation. Letters poured in by the hundreds, long, intimate, and terribly sad. Significantly, almost all the mothers expressed the hope that their daughters would avoid falling into the domestic trap.

The World of Our Mothers

Friedan's work spoke to a generation of women, mostly middle class and white, whose efforts prompted the second wave of the women's movement. The first wave had ebbed years before. Its roots were nourished in the early nineteenth century by the countless urban women, hoop-skirted and bonneted, defying tradition to work on behalf of prostitutes and women prisoners. These pioneers with an astonishingly modern agenda campaigned for broader access to education and jobs, better treatment in the family, property ownership rights, and more equitable divorce and rape laws. They articulated a sense of community among women, signing their letters, "Yours in the bonds of sisterhood."

Many of these first wavers joined the antislavery movement and later worked with Elizabeth Cady Stanton and Susan B. Anthony to win the right to vote in 1920. But if the first wave of feminism began as a broad-based movement only to narrow its focus almost exclusively to women's suffrage, the opposite is true for the second wave. Initially identified with Friedan's demand that women be allowed access to male-dominated careers, it became more inclusive and diverse over time. The addition of younger women whose political awareness was forged in the cauldrons of the civil rights and antiwar movements turned the second wave into a dynamic force transforming all of society.

Much of the impetus for change initially came out of the "other America," from African Americans frustrated by a hypocritical American society that rightly crushed Hitler's "master race" doctrine abroad while turning a blind eye to white supremacy at home. Over time, southern black men and women staged a series of protests—the Birmingham bus strike, the sit-in at the Woolworth's lunch counter—against systemized and brutal racial discrimination and striking at the heart of segregation.

As television brought pictures of orderly sit-ins, marches, and boycotts turned ugly by the violent intervention of white racists into living rooms across the nation, millions of Americans saw for the first time the cruelty and dimensions of racism on our own shores. The cause of black, or "Negro," rights became even more compelling, more critical. Donations and legal counsel flowed south. In county after county the black community organized. And women, whether they joined Martin Luther King Jr.'s Southern Christian Leadership Conference or the younger Student Non-Violent Coordinating Committee (SNCC), were crucial to the effort. "In every southwest Georgia county there is always a 'mama,'" one member of SNCC said. "She is . . . outspoken, understanding, and willing to catch hell, having already caught her share."

"The only thing they could do was kill me, and it seemed like they'd been tryin' to do that a little bit at a time ever since I could remember," Fannie Lou Hamer, then a southern sharecropper, said of her decision to join a voters' rights rally. Hamer, who went on to become a key member of the civil rights movement, lost her job and was trampled, jailed, and shot at, but she was never deterred. Her story is one of inspiring transformation, and like innumerable others it shattered the cultural representations of proper female behavior. "For the first time, I had role models I could respect," said a southern white woman after breaking with family tradition to fight segregation.

The civil rights movement originated with the southern black population, but SNCC's launching of the 1964 Mississippi Freedom Summer, a massive effort to free people of color from the death grip of racism by enabling them to vote and providing appropriate health care and education, brought hundreds of northern college kids to the state, then the poorest in the nation and with only 5 percent of eligible black citizens registered to vote. Black women and white women taught side by side in freedom schools established to teach academic skills, citizens' rights, and confidence; assisted in makeshift medical clinics; started libraries; and traveled through desolate rural hamlets registering voters.

Every day the women workers learned about bombs and fires set off at nearby churches and buildings. Under the veil of darkness the Ku Klux Klan fired into the shacks where they slept, forcing them to hide out in the grass. Beatings, arrests, and even death stalked their every move, but the women continued to demonstrate their courage, their skills, and their determination to ignore the harrowing risks. And yet their work was devalued. Few women ever assumed positions of leadership within the civil rights movement. Instead they were expected to do the typing, clerical work, and household chores. Joni Rabinowitz, a volunteer in the southwest Georgia project, wrote, "The attitude around here toward keeping the house neat (as well as the general attitude toward the inferiority and 'proper place' of women) is disgusting and also terribly depressing."

In hushed tones, young women shared their complaints about being used for the other "acceptable" female role—the sex object. The availability of birth-control pills in 1960 held out the promise of enjoying sexuality without worrying about getting pregnant. But liberation became ensnared in the age-old double standard. Women quickly found themselves harassed for saying no and morally suspect for saying yes. Progressive or not, men talked. Flora Davis, a historian of the women's movement, writes, "[I]n too many cases, the sexual revolution simply freed men so that they could use women."

As never before, young women of the 1960s openly began to question male authority. What had civil rights work taught them if not to value each person as an autonomous human being? To fight for the equality of those a bigoted society had demeaned and marginalized? Having witnessed how the unequal power structure between whites and blacks had truncated the lives of the latter, these women began to apply the same analysis to their relationship with men. They'd seen too much, learned too much, developed too much self-confidence to continue as doormats of the movement.

And this perspective spread. "The Uncle Toms of SDS" is how one woman described the female role in Students for a Democratic Society, among the largest, most visible organizations protesting the war in Vietnam. "Here were these men, so willing to go to the barricades to defend their Vietnamese brothers, treating us like slaves," she complained.

But it wasn't until an informal letter, "Sex and Caste," written by Casey Hayden and Mary King of SNCC, circulated among SDS members in 1964, that women began to forge a feminist critique of their experiences. Filmmaker Helen Garvey, in her moving documentary *Freedom Is Contagious*, captured the responses of former SDS members to the Casey-King memo. "I read it and felt moved as never before," Marilyn Saltzer Webb recalled. Suddenly all the bias she'd faced came thundering back to her: how she wasn't allowed to try out for Little League because she was a girl, how her professors wouldn't agree to be on her doctoral committee unless she slept with them, how her grandfather had been opposed to her graduate education. "For the first time women began talking to each other about what it was like to be in their own bodies, their own lives, to think about themselves."

"Until then, we'd never thought about women's issues," said Judy Schiffer of her female friends in SDS. And neither did her male colleagues. Mike Spiegel remembered how shocked he was when a woman coworker called him a male chauvinist. "As obvious as it later became, back then it had never occurred to me that women didn't have the same rights and privileges that I had."

Few men in the movement were willing to give women's concerns a fair hearing. It's an open question whether or not Stokely Carmichael, SNCC's leader, actually said "The only position for women in SNCC is prone," but the statement pretty much summarized the prevailing views. Constantly meeting with scorn and derision and unable to get any attention to the "women question"—unable even to get it on the agenda of the 1967 national convention dedicated to social justice held in Chicago—many young movement women reached a transforming and radical understanding: we can't free others until we, ourselves, are free.

It was a wrenching decision for activist women to put aside their civil rights and antiwar work, to break with the men with whom they'd faced tear gas, billy clubs, and in many cases even the threat of death. But following that Chicago meeting, with a poignant resolve to recast their lives, women formed liberation groups in cities across the nation.

"Seeds were spreading . . . as women understood their own oppression," former SDS member Carol Glassman said, likening the experience to putting on a new set of glasses and seeing the world completely differently. Exuberant, energetic, committed members of "women's lib" groups soon developed an organizing method that would become the hallmark of the movement: consciousness raising, or CR.

In small, intimate, and often informal settings, women like me, like my friends, shared our stories. One woman talked through her tears of discovering that an illegal abortion (the only kind then available) she'd had three years earlier, when she was twenty-two, had left her sterile. Another told about a doctor berating her for "getting hysterical" when she complained about persistent stomach pains. (She later was diagnosed with large fibroids.) A third woman with an enviable college record told how the top law schools had denied her entry because "she'd just end up having kids."

Consciousness-raising sessions disclosed the coherence and patterns behind problems we'd always thought of as individual. Secretly confronted troubles—Jenny's boss grabbing her whenever he passed—no longer seemed random or unique. These problems weren't simply our own but rather the result of a sexist society. Just as a racist society had legalized discrimination against people of color, a sexist society sanctioned the systematic and institutionalized subjugation of women. This is what we meant when we used the phrase "The personal is political."

CR sessions were painful and intense. And they were effective. Anyone could start one anywhere—living rooms, college lounges, neighborhood centers. I remember one beginning among a group of women on a New York City bus. By the early 1970s thousands of women were participating in these small groups. It felt right talking to one another, acknowledging our shared plight. Slowly we recovered and reignited the nineteenth-century language and sentiment of sisterhood. "There wasn't a thing we wouldn't and *didn't* discuss with each other," one woman, now a successful editor and grandmother, recalled.

All that we'd grown up with and accepted as natural was rethought and reevaluated. And we came to feel like we'd been duped. Sold a bill of goods. Why did women have to promise to obey when they got married?

Why were want ads segregated by sex? Why did we have to take cooking classes in high school while our brothers got electronics? Why did men make all the rules? Determine everything about us? Why were women supposed to be terrible drivers? Terrible athletes? Terrible at math? Terrible friends? *Why*? Because men said so!

As WOMEN FURIOUSLY questioned all that they'd been taught, they forged a radical redefinition of women's roles, far beyond what Betty Friedan had imagined. But turning that awareness into a movement for change proved daunting. In their enthusiasm, some younger women of the 1960s short-changed the contributions of those older than they. And both generations underestimated the entrenched opposition they would face.

Discussions started with morning coffee and went past midnight. How could the second-wave agenda reflect more than the experiences of white, straight women? How could it incorporate the voices and concerns of black women, many of whom were ambivalent about blaming males for their secondary status? What about Latinas? Lesbians? Working-class women?

From these debates, often vehement and heated, sometimes missing the mark but always striving for understanding and solutions, emerged a movement that would forever alter the landscape of women's lives and be overwhelmingly acknowledged as the most important social revolution of the twentieth century.

2

FEMINISM TAKES FLIGHT

We moved into the 1970s filled with optimism and energy. "Women's lib" became the big story. It dominated public discourse, and the press jumped to attention. The nightly television news and daily journals all told of a changing society. "The walls of economic and psychological discrimination against women in the American job market are beginning to crack under the pressures of the Federal Government, the women's liberation movement and the efforts of thousands of individual women themselves," declared a front-page article in the *New York Times* on January 31, 1970.

There were monumental successes and plenty of setbacks. But each victory encouraged and inspired others. The women who struggled so valiantly against oppression did so largely without recognition or financial support. What motivated them was a sense of injustice. Like the late Constance E. Cook—a Republican New York state assemblywoman who wrote the state abortion law of 1970, which was used as a model for *Roe v. Wade* three years later—many of their names are unfamiliar today. But their efforts on behalf of future generations are their legacy and precious gift.

Figuring Out Feminism

"I'm not a feminist," a lawyer and mother of two recently told me, echoing familiar words. Whether it's the young women I've taught or those I've interviewed, this disclaimer or its variation, "I'm not a *bra-burning* femi-

17

nist," is all but certain to get inserted into any conversation about work or families. The fact that these women are themselves beneficiaries of feminism, having graduated from previously all-male schools and holding jobs in professions once essentially closed to their sex, doesn't seem to matter.

Adoration, neutrality, uncertainty, animosity—the word *feminism* has seen it all. But lately it's fallen out of vogue. In 1998, 72 percent of the female high school students at an eminent New York prep school said they were feminists. Ten years later, in 2008, only 48 percent did. Some of the naysaying just goes with the territory. As historian Nancy Cott explained, "Like any great, hydra-headed, controversial, world-changing movement with outspoken and courageous leaders, the women's movement attracted derision and has been always subject to reductive portrayals."

Bra burning is certainly one such portrayal. Accepted as an incontestable truth, it's actually a total media fabrication. At a 1968 rally against the Miss America beauty pageant, demonstrators tossed hair rollers, spike heels, girdles, and an occasional bra into a "freedom trash can." LET'S JUDGE OURSELVES AS PEOPLE, the signs said. In *Moving the Mountain*, historian Flora Davis called the rally a protest against how "women in our society [are] forced daily to compete for male approval, enslaved by ludicrous 'beauty' standards." But nothing was set on fire. The only thing blazing that day was some reporter's imagination.

The bra-burner image got a lot of play. News outlets breathlessly depicted the movement as dominated by bad-haired, braless women screaming slogans while rejecting femininity and their families in one big heap. In reality there was no way to tell a feminist by the way she dressed. A few madras shirtwaists and penny loafers might pop up at rallies, but mostly there'd be young women in the blue work shirts and jeans of the protest movements, others in long skirts and embroidered vests, coarse-knit ponchos over skinny-legged pants, and always a sprinkling of Carnaby Street mod miniskirts and boots. Hair got longer, makeup lighter. Everything leaned in the direction of ease and comfort. If a fashion dictum existed, it was "Be yourself." But making feminists into caricatures has always been a way to trivialize their beliefs, leaving many women confused about the driving principles of the women's movement.

"I'VE NEVER BEEN able to find out precisely what feminism is," Rebecca West wrote sarcastically in 1913, "I only know that people call me a feminist whenever I express sentiments that differentiate me from a doormat."

Throughout history women articulated feminist views without giving them a name. "[There is] no feeling more universal among . . . human beings than the desire to be independent, to take care of themselves. [I]t's lamentable that there should be so large a portion of the human race so educated that they must be dependent on others," proclaimed the "Wrongs of Women" in 1854. The author concluded by mocking male objections: "'Oh, you deprive woman of her many charms if you make her self-reliant and give her independence,' exclaim the very many who are fearful of the encroachments of females upon their privileges and prerogatives."

Almost forty years after that article appeared, the word *feminist*, articulated at the First International Women's Conference in Paris in 1892, entered the English language as the translation of *féministe*. Today, as back then, the term means someone who believes in equality of the sexes. From that radical premise came the notion that women should be granted equal rights, equal treatment, and equal opportunities.

Feminism puts women's autonomy at the center of its agenda, insisting that all women be treated as fully human beings, not as appendages to men and creatures whose only identity comes from their roles as wives, mothers, daughters, and sisters. It looks forward to the day when women are free to define themselves rather than being defined by men and the culture they control.

We're not there yet, but we're much further along than we were before the 1970s, back in those dark ages when a girl's future was mapped out at birth, when you couldn't wear slacks without being excommunicated from your church, when you were expected to stop your education after high school so your brother could go to college, when you could be refused service at a restaurant if you were dining alone and refused a credit card or mortgage if you were single, when you couldn't refuse to have sex with a diseased husband, an abusive husband, any husband, when women "asked to get raped" and "needed a good slap."

The Personal Becomes Political

"I wish it was me. I wish it was me," my mother cried one evening in the spring of 1959.

I was afraid and confused. What my mother had just told me was terrible—my forty-six-year-old father had just been diagnosed with Parkinson's disease. Why in the world did *she* want to be the sick one?

"Because Daddy would be able to take care of me and the family," she explained. "What will I be able to do? I have no job, no income. How will I get him the best treatment? How will I support us?"

Then she looked at me gravely and said, "You must always be able to work. Do you hear what I'm telling you? Do you hear me?"

And I did.

At the time I didn't understand why my mother was so worried about finding a good job. I thought she was amazing. The daughter of immigrant parents whose income had fluctuated with my grandpa's factory work, she'd put herself through Barnard College working nights and weekends at Macy's Department Store. But then, I didn't yet know about the cultural noose around women's necks—the workplace discrimination, ghettoized jobs, and paltry pay strangling us into self-doubt.

Several years later, feminists fought to secure myriad employee rights for women like my mom and for the millions of others across America who wanted paying jobs. An early opportunity came with the Civil Rights Act of 1964, outlawing discrimination against race in the workplace. Women's groups lobbied hard to make it illegal to discriminate on the grounds of gender as well.

Ah, said southern congressmen, we'll support the addition, but *only* because it will ensure the bill's defeat. "Who's going to vote to protect women's rights?" they snickered among themselves. Imagine their shock and amazement when their cynical scheme backfired.

Title VII, the amendment to the act, banned sex discrimination in the workplace. A major victory, it applied to every kind of job and to the majority of American businesses. But the law was only as strong as its enforcer, and instead of Clint Eastwood, women got Howdy Doody. As Flora Davis reported, the Equal Employment Opportunity Commission

(EEOC), the federal agency set up to implement the new policy, had only one female commissioner and four men whose interest in stopping prejudice against women ranged from "boredom to outright hostility." And that's just what two flight attendants, or stewardesses, as they were then called, encountered when they arrived at the newly opened EEOC offices in 1965 to file their complaints. Barbara "Dusty" Roads and her colleague Jean Montague worked at "glamorous" jobs. Girls grew up dreaming to join airline cabin crews. Stewardesses blended the ideal feminine qualities—nurturing, serving, seeing to the comfort of men—with cheerleader good looks. One of the few positions available to women, it was considered perfect training for marriage.

"We wore high heels and hose, and we were supposed to wear girdles. Occasionally they'd do a girdle check . . . they come up and give you a little finger on the rear end. If you didn't have a girdle on you'd be called into the office," Roads recalled. Gaining weight resulted in firing. So did getting married.

The airlines capitalized on the image of the stewardess as young, single, and enticing. At one point, the uniform for Eastern Airlines' stewardesses consisted of skimpy hot pants. An airline executive explained the general thinking: "It's a sex thing. You put a dog on an airplane and twenty businessmen are sore at you for a month."

"I'm Cheryl [or Joan or Nancy]. Fly me," an attractive woman beamed in a $9.5 million advertising campaign for National Airlines. Stewardesses had to wear Fly Me buttons on their uniforms, prompting suggestive comments and sexual advances from male passengers.

But Roads and Montague hadn't come to the EEOC offices because of girdle checks or ad campaigns. They were protesting the airline's policy of firing women at age thirty-two. They didn't fire pursers or pilots or flight engineers at thirty-two—why stewardesses?

The airlines had a huge economic motive. With the average stewardess lasting only three years, they saved megamoney firing those young women before they had time to accumulate pay increases, vacation time, and pension rights. This left the stewardesses, unable to put away much if anything from their paychecks, with few options.

"I was twenty-eight . . . and absolutely hysterical," Lynda Oswald with American Airlines said, reflecting on the age policy. "I was trying to prepare myself for another job, but when I tried to get into a university, they wouldn't accept me as a part-time student. The whole climate was catch-22."

"It wasn't a question of being a feminist or not," Roads recalled. "It violated my sense of fair play." Once the facts came out, Roads predicted change would come immediately, a hope she later called naïve.

The case, derisively referred to as the Old Broad's Bill, languished. The women's cause attracted attention, but the wrong kind. Instead of talking about the discriminatory nature of the age rule, commentators focused on the women's looks. The central question became: at thirty-two, were they still appealing enough to keep their jobs?

When stewardesses from several airlines came before the House Labor Subcommittee, one of the members asked them to "stand up so we can see the dimensions of the problem." Finally, frustrated Michigan congress-woman Martha Griffiths blurted out, "[Are these companies] running an airline or a whorehouse?"

The involvement of Betty Friedan's newly formed National Organization for Women (NOW) ultimately helped put the spotlight back on the real issues at stake. "Supporting the stewardesses was a huge step back then," one early NOW member told me. "We kept our membership secret because we were afraid if our employers found out, we'd lose our own jobs."

NOW's determined lobbying of the EEOC, combined with the unre-lenting pressure from Roads and Montague's attorneys, finally paid off. After three years, the age and marriage restrictions both disappeared. Barbara Roads resumed flying, and NOW, along with dozens of organiza-tions such as the Women's Equity Action League (WEAL), continued their fight for workplace equity.

A Woman's Work Is Never . . . a Man's

By the early 1960s, 40 percent of all American women over age sixteen were employed, most in low-paying, low-status positions—secretaries, waitresses, salesclerks, nurses. Want ads were universally segregated by sex. The separate columns for "Help Wanted—Male" and "Help Wanted—Female" allowed for virtually no crossover. This policy kept women locked into what Betty Friedan described as gal Friday jobs.

For a great many this meant settling on careers well below their qualifications and interests. A woman with a degree in mathematics scanning the female help-wanted section in a newspaper like the *Pittsburgh Press* would find advertised positions for key punch operators, invoice clerks, or kitchen help, but never programmers or systems analysts.

Complaints brought to the EEOC went unnoticed. The commission agreed to get rid of the want ads separated by race—*that* they understood was unfair. But sex? No way. By and large, men resisted having to compete with women at work. They wanted to stick with the status quo—limiting the number of hours a woman could work, not allowing her overtime, denying her promotions if she married, and firing her when she became pregnant. Then they could point to her economic insecurity as a reason to deny her credit and a mortgage.

Male-only jobs became symbolic of male privilege and prerogatives, of maleness itself. My sex, one man explained at an EEOC hearing in 1968, has been forced to submit to the tyranny of women as children. We aren't about to submit to it again with women as our supervisors. Newspaper cartoonists had a heyday. Their sketches of angry women storming corporate men's rooms disclosed unspoken anxiety over the meanings and implications of gender equality.

It took almost a decade and a Supreme Court case in 1973 against the *Pittsburgh Press* before feminists could count the abolition of sex-segregated want ads among their victories. Women could now enter the forbidden occupations—airplane pilots, carpenters, engineers, mail carriers, orthopedists.

Other successes followed throughout the 1970s. Tirelessly going state by state, brief by brief, feminist lawyers fought to make it illegal for a prospective employer to question a woman about marriage and family plans during an interview. No longer could she be fired when she became pregnant, or discriminated against in promotions or salary. And married women could not be denied credit cards in their own names or the right to mortgages.

As the Twig Is Bent, So Is It Trampled

For all the workplace gains made by feminists during the 1960s and 1970s, one area remained untouched—nothing prohibited sex discrimination in *education*. And there was plenty of it, on all levels. From kindergarten through high school, school systems across the country educated, instructed, and socialized girls and boys as though they were polar opposites.

"Everything schools did back then was based on the assumption that boys were active, aggressive, analytical, and autonomous and girls were demure, docile, and fairly helpless," Barbara Sprung, codirector of the Education Equity Center, a pioneer in gender equity education, told me. "From kindergarten on, when girls were encouraged to play in the dress-up corner, draping themselves with beads and long scarves, and boys got to build with blocks, schools gave a particular social message." And it was reinforced again and again.

Teachers used readers for young children and textbooks for older ones filled with stereotypical images. But before the women's movement, no one seemed to notice. One survey conducted in the early 1970s of 134 school readers found boys to outnumber girls as main characters by five to two. And while men were portrayed in forty-seven different jobs, women hardly ever worked outside the home. They meandered across the pages as one-dimensional characters, insipid, unintelligent, uninspiring, too meek to make any decisions on their own.

"In the readers, boys are still adventuresomely, mischievously, athletically boys. They get into wonderful scrapes. They have fun. Mother and sister watch admiringly, pausing occasionally to shudder at frogs or snakes. Or elicit the advice of authority figures, doctors, teachers, savvy farmers, all of whom are male. In math textbooks, illustrations show girls baffled by simple measuring cup arithmetic," said Barbara Grizzuti Harrison, author of *Unlearning the Lie: Sexism in the Classroom*.

Among the most popular of the genre, the Dick and Jane series was updated in 1965 to include new African American next-door neighbors, yet its sexist messages were never modified:

Johnny says: Girls are no fun.
Dick says: Girls are stupid.

Janey says: Even though I'm just a girl, I'm not stupid, I want to be
    a doctor when I grow up, but I know a girl can't be a doctor.
Dick says: I will be an engineer.
Sally says: I want to be a Mommy.

A woman who started teaching in the New Jersey school system in 1967 and stayed for twenty years described what she called "a kind of tracking":

> There are so many things I could point to, but one really stands out: how we only coached male students to compete for the Westinghouse Scholarship. It was very prestigious, and our math and science teachers used to work with boys after school and on weekends with their projects, but I can't remember any of them doing that for a girl. In the same way, we encouraged boys to take advanced physics and biology and calculus courses. Typically if a girl was interested in science we'd steer her toward nursing. A lot of it was so subtle, we weren't even aware of it, like calling on boys more often than girls in our classroom, making them hall monitors and heads of committees, taking their questions more seriously, accepting that they'd be the leaders of student government, and of course, the way all the sports programs were totally geared to the boys.

"I can't remember ever playing a competitive sport," Marilyn Katzman, a graduate of Erasmus Hall High School—one of the largest in New York City—recalled of her school days in the mid-1960s. "Most of our gym periods were given over to learning about 'feminine hygiene' and practicing for the Miss Erasmus Hall Contest. . . . There was a huge gap between what boys and girls got to do. They played football and basketball, and the only way girls got on the courts was during halftime, cheering the guys on as 'Boosters.'"

All over the country, school curricula underscored this restrictive, secondary female role. No matter what the subject, women's viewpoints and contributions were entirely missing. In "Art Appreciation" you'd learn about Monet, Renoir, and Pissaro, but never about Cassatt. As for history—you could spend a whole year studying America's past, and the only women mentioned were "crazies" like the Salem "witches" and Lizzie Borden, the ax murderer, along with the "exceptional worthies"—Harriet Tubman or Eleanor Roosevelt. Great literature courses totally overlooked Virginia Woolf, Edith Wharton, and Maya Angelou in favor of Herman Melville, Thomas Hardy, and Edgar Allan Poe.

"Our schools view women's education as training for subservience rather than as equipping her to choose her own potential by exploring a wide range of possibilities," wrote author and educator Jenny Bull in 1974. "Role models for girls and young women wanting to break out of the mold barely existed, and certainly not in the school system."

Several years into the women's movement, men still held 80 percent of the elementary school principal positions (up substantially from the 1950s), 98 percent of high school principal positions, and 99 percent of supervisor positions. Women, of course, comprised the vast majority of public school teachers. In explaining these figures, some men cited the cultural assumption that the female role was to care for children, not to become administrators. In 1975 Dr. William L. Bitner III, the commissioner for instructional services of New York State's education program, expressed the most common thinking: school boards and schools are "run like the boards of directors of any big corporation—by men."

But as those working for sex equality in education pointed out, the male monopoly constituted a "subtle form of teaching." As women were shuttled into less academic, gender-specific classes, then refused entry into the most renowned schools and universities, then told they lacked the credentials for anything beyond traditional women's jobs, they were indeed being taught that it was a man's world, and they occupied a peripheral place in it.

Speaking out, protesting, and condemning treatment that most women accepted as normal took a tremendous amount of will. Just understanding you were discriminated against was a first and very difficult step. And if you took it, then what? Would you chance being criticized, even ostracized? But many women did take the risk for themselves and for others.

"No one wanted to be called abrasive or militant or unfeminine," Joanna said of her graduate school days in Michigan during the Vietnam War in 1968. "The male students were always asking, 'What's a girl like you doing in a place like this?' At first I tried to ignore it, but finally I got so angry I snapped back, 'One thing's for sure, I'm not avoiding the draft.' Why were my motives more suspect than theirs? I hated the implication that my only reason to be in there was to find a husband."

"Let's face it. You come on too strong for a woman," one of Bernice (Bunny) Sandler's colleagues explained when she was turned down, yet again, in 1969 for a full-time teaching position at the University of Maryland. Sandler had been teaching part-time for several years. Her qualifications, everyone agreed, were excellent, but she was never considered for any of the seven openings in her department. Her colleague's words sent her home in tears.

What did *too strong* mean? Sure, she had voiced her opinions with conviction at department meetings, but so did several men who got promotions. Still, Sandler accepted the label and vowed to be more soft-spoken. As for being discriminated against, she didn't buy it. Not yet. But when an employment counselor told her she wasn't really a professional, but just a housewife (with a Ph.D.) who'd gone back to work, and a research executive spent an hour telling her how he never hired women because they stayed home when their children were sick, she saw the pattern.

The existing laws, even the Equal Pay Act preventing discrimination in salaries on the basis of sex, exempted all professional and administrative employees, including faculty. But as a good researcher, Sandler kept digging until she hit upon something that made her cry out loud with joy.

An old executive order prohibiting "federal contractors from discrimination in employment on the basis of race, color, religions and national origin" had been amended, according to a footnote, by President Johnson in 1968 to include discrimination based on *sex*. Universities, colleges, secondary schools—all had federal contracts. The repercussions were huge!

Sandler sprang into action. Her first call to the Office of Federal Contract Compliance of the Department of Labor put her in touch with Director Vincent Macaluso, who'd actually been waiting for someone to use the executive order to challenge sex discrimination. Together they contacted the Women's Equity Action League. Soon afterward the organization filed a complaint, charging Sandler later wrote in a 1997 issue of *About Women on Campus*, "'an industry-wide pattern' of discrimination against women in the academic community." The authors of the complaint asked for an investigation in the following areas: admissions quotas to undergraduate and graduate schools, financial assistance, hiring practices, promotions and salary differentials.

What they found was astounding, Sandler recalled. "Many departments had no women at all, though women earned as much as 25 percent of the doctorates in those fields. The higher the rank, the fewer the women; the more prestigious the field, department, institution, the fewer the women."

Hearings, drafts of bills, and more charges followed. Working quietly and steadfastly, a team of dedicated feminists, men as well as women, within and outside of Congress, succeeded in amending the Equal Pay Act in 1970 to give it widespread coverage; and more significant, two years later, they passed Title IX of the Education Amendment of 1972 to the Civil Rights Act of 1964.

Title IX, mandating equal treatment in all arenas, including athletics, transformed the terrain of American education. However revolutionary its scope, the bulk of the backlash was at first aimed at sports programs.

High school administrators balked at having to take money from boys' teams to pay for girls' athletics. Then there was the whole question of space. Accustomed to using the girls' gym for male sports like wrestling and basketball, coaches like Ron Wied at a high school in Wisconsin were perturbed. "I think girls have a right to participate, but to a lesser degree than boys," he said. "If they go too far with the competitive stuff they lose their femininity."

As for girls playing against boys? Charles Mass, secretary of the Indiana State Coaches Association, wasn't so sure about that either. "There is the possibility that a boy would be beaten by a girl and as a result be ashamed to face his family and friends. I wonder if anybody has stopped to think what that could do to a boy."

Title IX made possible the admission of girls to Little League baseball and raised women's status in professional sports. The question of women's athletic talents culminated in the famous 1973 match between tennis hero Bobby Riggs and Billie Jean King. Thirty thousand viewers crammed into the Houston Astrodome—the largest crowd ever for U.S. tennis—to watch this "battle of the sexes." Las Vegas oddsmakers were five to two in favor of Riggs, but King won effortlessly.

But those who thought King's victory would put issues of equity in athletics to rest were sorely disappointed. School administrators and coaches continued to battle over implementing Title IX. Did *equal* mean girls having their own teams, budgets, and playing fields? Or, as some argued, should they be allowed to try out and, if good enough, play on the regular, previously all-male football and wrestling teams, knowing that most girls wouldn't make the cut? And some girls actually accepted on male squads had the same experience as Amy Mojica, who didn't exactly receive a warm welcome when she joined her high school's varsity lacrosse team. Several teams in their league refused to play against them, and when they did, the players would sometimes try to injure her.

Other parts of Title IX left less room for interpretation. If girls and boys, young women and men, were to have the same education, then books, admissions policies, and curricula had to be totally revamped. And many were. Previously all-male schools opened their doors to women, and the service academies slowly became coed.

History Through a New Lens

Along with women's advances in education and academia, women's studies courses, many supported by federal money, proliferated in colleges across the country—from seventeen courses dealing with women in 1969 to more than two thousand by 1973. Feminist scholars began reexamining academic subjects from the point of view of women, and there were plenty of surprises. The late Renaissance historian Joan Kelly (Gadol) hadn't really expected the Renaissance, always heralded as the great rebirth of learning after the Dark Ages, to have been any different for women than it had been for men. But at the urging of Gerda Lerner, a leader in the women's studies movement, Kelly agreed to take another look at her field.

What she found was transforming. The experience, she said, was akin to being plunged back into adolescence: "Profoundly frightening [with] all coherence gone . . . [but it] turned out to be the most exciting intellectual adventure. I knew now that the entire picture I had held of the Renaissance was partial, distorted, limited, and deeply flawed."

Kelly's groundbreaking 1977 article, "Did Women Have a Renaissance?" reveals how women actually lost economic independence and status during those years. Ironically, they'd actually been freer and more autonomous during the Dark Ages. Her article made crystal clear the extent to which the history everyone had been taught up until the 1970s rightly should have been called men's history, or white men's history. Written from the vantage point of the powerful, it drew only from their sources and reflected only their interests, goals, and successes.

This understanding was applied to every discipline, and it had an electrifying effect. So much of the received knowledge and wisdom, so much of what we all accepted, turned out to be one-sided, skewed, simply wrong.

Women's scholarship exploded all over the country and world. Seminars, conferences, journals, new professional organizations, articles, books, and women's bookstores proliferated. For me, teaching women's history at Sarah Lawrence College in those years under the direction of Gerda Lerner was an exhilarating experience.

My husband, Arnie, bought me a poster that proclaimed WOMEN'S HISTORY IS A WORLD WORTH FIGHTING FOR. I proudly hung it on my office door and have taken it with me every place I've taught since. And, in the beginning, it *was* a fight—to get our papers published in national journals, to be asked to review books, to be taken seriously. At professional conferences male colleagues, on hearing what I taught, would joke, "Oh, women's history? You must read the one book over and over again!"

Notwithstanding the wisecracks and put-downs, early feminist work did come in for some legitimate criticism. Missing from the analyses were the experiences of women of color, bisexual and gay women, and working women. Recent scholarship by and about women from a variety of backgrounds has done much to correct this imbalance and adds depth and a vital appreciation of the rich diversity of women in this country.

3

GENDER ROLES UNDER FIRE

Women's ongoing struggles for equal opportunities at work and at school, although laden with difficulty, didn't elicit the intensity of feelings brought out by the quest for equality at home. Challenging the conventional notions of femininity, motherhood, and domestic responsibilities as well as the power structure of male and female relationships, feminists encountered fury, pain, insecurity, and a lot of misunderstanding as they probed our deeply held beliefs and values about human nature.

Specifically, they asked: why should male babies be encouraged to be active and inquisitive while female babies be trained in passivity? Why should women be responsible for all the housework *and* the child care? Why should our popular culture, our very language, implicitly accept male superiority?

As women's groups of the 1970s and early 1980s recast accepted practices as *problems*, they stimulated a sea change in the way men and women talked and thought about their lives—not always happily or in agreement with feminist ideology, but certainly with a new consciousness of gender.

Homeward Bound

In the 1970 film *Diary of a Mad Housewife*, the most desperate of the early "desperate housewives" was Tina Balser (Carrie Snodgress), married to Jonathan, an arrogant, controlling, social-climbing attorney. Jonathan rules with a heavy hand, micromanaging Tina, whom he infuriatingly calls Teen. Nothing escapes his scrutiny: he tells her how to dress, how to style her hair, what to make for Thanksgiving dinner.

Jonathan's mean-spirited domination goes unquestioned. Only once does Tina timidly ask about his investment in what turns out to be a bank-rupting deal. His raging "How dare you question me?" effectively silences her.

Although she runs around the house doing Jonathan's bidding with the speed and repetition of a hamster on a treadmill, he faults everything she does. His special pleasure is demeaning her in front of the children. At the breakfast table with his daughters next to him, he mockingly asks, "Isn't it funny that Mommy managed to be Phi Beta Kappa at Smith, but doesn't know how to make four-minute eggs?"

The girls follow his lead. The older one, coming home from school and finding dog poop on the rug, tells her, "You bloody well better clean up this mess before Daddy gets home."

Slowly we see Tina, the quintessential housewife, driven crazy by the stultifying domestic realm. When finally she retreats into what Jonathan considers unresponsiveness, the audience understands—it is the sanest thing she can do.

In another take on the traditional marriage, *Up the Sandbox*, a belea-guered Margaret (Barbra Streisand) asks Paul, her college-professor hus-band, what she's getting from their marriage other than "stretch marks and varicose veins."

"You've got one job," she yells. "I've got ninety-seven! Maybe I should be on the cover of *Time*. Dust Mop of the Year? Queen of the Laundry Room! Expert on Tinker Toys!"

When Paul suggests maybe she'd be happier if she did more, she snaps. "Did more? I cook, I sew, I squeegee. I spend hours waiting in line for a sale on baby sandals just to save a few pennies. . . . I'm an errand boy, a cook, a dishwasher, a cockroach catcher, and you say I'd be happy if I did more."

And what about those women to whom "doing more" meant holding a paying job? In the 1978 book *Silences*, author Tillie Olsen articulated the deeply felt incompatibilities between motherhood and pursuing one's life work:

More than any other human relationship . . . motherhood means being instantly interruptible, responsive, responsible. Children need one *now* . . . the very fact that these are real needs, that one feels them as one's own (love not duty) . . . gives them primacy. It is distraction, not meditation, that becomes habitual. . . . Work interrupted, deferred, relinquished, makes . . . at best lesser accomplishment. Unused capacities atrophy, cease to be.

But how to resolve this conflict? Were women, as Olsen suggested, "obligated to shut off three-quarters of [their] being"? Or could there be other possibilities?

For many second-wavers, one answer lay in restructuring family roles. If men took on half of the domestic responsibilities, then women could fulfill their own aspirations—careers, hobbies, philanthropy, a fifteen-minute bath, whatever. And although feminism's detractors love to chide women for being simpering babies, complaining when they can't "have it all," we never envisioned doing everything ourselves.

That the traditional family would become more egalitarian was an article of faith. The second wave wasn't only about liberating women; we believed it would liberate men, too. "Fewer ulcers, fewer hours of meaningless work, equal responsibility for [the] children," Gloria Steinem said before the Senate in 1970.

So many women had only vague memories of their fathers as they were growing up, they wanted something different for their husbands and sons. "It wasn't until my dad retired and became a grandfather that I saw a side of him for the first time—how great he was with kids, how much he was enjoying himself," one woman told me. "I felt like I had been cheated, and I think he did too."

The Great "Nature Versus Nurture" Debate

To those who claimed—as many did—that iron-clad, distinct male traits, diametrically opposed to female traits, made it impossible for men to be nurturers, we countered with arguments of our own. Many of us had seen firsthand enough of the devastation wrought by the so-called scientific studies of "Negro intellectual inferiority" to discount such theories as biased. After all, as Gloria Steinem noted in her Senate testimony, scientists had justified English domination of Ireland for over a century by "proving" the "English were descended from angels and the Irish from the apes."

Scholars in every field, examining the teachings of biology, primatology, psychology, and anthropology, amassed mountains of evidence negating innate gender-difference theories. The idea that the disparities we saw between men and women related far more to socialization than to any inherent traits resonated widely. Study after study conducted during the 1970s revealed the extent to which gender imprinting began right after birth. And it went way beyond simply choosing pink or blue onesies. A whole constellation of ideas, attitudes, and behaviors—many handed down from generation to generation—descended upon the delivery room the moment the umbilical cord was cut.

"Doesn't he look like a bruiser?" "Isn't she beautiful?" Educational films of new parents revealed how fathers and mothers immediately began ascribing stereotypical characteristics to infants. What's more, parents treated babies of different sexes differently. Crying baby girls were picked up faster and held longer than baby boys. By six months, male babies were being bounced on fathers' knees and tossed into the air while baby girls were still nestled and soothed.

In one study, male and female toddlers, given a series of progressively difficult tasks to perform, tackled them with equal skill. Researchers, hidden behind one-way mirrors, watched parents consistently encourage their sons to persevere until they finished each project, but jumped in to assist their daughters, often completing the assignments for them. The same kind of interactions pervaded the playground. Caregivers kept a close watch on little girls and monitored their behavior. Not so little boys. They got considerably more latitude, allowed to venture farther and to choose more strenuous, challenging activities—rope climbing, playing on the jungle gym, and the like. From the get-go, boys learned to power through life, girls to be dependent and wary.

"I can still remember how envious I felt of my younger brother," Claudia, a forty-four-year-old woman I interviewed, told me. "He got wonderful adventure games, beautiful *National Geographic* magazines, a piggy bank so he could save his money for something special. All I got was this doll whose hair I could comb. Why was I born with an inquiring head if I couldn't use it? I thought. I wanted adventures, also."

When feminists of the 1970s peeked into the toy chest, they saw everything for girls was "pretty in pink" and lavender and pale yellow. Boys' playthings came in bold, brave, *manly* colors: green, navy, and black. Girls' toys encouraged passivity, nurturing, homemaking, and fashion: play kitchens, beadmaking, dolls. Boys' toys were all about action, strength, and ingenuity: erector sets, trucks, model airplanes.

While many parents insisted (and still do) that boys and girls "naturally" gravitate toward stereotypical "boys" or "girls" toys, Kathleen Alfano, manager of the Fisher-Price experimental laboratory, suggests a different reality. "[The fact is] girls and boys will play with anything— from toy trains to vacuum cleaners—until age three," Alfano said. After that, parents seem to push children into more gender-specific items. In the lab, little girls loved a fire truck equipped with a real water-squirting hose, but it ended up in the shopping cart of mothers with sons. And the play stove? Few parents would think of buying it for boys even though they showed far more interest in it than the girls.

However intimidating reversing these trends might have seemed, second-wavers had tremendous energy and optimism that we'd be successful. *Ms.* magazine, launched in 1972 under the leadership of Gloria Steinem and Robin Morgan, popularized feminist positions and provided monthly "Stories for Free Children," showing children playing with gender-neutral toys.

Unisex. Nonstereotypical. These words gained a lot of currency in the 1970s and 1980s. Schools began encouraging both boys and girls to play together with police cars and building blocks, and in the dress-up corner. Soon you were as likely to see attaché cases dangling from the shoulders of little girls as little boys, and children of both sexes wearing aprons in the "cooking" corner. Kindergarten teachers, who noticed little girls wearing party dresses to school, often sent letters home suggesting they wear "play-appropriate clothing."

For Halloween we dressed our children as black cats, ghosts, and goblins. Sure there were Cinderellas and Tarzans, but they weren't the majority. Looking through my own photo album, I see that in the early 1980s my daughter Alison went trick-or-treating as Little Orphan Annie and my son Andrew as Punjab, but the next year she was a scientist and he a rock star. The whole point was for our children not to be limited, to think outside of the gender box.

We listened for hours on end to the 1972 album *Free to Be . . . You and Me*, on which a star-studded cast saluted individuality and self-worth. Our family's favorite songs were about William, who wanted a doll so he could grow up to be a good father, and Atalanta, the fastest runner in the kingdom, who refused the king's command to marry her closest contender, saying, "Maybe I'll marry and maybe I won't. But first I'm going to travel the world." There was Rosey Grier, the football hero, telling little boys, "It's all right to cry," and Carol Channing's message to all families: "When there's housework to be done, do it together!"

Balking and Basking in the Blue Glow

When it came to challenging gender-specific roles in television and film, TV commercials, in particular, had to play catch-up. Sure, ads portray women equally, one reporter quipped. "Equally in a bad light." Domestic toilers, incompetents, sex objects—that's what NOW found in its 1972 survey of 1,241 commercials. In an advertisement for Downy, the fabric softener, a young woman anxiously asks her husband, "Did I wash it right?" He nods his approval, and she beams, "He noticed. I'm a wife!"

Complaints filed with the Federal Communications Commission and lots of negative publicity—NOW gave out "Old Hat" awards for sexist advertising—helped companies to imagine what should have been obvious: it's possible to sell products and entertain audiences without demeaning women. In the late 1970s and well into the 1980s we started seeing commercials showing moms leaving for work while dads cleaned up the kitchen.

Television producers, eager to separate themselves from Neanderthals, gave us series in which females hunted and males gathered. The feisty Mary Richards of the wildly popular 1970s sitcom *The Mary Tyler Moore Show*, "dumped" by her boyfriend after she'd put him through medical school, moved to Minneapolis determined to "make it after all." Ellen Burstyn portrayed a working mother who also happened to be a writer and a college professor in 1986's *The Ellen Burstyn Show*. Onscreen 1980s fathers such as Cliff Huxtable of *The Cosby Show* and Danny Tanner in *Full House*, raising three daughters with the help of his friends Joey and Jesse, showed us sensitive, nurturing men.

Director Martin Scorsese showed *his* sensitive side with the 1974 movie *Alice Doesn't Live Here Anymore*. Alice (Ellen Burstyn) once dreamed of becoming a famous singer but ends up married to a lout whose relationship with Tom, his adolescent son, is so vexed they're more strangers than kin. But when her husband is killed in a highway accident, Alice, with no resources or apparent talent for managing on her own, takes Tom across the American Southwest. Her trip, made with baby steps and lots of tenacity, is a stand-in for Everywoman's journey to self-actualization.

The same kind of awareness and fortitude are ultimately achieved by Erica (Jill Clayburgh) in 1978's *An Unmarried Woman*, after her husband of fifteen years announces that he's leaving her for a younger woman. Unlike Alice, Erica has a job—she works at a Soho art gallery—and she's supported emotionally by a daughter and women friends, some of them with worse problems than Erica's. Alice is eager to fall completely for a new man, but Erica remains wary. After a disastrous sexual adventure, she finds love again with a painter (Alan Bates), but this is no longer as important as finding herself.

The films of the 1970s and early 1980s didn't just show us women whose strength of character comes only after they've been tossed out of the domestic nest. We saw movies about women selflessly engaged in the most compelling and often dangerous issues of their times. *Julia* (1977) deals with fighting fascism, *The China Syndrome* (1979) with nuclear safety, *Norma Rae* (1979) with bringing justice to southern mill workers, and *Silkwood* (1983) is about the hazardous conditions at a plutonium-recycling facility. The heroines of these movies, many based on the lives of real women, possessed courage, persistence, and intelligence, qualities typically attributed only to men. They spoke out when it wasn't socially accepted, and they paid big time—with their reputations and sometimes their lives.

Toppling the Prestigious Pronoun

Attempts to weed out gender imprinting focused also on language, a constant, subliminal form of stereotyping. It seems like (or should seem like) the distant past when we all used the male pronoun to encompass females as well. But before the 1970s, the mighty *he* stood for both sexes. Women, after all, had no identity apart from men.

Look at any book on child care before the women's movement, and you'll only find advice on how to give "him" a bath, even—ridiculous as it sounds—when the passage is illustrated by a mother washing a baby girl.

Over time, the term *housewife*, literally meaning a woman married to her house, became replaced with *homemaker. Firemen* are now *firefighters, workmen's compensation* turned into *workers' compensation*, and *mailmen* are referred to as *mail carriers*. Some women, when they married, kept their maiden names, others hyphenated maiden and married names. And still others, reasoning that a maiden name is your father's and a married name is your husband's, took on completely new last names. Instead of differentiating women according to their marital status—*Miss* for the unwed set, *Mrs.* for married women—like Mr., *Ms.* is now used for both, and has become associated with women's autonomy.

Change limped along, uneven, incomplete, usually resisted. Horace Mann, a top-tier, all-male New York prep school that turned coed in 1972, retained its alma mater with the lyrics "As we *men* go forth" and "The truth that makes *men* free."

When I took a position as a dean there more than twenty years later, young women confided to me their discomfort. "It makes us feel invisible," they said. I became a faculty rep to the overwhelming male student governing council to see about initiating change. Naively, I thought it would be pretty easy. Just substitute a few words: as *we* go forth, the truth that makes *us* free.

Nothing could have prepared me for what I came up against. The old guard wouldn't hear of it. Didn't I understand about school tradition, honor, reputation? Exasperated, I tried to explain: "Women students don't see themselves represented in the alma mater."

"So?"

"Well, how would you feel if the song said 'As we *women* go forth?'"

The male students nearly rolled on the floor laughing.

"Who would want to be considered a woman?" They were incredulous. "Being called a man is a compliment."

They weren't joking; they were dead serious. And these were, in general, well-meaning, bright kids.

Four years later some of the diehards retired, and some of my colleagues joined the campaign. But what really got the school head's attention? The senior girls told me they planned to refuse to stand and sing the alma mater at the upcoming graduation. By the next day we had new words.

And a new generation of young women learned that sisterhood is powerful—a lesson they will have to draw upon to regain the rights we've lost, including those of reproductive justice.

4

DO NOT BEND, FOLD, SPINDLE, OR MUTILATE

We might not all have known that *spindle* means *impale*, but in the 1970s a lot of feminists started wearing buttons with the above inscription. Originally printed instructions on computer punch cards, the expression, to us, meant "Treat our bodies with care."

Even as we achieved more autonomy at work and school, we faced what seemed an intractable problem—gaining more control over our bodies. True, men dominated most professions, but their virtual monopoly over medicine, and consequently reproductive health and reproduction, gave them authority over the most basic aspects of a woman's being—sexuality, conception, abortion, pregnancy, adoption, motherhood, sterilization. The de facto arbitrators of which groups—classes and races—should have children and how many, doctors wielded power with a definitive, unquestioned hand.

Throughout most of the twentieth century, doctors occupied a revered place in our society, enjoying the support of the pharmaceutical industry and of most Americans. "He's a big man in the field," a common expression of the time, conferred status on the physician and patient fortunate enough to be in his care.

For their part, most doctors enthusiastically embraced the patriarchal role and expected women to accept subservience. Obstetricians seemed to be particularly condescending. When Cindy Martin, pregnant for the first time, brought her husband, Harry, to her appointment, she discovered how "irrelevant" she was.

" 'Does she have morning sickness? Is she tired?' My ob/gyn was directing all his questions to Harry, as though I wasn't even in the room," Cindy recalled. "They man-to-manned it for the entire visit, the doctor telling Harry all the things *he* might have to put up with—that I might be more emotional and irritable at times. It was so weird. Here I was, the one having the baby, being discussed in the third person."

Medical textbooks brimming with paternalistic, often condescending advice reflected the unequal power structure. Research I did in 1977 following a late miscarriage didn't shed as much light on what happened in my pregnancy as it did on doctors' attitudes:

[T]he frequency of intercourse should depend primarily upon the male sex drive. . . . The female should be advised to allow her male partner's sex drive to set their pace and she should attempt to gear hers satisfactorily to his.

Doctors should ask their female patients certain questions to appraise their character. Does she respond in a "feminine way"? or is she masculine, aggressive, [and] demanding in attitude?

There are two types of habitual miscarriers: "the basically immature woman or the frustrated independent woman."

Maybe this kind of training explained my then-gynecologist's response to my agitated phone call during my fifth month of pregnancy. "Something white that looks like a telephone cord is hanging out of my body," I sobbed. "You sound hysterical," he barked into the phone. "It's the urethra. Push it back in." It was my first pregnancy. I did what he told me to do. How did I know it had been the umbilical cord that prolapsed and that I should have been treated immediately?

Throughout the night my husband and I kept calling, pleading to go to the hospital. Almost twenty-four hours later an associate agreed to see me. By then I was in active labor, and the baby was dead.

For a long time afterward I blamed myself. Why didn't I insist the doctor take my symptoms seriously? Why didn't I insist he see me? Why did I have to be such a good girl? It wasn't until the book I wrote about my experiences connected me to so many women with similar stories that I began to understand what had happened to me in the broader context of women's medical care.

I did finally find a wonderful team of male doctors. Still, when a friend, eight months pregnant, was being examined by one of this fabulous team I'd recommended to her, he said, "You look great. Your breasts are so big. Your husband must be a happy man."

Our grandmothers and mothers put up with this kind of treatment. They saw no alternatives for themselves, but women of my generation had already started challenging authority in its many guises. Ironically, our stance against the male medical establishment was fortified by something heralded as a "major breakthrough for women": the birth-control pill.

The Pill: A Magic Bullet or a Deadly One?

When birth-control advocate Margaret Sanger asked a male physician why he opposed contraception, he said, "We will never give over the control of our numbers to the women, themselves. What, let them control the future of the human race? . . . [W]e make the decisions and they must come to us."

A public health nurse in the first decades of the twentieth century, Sanger was haunted by images of "those poor, weak, wasted, frail women, pregnant year after year like so many automatic breeding machines." She saw women die in childbirth, women who should never have become pregnant again, women who grabbed onto her skirt and pleaded for the "secret" to prevent conception.

To be married with an unwanted pregnancy was bad, but to be unmarried and pregnant, in most instances, marked you forever. And this was as true in 1910 as it was a half century later. "The scandal [of unwed pregnancy] was so intense," the singer Joni Mitchell recalled of her own experience in the early 1960s. "The main thing was to conceal it. A daughter could do nothing more disgraceful. It was like you murdered someone."

"It was all shame, shame, shame, *double* shame to be pregnant and not married," Mitchell's friend D'Arcy Case agreed. "Abortions were too dangerous. You'd hear stories from girls in our circle—a couple of them had frightening illegal abortions: you'd go in and there'd be this dirty old cot . . ."

Safe, effective birth control in a woman's own hands—not her husband's or boyfriend's—that was the way to protect women from unwelcome, repeated, and often deadly pregnancies, Margaret Sanger concluded in the early 1900s. But it took almost forty years before she gained the ability to act on that understanding.

Along with Katherine McCormick, who'd done the near impossible, earning a degree in biology from MIT, Sanger met with Gregory Pincus, a research scientist with a specialty in female fertility, in 1951 and asked him to produce a physiological contraceptive, backing up the request with McCormick's inheritance of over two million dollars. Six years later, after what turned out to be inadequate testing on groups of women in Puerto Rico, the drug company G. D. Searle released Enovid, "the pill," advertised as "safe and 100 percent effective." The FDA approved its use for birth control in 1960.

The definition of womanhood changed almost instantly. Chastity, of course, was still there, for those who chose it. But for others, sex could be embraced as pleasurable, fun, and freed from worry. Giving so much power to women (although they still needed prescriptions from their doctors) inevitably aggravated the political and social anxieties of the times. Rickie Solinger discusses the questions, both spoken and unspoken, percolating through society in *Pregnancy and Power*. Would the pill lead to promiscuity? To dwindling numbers of the so-called right kind of children? Could it be used to "curb social discord created by unwanted, out-of-wedlock birth [among] 'Negroes'"? Might it be the way to stop the population explosion?

Use of the pill clashed with the teachings of the Catholic Church and—as sociologist Joyce Ladner observed—with the longings of many poor women who saw motherhood as their only path toward recognition. Still, by the late 1960s millions of Americans of all backgrounds were getting prescriptions for Enovid. And no wonder!

In selling the birth-control pill, pharmaceutical companies instructed their salesmen to "weed out all the negative points," to talk down any links between the pill and such serious health side effects as thromboembolic disease, ocular problems, changes in thyroid and adrenal function, and, with long-term use, a higher risk of breast cancer.

Historian Elizabeth Watkin's research has shown how huge profits being raked in by Enovid encouraged the drug industry to continue short-circuiting testing and resist full disclosure. Here and there stories popped up of women on the pill who'd developed blood clots, who'd had strokes— all whitewashed by the FDA in its Report on the Oral Contraceptives in the summer of 1966. The media jumped on board. The *New York Times* and *Time* magazine applauded the pill's certificate of good health.

British medical researchers disagreed. Their studies, published in highly respected journals, gave evidence of higher than average rates of morbidity and mortality in women who used the pill. The late health reformer Barbara Seamen presented similar evidence in her groundbreaking book, *The Doctors' Case Against the Pill*.

With her intimate knowledge of so many accredited stories of death and disease attributed to the pill, Seamen should have been a key witness for the congressional hearings looking into the safety of the drug. Yet oddly enough, although she managed to be present, no one called upon her to speak.

"Why isn't Barbara Seaman testifying? Why aren't there any patients testifying?" a frustrated spectator finally called out.

"All the senators were men [and] all of the people testifying were men. They did not have a single woman who had taken the pill and no women scientists," one woman who'd been in the audience remembered.

The hearings caused a tremendous stir. Kansas Senator Bob Dole said:

We must not frighten millions of women into disregarding the considered judgments of their physicians about the use of oral contraceptives. . . . Let us show some sympathy for the beleaguered physician who must weigh . . . the emotional reactions of that woman which have been generated by sensational publicity and rumored medical advice.

Taking the Field Away from the Big Men

For many women, the hearings and new media focus on the medical problems associated with the pill *and* also with the "effective and safe" contraceptive the IUD, or intrauterine device, ultimately taken off the market because it led to infection and infertility (although back now in a supposedly improved form), confirmed what they had long contended: women needed to know more about their own bodies and what they put into them.

The drive to "demystify medicine" took as many forms as there were needs: newsletters; hotlines and referral services; women's clinics; campaigns against unnecessary hysterectomies—then the single most common operation performed on women—and against the forced sterilization of mainly poor African American girls; the movement for natural childbirth, home birthing centers, and the return of midwives (who'd enjoyed a virtual monopoly over delivering babies in colonial America) to obstetrics. Lesbians, women of color, and older women began calling for specialized medical care and started organizing their own health groups.

Also on the agenda were problems few people talked about—rape and domestic violence. One woman recounted the questions put to her at the police station following a vicious assault in 1974.

> *What were you doing walking alone at 10:00 P.M.?* (She was on her way home from the NYU library.)

> *Don't you think you're dressed provocatively?* (She was wearing leggings, boots, and a long sweater.)

> *Are you sure you weren't flirting with the guy?* (She was grabbed from behind by an unknown assailant, dragged into an alley, and raped.)

"Male officers grilled me mercilessly for two hours before I was offered any medical attention or advice. I was made to feel like I was the one who'd done something wrong," she said of the classic humiliating treatment given rape victims in the years prior to the women's movement.

Before the advent of twenty-four-hour hotlines, women, as soon as they got free of their attacker, generally rushed home to bathe, destroying evidence possibly helpful in their testimonies. But the majority of women, fearful of how they'd be treated in the courts, never reported the assaults anyway.

Until feminists began holding "speak outs" in the early 1970s, going public with their own experiences as rape victims, no one had any idea of the extent of unreported crimes. And the numbers were staggering. Concerned women established rape crisis centers across the country, offering counseling and legal help. Before the women's movement, date rape and marital rape were not even in our vocabulary. A wife couldn't legally refuse to have sex with her husband, even if he beat her, forced himself on her, or had a sexually transmitted disease.

With systematic determination, feminists lobbied state by state to make sexual assault within marriage a criminal offense. Domestic violence, another problem identified and named by women, took longer. When the Violence Against Women Act finally passed in 1994, granting $1.6 billion to investigate and prosecute instances of physical assault against women, many of us for years had been banding together to protect one another, establishing safe havens and sanctuaries for battered women and their children.

The seminal work *Our Bodies, Ourselves*, published in 1973, joined these different women's health initiatives together and put them on the cultural map. The book had its origins four years earlier when a group of women (none of them doctors) who called themselves the Boston Women's Health Collective stapled together 193 pages of newsprint. Women couldn't wait to get hold of this no-nonsense, nonjudgmental primer about their own bodies. Everything we wanted—no, *needed*—to know was in it. All the symptoms, all the questions—everything our doctors dismissed and belittled was here. The book became our bible, sometimes our lifeline. Word of mouth jacked its sales to a quarter of a million copies before the first commercial edition was printed.

Immediately right-wingers condemned the book; the late fundamentalist preacher Jerry Falwell labeled it "obscene trash." Some school libraries objected to the frank discussions of homosexuality and diagrams of genitalia and refused to order it. But the book went on to sell millions of copies and was translated into twenty languages and into Braille.

Whose Body Is It Anyway?

Of all the issues women have tackled, none has been as galvanizing or polarizing as their campaign for safe, legal abortion. The ongoing national debate, so deeply felt and rancorous at times, blurs an important understanding: abortion was actually accepted for most of our country's history, going back to colonial times. Even theologians seemed to turn a blind eye to the practice, generally considered legal before "quickening," the sensation of fetal movement, usually occurring toward the end of the fourth month. After that point abortion was treated as a misdemeanor, not even a felony unless it resulted in the death of the woman.

What's striking about abortion in the early nineteenth century is its very public nature. Books, manuals, and "ladies' guides" took a matter-of-fact approach, supplying abundant information on how to clear an "obstruction." Recommendations for such practices as "reaching too high, jumping or stepping from an eminence, strokes [strong blows] on the belly, [and] falls," appear frequently. The use of electricity "generally and locally applied . . . to restore the discharge" also gained its share of adherents. And all the authors had their favorite herbs and roots, such as jalap, scammony, bitter apple, black hellebore, and savin, known for their purgative effects. The demand for "remedies," far exceeding what women could concoct on their own, led to a booming pharmaceutical industry devoted to the preparation of abortifacients in the first half of the nineteenth century.

Abortion became a big business. Abortionists advertised freely in the popular press and used handbills and pamphlets to spread word of their clinics. Madame Restell, the celebrity abortionist of her time, spent upward of sixty thousand dollars per year—millions by today's standards—promoting her offices in New York, Boston, and Philadelphia.

But the publicity surrounding Restell and the others ultimately led to their downfall.

No one much cared if poor, unwed immigrant girls aborted their babies, but when it became obvious that Restell's clients were married, white, Anglo-Saxon Protestant women who were "distinctly upper class and wealthy," outrage spread quickly.

Making abortion illegal became the rallying cause for physicians who blamed it for the steep decline in the birth rate between 1840 and 1850. With the support of the newly formed American Medical Association, doctors saw a way to end unwanted competition, reestablish traditional gender roles, and "recapture their ancient and rightful place as society's policymakers and savants," said historian James C. Mohr. What he called "the physicians' crusade against abortion" paid off. By 1900 every state in the union had an antiabortion law. In Kentucky, the only exception, state courts forbid the practice. Once accepted and public, abortion now became something shameful, underground, and illegal.

And dangerous. More dangerous than ever.

But it didn't stop. Single women, poor women, women who already were caring for far too many little ones, women whose boyfriends or husbands would leave them if they had a baby, women who wanted to leave their boyfriends or husbands, women who wanted to finish their education or hold onto a job, were too young, too immature, too old, had been raped, were victims of incest, or just plain didn't want to be mothers—all found ways to end unwanted pregnancies.

The words of Dr. Edward Keemer of Washington, D.C., help us imagine the absolute desperation these women must have felt:

> I had treated a woman . . . [who] still had the straightened-out coat hanger hanging from her vagina. Some . . . died from air embolisms or infections. Over the years I was to encounter hundreds of other women who had resorted to imaginative but deadly methods of self-induced abortion . . . some would swallow quinine or turpentine. Others would insert a corrosive potassium permanganate tablet into their vaginas. . . . A sixteen-year-old girl . . . died after douching with a cupful of bleach.

During the 1960s, an estimated million women had illegal abortions. Of those who survived, untold numbers became sterile. By one count seven thousand women died from botched abortions in 1966 (compared to three thousand American deaths that year in Vietnam). Hard as it is to verify these statistics, what we know is that the deaths and disabilities from illegal abortions fell disproportionately on poor women and women of color.

Many wealthier women (although with no guarantee of the outcome) managed to get to doctors in Puerto Rico or Mexico or convince their own doctors of the need for a "therapeutic abortion"—permissible if a woman's life was in danger.

"My doctor was sympathetic," Gail recalled of her Cleveland gynecologist. "I already had a two-year-old, and my husband was physically abusing me. I couldn't imagine having a second child with him."

Gail's doctor got approval from the hospital board for a therapeutic abortion, but when she and her mom arrived at the scheduled time, the staff tried to turn her away. "Even though what I was doing was completely legal, they refused to admit me at first because I didn't have my husband's written permission."

Women's sovereignty over their own bodies heated up as a key issue for feminists who became the "shock troops" of the reproductive rights movement. Ignoring the risk of arrest, they counseled, gave referrals, and shepherded women back and forth for their procedures. And they held rallies and protests to bring national attention to the issue. In this, they received support from two unlikely places.

The first was the Sherri Finkbine case in 1962, which attracted the kind of media attention heaped on the Terri Schiavo lawsuit years later. Finkbine, host of the TV show *Romper Room*, was pregnant with her fifth child and had been given the medication thalidomide to alleviate morning sickness before unequivocal evidence emerged linking the drug to horrific birth defects. Finkbine's doctor scheduled her for an immediate abortion.

When a local newspaper did a piece on Finkbine's situation, the hospital cancelled the abortion. Finkbine became so vilified in the press and her children the target of so many death threats that the FBI had to protect her family. Appeals in this country proved futile, forcing Finkbine to Sweden for the procedure. The aborted fetus, with no legs and only one arm, confirmed Finkbine's fears. But the American public refused to forgive her. Upon returning home she was fired from her job, and her husband suspended from his teaching position.

The Finkbine case, combined with publicity surrounding botched and fatal abortions, pushed many doctors in a new direction. Once leading the antiabortion charge, in the late 1960s doctors became the second line of support, working with women's groups to change state laws and to put test cases before the courts.

By now women's organizations across the country were encountering fierce, well-coordinated opposition from antiabortion groups. To Catholics and others who believed life began with conception, abortion equaled murder. Also at stake were the complex relationships between men and women. Many who opposed abortion considered the mothering role nearly sacred—what imparted value and dignity to women.

For all the passionate arguments surrounding this issue, the Supreme Court ultimately decided *Roe v. Wade* on the question of privacy: Who gets to decide what kind of family life you have? Who gets to decide how many, if *any*, children you have? "To what extent may the government legitimately interfere in an individual's private life?" These were the issues informing the majority opinion written by Justice Harry Blackmun, who asserted that the "right to privacy . . . founded in the Fourteenth Amendment's concept of personal liberty and restrictions about state action . . . is broad enough to encompass a woman's decision whether or not to terminate her pregnancy."

Interestingly, the judicial decision of January 22, 1973, returned to women what had been theirs until the late nineteenth century. It made early abortion legal, and, as Davis points out, those past the point of viability (what used to be called quickening) could be prohibited.

Feminists hailed the law, although it was far from perfect. Too much authority rested with the doctor and not enough with the woman. Still, before a series of amendments and rulings in years to come would chip away at *Roe*'s boundaries, abortion remained equally available to women of all backgrounds.

Through both noisy, controversial battles, such as the one over abortion, and many far smaller and quieter ones, second-wavers tried to bring about a better world in which women—and men—lived, loved, and worked. Equitable rights and treatment for women—what we asked for seemed so simple, so just, so right, we approached the next decade eager to see our hard-won gains extended and amplified.

5

REAGAN AND THE GREAT REALITY CHECK

"I'm beginning to think that the women's movement was a revolution, except no heads rolled," one of my friends said toward the end of the 1970s. Yes, there'd been changes in schools, the workplace, and the home, but they fell far short of our hopes.

Every morning a vast army of women marched off to work in their dark blue pantsuits with mini bow ties around their necks, determined to be successful. Some of us had gone through assertiveness training programs, others had practically memorized books like *Games Your Mother Never Taught You* or *The Working Mother's Complete Handbook*, which warned, "Remember that people at the office want to hear you have this baby and see a snapshot once and that's all."

"The worst stereotype about women is the assumption that we will sacrifice the organization for our family because that's what we have always been taught to do," said Marcie Schorr Hirsch of Hiatt Career Development Center at Brandeis University.

"I never take a day off to be with my children," Susan Rabiner, now a New York literary agent, told me in the early 1980s when she was a senior editor with Oxford University Press. Thousands of other women followed this strategy, many staying at their offices when their children were sick and "worrying like crazy."

"Every day, no matter how busy I am, at four o'clock an alarm goes off in my head: Where are the boys? What are they supposed to be doing after school?" Betsy Gold, a corporate art consultant in Detroit, said. But back then, the tactic of separating work from family argued against Betsy making a quick call to check on her kids.

With job sharing and flextime not yet real options, the vast majority of women in the workplace had little choice but to twist themselves like pretzels to fit a culture still derived totally from male attitudes and behaviors and resting on the assumption that a full-time wife was minding the home.

On-site child care, a major solution to working families' problems, hadn't materialized in significant numbers. When Stride-Rite Corporation first opened its day care center in Roxbury, Massachusetts, in 1971, many hailed it as the wave of the future. The center saw almost immediate benefits in recruitment and retention and cuts in absenteeism, not only for its employees but also for lower-income families in the greater Boston area. Yet eleven years later only forty-two companies nationwide had followed Stride-Rite's example.

As for federally funded centers, feminists who'd been pushing for them since the early 1960s had gotten only scant results. Their best hope—Senator Walter Mondale's 1971 bill to establish a comprehensive national day care system—fell victim to President Nixon's veto. Child care threatens family stability by encouraging women to work and encouraging a communal approach to childrearing, Nixon said. As the *New York Times* editorialized, "Publicly funded day care [to Nixon] . . . was un-American, anti-family." In short, it would Sovietize the nation.

And what about changes in the family? Had roles become more egalitarian? Not quite. From what sociologist Arlie Hochschild reported in the late 1980s, 61 percent of American husbands needed to have Carol Channing sing "Housework" to them on a daily basis. That's the proportion who didn't pitch in at all. Hochschild found 80 percent of working women to be carrying the burden of an additional job in caring for home, kids, and husband. Through the 1970s and into the 1980s, the combination of work and domestic responsibilities kept American women constantly occupied fifteen hours more per week than men, adding up to "an extra month of twenty-four-hour days"—a "second shift," according to Hochschild in her book of the same name.

For all our efforts and many successes, feminists had made two major miscalculations—we'd underestimated both the resistance of male corporate America to change and the tenacity of idealized, traditional family life in the national psyche.

"Why would any man willingly give up his prerogatives?" one father asked during a parenting session at our children's nursery school. He made it clear: men didn't want women vying with them over the corner office and even less over whose turn it was to change the diapers.

And there were other complaints as well. Some women rightly charged the movement with continuing to be largely white, middle class, and heterosexual. And many women—full-time moms and those holding typical "female" jobs—felt belittled by what they believed was the second wave's emphasis on professional women.

But the women's movement was nothing if not a work in progress. More than most groups, we wanted to hear about our lapses and learn from our mistakes. In significant ways, a good number of feminists spent the late 1970s and early 1980s busily and conscientiously addressing our shortcomings.

Then, things started to change. Heads began to roll, all right. And they were *ours*. Women who believed in equal rights, who fought to make our society more free, more just, more inclusive, suddenly became the culprits in a nation weary of social upheaval and eager to play the blame game.

Of course we weren't the only upheaval in town. Civil rights, the student youth and gay rights movements, the war in Vietnam and the protests it incited, the assassinations of Robert Kennedy, Martin Luther King Jr., the fury of inner city riots—Watts, Detroit, Newark—all sent a collective shiver down the spine of what used to be known as "the Establishment."

The "age of Aquarius" was being trumped by a dawning age of conservatism as the "new right" marshaled its considerable forces in the 1980s to produce the most expansive, centralized, well-financed, and carefully orchestrated "message machine" ever found in a democracy. There were tracts and books like Milton Friedman's *Free to Choose* (1980), extolling the virtues of unfettered capitalism, visiting professorships secured at prestigious universities—Harvard, Yale, Stanford—and a flood of op-ed pieces. Over "100 captive printing presses" churned out newsletters and positions papers from such foundations as the American Enterprise Institute, the Heritage Foundation, the Federalist Society, the Independent Women's Forum, and Concerned Women for America.

Money poured in from trusts and wealthy businessmen across the country—"Richard Mellon Scaife in Pittsburgh, Lynde and Larry Bradley in Milwaukee, John Olin in New York City"—as well as from stalwarts of the Christian right. Many of these "new righters" were now becoming known as neoconservatives (neocons).

Defecting from anticommunist liberalism after the 1960s, neocons became obsessed with redeeming America's military prowess after the humiliation of Vietnam and allying with "America's religious core" to cleanse the nation of moral depravity and decay.

Huge swaths of this country, represented by Jerry Falwell's Moral Majority, joined in this condemnation chorus. Instead of taking a long, hard look at America's failings, they chose to blame acid-dropping hippies, disgruntled people of color, and hairy-legged women. Television evangelist Pat Robertson represented the new and increasingly common line of attack; feminists, he declared, encourage women to "leave their husbands, kill their children, practice witchcraft, destroy capitalism, and become lesbians."

By the time of Ronald Reagan's victory lap to the White House in 1980, his right flank had managed to put his opponents—those who sought to use government to promote the general welfare—on the defensive. Of course the GOP had always paid lip service to small government, but in fact Nixon and Ford had continued the legacy of the New Deal and had given ample federal support to social programs. Now the demonization of the word *liberal*—turning it into the dreaded *l-word*—became an integral part of Republican strategy.

Only twenty years earlier, John F. Kennedy had won an election under "the banner of a liberal, responsible Democratic party that believes in the people." Lewis H. Lapham, former editor of *Harper's* magazine, looking back at the time, noted: "The basic American consensus . . . was firmly liberal in character and feeling, assured of a clear majority in both chambers of Congress as well as a sympathetic audience in the print and broadcast press."

For sure, President Johnson's failure to be honest with us about the Vietnam War and Nixon's failure to be honest about Watergate yanked threads out of an ideology based on *trusting* the government to "do for people what people cannot do for themselves." But what really unraveled the liberal consensus was the right wing's deliberate, methodical strategy of and success in dominating the national discourse.

Hollywood Actor Plays Puritan Preacher

Before Nancy Reagan held her first tea at 1600 Pennsylvania Avenue, newly energized and financed neoconservative think tanks established themselves in Washington. With offers of huge salaries, ultraconservative intellectuals were pulled to the capital like metal filings to a magnet. It's uncertain whether these scholars actually read sociologist Emile Durkheim or his academic heir, Kai Erikson, but their polices and those that would mark the Republican party through the presidency of George W. Bush drew heavily on the sociological theories of deviance and its role in maintaining community cohesion.

Defining "deviant" behavior—or what is judged to be deviant behavior by any people at any particular time—can be a powerful tool in binding a society together. What constitutes deviance varies over time. In a sense it's made, not born. A heavy-drinking man might be said to be "partying" in one era, labeled an alcoholic the next. But once branded, certain conduct, activities, and ways of being become categorized as deviant, or "the other." This allows a culture to define "self"—what it stands for, its core values, its boundaries—by what it's not. Discrediting, devaluing, and making pariahs, even criminals, of those who disagree with its principles is a perfect way for a government to achieve social control over its people.

Kai Erikson draws upon these ideas to explain the witchcraft hysteria gripping Salem in the seventeenth century. Right before the outbreak, the Puritan way of life seemed to be falling apart. A spike in population put newcomers far away from the censoring, sharp-eyed leaders. At Sunday services, ministers peered anxiously at empty pews in their churches. Material gain and avarice were defiling souls. One sinner sported a lace collar; another was found lying with an Indian. Goodwives gathered in homes of false female prophets claiming to know the word of God.

Satan's face could be seen in Plymouth. Salvation of the glorious Puritan mission required . . . deviants! And the Puritan fathers found them in a vulnerable knot of giddy young girls playing with Tituba, a servant from Barbados. Hysteria spread; the maidens had been bewitched. They pointed fingers at their neighbors, older women, bent-over widows. Town criers called out news of the inquisitions, the spectacular trials, the public hangings. The epidemic howled through the wilderness, calling "the wayward" to conformity with community values, and sharpening, at least for a time, the Puritan identity.

Fast-forward to the 1980s, and we can hear the same strategies dropping from the lips of right-wing moralizers. Reagan may have been a leading man of Hollywood, but in Washington he risked playing a supporting role. Reading from the deviance script made him a superstar.

In front of the camera Reagan appeared affable and confident, posing in his well-creased Stetson pitched at a jaunty angle, his eyes squinting into the sun. This iconic image was more airbrushed than authentic—the newly purchased ranch was no more than a theatrical prop.

When Americans looked at our new president, we were supposed to think *heroic cowboy, rugged individual, self-reliant man*. After the weak-kneed administrations of Gerald Ford and Jimmy Carter, Republicans believed we were ready for a muscular foreign policy that would build up our military and stare down the communists.

But here was the Republican problem: most Americans weren't saddling up to be part of the posse. Reagan squeaked into office with the support of only 26 percent of the adult population. Conservatives needed to replace the collectivizing principles of Democrats with their own ideological glue. How could they gain adherence to the policies of their leader? Even more to the point, how could they rally the nation to an essentially negative program of cutting social services; weakening civil rights legislation, the labor unions, and environmental regulations; and strengthening the military, when the majority of Americans polled in 1980 were moving to the right on economic but not social issues? The answer? By labeling those who disagreed with them as deviants.

A glance at Reagan's famous 1983 "evil empire" speech shows how shrewdly the administration accomplished its goals. Steeped in anti-Soviet cold war rhetoric, the address ostensibly argued against a "nuclear freeze" resolution then being debated in Congress. But surprisingly, it wasn't delivered to any group remotely connected with foreign policy. And only the last two and a half out of a total eight pages related to armaments.

Reagan gave this famous and oft-quoted talk to the National Association of Evangelicals. Sounding like a revivalist preacher, the president spoke of a "spiritual awakening and moral renewal." The nation needed a "new political and social consensus," based on an end to reproductive rights, a return to "family ties and religious belief," and an amendment to restore prayer to the public schools.

Much like the Bush administration's later tactic of using the words *9/11* and *Iraq* in the same sentence to link Saddam Hussein with the terrorist attacks, Reagan artfully connected the pro-choice movement with infanticide, pornography, adultery, teenage sex, and hard drugs. These enemies of our society, he claimed, were attempting to "water down traditional values and even abrogate the original terms of American democracy." Their behavior was abhorrent, criminal. "Sin and evil at home" were analogous to communism—"the focus of evil in the modern world." Reagan gave Americans two deviants for one speech.

In what would become the hallmark of the Republican Party, disagreements over public policy, once considered simply differing viewpoints to be discussed and debated, even signs of a vigorous, healthy society, now were cast as a moral disease. Any divergence from the right-wing agenda immediately became a threat to our country's values and its survival. Enemies at home were as dangerous as those abroad.

In significant ways, America changed from a nation held together by a sense of collective responsibility to one held together by the fear of being cast as "the other." Neoconservatives and their preachers had found a mighty weapon in gaining adherents to their cause.

That they went after feminism isn't at all surprising. "The woman's liberation movement in the 1970s had become the most dynamic force for social change in the country," noted scholar Rosalind Pollack Petchesky, "the one most directly threatening not only to conservative values and interest but also to 'significant groups' whose way of life is challenged by ideas of sexual liberation."

"Women's lib is a total assault on the role of the American woman as a wife and mother and on the family as the basic unit of society," conservative activist Phyllis Schlafly wrote in 1972, positioning herself as the perfect person to toss right-wing grenades at feminist causes during the Reagan years.

"Satan has taken the reins of the 'women's liberation' movement and will stop at nothing," cautioned the American Christian Cause's fundraising letter. "Moral perverts," "enemies of every decent society," screamed the *Christian Voice*. "America's decline as a world power is a direct result of the feminists' movement for reproductive freedom and equal rights," it contended. And Jerry Falwell blamed feminists for orchestrating a "satanic attack on the home." In some pastoral New England cemetery, Puritan zealot Cotton Mather must have been smiling as the new right launched its modern-day witch hunt against women.

Tanya Melich, for years a loyal Republican insider, watched with dismay as the leadership of her party adopted an increasingly misogynist stance, exploiting antifeminist fears to win votes. Her book, *The Republican War Against Women*, is a chilling study of the strategies used by the Reagan administration to curtail programs and policies meant to empower women.

Almost at once, Reagan's economic initiatives plunged the nation into a recession and greatly increased the number of impoverished women in America. During his first term the poverty rate climbed 15 percent, the highest of the previous twenty years. Then, in a double whammy to women, Reagan also reduced social programs that could have helped them through the hard times ahead. Casualties included slashed funding for the Women, Infants, and Children's (WIC) program, which resulted in the loss of food supplements for one hundred thousand low-income pregnant women and young children, as well as three million children being dropped from school lunch programs. Hundreds of thousands had their welfare benefits limited or completely denied, and three quarters of all day care centers were forced to curtail their programs because of major cutbacks in federal funds to low-income families.

"I remember those years as being very hard," said Sandra Yaklin of Michigan. For Sandra, keeping her job at the *Flint Journal* depended upon finding good child care. "I went through government day care, then had a caregiver who turned out to be mentally impaired." Sandra ultimately was laid off and took in neighborhood kids to try and get by. She also did some sewing. "I became a seamstress," she said with a touch of irony in her voice. When Sandra did go back to the *Journal* she remembered hearing guys getting raises because their wives were pregnant. What about me? she thought. "My reviews were always excellent. I absolutely felt that because I was a female, I didn't get the raises."

How could we stop the kind of discrimination Sandra and millions of women across the nation constantly confronted? The answer, for many feminists, rested with the passage of the Equal Rights Amendment (ERA), which would guarantee equality in the Constitution. First introduced in 1923, the amendment, waxing and waning for more than fifty years, finally seemed on the brink of passage in the late 1970s. With congressional approval behind it, the ERA needed state ratification.

Immediately the right wing mobilized to prevent this renewed "threat" to our nation. Falwell swore with all his heart "to bury the Equal Rights Amendment once and for all in a deep, dark grave." Phyllis Schlafly and her Stop the ERA committee lasered in on the southern states with carefully concocted tactics designed to scare women into opposition. They painted dark pictures of unisex bathrooms filled with male predators lurking behind stalls, of women losing their children in divorce, of being drafted into combat (later discredited), and, stripped of all the protections accorded the "weaker sex," becoming "abject slaves" of their men. On June 30, 1982, the final deadline date for approval, the ERA still remained three states short of ratification, ensuring its defeat.

And, as Reagan had promised in his evil empire speech, he targeted reproductive rights. Already the process of chipping away had begun: the Hyde Amendment in 1976 prohibited federal funds from being used for abortions. But Reagan went further; he instituted the Global Gag Rule in 1984, banning even the *mention* of abortion in any women's clinic, here or abroad, receiving federal funds. This turned children and women into pawns of Reagan's ideological agenda.

With the president's blessing, the 1989 *Webster v. Reproductive Health Services* decision declared life to begin at conception. Immediately states drafted new laws requiring parental notification of abortion for minors and spousal consent for married women; some laws required women to be tested so the viability of the fetus could be determined, and others mandated a specific waiting period.

"It's simple—if you could afford to have children, you could have an abortion," Pulitzer Prize–winning cartoonist Herblock commented wryly. Poor women, many of them women of color, now faced a "damned if you do, damned if you don't" bind. Severely limited in their ability to obtain abortion services and cut off from vital support programs, many ended up on welfare. And then were condemned for it.

6

WELFARE QUEENS, HERCULEAN WOMEN, AND SEX-STARVED STALKERS

"**E**very woman is one man away from welfare!" declared Johnnie Tillmon, chair of the National Welfare Rights Organization, in 1972. "Welfare's like a traffic accident, it can happen to anybody . . . but especially it happens to women," she said, explaining why welfare is a woman's issue. "There's a lot of lies that male society tells about welfare mothers; that [they] are immoral . . . lazy . . . misuse their welfare checks . . . spend it all on booze and are stupid and incompetent. If people are willing to believe these lies," she asserted, "it's partly because they're just special versions of the lies that society tells about all women."

However persuasive Tillmon's words were, people *did* believe the lies, largely because they heard them incessantly. Many aspects of welfare, technically called Aid to Families with Dependent Children (AFDC), needed changing, but mostly what had to be changed were the stereotypes surrounding it.

President Reagan's vividly and frequently told but utterly fictional story of a welfare queen driving a Cadillac who ripped off $150,000 from our government through a bunch of fake IDs and four nonexistent dead husbands became part of our national ideology about welfare.

The pictures in our heads, journalist and political commentator Walter Lippmann believed, determine how we understand the world around us. And this picture—the slothful, scheming, unwed woman (whose race, unstated, was nonetheless understood to be African American)—was reinforced constantly and consistently by the mainstream media. This rankled many Americans. Patricia M. Smith, New York City's First Deputy Commissioner, who oversaw the welfare-to-work program under Mayor Giuliani, said, "The whole idea of the welfare queen got disproportionate attention."

In what at best could be called sloppy reporting and at worst deliberately misleading, print and television journalism from 1960 to 1994 peddled rather than pulled apart the myths. They overwhelmingly portrayed welfare recipients as African American women. A reality check of those years would have shown something quite different: children, not single mothers, were the largest group on welfare, and most of the women were in fact white. And for all the hype about women having large families in order to increase their benefits, the average size of a family of welfare recipients actually decreased from 4 in 1969 to 2.8 in 1994, with only a tiny percent of all welfare going to persons not entitled to it.

By demonizing welfare recipients as "welfare queens," the new right manipulated public opinion and framed the debate in its own terms. Alarmingly, but not surprisingly, we're starting to see the same rhetoric emerge during the present fiscal crisis. Robert Rector of the Heritage Foundation, quoted in the February 8, 2009, *New York Times*, labeled the proposed stimulus plan a "welfare spendathon" that doesn't address "the fundamental causes of poverty, which are low levels of work and lower levels of marriage. They just say, 'Give me more.'"

In the same way, during Reagan's administration, the poor economy, the cycle of poverty, racism, even the welfare system itself—none of these issues came under attack. Instead, the administration turned its big guns on individual women, those with "bad values," the deviants. Repeatedly, conservative pundits, joining political talkfests on shows like *The McLaughlin Group*, held welfare mothers responsible for rampant drug use and soaring crime rates.

The U.S. War on Drugs became a cause célèbre of the Reagan years, with Nancy Reagan launching her Just Say No campaign in the early 1980s. The widespread use of crack cocaine and the tragedy of crack-addicted babies came in for particular outrage and moral panic. "Wizened old men with terminal diseases"; that's what crack babies look like, and there are no less than 375,000 born every year—one in ten, ranted William Bennett, the federal drug czar. His statistics spread like wildfire throughout the mainstream press and created a sense of moral panic in the public mind. Caring for crack babies would cost society a bundle; wasn't it better to go after the mothers, who, by taking drugs while pregnant, had caused this problem? The administration and much of the public answered with a resounding yes.

Reacting to these sweeping anxieties, some twenty states began arresting mothers for the crime of transferring illicit drugs to a minor. *Scapegoating* is what sociologists Harry Levine and Craig Reinarman called it—turning national attention away from economic inequalities and injustices while allowing our conservative administration to pay lip service to law and order. Prison construction boomed, and under harsh new drug-sentencing laws, the incarcerated population jumped by more than one million between 1980 and 2000. The number of incarcerated women, the fastest-growing population, increased by 592 percent during roughly the same period.

The "drug crisis" became another stake on which to burn women. Welfare mothers were juxtaposed against the *real* Americans, the moral Americans who railed against feminism and abortion.

As for the crack baby, it turned out to be more of a media phenomenon than a medical one. The research correcting Bennett's mistaken information didn't get nearly as much attention as the mistake itself had, but in the early 1990s, doctors—even those who'd originally thought these babies, if they survived, would have compromised lives—now said "their average developmental functioning is normal." Dr. Claire Coles, studying the problem, said the crack baby became a "media myth" in part because crack is not used by "people like us." In fact, only recently, in January 2009, under such headings as "The Epidemic That Wasn't," have newspapers like the *New York Times* published the results of longitudinal studies showing cocaine to have only a minimal effect on the fetus.

If the values of the welfare mother who didn't work but stayed home with her kids came in for censure, so did the values of the working mom who—so the story went—selfishly abandoned her family for her own gain, without a thought of how her children would suffer.

Throughout the 1980s we were bombarded with what authors Susan J. Douglas and Meredith M. Michaels call "children in peril stories." Threats loomed everywhere. Cases of child abuse at day care centers, murderous nannies, runaway teens, and pregnant adolescents turned into "epidemics," sure signs of family deterioration threatening the fabric of society.

Of course molested or troubled children deserve our attention, but the media obsession with these issues, while ignoring stories about the thirteen to fifteen million American children during those years who went to bed hungry each night, after hunger had been basically eliminated in the 1970s, is nothing short of bizarre. Was it because reporting on the shocking prevalence of severe malnutrition not in a third-world country but right here in Boston and Appalachia might pressure our government to reinstate food programs, while sensationalized stories of honey causing sudden infant death syndrome and razors hidden in Halloween candies only induced guilt and fear in individual women? Maybe.

I vividly remember one mother who picked her daughter up after my son's tenth Halloween birthday party in 1988 saying, "I'm taking all the candy to New York Hospital to have it x-rayed before I give it to her," and another horrified that we'd let the kids bob for apples because they could contract AIDS from each other's saliva. Both ordinarily sane and sensible women, they'd gotten caught up in that month's media-induced panic with its everpresent subtext of what Douglas and Michaels refer to as the "risks and costs of feminist-inspired motherhood."

A 1987 *Fortune* cover story, "Who's Taking Care of the Children?" did its part to pull the rug out from under working moms:

> The first heady, breaking-new-ground phase of the social experiment called dual-career parenting seems to be ending. In its place: a more reflective, and troubling stage. More and more parents are asking

whether the higher salary, bigger title or extra professional recognition can make up for leaving a toddler in tears each morning or returning to a teen who is hurt and angry each night.

What about the majority of toddlers who *weren't* in tears each morning? Or the teens who *weren't* hurt and angry each night? They're not mentioned in this piece. Instead we learn of a recent Stanford University study revealing heightened anxieties husbands feel about their children if their wives are in the workforce. "A stay-at-home wife seems to insulate husbands from some of the stress," said the psychologist who conducted the research.

And while the article presents plenty of "experts" predicting poor development in children who are in group day care, we're hardly told about all the studies, like the one by noted Harvard psychologist Dr. Jerome Kagan, finding *no difference* between the children, even those who entered day care as early as three and a half months old, in bonding or attachment to their mothers than those raised exclusively at home. Or of pediatrician and psychologist Mary Howell's ten-year review of the literature: "[The] more closely children of working mothers are studied, the more they appear just like the children of mothers who are not employed," Dr. Howell said. "The main differences appear to be positive. . . . Children with two employed parents are less likely than children who have only an employed father to make sex-stereotypical assumptions about male/female roles and are more likely to be independent."

During these same years, my own investigation, for a book I was writing, of nearly one thousand working mothers from diverse backgrounds found them to be almost uniformly concerned and thoughtful about their children. Nowhere did I see evidence of the hard-driving, self-absorbed career woman, the kind the media loved to lambaste, who'd handcuff her kids to the playpen if that was the only way she could get to an important meeting.

The women in my study overwhelmingly believed their work had a positive effect on their children. When asked to give advice to other working mothers, Kathy, an advertising executive from Wisconsin, said, "Remember there's no one right way to do this. Just keep in mind how much your sons and daughters will benefit from having you as a role model, how much more you can give to them."

Contrary to the stereotypes, other working women had similarly self-less and child-centered thoughts and advice:

I love having something to talk about with my kids at the end of the day. I listen proudly to what they accomplished, and they listen proudly to me.

Hug a lot. Don't make mountains out of molehills. Have a sense of humor.

Talk to your children. Tell them you won't always make the right decisions and choices but that you're always trying to do what's best. It's how they'll learn and grow.

Enjoy the adventure and, above all, be able to laugh with your children and at yourself when things go wrong.

I believe you can have all you want, but not all at the same time; it's not instantaneous, it requires hard work and patience. It's been five years [of being a working mother], and I can finally say I am comfortable and can begin adding to my life materially, educationally, and spiritually.

Reading through these interviews even after so many years, I can still feel a palpable sense of energy, enthusiasm, optimism, and, most of all, realism. These women saw themselves as pioneers and groundbreakers, negotiators and planners, not as superhuman overachievers.

Still, the myth of the supermom, an expression of society's ambivalence and anxieties over women's changing roles, served as a prod to the 19.5 million working mothers in the mid-1980s. The message beamed out at us from every supermarket line. If you worked, you needed to compensate by excelling at all things—June Cleaver, Mary Kay, and Sophia Loren rolled into one ultrafabulous woman.

We've all read about some version of her—the woman who works all day, then comes home to color-coordinate her three children's drawers before sitting down with them to write a play the youngest can perform in his preschool talent show, and, with only twenty minutes before dinner, cooks a Daniel Boulay–level meal. The whole family eats together while discussing the upcoming presidential campaign—a debate continuing until she reads each child a different bedtime story and cuddles them to sleep, so she can spend some quality time with her husband.

As Laurel Parker West noted in her paper "Soccer Moms and Welfare Queens," "The implication that women who want it all must do it all—work for pay, keep the house, raise the kids, nurture the marriage" set an impossible standard for working mothers, in effect dooming them to failure. And once again, failure would be their fault, feminism's fault, rather than the fault of recalcitrant, unenlightened public policies.

Yet, flying in the face of all these pressures, a simple fact emerged: women enjoyed their multilayered lives. Mainstream magazines of the mid-1980s such as *Parents* published research showing that "the more roles the women had, the greater their sense of self-esteem. They felt more competent and proud of what they had achieved and they believed their lives were more interesting and satisfying." *Ladies' Home Journal* threw its considerable weight on the side of working mothers with this research: "[W]hen asked if they'd continue to work even if they didn't need the paycheck, 53 percent of employed moms said they'd stay on the job."

By 1986, a majority of women with children under the age of three were in the workforce, composing a sizable demographic to support policies for working families. The political right and their courtiers in the media needed to put a kibosh on their potential power. Having so recently drawn a portrait of the supermom, they proceeded now to give her a black eye. Soon the buzz filled our ears about the supermom *syndrome*: irritability, fatigue, impatience, messing up at home and at work.

This is the fate that befalls J. C. Wiatt (Diane Keaton), the corporate iron maiden of *Baby Boom*, when she "inherits" Elizabeth, a baby girl, from a distant relative. Before this calamity, J.C. and her equally driven boyfriend coexisted in an orderly, detached relationship. Lovemaking is allotted a full five minutes, squeezed in between evening work hours.

The appearance of the baby ends life as J.C. knows it. Her boyfriend moves out, and J.C., who can close a multimillion-dollar deal, can't figure out how to close a diaper. As love for Elizabeth finally awakens the heart within the steely breast, J.C.'s mind turns to pabulum. She's distracted at work and commits the cardinal mistake of bringing Elizabeth to the office. Her chance at partnership is nil, her high-profile client, Food Chain, is taken from her.

Undaunted, J.C. moves to a sixty-five-acre farm in Vermont. There she discovers love with Cooper, the town veterinarian, and proves herself to be a domestic diva. Her natural baby-food label becomes so spectacularly successful that Food Chain wants to buy it from her for a whopping three million. But thrilled as J.C. is to be "back in the game," she strides back into the boardroom only to reject the offer.

This is a pivotal moment in the movie. J.C. has a chance to blast all the smug former coworkers who'd mercilessly penalized her for Elizabeth. But she cops out. Tearfully, she tells the room full of pompous males about her new love and Elizabeth's happiness in Vermont. All is motherhood and romance. At last, she's become a natural woman, pure as the baby food she's producing. In the final scene, J.C. sits in a rocking chair reading to her daughter, curled up in her lap. Floral patterns on the walls and sofas complete the bucolic fantasy. Order and serenity have been restored to a life gone awry.

With J.C. nesting away in Vermont, the corporate culture has no reason to change. It's working mothers who have to accommodate, so unless you can afford acres of pastoral plenty and have a bunch of old family recipes up your sleeve, you're pretty much toast.

And that was fine with the hawkers of the supermom syndrome. They never had much sympathy for working moms, who presumably had brought their problems on themselves. It was far easier to stigmatize the whole lot as a bunch of self-involved, ambitious shrews than to acknowledge the majority of mothers stuck in low-paying, low-satisfaction jobs, having a tough time keeping it all together. The syndrome was a problem *only* because it presumably had a negative and lasting impact on a woman's children, dooming them to grow up pitifully unloved and permanently damaged.

Bad as a working mother might be, the single, childless career woman threatened the very soul of decent family folk. In 1987's *Fatal Attraction* Alex Forrest (Glenn Close), a successful editor, becomes infatuated with New York lawyer Dan Gallagher (Michael Douglas) after they have a ferociously passionate weekend affair. But when Dan refuses to see her again, the heat of Alex's fervor soars to the danger zone; she begins to stalk him.

Alex presumably is the quintessential woman of the 1980s. Sexually liberated and with an independent career, she's feminism's daydream. Except, of course, she's a nightmare. She's completely fixated on Dan, but even more so on his family. It's what she wants. And when she spies on the family all happily together, it literally makes her sick. Her obsession escalates into madness, her capacity for ruthlessness evident when she boils the family's pet rabbit alive on their kitchen stove.

Beth (Anne Archer), Dan's wife, tells her, "If you come near my family again, I'll kill you." And after a goose-bump-inducing scene in the bathroom, she does. Beth, whose name conjures up Louisa May Alcott's character, the embodiment of sweet domesticity, vanquishes Alex, the masculinized, aggressively toxic career woman.

Alex revved up such feelings of hatred in audiences watching the movie they screamed "Kill the bitch!" when she appeared. "[It] causes working women to reassess their lives, especially single working women," wrote film critic Emanuel Levy.

But nothing got to single women like the angst created by "The Marriage Crunch," *Newsweek*'s doom-and-gloom cover story in 1986 giving women who were still unwed at age thirty a 20 percent chance of tying the knot. Those over forty? Forget about it. You were more likely to be killed by a terrorist than to walk down the aisle.

Like so many stories geared to alarm women, this one had little hard evidence behind it. (Twenty years later, *Newsweek* admitted it got the numbers completely wrong.) But that didn't stop the story from earning raging headlines and "breaking news" coverage at the time. Initially women felt panicky and anxious; then, for many, resentment set in.

Laurie Aronson Starr, a happy single woman who enjoyed her career, travel, and a wide circle of friends, recalled reading the piece. "The statistics made me very angry. . . . Basically they kind of discounted me," she said. "I wasn't a person. And I felt I had a [meaningful] life. And it really made me mad."

REAGAN'S VICTORY—AGAIN—IN 1984 surprised and frustrated feminists. For the first time in our history a woman, Geraldine Ferraro, ran for vice president, on the Democratic ticket headed by Walter Mondale.

Some political analysts attributed Reagan's win to his "good news only" campaign. He'd earned himself the moniker "the Teflon president" because a newly manipulated media kept anything negative from sticking to him. Reagan's Strategic Defense Initiative, known as Star Wars, signaled the largest military buildup during peace of any president before him and appealed to those Americans fearful of attack from the "evil empire." Add to that the usual sound bites of a strong economy and no new taxes, and it amounted to a winning ticket.

By contrast, Mondale's campaign appeared grim and pessimistic; he didn't back off from the need to raise taxes and suffered for it. How much of his defeat related to his running mate remains unclear, but certainly the negative reaction Ferraro encountered suggests that it was a factor. Writing after the election, she confessed to having been unprepared for "the depth of the fury, the bigotry and the sexism [her] candidacy would unleash."

The conservative ascendancy, with its cynical heralding of rugged individualism and antiwoman cast, prevailed through the 1980s into the presidency of George H. W. Bush. For many of us the darkest days came during the confirmation hearings of Clarence Thomas for the Supreme Court seat vacated by esteemed civil rights leader Thurgood Marshall. Concerns about Thomas's experience and intellectual suitability for the position were forgotten when Anita Hill—an African American attorney like Thomas—came forward to charge Thomas with making uninvited and inappropriate sexual remarks to her over a course of years when they worked together at the Equal Employment Opportunity Commission. Before the Senate Judiciary Committee and a rapt television audience, Thomas balked at the charges. In a voice boiling with anger, he claimed to be a victim of a "high-tech lynching for uppity blacks."

The hearings sent seismic waves through the American public. Debate raged over whom to believe. It spilled out from the op-ed pages and universities to restaurants and street corners. Friends and colleagues walked away from each other baffled and dismayed. So many men, including the all-male senate committee, didn't understand the seriousness of Anita Hill's complaints. Women, overwhelmingly, did.

Listening to Hill's testimony catapulted me back fifteen years to a job I took in graduate school administering a financial aid program for a large university. Routinely, maybe three or four times a week, Ed Jones, my supervisor, a married man with children, would call me into his office, tell me to sit down, and reel off a series of suggestive and sexual remarks, inevitably followed by "When are you going to go to bed with me?" I dreaded going into his office. Every time I asked him to stop, he laughed me off. I lost sleep over it, but I never told anyone, not even Susan, my office mate, who would become a lifelong friend. Finally things got so bad I left the job, not happily and certainly not unscathed.

Four days into the Thomas-Hill episode, Susan called me: "I have something to ask you," she said, her voice low and raspy. "When we worked together, did Ed Jones ever hit on you?"

I drew in my breath. "All the time."

"He did it to me, too. *All the time.*"

Fifteen years plus one courageous woman. That's what it took for close friends finally to confront the degradation responsible for shaping and scarring our earliest work experiences.

Soon I began hearing from other friends about hushed, long-ago incidents far worse than my own. Janet's superior at the graphic design company where she worked constantly groped her. In desperation she complained to the head of the firm, who accused her of "not being a team player," told her she "should be flattered," and then fired her. Then there was Marie, a marketing executive whose boss came into her office one night and began to unzip his fly. Certain he planned to rape her, she picked up the phone to call building security. She, too, lost her job.

How can I explain the cloak of silence we draped around these stories? Shame, anger, overwhelming powerlessness, and, I think, resignation sealed our lips. Wasn't this what we, women, had to endure if we wanted to be part of the workforce? Wasn't this what we always got? Had to expect? Should've expected? We didn't know the words to describe it or the ways to stop it. Until the Thomas-Hill incident homeschooled the nation in sexual harassment, most of us didn't even realize that Title IX had made it illegal.

Senators who'd been uncertain about Thomas now flocked to prevent him from being brought down by a woman. The sexual harassment scandal actually sealed his nomination. He went on to become one of the most conservative, antiabortion justices on the bench, Hill to become an inspiring figure for women. Her testimony sparked a surge of female assertiveness. With nationwide studies confirming widespread sexual harassment on the job, women pressed their schools and offices to take a tough stand against it. Institutions feeling increasingly queasy about accusations of indifference rushed to get the mandated policies in place. They held workshops and designated "point persons" trained to hear complaints.

In a peculiar but not surprising twist, the popular motion picture *Disclosure* (1994) turned sexual exploitation in the workplace on its head. Meredith (Demi Moore), a rapacious corporate-climbing predator, attempts to seduce the unsuspecting VP of Production, Tom (Michael Douglas). When he rejects her thigh-throttling advances, she yells "harassment," effectively isolating Tom in the company, nearly ruining his future, and enlivening *Fatal Attraction*–like fears in the hearts of men. Career women are, at bottom, nastily ambitious was the clear message, and if they don't outright kill you, for sure they're going to humiliate and topple you.

Trying to strike as many blows as possible against women's liberation, the (George H. W.) Bush administration busily promoted itself up as the avatars of so-called family values. Vice President Dan Quayle, taking on this mantle, attacked the fictitious television character Murphy Brown for becoming a single mother. It was women like Brown, he claimed, who were responsible for our nation's "poverty of values. . . . [T]he anarchy and lack of structure in our inner cities," he claimed, "are testament to how quickly civilization falls apart when the family foundation cracks."

Quayle's wife, Marilyn, boasted of a Republican party representing those "women who do not want to be liberated from their essential natures as women." And to prove that, President Bush in 1991 vetoed the Family and Medical Leave Act, wiping out nine years of work by over one hundred different groups.

Thousands of women, like my colleague Kristen, pregnant at the time, found themselves caught between the proverbial rock and hard place: they had to leave either their jobs or their infants. And Bush's press secretary Marlin Fitzwater's totally out-of-touch advice to those unhappy with their companies' polices to "look for other jobs" only underscored their plight. They *needed* to hold onto the jobs they had. What it boiled down to was this: a great many moms, single as well as married, couldn't afford to risk their positions by staying out of work too long, but neither did they want to be away from their babies during those first exhausting and deliriously wonderful weeks.

Bush's veto had effectively taken away any viable choice for the majority of working mothers across America. And Kristen, with a husband still in graduate school, found herself back at her desk three weeks after giving birth. "I'd look down and see two wet spots on my blouse, where the milk had leaked through," she remembered, "and it took every bit of effort not to burst into tears."

Down but Certainly Not Out

The blue Thunderbird plunges to oblivion. My students gasp; a couple are teary. We're at the end of *Thelma & Louise*, the 1991 film about a buddy road trip gone hideously off course. When we first meet Louise (Susan Sarandon), she is a tough-talking waitress with a painful secret in her past. Thelma (Geena Davis) is a childlike wife married to a mistreating human slug. The women deserve a weekend of fun.

As the two embark on their getaway, symbols of male hegemony abound. Huge trucks overtake them; telephone poles, like phalluses, line and constrain their path. But actual male domination is rendered real in the form of a parking-lot rape. From that scene forward, Thelma and Louise's ongoing attempts to revenge male cruelty push them closer to their certain fate. Yes, the women have grown strong; yes, their friendship is wonderful to see. But to what end? As the final cut shows, these two victims of male abuse will never have their day in court. Encircled by a caravan of police cars stretching far and wide around them, Thelma and Louise reach the devastating conclusion: there is no place in America for women who resist male supremacy.

When *Thelma & Louise* came out it was considered by many joyful critics to symbolize a movement bombarded into retreat. In reality the reverse proved true. Invigorated and focused by the attacks from the right, the feminist agenda actually matured and strengthened in many respects during the 1980s and early 1990s.

NOW's membership, fueled by the battle for ratification of the ERA, grew from 55,000 in 1977 to 210,000 in 1982. Lobbying for the amendment translated into key political skills. In the midterm election held in 1982, nine women became U.S. senators, more than twice the number of women already there.

The same dynamic came into play with abortion. "Pro-life" protests, hitting pay dirt with the *Webster* decision of 1989, unwittingly sparked a remarkable outpouring of support for pro-choice organizations, putting the women's movement back in the news. Membership in organizations like the National Abortion Rights Action League (NARAL), committed to keeping abortion legal, soared. In addition to women, now men were suddenly fearful about the loss of reproductive rights and became so vocal that the media, several months after *Webster*, noted a decided shift in favor of pro-choice candidates and sentiments.

The more preachers on the right blasted women for abandoning their so-called predetermined biological roles as full-time mothers, the more determined women became to carve out for themselves different and additional kinds of experiences. During the late 1970s and throughout the 1980s the women's movement expanded its focus to address many of the issues faced by women of color, including high infant and maternal mortality and ghettoized housing and racism.

Looking back on the National Women's Conference held in Houston in 1987, Anna Quidlen remembered the "fierce sense of purpose and focus" and the "diversity of the delegates in terms of ethnicity, race, age and political affiliation."

Oppression, expressed through a range of voices and documented by different experiences, burst onto the literary scene. Eloquent, often angry, but always on target, the writings of African American, Native American, Chicana, and Asian American women were collected in the 1981 anthology *This Bridge Called My Back*. Novelists like Amy Tan, Toni Morrison, and Louise Erdrich brought expanded and compelling versions of feminism to the American public.

And while the press couldn't give enough airtime to such prominent conservative theorists as Phyllis Schlafly and Sylvia Ann Hewlett, whose book *The Lesser Life* damned the women's movement for "revil[ing] mothers and children," feminists were busy lobbying for better, affordable child care, family leave, and an end to discrimination against pregnant women.

What feminists wanted for women went far deeper than syrupy and vacuous Mother's Day rhetoric. "Show, don't tell," the proverbial advice given to writers, had an important application to feminist work. Real respect for women meant giving them agency and rights. As the title of Aileen S. Kraditor's book suggests, women needed to get *Up from the Pedestal*.

The Displaced Homemaker Network, providing counseling and job skills for women who because of death, divorce, or other changes in circumstance had to make the transition from stay-at-home moms to paid workers, fought to establish a permanent voice in Washington, D.C.

Lesbians still faced extraordinary challenges in being granted equality but managed to win the right to have domestic partnerships legally recognized in at least seven cities. Organizations dedicated to the needs of older women, women with disabilities, battered women, and the growing new population of women with AIDS sprang up all over the map.

Both ecofeminism, which emphasizes environmental concerns, and global feminism, a movement to support women's struggles around the world, got their start in the 1980s and are still vibrant today. And labor feminists, working with the Service Employees International Union (SEIU), scored important victories organizing home-care workers and university clerical workers at numerous well-known schools. Bank tellers from Minnesota, who picketed in frigid weather after the bank's president denied their requests for promotions with a dismissive "We are not all equal, you know," attracted media attention and inspired campaigns to unionize women in the insurance and banking industries.

As feminism moved to Main Street, its message that women could lead lives unrestricted by preconceived gender notions resonated widely. Groups like the YWCA and the Girl Scouts of America added programs to empower girls, enabling them to explore a range of possibilities for their futures. Activist organizations became accepted—and we thought then—*enduring* features of our political, economic, and social landscape.

In terms of the women's movement, author Susan Faludi was right to call the 1980s the "backlash years," but they should also be known as the "push-back years," for feminists mounted an impressive resistance against those who tried to sabotage their rights.

7

THE MIXED BAG OF
BILL CLINTON

During the 1992 presidential campaign, whenever the polls showed George H. W. Bush slipping against his rival Bill Clinton, the Republicans threw darts at Clinton's wife. Their long list of Hillary Rodham Clinton's deficits included using her maiden name, her failure to bake chocolate chip cookies, and her outspoken independence. But what really enraged them? According to Alessandra Stanley, writing in the *New York Times* on August 21, 1992, it was her career. She had worked full-time while being a mother. "An unwifely feminist," a Cruella de Vil with a law degree. It not only set her apart from other first ladies, it just about disqualified her for the role.

Many women—a good chunk of them among the 56 percent in the workforce—apparently rejected these slurs; they gave more votes to Clinton than to Bush, if only by a small margin.

For a lot of feminists the election signaled a new era of tangible political power. "More than half a century after women were granted the vote, a female block emerged; women were more likely to vote Democrat than Republican, favoring a greater governmental role in social services, men wanting less," reported historians Carole Ellen DuBois and Lynn Dumneil in *Through Women's Eyes*. Carol Moseley Braun took her seat as the first African American female senator, and women gained representatives in both the House and the Senate.

Initially, Bill Clinton didn't disappoint. Women played conspicuous and important roles in his government: Janet Reno, attorney general;

Madeleine Albright, secretary of state; Ruth Bader Ginsburg, second female member of the Supreme Court. More than 40 percent of his appointments went to women, and his administration oversaw record funding for women's health programs.

I remember the excitement when my colleague Kirsten called to say, "He did it!" The "it" referred to passage of the Family and Medical Leave Act, the first piece of legislation Clinton signed.

The most prominent of the new act's several clauses made it mandatory for companies of a certain size to give both men and women at least twelve work weeks of unpaid time off from their jobs each year for the birth or adoption of a child or the addition of a foster child to a family. Our next push would be for *paid* leave, but this constituted a good first step to becoming a country acknowledging, understanding, and even supporting the needs of mothers in the workplace.

Other successes followed. Clinton rescinded Ronald Reagan's Global Gag Rule and signed the Violence Against Women Act, finally recognizing domestic violence as a major public policy concern.

Then his agenda hit the skids.

His pledge to allow openly gay men and lesbian women to serve in the armed forces collapsed like a poorly made soufflé. The Don't Ask, Don't Tell policy effectively said to servicemen and -women, "It's OK to be gay, just keep quiet about it," and proved unappetizing to both the military and homosexual communities. The armed forces thought the policy was insensitive to their needs, and gays criticized it as too cautious.

As for health care reform, with its much-needed provision of universal coverage? The plan, spearheaded by Hillary's task force, ultimately went belly up under the well-coordinated attack from conservatives, the American Medical Association, and the health insurance industry. While pundits and policy wonks dissected the failed proposal, the number of uninsured Americans rose from 34.7 million to 42.6 million by the end of the 1990s. The human faces behind these staggering numbers will haunt anyone who reads through the transcripts of the regional hearings the American Cancer Society conducted during those years. For those lacking insurance, the words *second opinion* and *early detection* are little but cruel taunts from an exclusionist world. At forty-one,

Anna had stage four cervical cancer, a disease easily diagnosed by a pap test, if only she could have afforded one. And Marge, terminally ill with breast cancer, had worried for years about the lump she'd found, but the money for a biopsy, surgery, maybe chemo—where would she get that with three children to feed?

Next came welfare—a topic so demonized by Republican rhetoric by the time of Clinton's presidency that any meaningful debate on its merits became impossible. Once he signed the reform bill in 1996 under the who-could-criticize-it title "The Personal Responsibility and Work Opportunity Reconciliation Act," the sixty-year-old safety net for the poor fell apart. However fair the bill attempted to be, there's no way to see its first sentence—"Marriage is the foundation of a successful society"—as anything other than a swipe at many of those it presumed to help.

Welfare and work programs now became the responsibilities of individual states, with financial incentives to reduce their caseloads. Recipients had to find work—thirty hours of it per week for parents with children over age six—within two years or be cut off from aid. No one could receive cash assistance for more than five years, and states could deny benefits to women who had additional children while receiving welfare. A patchwork of provisions helped ease the transition for welfare recipients, and the vigorous economy did its part to enable some women to find moderately well-paying jobs. Others stayed poor, desperately poor. With so much likely to be stacked against them—little education, few employable skills, abusive partners, limited access to child care—it's no wonder many women reported cutting back on or skipping meals so they wouldn't run out of food before the next paycheck.

That Clinton had a bellicose Republican Congress hurling a wrecking ball into all his social policies didn't give him a pass in the eyes of many feminists. His welfare "reforms" signaled a betrayal. "He was the man we hoped would bring back social responsibility, a sense of community to our country," one of my colleagues said, her voice filled with disappointment. Instead, he'd taken a page from the GOP handbook with unfettered individualism written all over it. Patricia Ireland, then the president of NOW, led a hunger strike protesting the new law. NOW activists joined hundreds of others picketing in front of the White House in what they called a Hungry for Justice campaign.

Clinton's veto of a bill outlawing dilation and extraction, a type of rare late-term abortion approved by numerous organizations including the American Nurses Association, helped to redeem his image with many women, but it set him on a crash course with Republicans who vowed to end this kind of abortion in any way they could. And though few of us realized it at the time, Clinton, with his sexual escapades, had as much as tied himself to the train tracks.

THROUGHOUT 1998 WE began hearing about an alleged relationship between Clinton and a young White House intern, Monica Lewinsky. The steamy media spectacle that ensued refused to budge; it squatted like a toad on the public consciousness, kept there by a press wallowing in the smutfest.

But even when the president confirmed the validity of reports, most of the women I knew abstained from judgment, taking an "If Hillary doesn't care, why should we?" attitude. Interestingly, at the time, Hillary, in the role of the poor deceived wife standing by her man, won far greater support than Hillary the would-be policy maker. Her approval ratings soared.

Of course many of us responded with outrage, deploring Bill's womanizing, his appalling inappropriateness, his inability to "keep it zipped"— but impeach him for it? You've got to be kidding! One of my friends hung a sign in his office reading It's the Nation's Welfare, Stupid. Still, Newt Gingrich, House speaker and determined foe of everything Clintonian, steamrolled ahead, putting substantial resources into the search for snippets of titillating evidence against the president.

Known feminists and women politicians whose opinions hadn't been sought on any number of issues, from gun control to minimum wage, suddenly became grist for the media mill. The press hammered high-profile women who refused to call for Clinton's impeachment, calling them hypocrites, opportunists, and worse. When former congresswoman Elizabeth Holtzman, appearing on Chris Matthews's *Hardball*, wouldn't label Clinton's behavior as sexual harassment because Lewinsky was a consenting adult, another guest, Michael Barone, senior Washington editor for *Reader's Digest*, likened the women's movement to prostitution. And Larry King invoked Hitler's name when Patricia Ireland, on CNN, argued against overturning the election—especially one determined by women—because of Clinton's irresponsible behavior.

Feminist theorists Andrea Dworkin, Susan Brownmiller, and Barbara Ehrenreich all spoke out against the president. But many other advocates of women's rights, while condemning his actions, expressed deep concern about an ultraconservative agenda. Numerous leaders of the women's movement put out a joint press release in 1998:

> We are witnessing a relentless campaign—both inside and outside the government—to hound President Clinton out of office. . . . And some of those who are leading the charge . . . are among the worst foes of women's rights. The opponents of the President have a political agenda that will harm women long after the scandal has faded from the front pages.

For certain, Clinton's scorecard on women's issues hadn't been perfect, yet he'd done more for us than any president in recent memory. His unfinished program, including raising the minimum wage, ensuring pay equity, giving twenty-one billion dollars to child care initiatives, expanding health services for women, and numerous antipoverty remedies, lay fallow in a Congress totally preoccupied with reaping the political rewards of the revelatory semen-stained dress.

And it *was* preoccupied. And partisan—splashing the secret grand jury testimony all over the news, rushing to publish the report of independent counsel Kenneth Starr well before the decision to proceed with impeachment hearings had been reached. The moralizing right, wringing its hands over Clinton's salacious behavior, simply couldn't get enough of it. Peculiarly, they wanted the public to join in their voyeuristic orgy—445 pages filled with sexually explicit language and X-rated descriptions.

When Hillary Clinton, in the midst of the Lewinsky scandal, claimed "a vast right-wing conspiracy" had been against her husband since his election, most Americans shrugged it off. And while there was no coordinated, top-to-bottom plot, she wasn't that far off the mark.

The reports of numerous esteemed journalists described a well-financed, organized, conservative attack machine bent on destroying progressive candidates and policies. David Brock's bestselling tell-all *Blinded by the Right* revealed how he received huge sums from firebrands of the right to trample truth in a brazen but highly successful smear campaign against Bill Clinton. And Anita Hill. And Hillary. (That Brock's exposé of A-list conservative participation in these nefarious schemes didn't result in any slander or libel suits against him goes far to affirm the validity of his charges.)

Still in the future were the damning disclosures about Clinton's leering enemies: Henry Hyde, head of the Judiciary Committee, responsible for deciding whether to refer Clinton's case to the House for impeachment proceedings, had a long affair with a mother of three, ending her marriage, although not his own. And Newt Gingrich took time out from self-righteously megaphoning his disgust at Clinton's behavior to have sex with a young congressional aide. Quite likely, the Peeping Toms on the right went after Clinton as a way to expiate their own guilt.

The disproportionate attention given to l'affaire Lewinsky—the formal impeachment ceremony, the public shaming of the president—was a definite and deliberate attempt to draw the public together by casting Clinton as a deviant. Clinton's serial womanizing became a wonderfully suited launching pad from which to rocket off a newly fueled "family values" agenda. See what happens in a marriage when a wife works outside the home? See what happens to a country embracing debauchery instead of morality? demanded the outraged and often hypocritical voices of Washington.

When the Senate voted against convicting Clinton in 1999, the majority of Americans—according to the polls—expressed relief. More than forty million taxpayer dollars had been spent, attention to important issues diverted, precious legislative time squandered.

Most of us didn't realize at the time how much all the brouhaha surrounding the impeachment hearings emboldened and played into the hands of the political right and their champions in the media. But we were going to find out soon enough.

Finding Our Way in the Millennium

As the new century turned, Americans felt optimistic and secure about their futures. The 1993 World Trade Center bombing, never evoking deep feelings of vulnerability, had begun to fade in memory. The U.S. embassy bombings in East Africa five years later, while horrific, didn't seem a direct threat to U.S. citizens, and the attack on the *Cole* was still ten months away.

As much as Clinton's detractors had painted dire scenarios of a nation plunged into ruin, by the end of the 1990s life had improved considerably for the majority of Americans. Daring to raise taxes, Clinton had helped close the budget deficit. He left a budget surplus of $127 billion, projected to swell to $5 trillion over the next ten years.

America had more jobs than we'd had for decades. "Between 1992 and 2000 U.S. companies added 32 million workers to their payrolls, driving unemployment to a 30-year low. Productivity—the amount produced per worker—responsible for higher wages, soared. By the end of Clinton's term it was rising faster than ever before in our history," according to economist Paul Krugman.

For the first time since the 1960s, poverty rates declined. Families finally had a chance to break free of the generational stranglehold keeping them down. Two especially vulnerable groups—children under eighteen and single mothers, particularly those with young children—saw a substantial increase in their standard of living from 1989 to 1999.

More jobs and more money translated into a healthier society. Serious crime, including sexual assault, dropped dramatically. The availability of new treatments for breast cancer resulted in a higher survival rate for women with the disease, although better outcomes for white women than black pointed to the need for more funding. The death rates from lung, prostate, and colorectal cancers also dipped.

Not surprisingly, there were fewer teen pregnancies occurring in all states and among young women of all ages, races, and ethnicities. This trend, as a study on youth risk behavior from 1991 to 2001 made clear, resulted from improved contraceptive availability and practices.

High school sex education was at an all-time high. Those of us who taught adolescents told them straight out: there's only one sure way to avoid pregnancy and sexually transmitted diseases—no sexual intercourse. But being realists, we spent hours in workshops learning how to talk with teens about sex and how to teach contraception. Then we took our show on the road, meeting with small groups of students, excusing those whose families opted out of the program. With plastic models at the ready, we demonstrated how to use both male and female condoms. The bravehearts among the faculty play-acted ways to say no and ways to say yes *safely*. Our mantra: "Don't die from embarrassment." And similar scenarios played out all over the country.

Women's groups scored impressive victories in getting more insurance companies to cover contraception, making it widely available to those who wanted it. And in what might have served as a public policy lesson for future administrations, abortion rates plunged under the watch of our first pro-choice president. By the end of Clinton's presidency, 180,000 fewer abortions were performed nationwide than when he took office.

By the mid-1990s mothers of young children accounted for more than 59 percent of the workforce, and longitudinal studies of how everyone was doing began to roll in. One, by the Society of Early Child Care, following over a thousand children from birth to three years of age at ten different locations in the country, confirmed earlier findings: these children benefited from their mothers' involvement in the outside world. Good child care experiences—whether in a center or with relatives—had a positive impact on emotional and social development.

Still, lack of a comprehensive federal policy regulating child care facilities meant far too many children spent time in centers exceeding the recommended ratio of five children to one adult, but the narrowing of the wage gender gap and a drop-off in the number of divorces (on the uptick until the Clinton years) meant many more families would be able to afford quality child care than previously.

Not surprisingly, households with a better financial outlook, no matter the source, enjoy a better quality of life. A compilation of some twenty-odd analyses showed no difference in marital happiness of couples with employed and nonemployed wives, and, all other factors being equal, a woman was generally more satisfied if she had an income. The old adage—men don't want their wives working—just didn't hold up.

Even television began to reflect an increasing acceptance of female independence. After the feisty detective-friends Cagney and Lacey were yanked off the air in 1988 because, as one CBS executive told *TV Guide*, the heroines "were too harshly women's lib," viewers in the 1990s hunting for female characters with some oomph found two.

Roseanne, the overweight, tart-tongued working wife and mother in the Emmy Award–winning show by the same name, struck a responsive chord with women across the country as a welcome alternative to the typical saccharine sitcom heroine. Even with her string of jobs—cashier, telemarketer, waitress, clerk—Roseanne and her husband, Dan, struggled constantly. Financial difficulties dogged them as they did so many working families. But more than that—the series showed us a world where life happened. In the face of the gritty realities of abortion, domestic violence, and infidelity, the female characters supported one another. They weren't afraid to speak up, sometimes at an ear-splitting pitch, and when they did—miraculously for TV—they got respect, not rejection.

To link Buffy, the slender, young, blond vampire slayer, with Roseanne seems, at first glance, odd. But like Roseanne, Buffy, who vanquished the forces of darkness, also defied existing gender stereotypes. The show's writer, Joss Whedon, set out to invert the Hollywood formula of "the little blonde girl who goes into a dark alley and gets killed in every horror movie." He wanted his character to personify the "joy of female power: having it, using it, sharing it." Back in 1997, executives at Channel WB (now home to such female-undermining series as *America's Next Top Model*, *The Search for the Next Pussycat Doll*, and *Beauty and the Geek*) had been looking for a series empowering young women, and they picked up the show.

Buffy's age—she was a high school student—made her a bit young for a superhero, but it also created a lot of her appeal. Some of her monsters had real faces and names: Spike, Drusilla, Oz. But other demons she had to conquer were far more pervasive and elusive: the harrowing obstacles confronting adolescent girls.

Sunnydale High, Buffy's new school, may have been perched on top of a "Hellmouth," an entryway to evil's domain, but every high school can be a dangerous place for teenage girls as they try to negotiate the risky complexities of their own sexuality and autonomy.

Film critic Hannah Tucker, then seventeen years old, described Buffy's appeal. "For some . . . [it's the] brutal portrayal of high school . . . for others, it's the pop culture references . . . and for some, the lure of a Wonderbra'd blond chick fighting vampires, and that's fine with me. Because the basic truth about Buffy herself is known to all who appreciate her: She's the intelligent, youthful hope."

Tucker's words could well be part of the mission statement for third-wave feminism. The movement began in the 1990s, largely among women in their twenties. Some took their inspiration from the activities of riot grrrls, the music movement of punk bands like Bikini Kill and Bratmobile. Others wanted to accomplish the unfinished work of the second wave: raising the minimum wage, gaining affordable, accessible child care, fighting rape and domestic violence.

But however they began, third-wavers have concerns unique to their generation. In *Manifesta*, the wave's quasi-bible, authors Jennifer Baumgardner and Amy Richards list "equal access to the Internet and technology, HIV/AIDS awareness, child sexual abuse, self-mutilation, eating disorders, body image and globalization" as priorities. The movement calls attention to the treatment of women in the army and women in prison, two significant and often overlooked sites of inequity.

Accepting and expanding upon much accomplished by my generation, third-wavers can be gently (and not so gently) critical of the movements before theirs. To distance themselves from what many see as the white middle-class centricity of the second wave, they ask: Whose Personal? Whose Political? Their movement is widely inclusive, battling all forms of discrimination simultaneously: sexism, racism, classism, ageism, and homophobia. They may not have any clear-cut icons, but neither are they a few lone cheerleaders twirling the baton of change. Over five thousand members form the Third Wave Foundation alone, raising money for women's organizations around the world.

Third-wavers call to mind the chant arising from the march against the imminent invasion of Iraq, in New York City, February 13, 2003, a month before the spectacularly wrong-headed Shock and Awe campaign. Protesting the high-handed tactics of the Bush administration, tens of thousands, representing all races, classes, ethnicities, and ages, cried out, "*This* is what democracy looks like."

In much the same way, third-wavers working to give a better life to the gray-haired and the bottle-blond, the sexy and the wallflower, the stay-at-home mom and the lesbian mother, the Hollywood producer and the factory worker, are saying loud and clear, "*This* is what a feminist looks like."

They remind us again: there is no one-size-fits-all feminism, but a uniting of all politically conscious women in their quest, to use bell hooks's phrase, for "gender justice."

So that was where we were at the dawning of the new millennium: second-wavers still strong, the third wave pushing after us, all gaining momentum, when we came crashing into something huge and formidable, something that was, without doubt, one of the most bizarre and prophetic episodes in American history—the election of George W. Bush.

8

BUSHWINKED TO
BUSHWHACKED

My daughter Alison called me, crying. It was December 13, 2000. She had just finished watching presidential hopeful Al Gore's concession speech. The outrage and disillusionment of my newly political, idealist daughter were no greater than those of people who'd been voting for years. In the thirty-six days since the election, the nation had gotten a crash course in partisan politics. And it wasn't pretty. Underneath all the talk of butterfly ballots, hanging chads, and future career plans of Katherine Harris, Florida's secretary of state, lurked a *really* inconvenient truth: Al Gore had won the popular vote and quite possibly the election, but George W. Bush was going to be our next president.

The weeks following the election found us all riveted to the news as teams of high-profile lawyers flocked to key Florida counties. At stake: the right to a manual recount of ballots in counties where voting irregularities and confusion might have skewed the outcome. Shouting matches, shuffles, cries of foul play punctuated the legal proceedings. Two weeks into the fast-developing web of suits and countersuits, Florida's high court ruled in favor of the Democrats by allowing the hand counts to continue. Then came the staggering news: the U.S. Supreme Court, throwing states' rights to the wind, agreed to hear Bush's appeal of the Florida decision.

History will decide if the Supreme Court ruling—ordering a halt to the recount—ranks "as the single most corrupt decision in . . . [its] history," as famed constitutional lawyer Alan M. Dershowitz charged. The way the justices' votes split along partisan lines, and the tiny size of Bush's lead over Gore—some 286 votes out of more than 5.8 million cast, according to estimates by the Associated Press (other sources judged the lead to have been nine hundred votes or slightly higher)—shocked a nation that believed in the detached impartiality of our courts. But looking at the decision in the context of the presidential campaign, it shouldn't have been unexpected.

The Republican candidate, George W. Bush, was generally considered a nice, if not particularly bright, guy. His handlers had tried to create a steadfast cowboy persona out of the former frat boy. Like Reagan's advisers had done, Karl Rove had seen to it that the requisite ranch, in this case in Crawford, Texas, was purchased before the election. But aside from the Photoshopped Marlboro man image, Bush didn't have much to recommend him or give him an edge over Gore. Luckily for him, he didn't need much. He had the press.

All The News That's (Un)Fit to Print

The "mediathon" is *New York Times* columnist Frank Rich's term for the 24/7 barrage of what passes as news these days. The consolidation of the news industry in the 1990s put about 90 percent of what most of us see and read into the hands of some eleven companies, entertainment biggies like Disney, Viacom, and Time Warner. Over the past few decades, two thirds of independent newspapers in this country have disappeared, while one whale of a company, Clear Channel Communications, has swallowed up more than one thousand radio stations.

As corporations vie with each other—and the Internet—for an audience, journalists leapfrog over facts, scattering hard-nosed reporting and critical analysis to the wind. In their mania to saturate the airways with round-the-clock cable and talk shows, the media latches onto a snippet of information and spins it into a sensational story, instantly morphing into *the* story of the day, often of the week. Instead of communicating news, the press, with a sharp eye to advertisers, is shaping and creating its own version of current events.

And even though we spend endless hours surfing the Web, most of us still learn about our world the old-fashioned way—through radio, television, and newspapers. But what's *new*-fashioned is the press's unprecedented influence over the American mind. As Gerald Levin, then chief executive of AOL Time Warner, said, global media giants "might, in fact, become more powerful than government."

"The only security of all is in a free press," the perspicacious Thomas Jefferson said, simultaneously bequeathing a gift and a warning to the new nation. He'd be horrified to see how compromised our once fiercely independent press has become. Instead of presenting divergent viewpoints vital to the survival of a democracy, the media, after the consolidation of the 1990s, took a sharp turn to the right, nearly eclipsing objective reporting. It is axiomatic that corporate conglomerations will inevitably support those candidates whose policies won't threaten their bottom line. But the fervor and frenzy of the new millennium press roared out of a well-oiled attack machine, revved up (or pretending to be) over Clinton's bad behavior two years earlier. And it clamored for a regime change at home.

Clinton's sex scandals and impeachment hearings fed the insatiable maw of the right-wing partisans in a way few of us at the time could have imagined. With communism no longer a menace, like-minded conservatives—evangelicals and politicians—needed to focus on other deviants, other threats to "American traditions and values of faith." They found what they were looking for, as they had before, in "radical feminism," "environmental extremists," and the "purveyors of sex and violence"—the Clinton-Gore, soon to be the Gore-Lieberman, agenda. But now they were newly energized with proof of "corruption at the top." Fearfully powerful, the right exercised a virtual chokehold on the press, giving them unprecedented control over public discourse and effectively flatlining dissent.

Under the tutelage of able right-wing theoreticians, the cold war morphed into the "culture war." This handy term, popularized by Pat Buchanan, sprang off Republican lips to describe a largely manufactured divide over "hot button" issues—abortion, women's rights, gay rights, separation of church and state, stem-cell research—allegedly splitting the nation into two hostile camps. It wasn't that there were several views on these issues, or that someone might support, let's say, gay rights but not stem-cell research. There could be no in between, no middle ground. It was an all-or-nothing deal.

The political right pummeled the nation into believing an ideological barbed wire separated the Bush and Gore camps. And as Reagan had done, the Bushies, filled with righteous indignation, claimed to speak for the true Americans, for those shielding our nation from "the gathering storm" of moral decay.

Words like *decadence* and *immorality*, beaten into a platitudinous pulp by years of right-wing usage, suddenly became animated with reverential meaning. Bush might not yet have had a proverbial bloody shirt to wave, but he had a defiled dress, and he used it mightily. When during a campaign speech he talked about bringing honest people to government, people who wouldn't "stain the house," the American public immediately conjured up images of Lewinsky's semen-smeared dress. But Gore, not Clinton, was the candidate; Republicans needed to tarnish *his* image, and this put the slander-panderers in a bit of a pickle.

Before his ecowarrior days, Al Gore was Bill Clinton's squeaky-clean boy scout of a vice president. Happily married to his high-school sweetheart, Tipper, with whom he'd had four children, Gore could match his bedrock-solid family-values credentials with any red-state candidate.

Here is where the fabulously endowed right-wing think tanks came in. Organized and disciplined, meeting weekly to set movement priorities and plan strategy, they adopted talking points for the media to use, wittingly or not, against Gore. According to archconservative strategist Grover Norquist, it was not good enough to win; it had to be a painful, devastating defeat. "We're sending a message here," Norquist said. "It is like when the king would take his opponent's head and spike it on a pole for everyone to see."

Under the right's onslaught, Gore allegedly became someone so uncomfortable in his own skin that he had to inflate his achievements. He'd lied about being used as an inspiration for the book *Love Story*, he'd lied about inventing the Internet, said conservative pundits. And when he said he'd never made either claim? He was lying about that, too. Could a man so fake, so delusional, so filled with grandiosity, a man with such major character flaws, be trusted as president?

A reread of the press coverage of Al Gore's campaign is a study of misquotes, misinformation, and misuse of the public trust. "Fictional," "nasty," "spun to sound like something corrupt" is how Sharon Francis, executive director of the Connecticut River Joint Commissions, put it after reading the distorted reports of Gore's trip to her state.

"You can actually disprove some of what Bush is saying if you . . . get out your calculator or you look at his record in Texas," said *Time* magazine columnist Margaret Carlson. "But it's really easy and fun to disprove Gore. As sport and as our enterprise [it's] . . . greatly entertaining to us."

It took Al Gore's winning the Nobel Peace Prize in 2007 and the disastrous presidency of George W. Bush for the press to issue its string of mea culpas. "We mocked him in 2000," confessed Bob Herbert. Why? Not because of his politics, but because of his clothing. "In the race for the highest office of the land, we showed the collective maturity of three-year-olds." Other journalists made the same admission, with the same regrets. Back then, the defining factor of which candidate the media supported was reduced to whom you'd rather sit next to at a barbecue.

All this—the intimidating muscle-flexing of the right, the caving in of liberals and the left, the abysmal failure of the press to do its job—made the Supreme Court's decision as predictably shameful as the campaign it ended.

In his concession speech, Gore called on the nation to end its partisan rancor, to focus on what unites us rather than on what divides us. But he might not have realized—most of us didn't—that we had the great divider headed to the White House. Consensus was not in the Republican play list.

Thanks to "barbecue journalism," we didn't know much about Bush's plans for the country. When he talked about his relationship with God, most of us assumed he was describing private worship, not public policy. We didn't appreciate how the word *values* was really a code, telegraphing to the Christian right his intentions to rid the country of what evangelicals call "radical Christ-hating" feminists.

We understood, in a generalized sense, he wasn't in favor of abortion, but we believed Laura Bush when she said on television she didn't think *Roe* would be taken away. And some of us really bought into those campaign slogans, such as "W is for Women." Little did we realize the W stood for *Whacked*. If we knew then what we know now, a lot more of us would have been crying along with my daughter that cold December night.

GEORGE W. BUSH presided over an administration responsible for rolling back women's progress in profound and frightening ways. Much of the assault was secretive and often hidden. "We know that life is harder, more difficult. . . . We're struggling more and getting less of everything in return, but we're not sure why," Wendy, a mother of two young children, said. Her words were echoed in a 2006 study finding that for the first time since the 1970s women were less happy with their lives than men. The happiness gap was also found among high school students.

Researchers mulling over these results came up with a "the fault, dear Brutus" type of explanation: *we* were to blame. The reason? Women today want more, whereas in the 1970s and 1980s "they had narrower ambitions."

Not only is this historically inaccurate, it misses the point—an important one made in 2007 by the Global Gender Report documenting the United States' shameful slip in gender equality from twenty-fifth to thirty-first out of 128 countries, representing 90 percent of the world's population. All those countries in the top twenty narrowed the gap from the year before. This is what the researchers had hoped and expected to find. But the United States had the ignominious distinction of going backward, beaten out by South Africa, Cuba, Namibia, and Lesotho. It's hard to advance our scores when we have the second-worst rate of newborn mortality in the modern world. So if we, women, aren't satisfied with our lot these days, it's not because we *want more*, it's because we're *getting less*—economically, educationally, politically, and medically.

This erosion of women's rights didn't happen overnight. We've already seen the pieces in play starting in the 1980s. Bush and his crowd didn't invent antiwoman attitudes, or antiwoman policies, for that matter. Sexism, it's fair to say, is America's default setting. But without doubt, W. had the worst record on women of any president in memory.

What's happened to women in this country goes even deeper than all the legal setbacks, the programs slashed, the budgets cut. Distorted views of women pound through the popular culture and public consciousness like a war drum. Unadulterated wrath against women's progress was unleashed (and continues to be) by numerous ultraright foundations and organizations, including the Sarah Scaife, Olin, Bradley, Carthage, Castle Rock, and American Enterprise foundations. Three in particular have been funded with the express purpose of marginalizing and demeaning women. The Susan B. Anthony List raises money for antichoice and other like-minded candidates. The Claire Booth Luce Foundation targets young women, especially on college campuses. With vitriolic attacks on women's studies programs and feminist initiatives, it blames all the ills of humankind on women's quest for independence. Bashing feminism is a particular skill of the members as they eagerly try to erase all its gains. The foundation woos adherents to the retrogressive agenda by generous paid internships and mentoring programs. Conservative political activists and right-wing analysts such as Ann Coulter and Laura Ingraham are supported while the next generation of Phyllis Schlaflys is being groomed.

The Independent Women's Forum, whose board is stocked with Washington heavy hitters, many of whom hold prominent governmental positions, takes delight in running roughshod over feminist causes. It spends megasums publishing antifeminist newsletters, books, and periodicals; lobbying against affirmative action; and hyping the purported "myths" of the gender wage gap, the glass ceiling, date rape, and domestic violence.

Back in 2000, few of us realized the extent to which neocon billionaire backing made certain that the most familiar and prolific political voices were on the right, poisoning the mediasphere with antiwoman sentiments. The mainstream press, when it roused itself into writing about women at all, simply circulated reports filled with misleading information and inaccurate data, some supplied by these very foundations or by the self-serving Bush administration. While our attention was riveted on the traumatic events of the times, with cynicism and stealth the Bushies, by embracing evangelical Christians, reactionary politicians, and the media they control, wrapped misogyny in the gloss of respectability and gave it a life of its own.

IN THE NARRATIVE of what happened between the third wave's invigorating thrust in the 1990s and our present struggles to regain hard-won rights, Bush's lack of a mandate when he took office also played a significant part. The newly anointed president needed to find legitimacy and authority.

And he needed to pay off his political debts. As bestselling author Nina Easton explains, "The Christian right's sway within the Republican party . . . made it an influential power broker in the neck-and-neck 2000 presidential race."

From the moment born-again Bush declared Jesus Christ to be his favorite philosopher, evangelicals threw their large and organized grassroots constituency wholeheartedly behind him. This was no case of strange bedfellows but rather of kindred sprits. Still, the speed with which Bush took on the mantle of fundamentalist Christians smacked of payback with a sharp eye toward expediency. As the late Molly Ivins used to say, "In politics you've got to dance with the one that brung you."

A newly renovated "family values" program became the creed of his administration. It signaled Bush's commitment to return our country to what his supporter evangelical Jeff Robinson calls a "biblical patriarchy that restores the male to his divinely ordained station as head of the home and church." When Bush called upon "All of us . . . to work together to counter the negative influence of the culture," there was no mistaking what "culture" he had in mind. He was launching a moral crusade against feminism, reproductive freedom, and homosexuality.

By firing off sorties against progressive-thinking Americans (and having his loyal henchmen do it also), Bush was rallying his base to his side and setting up boundaries, articulating the "us or them" philosophy we've come to know so well.

His first day in the Oval Office, he reinstated the Global Gag Rule. Following in short order he made known his intention to get rid of *Roe v. Wade* and eliminate contraceptive coverage for female federal employees and their dependents. His administration restricted Medicaid funding for mifepristone (formerly known as RU-486 or the "abortion pill"), and in the first of his many bizarre appointments, Kay Coles James, a former dean of Pat Robertson's Regent University and a fierce antiabortion, anti–affirmative action activist, took over the directorship of the U.S. Office of Personnel Management, in charge of hiring and firing and discrimination complaints in the entire federal workforce.

Then, notably, he asked John Ashcroft, who while in the Senate had tied with Senator Jesse Helms as the most conservative senator (scoring 100 percent ratings from every far-right group), to be his attorney general.

A Pentecostalist, Ashcroft held daily prayers in the Justice Department. He became the butt of many jokes after he spent eight thousand taxpayer dollars to cover the exposed metal breast of the Spirit of Justice statue that had stood in the Great Hall for sixty-five years. But his other actions were no laughing matter. From the get-go he showed his outright hostility to women's safety—backing away from providing security to abortion clinics, closing the Violence Against Women Office, and picking Nancy Pfotenhauer, formerly CEO of the Independent Women's Forum, vocally opposed to legislation protecting women from domestic violence, for a task force studying that exact issue.

But his lifetime appointments are what will be remembered as his most damaging deeds. Drawing heavily from the ultraconservative Federalist Society, whose legal philosophy is represented by Supreme Court justices Antonin Scalia and Clarence Thomas, Ashcroft, in his first six months in office, stacked the federal judiciary with right-wing ideologues known for opposition to reproductive rights.

Similarly, vice president Dick Cheney, in charge of Bush's transition team, crafted a testosterone-fueled inner circle, a veritable who's who of A-list neoconservatives: Donald Rumsfeld, Paul Wolfowitz, Douglas Feith, Richard Perle, John W. Bolton, and Lewis "Scooter" Libby. Off to a sure-footed start in the 1980s, neocons had shaped Reagan's militaristic ideology and served in Bush I's administration. Out of favor in the Clinton years, they used the time to secure funding and sharpen their message. In 1997 a core group of these men—Cheney, Libby, Rumsfeld, and Wolfowitz—along with top political operative Karl Rove, Christian Conservative leader Gary Bauer, and William Kristol, editor of the powerful right-wing journal *The Weekly Standard*, founded the think tank Project for a New American Century (PNAC). This double-dipping just about ensured PNAC's overzealous agenda a prominent place in American foreign policy. PNAC called for a Pax Americana—the United States as sole superpower, a benevolent "hegemon," CEO to the world.

What they wanted, simply put, was for America to go *mano a mano* against the rest of the planet and come out on top. To accomplish this we had to beef up our armed forces, necessary to regain prestige after "wimping out" in Vietnam. And we had to embrace religion, necessary to give a moral imperative to our mission: dominating the globe's major developed economies, unilaterally and, if need be, with force.

Their plan was so big stick it made Teddy Roosevelt's look like a weenie. Although PNAC members would have to sit tight before seeing their pet project—a war with Iraq—put into place, they brought their considerable clout to President Bush's early policy moves. We can see their pumped-up-go-it-alone approach in Bush's walking away from the Kyoto Protocol to reduce greenhouse gas emissions, abandoning the Anti-Ballistic Missile Treaty, and opposing the International Criminal Court.

Even then, Bush's unilateral polices worried our allies across the Atlantic. A study conducted by the Pew Research Center and released in August 2001 found people living in several Western European countries to have little more confidence in the president of the United States than in Russian president Vladimir Putin.

But no matter. Real men go it alone. The muscle-flexing America of the new millennium exalted dominance, aggression, and control. It was after all Colin Powell, Bush's secretary of state, who said, "I want to be the bully on the block."

Lord Guthrie, a former British diplomat, noted how "peacekeeping . . . [was] something for wimps." All the talk, Guthrie said, was "about the warrior ethic." It's hard to escape the gendered implications of our new mantra: macho abroad, macho at home. In both realms, men ruled, as they did in the 1950s. The *P* of PNAC might just as well have meant *Patriarchy* for a New American Century.

Phallic politics would bring about a stunning reversal of women's progress, craftily sabotaging our rights, curbing our autonomy, and re-creating traditional roles. But back then, no one was reporting on women's diminishing prospects. Capturing the news instead was the mysterious disappearance of congressional aide Chandra Levy. It was a portent.

As we dashed off for our Labor Day vacations, dark clouds blotted the horizon. The perfect storm of sexism was already brewing. We just didn't see it coming.

9

9/11 AND WOMEN

I t was almost impossible to understand what had befallen us on September 11, 2001. That my twenty-three-year-old nephew escaped from the north tower only minutes before it fell added, for my family, an overpowering immediacy to the shocking events of that day. As we kept vigil at my sister's apartment, we asked the questions, I would later learn, that fell from the lips of Americans everywhere. "How are we going to get through this?" "How will our lives change?"

In the immediate aftermath of the attacks, we felt we'd never be the same. And on that heart-scalding day, tens of thousands of lives *were* tragically altered forever. For countless others, 9/11 affected the way we went about our daily lives, the way we thought of ourselves and our country. But while we can now see there have been significant changes in our nation, these were neither sudden nor radical departures from policies and trends already in place.

"That moment and the actions that followed reflected a view of the world that was there before 9/11 and was implemented after 9/11, and it's still there," Ivo Daalder, a foreign policy analyst with the Brookings Institute, said recently.

What 9/11 and the subsequent war on terror accomplished—and accomplished in a major way—was to enhance and accelerate the conservative agenda and make it palatable to increasing numbers of Americans. This was true on both fronts: domestic and foreign. The absolutist way of thinking—self versus other, the push for unilateralism, the undermining of women's progress, the veneration of maleness—all these had become bullet-pointed parts of our public policy and thinking well before the planes were airborne.

But in ways blatant and obvious, subtle and insidious, women have become collateral damage in our war against terror. Sexism is now applauded like the comeback kid, newly equipped and stronger than before. Massively destructive, it's brazenly obliterating years of women's progress. The new normal should really be called the new *old* normal. We're living in a society that is turning back the clock, eagerly reconstructing traditional roles for men and women, with and without our complicity.

This didn't happen because of one day or even one year. The footprints lead back to Reagan. But after 9/11 those on the right no longer needed to pick their way around the obstacles to their goals. Now they could throw their energies into high gear and zoom ahead. And amazingly, no one stopped them.

Of course, anything resembling feminism still evokes vehement hostility, but under the fog of war, *all* women have been cast *and* treated as "the other." Whether as damsels in distress, sacred homemakers, or sexy arm candy, women have come to symbolize weakness, dependence, and passivity, diametrically opposed to men's virility, rationality, autonomy, and activity. And it's probably not a major surprise that, in the haunting shadow of catastrophe, masculinity became the embodiment of a new America.

Even as the embers still smoldered, the body search continued, and sirens screeched throughout the night, the media began its group swoon over our rescuing heroes.

"The Hunk Factor: Manly Men and Their Uniforms Muscle onto the Scene," blared a headline of *USA Today*. Manly men are "suddenly chic." "Blue-collar cops and firefighters, tradesmen and soldiers across the USA have been transformed into heartthrobs and hunks." It's a girl thing, Sam Keen, author of *Fire in the Belly: On Being a Man*, observed. "In times of danger women gravitate to the protectors. They want the guy who can kill the saber-toothed tiger."

Maureen Dowd also thrilled at the return of the macho man. "In three decades, feminism has done a back flip. Once men in uniform were the oppressors. Now they're trophy mates."

"I miss John Wayne," Peggy Noonan, Reagan's former speech writer, mused. "But I think he's back. . . . A certain style of manliness is once again being honored and celebrated in America since Sept. 11. You might say it suddenly emerged from the rubble." And social critic Camille Paglia gushed over the "robustly, dreamily masculine faces of the firefighters."

In this national crisis, masculinized saviors of the attacks loomed large in the public mind. At first glance, the reasons seem obvious: the veneration of "manly men" represented our nation's gratitude for the sacrifices and services they unsparingly gave. But a closer look suggests something different—a rush to defend and bolster an American manhood compromised and belittled by the attacks.

The amplified machismo of the zeitgeist betrayed the national anxiety that somehow we weren't manly *enough*. In the horrible, shocking aftermath we couldn't see it this way, but in retrospect the signs were everywhere—in the 24/7 talk of the "new cultural icons," in the popular cartoon *Our Towering Heroes* showing the World Trade Center in the form of the bodies of a male firefighter and police officer. And, significantly, in post-9/11 news reporting.

"I was immediately struck by the total invisibility of women in the media coverage of the rescue and recovery efforts in New York," Captain Brenda Berkman of the NYFD said. "And I was not the only one. Women rescue workers found that our own agencies were even ignoring our presence at the countless funerals for their coworkers. After twenty years of women working as firefighters in the NYFD and much longer in the NYPD and EMS, it was frustrating and demeaning to have our contributions ignored."

This lapse also angered two California women, Mary Carouba, a former social worker and investigator into child abuse, and Susan Hagen, who'd been a firefighter with the Sonoma County Fire Department. "After the attacks we were glued to the television like everyone else, but we kept wondering: where are all the women rescue workers? Why is the media going back to talking about fire*men* and police*men*? And why isn't anyone correcting this?" Carouba and Hagen became determined not to "let all the work women had done simply vanish." They pooled what little money they had and set out for New York, a city they'd never seen, where they had no contacts and no friends.

Their search for women who'd been part of the rescue and recovery effort didn't take them long. Newly arrived in Manhattan, they walked into a smoky restaurant in downtown Manhattan, near "the pile," crowded with exhausted, off-duty female police officers. Mary said, "We want to write a book about the women at Ground Zero." First there was dead silence, then tears.

In the following weeks they would hear the stories of Terri Tobin, a member of the NYPD who pulled people to safety even though she had a chunk of concrete stuck in her skull and a shard of glass piercing her back. Of police officer Mora Smith, killed while evacuating people from the second tower. And of Yamel Merino, an emergency medical technician and mother of a ten-month-old daughter, buried under the collapsing debris as she cared for the wounded. And more. So many more—women firefighters, police, doctors, nurses, clergy, military, Red Cross workers, and volunteers by the dozens who rushed to Ground Zero after the first plane hit and continued to come in the weeks after.

"These women shared their stories for only one reason," Mary told me. "Not for fame, not for thank yous. They wanted other women, younger women, girls, to know what was possible. They wanted to be role models, and they knew they'd never be counted by the mainstream media."

The coverage women got was a direct result of who was giving it. Numerous commentators, the British newspaper *The Guardian* among them, have noted the virtual disappearance of women from newspaper pages and television screens after 9/11. To be sure, women never have had anything like equal representation on the Sunday morning talk shows, accounting for only 11 percent of the guests on the big five—ABC, NBC, CBS, CNN, and Fox—between January 1, 2000, and June 30, 2001. But right after the attacks, the number fell to 9 percent.

In print, women's stories were nowhere to be found. Of the 309 bylined op-ed pieces published by the *New York Times*, the *Washington Post*, and *USA Today* in the month after the attack, 92 percent were by men.

Projecting male voices and ideas was part of our frantic scramble to show the world—and ourselves—that we were a nation of don't-mess-with-us-again überstuds.

Praising female rescue workers, of course, in no way diminishes the rightful praise due to the male rescue workers. But to do so would have acknowledged that women, too, could possess courage, fortitude, and daring. And this would muddy things up for a society bent on re-creating specific gender roles.

Damsels in Distress of the New Millennium

The women we *did* see on TV were the widows of men killed in the attacks. These 9/11 victims presaged a different way of thinking about women in this country. Women like Lisa Beamer, whose husband was one of the publicly acclaimed heroes of doomed flight 93, was lauded by the media as "virtually saint-like," a "victimized mother and wife." She needed protecting; her plight called out for retaliation. And, after Laura Bush used the president's weekly radio address to describe the decimated lives of women in Taliban-dominated Afghanistan, they, too, were high-profiled in the press as terrorists' prey, although their plight had been completely ignored by both the administration and the media before 9/11. Avenging wronged women served as a powerful subtext for our attack on Afghanistan. But relegating women to the role of victims of war, while men are accepted as the warriors and heroes, inevitably brings about a power imbalance in society. The concept of masculine protection allows men to be on the front lines, the public realm, while women are sheltered "somewhere in the background . . . in the private sphere," writes Lorraine Dowler in "Women on the Frontlines: Rethinking War Narratives of Heroism Post 9/11."

For those who may have doubted that women really needed sheltering, there was plenty of backup for the claim. In a rush to publish, researchers, just three months after the attacks, had already documented the differences between the male and female reactions to them. Pew Research Center found that "four in ten women felt depression after September 11; only one in five men reported the same thing." A little more than 50 percent of women told Pew researchers that they're very or somewhat concerned about a new attack; only 30 percent of men did. Similar results came from a mid-November issue of the *New England Journal of Medicine*, noting higher stress reactions in women.

"The Great Worry Divide" headlined the *Washington Post*. "[M]en and women have taken their places on either side of an emotional gap," said staff writer Paul Farhi. Could this "worry gap" translate as Man: rational. Woman: emotional? Farhi wondered in his piece. He admitted it might be a "cheap stereotype." "But," the article says, "that doesn't mean it isn't generally true."

And another study, conducted by the universities of Buffalo and California, found women to be sadder and men angrier about 9/11. But the researchers' conclusions—women were more likely than men to respond to the attacks with emotion—seemed to ignore the fact that *anger* is just as much an emotion as *sorrow*. Even before we could fully process how the terror attacks affected our lives, a master narrative was taking shape, one that insisted on seeing women as passive, vulnerable, overwhelmed by feeling, and needing to be safeguarded and men as tough, in control, and ready for war.

The chant began almost immediately. "In the wake of the terror attacks, 'Bridget Jones' may well be eager for marriage and less interested in finding fulfillment through work," predicted *The Economist*. And journalist Chris Black, looking at the impact of 9/11 on the members of the Independent Women's Forum, wrote, "From their standpoint the terrorist attacks on the United States turned the feminist tide and brought back traditional values, a retreat to the home and hearth."

Parallels to the cold war era abound. We can hear the echoes of communist spies lurking among us in the warnings of sleeper cells tucked away in our neighborhoods. And the danger falling from the skies, so menacing to the 1950s generation, became excruciatingly real to our own.

The climate of fear and uncertainty pervading both societies resulted in strikingly similar calls to reconfigure traditional masculine and feminine roles—a phenomenon we've seen throughout our nation's history. From the urbanization and industrialization of the antebellum period to the cold war of the 1950s, male insecurity has manifested itself in an assault on women's autonomy and a revival of that citadel of masculine authority—the patriarchial family—along with its counterpart—the esteemed stay-at-home mother. The noncompetitive woman tending the hearth has always been a surefire way to soothe the wounded male psyche, enhancing feelings of virility.

In the 1950s an outsized campaign pried the acetylene torches out of women war workers' hands and replaced them with upright Hoovers. A half century later, the "new normal"—economic and homeland *insecurity*—played upon guilt and fear to get women back home.

"It would be easy for terrorists to cook up radioactive 'dirty bombs' to explode inside the U.S.," secretary of state Colin Powell said. Department of Homeland Security secretary Tom Ridge predicted, "The near-term attacks . . . will either rival or exceed the 9/11 attacks." News of imminent strikes raising the threat level to "code orange" put most of us on red alert—and kept us there, say the researchers at Columbia University's School of Journalism, "by the media viewing fear-mongering as payday and senior politicians seeing it as good political strategy."

Like marionettes we were constantly yanked into hypervigilant dread by an administration callously pulling our emotional strings. Looming diabolic plots to demolish bridges, railroad systems, public buildings, apartment houses, hotels, malls, water supplies, and nuclear power plants by hijacking tourist helicopters, vans, school buses, and airplanes and annihilating untold numbers with ricin, smallpox, or radioactive chemicals kept women scrambling to protect their families.

I know I'm far from the only one who searched for gas masks for her children after one toxic chemical warning—the first five online sites I tried were completely sold out. And although I realized how absolutely useless duct tape and plastic sheets would be (the old 1950s "duck and cover" was now *duct* and cover) in a poison gas attack, I still waited an hour in the cold to get into my local hardware store to buy them.

"Just talking about the terror alerts brings chills down my spine," a New Jersey mother of three told me. "We were all frantic to get our hands on prescriptions of cipro. All the mothers at my children's schools had their own private sources; even though we weren't supposed to stockpile it, we were."

Families packed emergency kits, sent their children to school with a change of clothing and a supply of medicines in the event of lockdowns, and decided on meeting places in case their homes were destroyed. And many women, remembering the wrenching cell phone calls mothers, doomed in the towers, made to their husbands telling them what time to pick up the children at school, told me that for years after the attacks they posted detailed daily schedules on their fridges. Some mothers confessed to buying HazMat suits; others thought about constructing basement hideaways.

Interest in home security devices surged following the release of the movie *Panic Room* in 2002. Although the plot bears no resemblance to the al Qaeda attacks, it resonated with our deepest post-9/11 fears: unknown and unexpected terror strikes at our homes and families, impelling us to do everything in our power to try to keep our children from harm. And even then, we might not be successful.

We meet the fictitious Meg Altman (Jodie Foster) and her daughter Sarah (Kristen Stewart) right after Meg's divorce when they are about to purchase a magnificent townhouse with a unique feature—a fully equipped panic room off the master bedroom. But there is no real protection. Robbers enter the house the night they move in, and although the mother and daughter make it to the panic room, they're hardly safe. The thieves are after money stashed exactly where they're hiding.

"The appeal of the panic room," said the *Washington Post*, is as a "perfect encasement of safety in a world that's so suddenly turned hostile." One security system designer said, "Today's panic rooms are yesterday's fallout shelters, although much more hi-tech than their cousins of yesteryear."

Just as most Americans didn't build fallout shelters, most of us aren't sequestering our families in rooms costing anywhere from ten thousand to over one hundred thousand dollars with wrap-around cameras, ten-day food and water supplies, and decontamination stations for chemical or biological attacks, but every time Homeland Security issued an alert, many women told me, they considered some version of it.

That the Bush administration used these panics much the way other presidents had done to manipulate the public and gain support for their policies wasn't widely evident at the time. The press, no longer accustomed to exercising an independent voice, fell into step with the administration and toed the party line. Typically the "credible report" or taped message by bin Laden or al-Zarqawi got almost incessant coverage, but when the threat passed or turned out to be bogus, it barely made the news. As for the public, pummeled by these accounts, we slept less, ate more mac and cheese, and worried about our families and our jobs.

Women's jobs in such hard-hit industries as air transport and travel service, retail trade, hotels, and manufacturing were more likely to be affected than men's by the attacks. Lower-wage workers—a group in which women are overrepresented—suffered considerably. With 2.5 million jobs lost in just the first eighteen months following 9/11, women, often employed on a precarious, temporary basis, were the first let go.

Even before 9/11, women workers had far more part-time jobs compared to men. And part-time workers are much less likely to have pensions, health benefits, or unemployment insurance. (Forty-three states don't pay unemployment benefits to part-time workers at all.) Add to that other complications and restrictions in their unemployment insurance, and it amounted to a lot of women, often heads of family, unable to put food on their tables. In the two years following the attacks, the unemployment rate for single mothers rose by 74 percent.

Before 1996 many of these women could have qualified for public assistance, but in post-9/11 America that was no longer the case. As the authors of an analysis for the National Jobs for All Coalition observed, "The unemployed and underemployed fell into a safety net, never very supportive, that had been tattered—if not battered—in the preceding decades."

"We were ignored long before 9/11. We shouldn't expect that it'll be any different, even after such a tragedy," said one woman.

And the difficulties persisted. One study, conducted in 2000 and again in 2002, found that women in new-economy companies who kept their jobs through the start of recession experienced heightened insecurities and difficulties after the attacks. Where once they'd felt exhilaration coupled with exhaustion, now they felt only exhaustion. As they watched their earlier gains—rapid advancement, flexibility, reduction of gender-related obstacles—disappear, workplace stress *and* life stress soared.

The same held true for women in newly hazardous positions. From physicians to mail carriers, many women felt threatened on their jobs, more likely than men to say work had become more dangerous in the face of possible biological and chemical attacks.

"I felt like I was living through *Apocalypse Now*," Jennifer Capla, who was a third-year surgery resident in 2001, told me. "Every time I saw a bunch of docs running down the corridor I thought, 'this is it.'"

Fear. Anxiety. Insecurity. I don't know anyone who didn't feel them. But the big question we have to answer is this: considering all of women's post-9/11 worries about our families and our workplace, did it change us? Did we actually become a bunch of surrendering homebodies?

Fewer stories have gotten more currency than the one about women reevaluating their priorities after the attacks and deciding to quit their jobs and stay home. This scenario works on many levels, fulfilling unexpressed insecurities, ambivalences, and agendas. But, like the tale of the nonexistent post-9/11 baby boom, it just isn't true. Many women *did* lose their jobs after 9/11, but this was hardly their choice. And interestingly, about a third of working Americans said their job was *more* important to them than before September 11, while "two-thirds . . . said there had been no change in their values relating to the importance of their jobs," sociology professor J. Timmons Roberts concluded from his study of the topic.

The tragedies inspired some women to become pregnant and others, who could afford it, to quit work or go part-time, but there was no stampede back to the nest. One year after the attacks, 70 percent of couples with children had both adults in the workplace.

What became obvious to me after listening to scores of women and reading hundreds of responses to my online survey is that women did see 9/11 as a turning point in their lives—a chance to do something important, but not necessarily domestic.

"I've always felt a tug between my work and a commitment to doing other things," Abby Shuman, a clinical psychologist living in Boston, told me. "September 11th made me question what constitutes a meaningful life. And I felt compelled to become active again in politics."

Kim, a thirty-two-year-old corporate marketing executive, was one of many who changed careers to do something she believed was more socially useful. For Kim it was becoming a teacher. For Angela, who'd just started her dream job with *InStyle* magazine, it was leaving to work at New York

Cares. "I wouldn't have had the courage to do this before 9/11," Angela admitted. "I realized I wanted to help society or the city. Now, I feel like I'm making a difference."

"September 11th made me want to change my life, and I did . . . from Wall Street. I used my savings and worked for myself a couple of years. It was good for my soul." One woman, a tax lawyer, switched to a position with the Legal Aid Society, another began working with the Coalition for the Homeless, a third went back to school to become a nurse, and a fourth took a one-year leave to study Middle Eastern religion and society.

"September 11th was a wake-up call," Dr. Jane Greer, a New York psychologist and author of *Gridlock: Finding Courage to Move on in Life, Love and Work*, told me. "For many people, it became a clearinghouse for values and meaning. This was particularly true for those who were disengaged. They saw how fleeting life could be and no longer wanted to waste time."

"AFTER 9/11 WE began to hear from many readers that they felt a sense of dismay, a kind of generalized feeling that they wanted to do something, but weren't sure what," Susan Shulz, then editor in chief of *CosmoGirl*, told me. "We began thinking about ways to empower girls, and it was a big factor in our launching Project 2024." Initially starting as a campaign to get a woman in the White House by that year, the project provides leadership training to young women and paid internships in a variety of fields. It profiles women in positions of power, many who've overcome hardships, to make a difference in the world.

"If I survive this, I can survive anything," twenty-five-year-old Suzanne McKenna thought after she was evacuated from the north tower. So much of that day remains as blurred to Suzanne as the sky she gazed at from in front of J&R Music, a block away from the fallen Trade Center, where she paused to catch her breath. But about this, she told me, she's very clear. "I felt it then, and I still do. It made me stronger. It made me feel I could do anything I set my mind to."

Over and over, the same message comes through: "Since that day I've traveled to ten countries and sampled jobs around the world. I've come to accept myself more. I realize there's no point in being afraid of doing things you want. Why wait?"

"After 9/11 I reconnected with my father. . . . [It] has boosted my self-esteem and helped me to be a better person."

What all the research suggests is this: after the terror attacks, women most definitely did *not* feel weak and powerless. September 11 didn't signal a retreat from the world as much as a renewed engagement in it.

Why, then, were we bombarded with news of women eagerly fleeing the workplace to embrace their inner homemaker? How did an idea so at odds with the majority of women's lives gain so much traction and become part of our common wisdom? And if so many women wanted to press forward effectively and energetically, why were our rights withering, our autonomy diminishing?

10

9/11 AND MEN

If the post-9/11 climate for women has been artfully misunderstood, the same is true for men. The immediate gendered analyses of the rescue and response suggest something far more complicated than a society grateful to its male firefighters and police. What happened on that tragic day was experienced as an assault on the virility, on the *maleness* of our nation, sorely compromising the traditional male role of protector and provider.

The twin towers, whether we consciously made the connection or not, were the phallic symbols of the whole nation. They stood for American prowess. Soaring, tall, a sign of our dominating financial strength and world position. Then, monstrously and suddenly, they were cut down. Less spectacular but equally devastating was the attack on the Pentagon, the heart of our military power. The loss of life was transforming. And so was the loss of face, although few of us dared to say it.

Our nation had been in effect "castrated," leaving us fearful, threatened, impotent, humiliated, and ineffective. The assumptions around which we organized our lives collapsed. No longer could we think of ourselves as strong or secure. We couldn't escape the feeling that our leaders had failed miserably to protect us. Strangers on the street asked each other, "How could this have happened? How could our security have been so penetrated?" And that it had been done by Osama bin Laden, a man who'd taunted America as being *feminized*, who'd scoffed at the "weakness, feebleness, and cowardliness of the U.S. soldiers" in Somalia, made it even more galling.

September 11 didn't make *women* feel weak and vulnerable, that was how it made *men* feel. But few things are more verboten in the canon of maleness than to acknowledge inadequacy and fallibility. So rather than admit those feelings, men projected them onto women, and our nation set out to establish its macho bona fides with all the excessive showmanship of the insecure.

Proving to the world and to ourselves that we weren't a bunch of ineffectual eunuchs became a key issue for our leaders as they debated an appropriate response to the terrorists. *Washington Post* columnist George Will warned against "appeasement tarted up as reasonableness," Rear Admiral Kevin P. Quinn worried that the attacks "left many of Washington's power players feeling impotent," and Senator John McCain spoke heatedly of the dangers of returning to the "soft," emasculated foreign policy we'd had during Vietnam. Using sexualized comments like these, our leaders constructed the conflict as a way to prove our nation's masculinity.

To read through our top officials' speeches in the wake of the atrocities is like looking at language on steroids. Muscular and bulked up, the rhetoric deliberately invoked images of strength, men of decision, the hero, and the cowboy. We talked of a "bold response," "extreme action," our "steel resolve," of it being "the warriors' time," of "smoking 'em out," of getting bin Laden "dead or alive," and of "full-spectrum dominance."

When "*men* [becomes] the operative word, [b]rawny, heroic, manly men," to use journalist Patricia Leigh Brown's words, women are demoted to ancillary and decorative. Before 9/11, those on the right castigated femi*nist* leaders, ideas, and agendas. Now anything femini*zed* was tainted.

Our new machismo made us scornful of men who have "become feminized due to legislative actions and by law-makers" to the "touchy-feeliness of Alan Alda," and the "vaguely feminized man-child Leonardo DiCaprio," said a variety of reporters. But nothing produced masculine disgust as much as our feminized military. Strong women made men soft. Military analysts, especially those who've always opposed women in the armed forces, like Gerald L. Atkinson, a former commander in the U.S. Navy, raged about how the terrorist attacks had exposed our nation's major vulnerability: the "feminization of our nation's combat arms."

We can almost hear the echoes of ancient cultural taboos about women, especially menstruating women, who allegedly contaminated food and rendered weapons useless, as men rushed to differentiate themselves from the "weaker sex." In their femophobic haste, they ran roughshod over gender equality as a concept, a fact, a goal.

Hypermasculine war whooping eclipsed traditional military values of valor, loyalty, and justice and turned our fight against terrorism into a messianic, patriarchal, punishing crusade. Any alternative to military action—negotiation, peace—smacked of womanliness, therefore totally unacceptable.

The assault on Afghanistan, fought under a virtual media blackout, hid from sight images of the Afghan women we were "saving," injured, bereaved, and rendered homeless by our attacks. But even the collapse of the Taliban with the fall of Kabul right before Thanksgiving in 2001 in no way spelled peace. A quickly assembled string of terror alerts seized the news. The menace stayed real, our siege mentality everlasting. Afghanistan represented just the opening salvo in the global war on terrorism. We were in this fight to the end.

"Men make war for many reasons, but one of the most recurring ones is to establish that they are, in fact, 'real men,' " historian Barbara Ehrenreich wrote in the late 1990s. Her words are particularly applicable to 2001. With bin Laden effectively cave-hopping, the saber-rattling began again.

After saying flat out a week after the attacks that Saddam Hussein had no connection to them, Vice President Cheney reversed himself. On December 9 on *Meet the Press*, he told Tim Russert of new developments since they'd last talked. It was pretty well confirmed that one of the hijackers had met with senior Iraqi intelligence service in Prague several months before 9/11, he said.

Immediately the story spread and magnified. The *New York Times* carried a front-page article with enough details about Saddam's program of weapons of mass destruction to send scores of Americans dashing off to their doctors for sleeping pills. No matter that the details were false and the source a liar, no matter even that the administration most likely knew all that at the time, this was the war the neocons had long dreamed about. Rumsfeld started lobbying to bomb Iraq right after 9/11, not only because it had more high-profile targets than "moonscape" Afghanistan but because it was step one in Project for a New American Century's grand imperialistic design.

With 80 percent of the talking heads on television drawing from conservative lines, supported and coached by powerful think tanks and foundations and all reading from the same doomsday script, the stories of annihilating weapons of mass destruction came at us all the time, everywhere we turned. But Americans weren't buying it completely.

As a people, we've always been steadfastly committed to the idea of a just war, a defensive and necessary war. So the powerbrokers ratcheted up their pitch and started the hard sell, opportunistically manipulating our 9/11 grief and outrage into support for an unprovoked, unilateral invasion of Iraq.

Bush said it; Cheney said it; Powell said it: a definite link existed between 9/11 and Saddam Hussein; Iraq had inspired and financed the plan. And slowly, we began to believe it. Two weeks after the terror attacks only 6 percent of Americans thought there was a connection, but by 2003, right before we invaded Iraq, 70 percent were convinced, with a good number even (falsely) accepting that several Iraqis had been among the hijackers.

The lead-up to war gave the neocons and their Christian conservative allies unprecedented authority and legitimacy in the government. Evangelicals supported the war and became "an ardent lobby for the U.S. military." Fundamentalists believed, as did our president, that God, putting him in power at this particular time in history, was directing Bush's actions.

When asked, Bush repeatedly said his advice comes from his "higher father" (as opposed to his real-life one, the senior Bush). With God on our side it was easy to see the war in terms of good versus evil, us versus them, with us or against us. Terrorists, and nations sponsoring them, replaced the communists as our enemies, as those actively plotting our destruction. Scarier, more diffuse, and less predictable than the reds, terrorists became the new foreign deviants. Bush's phrase "the axis of evil" was a clear and purposeful reference to Reagan's evil empire.

President Bush may have stopped short of blaming abortionists, feminists, and gays for 9/11, as Jerry Falwell did, but Bush did link abortion to terrorism. Having declared the anniversary of *Roe* "National Sanctity of Life Day," Bush said, shortly after the attacks, "On September 11th we saw clearly that evil exists in this world, and that it does not value life. . . .

Now we are engaged in a fight against evil [the pro-choice movement] and tyranny to preserve and protect life."

As Reagan had done, Bush adroitly joined together our "enemies" abroad and at home to affirm what his administration believed to be the core values of society. And, as we launched our war on terror, those values increasingly became aggression, domination, violence, and control, the driving force of the new military. Women, if they figured at all in this scenario, were victims, helpmates, supporters. Still largely out of sight. And, again, the other.

The sidelining strategy is evident in the 2002 State of the Union Address. Assessing our victories in Afghanistan, Bush declared, "mothers and daughters were captive in their homes, now they are safe." The president honored Michael Spann, a CIA officer who died at Mazar-e Sharif, and his wife, Shannon, the brave widow, in the audience. He also paid tribute to the heroes of 9/11: a fireman whose two sons died at Ground Zero, a little boy whose football-playing father did as well, and the "fierce brotherhood of firefighters."

When I asked Mary Carouba, coauthor of *The Women of Ground Zero*, why, even months after the attack, women rescue workers still hadn't gotten any recognition, she said it was a "deliberate effort to make them invisible and bring [certain groups] back to where they want to be. It reverts the nation back to patriarchy. The focus on the war epitomizes big strong guys."

Big strong guys have big guns. And we fixed them on Iraq. Our Shock and Awe strategy, known militarily as rapid dominance, wasn't about getting Saddam or finding his weapons cache. It was all about mounting an assault so intimidating, inflicting such damage on Baghdad, it would compel the people to submit. The excessive use of force against a nearly unresisting population resulted in far more devastating civilian casualties than what we would have imagined from the televised high-tech "clean strikes."

Colin Powell's wish proved prophetic: we'd become the bullies on the block. The alpha men in Washington reveled in our new status. Bush had already perfected his swagger and straight-shooter look to the applause of the media machine, which lauded his muscular foreign policy, religious righteousness, and steadfast opinions. His chest-thrusting style let it be known that he was the decider (even as events have since shown that he'd decided little). Those who dared to disagree with him were sissified and branded as "girlie-men," the fate that would befall his opponent in the 2004 race, John Kerry, a Vietnam veteran who was decorated for his valor.

But Bush's *Top Gun*–style landing on the *USS Abraham Lincoln* back in 2003 was without a doubt *the* testosterone moment of his presidency. Numerous pundits have commented on the staging of that event, timed just perfectly so that when the president walked across the deck, the sun illuminated the crotch of his fighter-pilot uniform.

G. Gordon Liddy, of Watergate notoriety, was positively giddy at the way Bush's parachute harness "ma[d]e the best of his manly characteristic." It showed him to be "virile" and "hot" and "powerful," an excited columnist gushed in the *Wall Street Journal*, while Richard Goldstein, writing for the *Village Voice*, thought that flaunting his balls was a defining moment in the president's troubled quest for manhood.

When Bush donned the uniform of the warrior he never was and told us of a mission accomplished, with the real slaughter just beginning, it *was* a defining moment. Defining because it hinted at the deception, the artifice, the cynical use of the press and of our nation's money and good will to advance a single and dangerous agenda.

11

MILITARY MADNESS

Artifice reigns in how women are portrayed and treated in our military. Underneath the lip-service comments of our "brave men and *women* in uniform" lies a hidden reality of disrespect and exploitation.

If you ask a random group to tell you what they know about the women in the Iraq war, you're likely to hear the same two names I heard: Jessica Lynch and Lynndie England.

Jessica Lynch's story is the stuff movies are made of. And they have been. The nineteen-year-old Lynch from West Virginia enlisted in the army with the hopes of getting an education, but two years later she found herself in Iraq. When her convoy was ambushed after making a wrong turn into enemy territory, her vehicle crashed and was surrounded. Initial reports claimed she'd gone down firing. With life-threatening stab and bullet wounds she had been taken captive and subsequently moved to the hospital in Nasiriyah.

Her spectacular rescue by U.S. Special Operations forces—the media dubbed it "Saving Private Lynch" in a conscious reference to the popular movie *Saving Private Ryan*—played and replayed on television throughout the world. Who can forget the picture of the pale, blond, wounded Lynch being carried on a stretcher to safety by our strong, fearless military?

"Some brave souls put their lives on the line to make this happen," said general Vincent Brooks. The story of an angelic damsel in distress snatched from the forces of destruction by righteous saviors so perfectly conveyed the American version of the war, of good trumping evil, it could have been scripted. And it was.

Not long after the events, Jessica Lynch began to refute the accounts. "I did not shoot, not a round, nothing." (Her weapon jammed, as did all the weapons systems assigned to her unit.) "I went down praying to my knees," she told Diane Sawyer. Her injuries—a broken arm and thigh and a dislocated ankle, not gun or stab wounds—came from the crash, not the enemy. "They used me to symbolize all this stuff. It's wrong. I don't know why they filmed [my rescue] or why they say these things." And later, in 2007, testifying before Congress, she called the reports "hype and misinformation."

In time, other parts of the tale would also unravel. For all the stealth and heavy metal employed in the raid, our forces knew in advance there'd be no resistance—the Iraq military had fled the hospital twenty-four hours earlier. Equally surprising was the revelation that an attempt by Dr. Harith al-Houssona, the physician taking care of Lynch, to deliver her by ambulance to our troops two days before was bungled by our soldiers.

So if the story of our shining military moment in Iraq was "one of the most stunning pieces of news management ever conceived," as the BBC claimed, what can we say about our most tarnished, the Abu Ghraib scandal? It too revolved around a woman, Lynndie England, also a private, also young—twenty-two. If Lynch came from a poor background, England's was difficult as well. Oxygen-deprived at birth, and under the longtime care of a psychologist, she suffered from reduced mental capabilities, making her easily swayed by authority. Her picture also is embedded in our minds. Holding the leash of a naked Iraqi prisoner, she became—for the entire world—the face of American torture. Torture revolving around the emasculating and humiliating of male prisoners.

Whether you buy England's version—her superiors gave her specific instructions on how to pose for the photographs so they could be used to "soften up" more valuable detainees—or not, it's clear that she was made the scapegoat for a series of abuses more far-ranging and damaging than her own. The confusion of command at the overpopulated prison, the domineering role of her boyfriend, Private Charles Graner, who admitted his influence over her (she was pregnant with his child during the trial), the likelihood our Defense Department knew about the practices in our detention centers, all suggest enough blame to go around.

Seven soldiers were sentenced in the Abu Ghraib scandal. Do we know their names? Can we picture them? The media relished showing us Lynndie England. In our collective consciousness she became the "bad girl" to Jessica Lynch's "good girl." Neither one portrayed exactly as she is, both became iconic images of the war. They formed the classic madonna/ whore syndrome, reducing women to the stereotypical: either vulnerable, virginal, and innocent or damaged, sexual, and dangerous. It's an easy, dehumanizing shorthand, one consistent with a community lacking real respect for women, undervaluing their contributions, and all too often ignoring their dreadful treatment.

As of 2008 more than 25,600 female soldiers have been deployed to Iraq, Afghanistan, and other countries supporting America's war on terrorism. Women are flying fighter jets, serving on patrols and supply lines, and analyzing intelligence data. Every day they put their lives in danger.

Staff Sergeant Dawn Moreland was in Afghanistan for nine months and Iraq twice. "I've been attacked and shot at as well as seen people strap bombs to themselves and blow themselves up," she told me recently.

While women are still generally limited to combat-support roles in war, our present battles, eliminating any distinction between combat and support units, have resulted in high numbers of fatalities and horrific injuries. "Frankly one of the most dangerous things you can do in Iraq is drive a truck, and that's considered a combat-support role," said Matthew Friedman, executive director of the National Center for Posttraumatic Stress Disorder.

Talk to women in the military and they'll tell you about the dangers, not only from roadside bombs but also from their own comrades in arms. A report sponsored by the Department of Defense in 2003 found that one third of female veterans seeking health care through the Veterans Administration said they'd experienced rape or attempted rape during their service. Within one year, accounts of sexual assaults have jumped 40 percent. Over five hundred cases among U.S. troops in Afghanistan and Iraq were reported during 2006.

"Saying something [about abuse] was looked down upon," said Amorita Randall, who served in Iraq with the navy in 2004. "I don't know how to explain it. You just don't expect anything to be done about it anyway, so why even try?"

Randall's expression of the futility endured by abused women in the armed services has been repeatedly confirmed. "Evidence is not being collected in some cases, and they are not getting medical care and other services," said Christine Hansen, executive director of the Miles Foundation, an organization assisting sexually abused women in the military. Women are frequently left in the same units as their accused attackers, putting them at greater risk of future abuse. Even their requests for emotional and legal counseling are ignored.

Danielle is a military officer who was stationed at Camp Udairi in Kuwait, fifteen miles from the Iraqi border. She was in training before deployment and had just finished guard duty at 2:30 A.M. when she was hit on the back of her head and knocked unconscious. She awoke with her hands tied, her own underwear stuffed into her mouth, and a man raping her. As she struggled, he slammed a heavy object between her eyes, causing her to black out again.

When she finally came to, she found herself alone. Gagging, bleeding, and naked, she ran into camp. A rape examination was performed at an aid station, but Danielle's other injuries were left untreated. There was no trauma counseling and no opportunity to meet with a chaplain (even though she asked to see one), and her superior officers wanted her to take a polygraph exam and get back to work in spite of her condition.

"I feel like my chain of command betrayed me," Danielle said. "I gave four years to that unit, and I feel like it kicked me in the teeth when I was down."

There has been no shortage of testimonies and information—some eighteen major reports on sexual abuse have been issued in the past few years—but military women continue to get a cold shoulder from those in power.

"Why is there no outrage about this?" Senator Ben Nelson asked a group of military leaders at a hearing on the prevalence of sexual assault and harassment in our armed forces and service academies.

So far no one has given him an answer.

A culture of hostility to women is evident throughout the military, starting with the recruiting process. More than a hundred young women interested in joining the military were sexually attacked by their recruiters in 2006, according to a CBS News report. "Women were raped on recruiting-office couches, assaulted in government cars, and groped en route to entrance exams." And it's happening to girls still in high school, the result of a hidden provision in Bush's No Child Left Behind (NCLB) Act of 2002—called by one irate father "the most aggressive military recruitment tool enacted since the draft ended in 1973."

Most parents don't realize it, but their children's public schools, under the NCLB Act, are required to provide the military with personal data on their students, including birth dates, social security numbers, e-mail addresses, phone numbers, and grade-point averages. Dossiers, shared with private companies, are being maintained on millions of young Americans, making them easy targets for military recruiting. Equipped with all the necessary information, recruiters are now able to bypass parents and contact students directly. This policy enables ill-intentioned men—like Indiana National Guard sergeant Eric P. Vetesy—to pick out young women who would be especially vulnerable to authority. Vetesy, who's been accused of sexually assaulting six female recruits, preyed on girls from single-parent homes, with no father figure present.

"It doesn't surprise me," Michael Berg, director of the Carolina Peace Research Center, said about the increasing incidents of sexual misconduct. "I don't think, in general, we should disparage all recruiters as sexual predators. However, they have undue influence and access to our schools. . . . Regulations to protect students go by the wayside when it comes to recruiters."

When you put young women eager to join the military together with the persuasive power and authority of older men in uniform, you have conditions ripe not only for exploitation but for keeping quiet about it.

Berg's organization is working to limit recruitment in schools, but it's not likely to happen. During the past several years the military has extended its reach into our everyday lives. Part of it comes from the enormous pressure to increase military enrollment numbers, even giving waivers to those with criminal records and histories of drug and alcohol problems. And part comes from the government's interest in getting Americans to accept the concept of ongoing war.

GI Joe Is Back, and He Is Us

Once confined to certain subgroups of society, military values now permeate our entire culture. Militarization occurs on many levels, making it appear by turn fun, "in," powerful, and normal. Some indicators seem fairly innocuous—the popularity of Hummers and camouflage (camo) clothing, the new buzzwords coming from soldiering, like "a navy shower" (for a short shower), bantered around in mainstream speech. But other aspects are especially worrying, inculcating our young men and boys in a world of violence while inflaming sexism and accelerating the marginalization of women.

Media experts and scholars are starting to talk about the "military-entertainment complex" to describe an enormously successful and profitable new alliance. Commercials disguised as docudramas are shown with disturbing regularity when you turn on the television or sit in a movie theater waiting for the feature presentation. The singing, music, special effects, and action depict troops of brawny men engaged in romanticized battle. As a mosaic of airbrushed images flicker across the screen, we're being sold on war, and our children, especially those of the working class, are being sold on fighting in it.

Then there are the movies themselves. Two post-9/11 films in particular, *Black Hawk Down* (2001) and *The Sum of All Fears* (2002), are noteworthy examples of our armed forces' participation in Hollywood. The Pentagon invited the actors of *Black Hawk Down*, a movie glorifying our botched mission in Somalia, to train at military bases. With Donald Rumsfeld's personal intervention, eight helicopter pilots and more than one hundred U.S. rangers were sent to support the filming in Morocco, making it the first time in history that our military actually assisted in a movie's production.

"*Black Hawk Down* is a self-conscious attempt to recuperate the collective memory of this raid—to claim it as a stunning example of the valor and heroism of U.S. soldiers," said sociologist Jonathan Markovitz. Although production had started before 9/11, the movie speeded to release because Somalia initially ranked high on the list of possible targets.

Like *Black Hawk Down, The Sum of All Fears*, vividly portraying a nuclear assault on the city of Baltimore, premiered not in Hollywood but in Washington. And it too had political value. The Monday after the movie's second successful weekend, Ashcroft announced the arrest of "shoe bomber" Jose Padilla, charged with trying to make a radioactive bomb. Since Padilla already had been in custody for a month, it's likely the government timed its broadcast to the movie hoping to spike our worries of nuclear annihilation as it paved the way to war in Iraq.

In the wake of the attacks, a new brand of reality TV, with unprecedented access and support of our Pentagon, burst on the scene. A-list producers such as Tony Scott of *Top Gun*, well known for promilitary movies, could be counted on to deliver a heavy duty patriotic message and keep the public interested in an open-ended conflict.

VH1's *Military Diaries* gave sixty members of our armed forces video cameras to take with them on their missions, talk about their daily lives, and describe how music helped them cope. *American Fighter Pilot* follows F-15 pilots through training. Although short-lived on television, the series has enjoyed widespread popularity on DVD. And *Profiles from the Front Lines,* produced by Jerry Bruckheimer of *Pearl Harbor* and *Black Hawk Down*, told the personal stories of our soldiers abroad.

The foray into feature-length movies and television proved to be just the beginning of "militainment." Columbia University's Nick Turse, writing about this trend, believes our military has scored its greatest victories where our "most vulnerable population—children—resides. . . . Through toys, especially videogames, the military and its partners in academia and the entertainment industry, have not only blurred the line between entertainment and war, but created a media culture thoroughly capable of preparing America's children for armed conflict."

The younger ones can choose from a selection of military bears called Faithful Fuzzies, toting M-16s, or the Shock and Awe twins. For their older brothers, the selection is virtually unlimited. There's Battle Command Post Two Story Headquarters—a militarized dollhouse, complete with a gun rack, sandbags, a talking, bloodied, about-to-die Uday doll who cries out in pain for his father, Saddam Hussein, and an updated assortment of action figures. Toy GIs, furloughed after Vietnam and heading for retirement, are now back on the scene and more realistic than ever. In combat gear pegged to our current battles, a top line manufactured by the U.S. Army depicts actual soldiers with names, ranks, and serial numbers.

Without a doubt the most dazzling, innovative toys are the military videogames. Developed by top-notch military analysts at the best training centers and schools and fully funded by our military, these games immerse children in the barrage of noises, violence, and destruction of modern combat. Every one of the armed forces, even the CIA, has its own high-tech version. America's Army, Full Spectrum Command, Full Spectrum Warrior, and Rogue Shield rank among the most popular games played online. Children can blast the enemy to smithereens, endure the sweaty rigors of boot camp, fight hand-to-hand in urban settings, or hunt after bloodthirsty terrorists in mountainous terrain, all from the privacy and comfort of their own bedrooms. As recruiting and training devices, these games are hugely successful. More problematic is the impact on millions of American kids.

"This toy states to me: war is the only way," said Mike Brody, a child psychiatrist and the media committee chair of the American Academy of Child and Adolescent Psychiatry, commenting on one of the military PlayStations. "These toys are normalizing the concept of war for the next generation of Americans."

The new war toys "represent a troubling new paradigm in play itself," said Brody, because they're linked so closely to actual events, making it harder for children to distinguish between real and pretend and, according to many experts, harder for them to control aggressive behavior. Numerous studies have documented the association between participation in violent gaming and belligerent behavior. One, coming out of Indiana University's School of Medicine, studied the brain waves of adolescents playing a violent wartime video for a half hour and found an irrefutable physiological connection between the games and aggressive thoughts and antisocial behavior.

"Murder stimulators!" That's what Lieutenant Colonel David Grossman, a former West Point psychologist and army ranger, calls violent videogames. Grossman, author of several highly acclaimed books dealing with teen violence, is a world-renowned authority in the new scientific field of "killology." Human beings, he says, aren't born to be violent. We have to be taught. And the best way, according to our military? Through the kinds of video games being marketed to our kids. These games teach recruits to kill on command, and to do it repeatedly until it feels natural—kiddy versions of *Manchurian Candidate*. Grossman is worried because he sees children at very young ages increasingly attracted to violence, simultaneously learning the mechanics of killing while becoming immune to its consequences.

"Does this toy represent the values American parents want to instill in our young people?" an aghast Carrie Lybecker of Washington asked about J. C. Penney's Forward Command Post (precursor to the Battle Command Post), advertised for children five years and older.

Carrie's question is one we all should be asking. Consciously or unconsciously we have accepted the values of the warrior and discarded the ideals of compassion, understanding, cooperation, and empathy—time-honored principles and, until recently, proud parts of the American national character. Our hypermasculinized, femophobic society is dangerous to all of us. Sexism has continued virtually unchecked for so many years that it's become part of our national consciousness.

President Obama brings a gentler, more collaborative tone to Washington, emphasizing diplomacy and engagement with the world. But this in itself, without the efforts of every one of us, isn't enough to alter deeply entrenched and distorted views of masculinity and femininity—a change mentioned neither by the administration nor the media, but one that is surely needed.

12

STARVE THE BEAST, SINK THE NATION

I t's virtually unheard of to cut taxes at a time of war, thundered Nobel Prize–winning economist Paul Krugman. Krugman smelled a rat. A big one. Deceit and deception, brought to us by the same flimflammers who swindled the American public into backing the war in Iraq, have destroyed our economy. And it's having a disastrous impact on women. The creature Krugman smells is "the beast"—Republicanspeak for government, and they want as little of it as possible. The whole idea of starve-the-beast economics is to "shrink the government down to the size where you can drown it in the bathtub," according to archconservative Grover Norquist.

The strategy involved pushing through huge tax cuts to deprive the government of crucial revenue, then crying out "Oh my god! We have huge deficits, we have to cut vital social programs, we have to cut domestic spending. We're good guys, we're compassionate conservatives, but, hey, what else can we do?"

Bush gave a number of spurious explanations for slashing taxes back in 2001 and again in 2003, but the real reason, said Krugman, was to advance his radical right-wing agenda. The hawks of his administration certainly realized how much wars cost. As of September 2007 our forays into Iraq and Afghanistan totaled $604 billion. An additional $200 billion was added in 2008, and the estimate through the next decade is a whopping $3 trillion. And we already had a big deficit before we went into Iraq.

In our nation's past, we all shared the burden of armed conflict. But not under the Bushies. We lavished huge benefits on the wealthy—many of whom gained directly or indirectly from the war—while asking the children of our poor and working families to die for our country.

A more cynical mind than mine might question if impoverishing millions of American youths was part of a grand plan to supply our nation with an underclass for whom the military beckoned as their only option for a better life. But even if that wasn't a motivation for Bush's callous policies, they've had that effect. We've become a nation of vast and harsh extremes; the gap between the very rich and the rest of the nation has grown dramatically.

Before the economic catastrophe of 2008, social commentators talked about a new Gilded Age, a time of excessive and ostentatious wealth concentrated into the hands of the top 20 percent of American families, who built mansions in three or four different locations and flew back and forth between them in private jets.

At the other end of the scale, barely noticed, are some thirty-seven million Americans, many of them women and children, officially classified as poor. That's roughly one in eight of us without adequate food, shelter, and clothing. The poignant struggles of another fifty-seven million barely hanging on one rung above the "officially" poor are depicted in Katherine Newman and Victor Tan Chen's book *The Missing Class: Portraits of the Near Poor in America*. Poverty is a kind of banishment in this country. It translates into subpar education, deteriorating health, and dim prospects. The poor and near-poor of our nation toil at jobs the rest of us wouldn't even consider. Their wages are subsistence, their benefits nil. And now even these jobs are most likely gone.

It wasn't always like this. The poverty of the 1950s and 1960s was considered a blight upon our nation. People of good will, compassion, and courage resolved to combat it. And, to a large extent, they did. President Johnson's War on Poverty resulted in real gains, especially for children. Their poverty rate fell from 23 percent in 1963 to 14 percent in 1969. Back then we had a solid middle class, composed of middle managers, academics, lawyers, and many unionized blue-collar workers.

Not too long ago CEOs ascribed to a social code of behavior as described by John Kenneth Galbraith. "Management does not go out ruthlessly to reward itself—a sound management is expected to exercise restraint . . . [otherwise] the corporation would be a chaos of competitive avarice." We need only remember such scandals as those surrounding Enron, World-Com, the New York Stock Exchange, and Tyco; the luxurious weeklong retreat executives of AIG enjoyed at the plush St. Regis Resort in Monarch Beach, California, piling up a tab of $440,000; *and* the outrageous bonuses AIG paid its executives after the federal government offered the giant insurance company an eighty-five billion dollar bailout; or the chutzpah of the three automotive companies' CEOs flying in separate private jets to Washington, D.C., where they pleaded corporate poverty, for us to conclude that no one is reading from Galbraith's manual.

And even when they're not raking in a fortune at the expense of their workers, CEOs of most major companies are granted huge perks, like fully stocked apartments, limousines with chauffeurs, home security systems, country club memberships, and other benefits totaling millions of dollars a year.

Executive compensation is set by boards of directors who are elected by investors/shareholders. They could change these astronomical numbers if they wanted to. But as long as they're happy with their returns, they have little incentive to put on the brakes. A report conducted by the Associated Press in December 2008 found that even failing banks and companies awarded huge handouts at taxpayer expense continued to grant their executives multimillion-dollar pay packages. Of the 116 banks receiving federal help at the time of the study, the average top executive went home with $2.6 million in salary, bonuses, and benefits. Former Merrill Lynch CEO John A. Thain (of the $1,400 wastepaper basket) earned $83 million in 2008, making him the leader of the pack, but not by much. Most significant companies also have extensive pay-deferral plans, allowing executives to stash away tens of millions of dollars into tax-free pots.

This extraordinary wealth translates into political clout. It's more than a matter of colossal contributions to business-friendly candidates. Conservative think tanks have shaped public opinion and understanding in ways that favored letting the rich accumulate fortunes and—if the estate tax is eliminated—pass them on intact to their children. And although President Obama wants a cap on the salaries and bonuses of top executives whose companies receive federal funds, there are untold ways to circumvent any pay restrictions.

NUMEROUS STUDIES AND economists have shown the mammoth tax cuts of the past thirty years, both Reagan's and then Bush II's overwhelmingly benefited the rich, parceling out only a little to the rest. The tax-cut bill President Bush signed in May 2006 granted millionaires an average break of nearly forty-three thousand dollars. It gave households with incomes below seventy-five thousand (more than three-quarters of all households) a tax cut of approximately thirty-one dollars, not enough these days to pay for half a tank of gas. The average single mother with a median income of just $23,428 got a mere ten dollars.

Bush's tax policies asked "the most vulnerable people in society to tighten their belts so that the most affluent can have a tax cut," said Paula Roberts, a senior staff attorney at the Center for Law and Social Policy in Washington, D.C.

Working Americans, traditionally honored as the backbone of our country, got short shrift, squeezed again and again. The federal minimum wage of $5.15 an hour hadn't been raised in nine years—the longest period in our history without an increase. After the midterm elections of 2006 brought in a (barely) Democratic Congress, tackling this issue became a priority. Because of entrenched opposition, the bill had to go through numerous drafts, each giving less to the workers than the previous one. When finally passed in May 2007, it prescribed a three-step increase over two years before reaching the final $7.25. (The tipped federal employee wage is still stuck at $2.12). And as part of the deal, $4.8 billion worth of tax breaks are being handed to small businesses over a ten-year period.

This is nothing short of shameful—a nation like ours, the richest in the world, allowing corporate bonuses to spiral to hundreds of millions, and bickering for years over a bill giving only a paltry increase in the minimum wage to working Americans, most of them women, many the sole supporters of their children. And then making them wait more than two years for it.

How did this happen in America? How did we become a country in which the real average annual compensation of the top one hundred CEOs is more than one thousand times the pay of ordinary workers? Since 2001 the number of people in poverty has increased by 4.3 million. And with the recession of 2008, it's only gotten worse. Raging avarice is a major culprit, and it was given wide latitude by acolytes of the Reagan Revolution's antiregulation dogma. As the *New York Times* noted on September 28, 2008, over the past several decades crucial laws have been abolished, the passage of vital new regulations prevented, reckless risk-taking encouraged, and gross malfeasance and ineptitude simply ignored.

Democrats as well as Republicans have had a hand in dismantling key legislation and contributing to the culture of greed. But Bush II's administration, by making antiregulation and deregulation the twin pillars of his fiscal policy, bears a unique responsibility for precipitating one of the worst economic crises in our country's history.

INDIFFERENT GOVERNMENTAL POLICES are largely to blame for our financial mess, but they're not the whole story. Just as our nation has lost its way abroad, we're lost at home. Our moral compass is askew. Our sense of social responsibility, weakened under the polarizing tactics of the Reagan administration, gave way, under Bush, to grasping and competitive individualism. Compassion, empathy, and caring were demeaned as the feelings of the weak, the womanly. They carried little weight in our macho-militarized society. On a personal level, as in foreign affairs, we became obsessed with self-preservation, unilateralism, and a heightened sense of exceptionalism. All this allowed and at times even encouraged us to turn our backs on those in need. When news appeared in June 2007 about little Deamonte Driver of Maryland, who died from an abscessed tooth because his mother couldn't afford the eighty dollars to have it pulled, a lot of us were shocked and outraged. But how many of us decided, right then, to give some time or money to support those trying to make health coverage a reality for all our children? (I know I didn't.)

Not too long ago women fought and lobbied for those less fortunate than themselves. But in these Darwinian times, talking about sisterhood makes you akin to a tyrannosaurus. We've taken on the mantra of the "war on terror." "Us or them" has become the creed by which many American families live, and this attitude has only been exacerbated by the deepening financial collapse. "Sometimes I feel like my whole existence is one big *Amazing Race*," a mother of two admitted. "I feel like we're always vying with one another for getting our kids the best positions on their teams, for making the most elaborate birthday parties, for having the biggest homes, the most number of cars."

Understandably, September 11 and our fears of imminent death unleashed feelings of hedonism. For those who could indulge them these feelings translated into the urge to spend, buy, have, own—to achieve a sense of security and status by surrounding ourselves in the comfort of material goods just as we did in the 1950s. And the Bush administration's policies made it easy for some of us to do just that, right up until the financial collapse, when most people across the economic spectrum started exercising some restraint.

For other Americans, governmental actions have made day-to-day life a near-impossible struggle, heightening our anxieties about job loss, home foreclosures, and food insecurity. Women have been especially hard hit. The subprime mortgage debacle has disproportionately affected African American and Hispanic women, a significant number the single heads of their families who were trying to create stable environments for their children. Many of these women started out with low interest rates, only to see those rates skyrocket way beyond what they could afford. And studies conducted by the Consumer Federation of America have revealed how subprime lenders charged Latinas and black women higher rates and fees than men of all races across all types of loans. Elderly women especially are at risk of becoming dependent on social services and of joining the permanent population of homeless, said Brandeis law professor Anita Hill.

While much of the press has bemoaned the loss of male jobs, especially in the financial sector, as award-winning professor of social policy Mimi Abramovitz, writing in Women's eNews, points out, a greater percentage of the sixty-eight million working women in this country have been laid off than men and have experienced a larger drop in wages. The current recession is really hitting women's jobs, agrees Rebecca Blank, a senior fellow at the Brookings Institute. And for many of these women there is no safety net. Low-wage-earning women usually don't qualify for unemployment insurance benefits because they tend to work intermittently and part-time. Twenty years ago, these workers would have found help in the traditional welfare program. But, says Blank, "[o]n that front, the news in not promising at all." It is more than a bit ironic that the same folks who applauded government investment in our failing banks, calling it "recapitalization" rather than nationalization, are the first to scream "Socialism! Socialism!" at the notion of expanding social services.

Some of the ways women are being hurt by the financial meltdown are obvious and immediate, others less so. Throughout our nation's history, periods of economic insecurity have always resulted in setbacks for women. Beyond all the trappings of masculinity—being a good athlete, a decision maker, a soldier—what really makes men feel like men? "Being a good family breadwinner," says a two-decades-long survey conducted by the *Yankelovich Monitor*, reinforcing numerous academic studies showing male identity linked to occupation. "A Crisis of Confidence for Masters of the Universe" is how Dr. Richard A. Friedman, a psychiatrist writing in the *New York Times*, assessed the impact of the current economic debacle on the male ego. Friedman was referring to Wall Street high rollers, but men of all economic backgrounds are shaken by losing their livelihoods.

THREATS TO FEELINGS of masculinity generally result in greater subjugation of women—everything from a further rollback of our rights to heightened gender discrimination to shifts in family dynamics to increased domestic violence. Not surprisingly, violent crimes against women have multiplied dramatically over the past two years. And this is on top of the misogyny already running rampant in the nation, eroding our progress in every area: not only in achieving financial independence but in health and reproductive rights, the ability to succeed in school and at work, and diminishing our sense of ourselves as autonomous, self-determining individuals. The process, for the most part, has been deliberate. And it's been effective. Until I began writing this book, I didn't realize how effective. It began with Reagan, lay dormant under Clinton, and got rebranded under Bush. It's happened over years, and it will take years to return us to where we were in the 1970s.

Our most powerful and enduring institutions have become inimical to real gender equality. As antiwoman as W. was, we elected a Congress in 2006 that accepted, even endorsed, his policies. Cowardly, fearful of being called unpatriotic, it remained a silent witness to the destruction of necessary social programs, hurting millions of lives. And the press followed right along. "Women's issues have been demoted to untouchables," one journalist said. Occasionally, "family issues" make the news, although usually buried in the styles or living sections, signaling that it's still acceptable for us to advocate for our children but not for ourselves.

When the media has covered women, it's been to hype bogus battles between us, magnifying the differences and pitting one against the other, as in Hillary supporters versus Obama supporters, or gleefully exposing the latest Spears family scandal, all the while ignoring the hard realities women endure all over the country.

But we can't ignore it any longer. Americans of good faith, patriotic Americans who honor the real meaning of democracy, who believe in caring for our nation's future and for one another, must take a stand. We can't allow divisive politics, pushing women to the sidelines of society, labeling us as the other, telling us we don't matter, make us *believe* that we don't matter. We can't let the fearmongers, the anxiety pushers, and the lack of a clear spokesperson for women keep us passive.

In Barack Obama we have a president who promised to be sympathetic to our concerns. He faces an enormity of complex problems demanding immediate attention. That's why it's crucial to make his administration aware of all the rights women have lost over these past decades, to make sure that women's issues aren't shoved aside and forgotten about. *Again.* To start, we need to understand what those issues are today.

The truth might ultimately make us free, but first it's going to make us pretty unhappy.

I hope it also makes us fighting mad.

13

BODILY HARM

"I have some bad news," the voice on the other end of the phone said. There was a pause, and as Alison Rein's heart started pounding, the doctor said the unimaginable: "It's malignant."

"I almost dropped the phone. How could this be? I was twenty-nine years old and just told I have breast cancer," Rein said.

The news was equally devastating and terrifying. Alison sat in her office, unable to absorb what the doctor had said. Finding the words to tell her boyfriend, Matt, seemed impossible. Finally she picked up the phone and dialed. "But as soon as I heard his voice," she said, "I completely lost it."

At first it felt as though her world were crashing down on her. What would happen to her job as a public policy analyst in Washington, D.C.? Her relationship with the man she planned on marrying? Her dreams to one day be a mother? Lurking in the background was the uncertainty she didn't dare express: would she have a future at all?

Years ago, the answers to these questions would have been pretty grim, but Alison was lucky to live in an area known for top-notch physicians and hospitals. Even so, her first round of appointments left her in despair. Doctors at both Johns Hopkins and George Washington hospitals suggested chemotherapy, in effect knocking out her ovaries.

Alison kept looking until she found a doctor who tailored a protocol—lupron injections, tamoxifen, and radiation—to fit her life hopes. Today, Alison has been cancer-free for eight years, is married to Matt, and has recently given birth to a robust nine-pound baby boy.

"I'm one of the lucky ones," Alison said. "My insurance plans allowed me to see several doctors, and I benefited from research yielding generations of effective treatments. I used to be part of the Young Survival Coalition of breast cancer patients, women who had reoccurrences two, three times for whom there are no real options, no real clinical trials being done on medications that might help them. A lot of them . . ." her voice trailed, "I don't know if they'll make it."

Most women, no matter their age, are, like Alison, terrified of this disease. The day their mammograms approach, they tell me, they're filled with dread. Women in my online survey overwhelmingly listed it as the most pressing medical concern facing our sex. Twice as many women die of heart disease in America, but it's breast cancer we fear. Approximately one in eight will be diagnosed with the disease this year. I'm sure that every one of you—like me—can immediately come up with a long list of coworkers, friends, and relatives who've battled it. I recently asked Dr. Hiram Cody III, a breast surgeon at Sloane Kettering Memorial Cancer Hospital, if we're in the midst of a breast cancer epidemic.

"I don't think so," he said, pointing out that early detection and better screening have enabled the medical profession to identify and care for more cases. He and other physicians have emphasized that with new treatments, fewer women will die from the disease.

The American Cancer Society has recently reported a decline in the death rate from breast cancer (some of it possibly linked to women going off hormone replacement therapies), but long-term outcomes continue to be better for white than for black women. Even with the current drop, altogether some 40,900 American women will die of the disease in 2009. These numbers represent our grandmothers, mothers, sisters, daughters, our best friends. Their hopes, their chances of survival, depend on scientific progress, on work to produce new drugs like abraxane, being used effectively to combat the disease in its advanced stages.

Under the Bush administration, scientific research stalled. For the first time since 1970, the budget of the National Institutes of Health (NIH) was cut, including the National Cancer Institute (NCI). This affects not only funding for breast cancer research but for cervical and ovarian cancers as well.

"We're at jeopardy of losing a whole generation of scientists, of cancer researchers, and that's undoubtedly going to have an effect ten years down the line," said Dr. Ben Ho Park of Johns Hopkins' Kimmel Cancer Center. Park is in the midst of valuable breast cancer research and is concerned that the cuts—his lab budget has been reduced by almost 30 percent—will result in an increase in the death rate again. "Right now it's a shame because we're really poised with our knowledge base of cancer to make really great inroads into this disease as far as therapy and treatment," he said.

As women learn of these cutbacks, they're horrified. "I watched my own mother die of cancer in 1985 and three years later lost my mother-in-law to it also. In 2004, I was also diagnosed. . . . How does anyone . . . even consider cutting funding this research?" one wrote.

"INDIGESTION, THAT WAS the main thing. And I felt overwhelmingly tired and dizzy, with occasional shortness of breath," Marcie Pollock recalled.

"I phoned my doctor repeatedly, but he insisted that it was stress. My only stress was that I wasn't feeling well."

Even though both of Marcie's parents had died of heart attacks at relatively early ages, and her brother, at forty-five, only a few years older than she, had already had triple bypass surgery, her doctor, a well-known internist with a cardiology specialty, kept dismissing her complaints. "Maybe it's a hiatus hernia," he allowed, "nothing more."

Two weeks of these warning signs later, Marcie collapsed on her bedroom floor. Miraculously, her husband was late going to work that day and immediately called for an ambulance. It saved her life. She was rushed to the hospital and diagnosed with a myocardial infarction (heart attack). After a week in the ICU and a double bypass, she slowly recovered.

Her physician remained unapologetic. "Your symptoms were atypical," he kept insisting.

Actually, Marcie had very common warning signs of a heart attack *for women*. It's men who present with chest and arm pain, and while heart attack rates for men have leveled off, they're increasing for younger women.

Obesity and its twin, diabetes, both on the rise across the country, are largely responsible for the spike in cardiovascular disease (CVD). And women, particularly African American women, have a higher risk of developing diabetes than men do. CVD in this country kills a woman every minute, and we're more likely than men to die of a first-time cardio-vascular event. The reasons for this are twofold. The first is because, like Marcie's doctor, most physicians aren't familiar with our symptoms or the therapies appropriate for women. The second is suggested by research-ers at Tufts Medical Center in Boston, who found female cardiac patients endure more delays than male patients at the hands of emergency medical workers.

With heart disease, many cancers, immunological disorders, and HIV, women present symptoms unlike men's and respond to different medica-tions and dosages. Knowing this is absolutely crucial to prevention, diag-nosis, and treatment, but before the formation of the Society for Women's Health Research in 1990, no one paid attention to these disparities. Even when women had been included in clinical trials, the results weren't being analyzed.

"One of the Society's most important goals is to ensure women's inclu-sion and retention in clinical trials," said its president, Phyllis Greenberger, who is considered to be among the most influential women in medicine today.

There are offices of women's health in both the NIH and the FDA. They collaborate with medical and scientific communities to support fund-ing for research on women's illnesses and encourage the advancement of women in medical fields. But however vital their work, these offices are in constant danger of being budget-cut to extinction. Recently, only an eleventh-hour campaign prevented the FDA's Office of Women's Health from having to curtail all its research in 2007.

An act of Congress granting the offices of women's health in our fed-eral agencies permanent status would give them some immunity from political maneuvering. The Society for Women's Health Research has been pushing for over eight years for such a mandate. But, says Greenberger,

> While these offices are important, nothing will substitute for more atten-
> tion to and funding for conditions that affect women disproportion-
> ately and differently. Continued pressure is needed to include women

and minorities in medical research and analysis by sex and ethnicity, and we need to convince the medical and research establishment that understanding sex differences is important in ensuring the provision of appropriate care. For too long, women have been treated as "little men," without an appreciation of the differences in prevalence and symptoms among various conditions and what those differences mean for diagnosis and treatment. What it amounts to is women's health getting really short shrift.

In the meantime, efforts expended in just staying afloat could be putting their programs (those that could save women like Marcie from near tragedy) in jeopardy.

"MAMA, PLEASE HELP me! Please take me to the E.R.," cried the thirty-one-year-old Tennessee woman, Monique "Nikki" White. Skin lesions from untreated lupus were spreading over her entire body, her stomach swelled, and the pain was unbearable. But when her mom said, "OK, let's go," Nikki held back. With no insurance and still owing money from her last visit, her fears of being turned away kept her from getting help.

The next day she suffered a seizure and was rushed to the hospital, but the care she received came too late. Significant organ damage had taken its toll. She died shortly afterward.

Since receiving her diagnosis ten years earlier, Nikki had waged two equally arduous battles—against her disease and for medical insurance. Both were doomed.

As one of the forty-seven million Americans uninsured because they don't qualify for Medicaid and are unable to purchase insurance on their own (up by nearly 8.6 million between 2000 and 2006), Nikki did not have ongoing, coordinated medical treatment.

If her illness had been managed appropriately, if she'd been treated by a specialist and given appropriate medication, she might not have died, like some twenty-seven thousand other Americans whose deaths in 2008 alone would have been preventable if they'd had insurance, according to a recent study by the Urban Institute.

Women without insurance (Latinas and African American women are two to three times more likely to be uninsured than white women) "typically postpone needed care, skip important screening services, are diagnosed at more advanced disease states and receive less therapeutic care," a 2007 study by the Commonwealth Fund revealed. "Holding on to my insurance is the reason I'm sticking with a job I loathe," one woman wrote on my survey, expressing the views of many. In an AFL-CIO poll of over twenty-three thousand women of all ages and nationalities, concern about health care and finding affordable insurance ranked as the top concern. And startling new evidence, reported in the October 30, 2008, *New York Times*, has revealed a large gap in the cost of health insurance plans between what women and men pay, a difference amounting to hundreds of dollars more per year for women. As Marcia D. Greenberger, copresident of the National Women's Law Center, said, just as we don't allow for race to be a factor in setting rates, we shouldn't allow gender to be, either.

This disparity may explain why women with insurance often have to ignore serious medical conditions because they can't afford to treat them. Elizabeth M. Patachias and Judith G. Waxman, also of the National Women's Law Center, note that women have greater health care needs, take more prescription medications, and have lower incomes than men. Many with policies are underinsured. And faced with the high cost of premiums and health care services, women report avoiding care altogether or getting far less than they need.

In the current economic meltdown, with such horrific job loss, more families are buying individual insurance. But as Dawn Foiles found out, this might result in no insurance at all.

Dawn did all the right things. She found a surgeon on her plan, then got Blue Cross's authorization for her back and neck operations. But while she was just starting to recover, the company pulled her coverage, leaving her and her husband with one hundred thousand dollars in medical bills. Blue Cross accused her of failing to disclose an earlier back surgery in 1997. Dawn has the documents to prove them wrong, but the company still refuses to reconsider. The last thing in the world the Foiles want is to sell their California home and live with her husband's mom in Idaho, but that might be their only option. "I've never been this stressed out in all my life," Dawn said.

DUMPING PATIENTS AFTER accepting them and then claiming their initial applications were misleading or erroneous is a growing trend among insurance companies as they maximize their profits at the expense of patients. Health insurance companies are growing at a rapid pace, soon to take over manufacturing as America's largest industry. There are four health insurance lobbyists for every member of Congress. We're spending more on health insurance than almost every other wealthy nation, and getting less care. A universal system, equally responsive to the health needs of women as it is to men, and to the poor as to the well-off—with meaningful and equitable access for everyone—would go a long way toward preventing these medical horror stories.

Warning! This Country May Be Dangerous to Your Health

Many pregnant women enjoy their final trimester as a time of planning and fantasizing about the new baby. For African American women, those daydreams often lead to heartbreak. They are four times as likely as white women to die in childbirth, and for every one thousand live births, nearly fourteen infants will die. These numbers, two and a half times what they are for white women, are rising in many states. In our nation's capital, the mortality rate is four times as great for black infants as for white ones. The gap between white and black babies expanded in twenty-five states between 1989 and 1991 and 2002 and 2004, coinciding with the Bush I and II years.

The causes are the usual suspects: low socioeconomic status, poor nutrition, and lack of access to prenatal care. And Bush's fiscal irresponsibility and misguided wars hurt attempts to reverse our staggering rate of infant mortality.

A cut of more than six hundred million dollars compromised WIC's ability to subsidize the diets of low-income pregnant women and nursing mothers. Two other vital programs, one giving medical care to women during and after their pregnancies and the other (the Healthy Start program) to their babies, were slashed.

When President Obama signed a bill to expand coverage of the State Children's Health Insurance Program (SCHIP), he undid some of the damage caused by his predecessor's veto of the expansion in 2007. But there is still much more to do. Over the course of W.'s terms in office, he cut programs to help youngsters scarred by domestic violence, as well as those struggling with substance abuse, physical disabilities, and severe emotional disturbances, according to a report by the Children's Defense Fund. Bush's budget of 2008 even ignored the Department of Health and Human Services's positive findings: an impressive 90 percent of children included in the Children's Mental Service Program attended school, and almost 70 percent had no contact with law enforcement agencies.

Attracting less attention but also inflicting hardship are recent rules making it harder for children, who comprise one third of the beneficiaries, to be enrolled in Medicaid, and cuts both in programs to improve emergency medical services for minors and training for health care professionals to staff freestanding children's hospitals. What's important to remember is that children's welfare is determined by the families they grow up in. When kids' parents are poor, they are poor.

Under Bush's administration a series of reductions in Medicaid totaling some $12 billion effectively shredded the safety net for moderate and low-income families. Obama's $787 billion stimulus package provides $87 billion for Medicaid. It will help, of course, but it's not as generous as many governors had hoped.

INCARCERATED WOMEN, PROBABLY the most invisible group in our society, are also among the most vulnerable. They're being seriously hurt by Medicaid rulings mandating delays upon release from prison to reapply for its benefits—a process that can take upward of ninety days. The majority of imprisoned women are there for nonviolent crimes: drugs, prostitution, check forgery—and most are mothers, incarcerated at great distance from their children. Many of these inmates have long histories of abuse and suffer from myriad mental and physical illnesses.

Hypertension, diabetes, heart conditions, asthma, HIV/AIDS, substance abuse, and depression afflict female prisoners at an alarming rate. Being put behind bars *is* the punishment, but women are punished even further by appallingly neglectful medical care. The blood-sugar levels of diabetics aren't routinely tested, resulting in life-threatening seizures; inmates with newly detected cancers are ignored until they're deathly ill with stage four metastasized malignancies. "[S]ubstandard care and unconscionable delays" is how one former prison doctor characterized the jumble of apathy, incompetence, and outright deliberate refusal to diagnose and treat seriously ill incarcerated women. As Ross Sears, a retired Texas appellate judge referring to Carswell, a federal prison in Fort Worth, said, "Far too many inmates have died unnecessarily and their pleas for help ignored."

Whatever chronic conditions women bring to imprisonment, it's safe to say they'll have them, or worse, if they survive their time inside. For many of these women being on the "outside" is a risky proposition. Lacking homes, jobs, embracing families, and health care, the experience can be fraught with anxiety.

Tina, a young mother and a former alcoholic, desperate to stay sober, found herself returning to her earlier destructive patterns. "I wish someone had told me how to take care of my health," she said of her time in prison. "I wish people would have told me about getting regular checkups. You didn't get that inside. You were never told anything. I wish people had told me to make sure I was OK."

Continuity of medical treatment is especially vital for this neglected population. By the time they're able to access Medicaid again, many face deteriorating conditions, compromising their ability to lead productive lives and making recidivism more likely.

FORMERLY INCARCERATED WOMEN often feel discounted by a medical establishment holding their past against them. If this is true, then the reverse should prevail for women in our armed services. We'd think they'd be granted superlative care. But, sadly, this isn't the case.

When female veterans return home, they have to depend on deficient services. Like men, they often face shockingly unsanitary conditions and indifferent treatment, such as those reported at Walter Reed and other VA hospitals. And while the numbers of wounded are less than those of the men they serve with, women have a significantly higher incidence of serious posttraumatic stress syndrome (PTSS).

PTSS can result from multiple deployments, from injuries, from the trauma of combat, or from sexual abuse while serving. Interestingly, studies have shown that sexual harassment is so damaging to women it causes the same level of posttraumatic stress that combat does for men. But programs to help treat PTSS "were designed with men in mind," and women are not getting the psychological care they need, a Memorial Day editorial in the *New York Times* (2008) noted. "Women who have been raped or sexually assaulted often cannot face therapy groups or medical facilities full of men."

Major Tammy Duckworth, assistant secretary of public and intergovernmental affairs for the U.S. Department of Veterans Affairs, said, "I don't think the mental health care system is ready for [female veterans]." Some eight hundred thousand of them are homeless, the majority because they have children and no child care and are suffering from mental distress.

Even though the cost of caring for returning veterans is soaring, the Republicans under Bush put in place a budget severely reducing funding for their health care in 2009 and again in 2010, and then freezing it afterward.

BUT BUSH'S LARGEST cuts—$105 billion over ten years—came from Medicare, which provides health care coverage to forty-three million senior citizens and people with disabilities, the majority of whom are women. The bill that passed in July 2008 will help ease the difficulties in accessing care of those who reside in rural areas but will not remedy the damage already done. Nearly one third of women living alone over the age of sixty-five are classified as poor. Women are less likely than men to have had health insurance through their jobs, and they're more likely to have worked part-time jobs or to stop working entirely to care for family members.

A significant number of these women have to postpone or forego necessary care for themselves. In many cases they are no longer able to afford the medications they require. Although secrecy has surrounded the pricing of the new prescription drug plan, high-level congressional investigations have disclosed that using private insurers is actually driving up the cost of drugs for our nation's senior citizens. Each of the seven largest U.S. publicly traded pharmaceutical companies are spending much more on marketing and advertising than on research and development.

However disparate the health needs of pregnant woman, infants, children, the impoverished, and the elderly, they're bound together in one unhappy way—they all have high incidences of food insecurity. Or, put less euphemistically, hunger.

What really turns the bright lights on the moral priorities of the Republicans in Washington is their cavalier cuts in necessary relief to our most susceptible populations. Some three hundred thousand low-income working families were eliminated from receiving food stamps, and the Commodity Supplemental Food Program was put on the chopping block so that more funding could be thrown into the money pit of war.

"It's zero degrees of separation between those struggling to put food on the table and those serving up three-course meals," David Goodman, executive director of the Redwood Empire Food Bank, in Sonoma Country, California, told me.

"My sister has MS."

"My husband lost his job."

"My daughter was diagnosed with viral pneumonia."

Such unexpected life events can throw off a tight family budget, creating dire food shortages for families. Households with children, the elderly, and the disabled are at greatest risk. Having a job is no guarantee of having enough food for your family. The majority of children who go to bed hungry have at least one parent working; nearly half live in two-parent families. And even though spiraling prices, especially at the gas pump, only brought forth a cosmic shrug from the Bush administration, those dependent on their cars to get to work have often had to choose between their jobs and food. And the high cost of gasoline has kept aid workers from reaching some of the neediest, most malnourished populations.

"These families," Goodman explained, "are always negotiating their diet." Having food is never a given. People will move from location to location because of food availability. One way of gauging hunger in America is to consider Redwood's experiences. In 2003 they served 4,000 summer lunches (this is outside of meals given in summer school); four years later they were serving 53,900. And, not surprisingly, the economic collapse is having a harsh impact on a family's ability to find adequate nutrition.

The most recent figures available, according to the *New York Times* of December 26, 2008, show a 60 percent increase in children pushed into food insecurity.

Hunger is a predictor of problem pregnancies and of infants' failure to thrive. For children it means overall poorer health, compromised ability to resist illness, greater incidence of hospitalization, impaired cognitive functioning, and diminished learning capacity. In the elderly it "exacerbates disease, increases disability, decreases resistance to infection, and extends hospital stays," reports the Center on Hunger and Poverty at Brandeis University.

Food insecurity is another thread in the rope choking off the lives of American women. "The outlook for women's health is grim and no where near approaching the nation's goals for 2010 set by the U.S. Department of Health and Human Services initiative," said Dr. Michelle Berline, associate professor at the Oregon Health and Science University. Not one state in fifty received a satisfactory grade in a women's health report card issued by the National Women's Law Center. The United States overall received a failing grade when evaluating how well it met benchmarks for women's health.

Americans, amazingly enough, aren't competitive in the longevity game. We rank forty-fifth in life expectancy in the world, behind Bosnia and Jordan. And for the first time since 1918, women's life expectancy is dropping. Emphysema, kidney disease, lung cancer, and diabetes are taking a huge toll among women of all races in Appalachia, the Deep South, and the lower Midwest. Where disparities are the greatest, families at the lower end struggle against the almost impossible odds of poor diets, rampant cigarette smoking, and failure to treat chronic illnesses.

Dr. Majid Ezzati of the Harvard School of Public Health questions how quickly America will stem the rising death rate for women. As he notes, "policies aimed at reducing fundamental mental socioeconomic inequalities are currently practically absent in the U.S."

Also missing are policies preventing loss of life from a *deliberate* cause—murder.

Battering the Already Battered

"You can run, but you'll never get away."

These chilling words from Darlene's abusive husband were left on her cell phone as she hid in her sister's apartment. Even with a bloodied gash on her face and several broken ribs, Darlene was too terrified to go for treatment. Several times before, her husband had torn through the area emergency rooms until he'd found her.

Darlene eventually did make it to a shelter; others aren't so fortunate. Four women are killed in this country each day by their husbands or boyfriends. And an estimated 1.5 million women are physically or sexually assaulted by their intimate partners every year.

Battered women live in constant fear, never knowing when the next attack will come. And when it does, as it is certain to, whether they'll survive it. The most dangerous time, experts say, is when a woman is trying to get out of the relationship. This act of independence and self-preservation sets off a rage in the abuser, who feels his control is threatened.

When a woman leaves an abusive relationship she is literally running for her life and sometimes the lives of her children. Usually it means parting with possessions and—if she has one—a job. Shelters are only temporary. It's either find a place to live or become homeless. For this reason battered women and other displaced families are recognized as having priority access to federal low-income housing and, in the past, have benefited from the Section 8 Housing Voucher Program to help pay the rent. But Section 8 was decimated by the Bush administration. "The lack of available housing is a key element in forcing women to return to abusive partners," Beth Silverman Yam, clinical director of Sanctuary for Families, told me.

The Bush Administration consistently weakened the enforcement programs of the Violence Against Women Act, including cutting funds for such vital services as bilingual crisis hot lines, emergency shelters, counseling, support groups, and other forms of assistance. It refused to include important protections for domestic violence victims in marriage promotion programs and has failed to protect battered women from gun violence. And in 2008 it sought to transfer the overseeing of how funds are spent from Congress to the Department of Justice—making it possible for the administration to eliminate even more antiviolence programs.

"It's a nightmare," said Jill Morris, public policy director at the National Coalition Against Domestic Violence, commenting on the Republicans' antagonistic response to the real needs of abuse victims.

Without governmental support, women in brutalizing relationships have to rely on local volunteer groups for help. Many of these are terribly short of funds, especially in the poorest areas, where higher rates of unemployment and alcoholism trigger abuse and where need is the greatest. American Indian women, for example, experience the highest rate of violence of any group in the country. Homicide is the third-leading cause of their death, said sergeant Daren Simeona with the Navajo Police Academy in Toyei, Arizona. Like other poor rural communities, most reservations lack safe havens, so abused women are cramped into friends' homes and makeshift shelters. "It's a band-aid approach," said Simeona.

But a band-aid can't fix a gunshot wound or a slit throat.

14

BIRTH-CONTROL ACTIVISTS, PLEASE PHONE HOME

"**H**ow many millions of dollars must be spent on this program? Research has shown over and over, it just doesn't work. Kids are more likely not to use anything and end up pregnant or with STDs. Our job is to give kids what they need, not what politicians think they should have."

I've just asked Dr. Angela Diaz, director of the Mount Sinai Adolescent Health Center—the largest in the nation—who works with young people around issues of reproduction and sexuality, about abstinence-only programs, and she can hardly keep the anger out of her voice.

"Of course we talk about abstinence," she said, "but many teenagers nationwide engage in sex at a very early age."

At the Sinai Center they see about ten thousand teenagers a year and hand out thousands of condoms and other forms of birth control. "Many of our kids are poor, abused, and underserved," Dr. Diaz said. "They come here with so many problems. Our biggest challenge is to help our teenagers make the most of their lives."

Without putting too fine a point on Dr. Diaz's remarks, this country is currently spending about two hundred million dollars a year on abstinence-only courses, and they've been proven completely ineffective. Students who received *comprehensive* sex education are half as likely to become teen parents as those who were in abstinence-only (AO) programs.

What's more, AO does *not* delay teen sexual activity. A new study by researchers at the University of Washington found that teens are actually having "more sex than they were in 2001, and condom use declined after the U.S. government increased spending to promote sexual abstinence."

The right's faith-based, blundering intrusion into school sex-ed classes has resulted in a rising teenage birth rate in this country, the first time since 1991 and the highest rate in the developed world, on a par with Ukraine. Abstinence-only courses are most likely also responsible for the increase (the first in thirty years) in syphilis and gonorrhea and for the staggering incidence of other sexually transmitted diseases (STDs) among girls and young women.

One out of four adolescent girls has been found to be infected with the human papilloma virus (linked to cancer), genital warts, or chlamydia, and 15 percent with more than one. The numbers fall with particular weight on women and girls of color. Half of all African American and impoverished young women between the ages fourteen and nineteen have at least one of these diseases. For this population the accidental pregnancy rate has gone up by 30 percent since 1994.

While evidence of abstinence-only programs' danger to our public health continues to mount, astonishingly, the Democratic Congress in December 2007 approved a twenty-eight-million-dollar increase for it. Ostensibly the program's goal is to prevent young people from becoming sexually active. It attempts to accomplish its aim at all costs, even if that means spreading gross misinformation, substituting religious thinking for scientific fact, and advocating antiquated, misogynist gender roles.

The abstinence-only curricula (the *only* form of sex education available in 35 percent of public schools across the country, according to a survey by the Alan Guttmacher Institute) do everything possible to put "holes" in condoms' effectiveness. The courses exaggerate condom failure rate in preventing pregnancies, putting it at 14 percent instead of the 3 percent shown repeatedly by independent studies when condoms are worn consistently and correctly. And even though the *New England Journal of Medicine* found that "in 15,000 acts of intercourse with consistent condom use,

HIV was never transferred from an HIV positive individual," AO denies condoms provide a barrier to the HIV virus.

When it comes to abortion, no fundamentalist Bible class in America could compete with the "pro-life" lessons our children are learning in *public* schools. If our youngsters aren't scared enough by the inaccurate figures of abortion-induced sterility (largely culled from stories of illegal procedures), premature births (supposedly a major cause of mental retardation), and suicides of the young aborting mother, the guilt trip will surely get them.

"A *baby* begins at the moment of conception," say the most popular of the AO courses, and everything following that questionable assertion flies in the face of long-known and accepted scientific knowledge. "Six days later [after conception], the baby snuggles into the soft nest of the mother's uterus." At forty-three days "this new life may be thought of as a thinking person. . . . Ten to twelve weeks after conception he/she can hear and see."

Questioning such erroneous statements about fetal development is discouraged by the antisex cabal with its insistence on female passivity and subservience. There are enough gender stereotypes in the curricula to make you think you've picked up a tract from the Victorian era: "Girls are less able than boys to focus on one task at a time," says one, while another insists "they need protection and that is why a father gives a daughter in marriage to a husband, another man who will take care of her."

A popular feature of AO literature is cautionary tales, such as the one about a princess who offers the knight advice on how to kill the dragon. Obviously too smart for her own good, she's jilted for a know-nothing village maiden. Just in case the kids miss the moral, it's clearly stated: occasional advice may be acceptable, but "too much will lessen a man's confidence or even turn him away from his princess." The books, pamphlets, and syllabi of faith-based AO programs show millions of children a world in which men are the resourceful, dominant, and often aggressive protectors while women, unfailingly, are weak, subordinate, easily distracted, and limited in every way. Including their reproductive rights.

The New War on Contraception

"It may be news to many people that contraception as a matter of right and public health is no longer a given, but politicians and those in the public-health profession know it well," said William Smith of the Sexuality Information and Education Council of the United States, an organization dating back to 1964.

Judging by the women I interviewed, Smith is absolutely right. Among all the issues they saw as vital to women's ongoing progress—keeping abortion legal loomed high on their list—not one worried about contraception. In reality, though, we're in the midst of what experts are calling a war on contraception. The most recent assault was the Bush administration's eleventh-hour issuance of the Right of Conscience Regulation, broadening the definition of abortion to include many kinds of birth control, especially oral and emergency contraception, and allowing health care providers to withhold available medical information if it conflicts with their moral or religious beliefs. Numerous organizations, including the American Academy of Pediatrics, have urged the Obama administration to repeal this regulation, and President Obama has taken the first step toward doing so.

Conservatives, energized by the success of their antiabortion drive, are ratcheting up their offensive. They're doing it in their churches and in faith-based organizations and with the help of numerous point people in Congress. Those on the right claim they're honoring women by preserving the sanctity of motherhood, but their real beef is the freedom birth control affords women to enjoy a healthy, safe sex life while avoiding unwanted pregnancies. That speaks for the forty-two million—or seven out of ten—American women in their childbearing years who are sexually active and don't want to get pregnant.

Whether it's to finish high school, study to become an accountant, or go mountain climbing, a woman's ability to fulfill her dreams and be self-actualizing depends upon her control over the decisions of whether and when she has children. And while old-schoolers may wring their hands about the debauchery of present-day America, the number of people who are sexually active before marriage has remained pretty constant since the 1950s. As one writer sardonically noted, "even Grandma had premarital sex."

Misinformation about what constitutes safe, effective birth control is an ongoing problem. Bayer, the maker of Yaz, the most popular oral contraceptive in contemporary America, has been reprimanded for not revealing the pill's serious health risks in advertising it, according to the Department of Health and Human Services. Bruce L. Lambert, a professor of pharmacy administration at the University of Illinois at Chicago, was not optimistic that we'd see the end to this kind of misleading advertising any time soon. It's all too reminiscent of the underreporting of health concerns associated with Enovid. Apparently when it comes to women's well-being, we haven't advanced much over the past fifty years.

In fact, in some ways we're actually going backward. Challenging contraception at the highest levels of government was the task of several high-profile Bush cronies, whose appointments made about as much sense as putting former Yugoslavian president Slobodan Milosevic in charge of a commission charged with ending ethnic cleansing. There was Dr. W. David Hager as head of the FDA's Reproductive Health Drugs Advisory Committee, who uses Jesus as a model of chastity to treat his gynecological patients. And Eric Keroack—an anti–sex education, anti–birth control zealot—appointed to oversee the federally funded family planning programs at the Department of Health and Human Services, later replaced by the equally anti–reproductive rights Susan Orr, who called contraception part of the "culture of death."

These key players waged a battle against emergency contraception, or Plan B. The Plan B pill works by stopping ovulation or fertilization. Because in some rare cases it may prevent a fertilized egg from implanting in the uterus, right-to-lifers have jumped all over it, claiming it's a form of abortion, although every independent medical organization disagrees.

The pill would encourage adolescents "to form sex-based cults centered around [its use]," Hager wildly predicted. He and his team used every possible ploy to block FDA approval for over-the-counter sale of Plan B. Numerous large-scale studies by nonpartisan organizations found his hysterical charges completely without basis: the availability of Plan B did not in any way lead to increased teen promiscuity. Besides, the FDA's mission is to pass judgment on a drug's safety, not its impact on sex in America.

That something was foul in the FDA led to calls for an investigation. The Government Accountability Office released its findings in 2006: the FDA's handling of Plan B was *inconsistent* with its approach to sixty-seven other prescriptions that were switched to over-the-counter status between 1994 and 2004. Religiously motivated politics were allowed to affect decisions impacting millions of lives. Forty percent of women who become pregnant in the United States are under twenty years old, and 80 percent of them will end up on public assistance. You really have to wonder what these folks were thinking.

Finally, at the end of 2006, after a three-year stall, Plan B received FDA approval. Initially women under eighteen needed a prescription, but in March 2009 a federal court lifted the Bush administration's restrictions and ordered that Plan B be available over the counter to those seventeen and older. Still, its price—almost forty-five dollars—puts it beyond the reach of many. And although it's technically available over the counter, it's actually kept locked *behind* the counter, requiring a willing pharmacist to give it to you.

Some young women, especially those in small towns, may be uncomfortable asking someone they may have known their entire life for the contraceptive. Others get a whole lot more than the pills when they ask for them. Cathy, a twenty-five-year-old from the Midwest, ran to her drugstore after her boyfriend's condom broke. "I had my driver's license, so there was no problem with eligibility," she said. But before the pharmacist handed her the packet, he said, "What you're doing, young lady, is against humanity. You should be ashamed of yourself."

Cathy paid for the contraceptives and left the store with tears streaming down her face. "I know he had no right to speak to me that way, but I was feeling so vulnerable and frightened to begin with, he just made everything much worse."

Wal-Mart stores—in many parts of rural America the only pharmacies available for forty or fifty miles—like several other big chains initially refused to stock the pill on moral and religious grounds. Because the pill must be taken as soon as possible after unprotected intercourse, having to travel long distances to obtain it could result in an unwanted pregnancy.

Only when faced with unremitting pressure from state legislatures did Wal-Mart agree to dispense the pill, but they've allowed pharmacists to opt out of filling prescriptions for those under eighteen, a policy Pope Benedict said in 2007 he wants implemented throughout the country. A new trend is "pro-life pharmacies" that refuse to stock Plan B or any birth-control pills or condoms whatsoever. As the *Washington Post* reported on June 16, 2008, many of these drugstores are indistinguishable from typical drugstores in heavily populated shopping plazas with pizza parlors and coffee shops. Except these pharmacies are "walling off essential parts of health care," asserted Marcia Greenberger of the National Women's Law Center. Some sell Viagra but refuse to stock contraception for women. Critics of these pharmacies are concerned about women who may unknowingly go to one of them and be humiliated or, in the case of those needing emergency contraception, waste precious time. In addition, at this point less than 40 percent of hospitals—Catholic as well as secular—in eleven states surveyed provide Plan B on-site to rape survivors.

Difficulty accessing emergency contraception isn't the only obstacle facing young women. Soaring costs for regular prescription contraceptives due to a recent change in federal law are hurting college students as well as poor women who use community health centers. "The potential is that women will stop taking [birth-control pills], and whether or not you can pay for it, that doesn't mean that you'll stop having sex," said Katie Ryan, a senior at the University of North Dakota. A huge number of the students affected have little disposable income, relying on scholarships or Pell grants. "For them," as one activist put it, "this is like a choice—groceries or birth control."

Anticontraception policies have already resulted in the spike in teen pregnancies and an uptick in abortion rates. In Western Europe, Canada, and around the world where abortion is legal and contraception widely available, abortion rates plummet. (Americans are 38 percent more likely to get abortions than Canadians.) Places that outlaw abortion—Africa and Central and South America—have the highest rates. This isn't rocket science. It's common sense. Once our nation prided itself on how far ahead we were of the pack. Now we're falling backward. I'm not sure if this is a sign of our unilateralism. It's certainly a sign of our misogyny.

The New Right's Assault on Choice

Imagine the fetus you're carrying inside you is sloughing off its skin, its skull is already collapsing, you've started bleeding heavily, and you have to either wait days for a chemically induced labor to start or find a physician who can safely perform the dilation and extraction (or evacuation) (D&E).

This harrowing situation is what Pulitzer Prize–winning journalist Martha Mendoza faced in 2004 when she learned her once-thriving nineteen-week fetus was dead. For nearly a week, Martha was bounced around from one doctor and hospital to the next, still bleeding and growing increasingly fearful that the dead fetus would simply fall out while she cared for her three young children.

Her own doctor refused to perform the procedure, and she couldn't find anyone else who would. Although Bush had signed a ban on late-term abortions in 2003, technically a doctor could surgically remove a dead fetus from a woman. But so much negative right wing–inspired publicity surrounded the procedure, accompanied by physical attacks on abortion providers, that physicians were wary. Only 7 percent of all doctors in this country are taught how to do a D&E while in school. D&E is a safe, rare, and effective way to terminate a pregnancy in the second trimester, when by all accounts a fetus could not survive outside the womb.

From her research, Martha knew that with a D&E she'd be less likely to have bleeding requiring transfusions, less likely to require intravenous antibiotics, and less likely to endure organ injury and cervical laceration requiring further hospitalization than with a regular vaginal delivery. Finally Martha found a doctor, but up to the very last moment, when she was already in active labor, the hospital staff pressured her to change her mind. Still, Martha insisted on having the D&E. She had no complications, and her next pregnancy resulted in a healthy baby girl. But what of other women who must cope with similar heartbreaks?

A recent Supreme Court ruling upholding the ban on this form of late-term abortion has doomed them to face the chances of greater physical injury and more emotional pain.

How did this happen?

As we've seen, from the moment George W. Bush took office he began to undermine a woman's ability to control her childbearing and her body.

He packed the federal judiciary and state courts with known ideologues committed to overturning *Roe v. Wade*, and nominated like-minded Justice Roberts to the Supreme Court.

With John Roberts securely at the helm as chief justice, right-wingers needed a fifth vote against abortion on the court. And they found it in Samuel Alito, who'd devised a plan to destroy *Roe* while part of Reagan's administration. Ten years ago his background would have called forth torrents of condemnation and cries for investigation. But not now. The media has dramatically fallen away from its fierce support of reproductive choice.

In the weeks following the announcement of Bush's selection, 50 percent of the coverage of Alito was positive, according to the Center for Media and Pubic Affairs. A look at the *New York Times* in the period leading up to the Supreme Court decision on D&E reveals its op-ed pages giving an almost exclusive platform to the "views of pro-life or abortion-ambivalent men, male scholars of the right, and men with strong, usually Catholic, religious affiliations." Amazingly, between March 2004 and March 2006, 83 percent of the pieces discussing abortion appearing on that page came from men.

And during Alito's confirmation hearings—when women needed all the support we could muster—only twenty-five senators stood up for us. Alito sailed into office. Barely had the two new justices settled in before they were deciding one of the most important abortion cases since *Roe*.

At issue was the legality of the federal ban on D&E, what the right inflamingly calls partial-birth abortion. Only 10 percent of all abortions in the United States are performed during the second trimester. Those performed in the third trimester are even rarer, and doctors have to prove the pregnancy is incompatible with the mother's health or life. An impressive array of physicians, including the leading medical group in the field, the American College of Obstetricians and Gynecologists, oppose the ban. "These procedures are selected generally, at least in my experience, on the basis of what is best for that woman . . . and the situation she's in," said Fred Frigoletto, past president of the college. Bill Clinton vetoed this bill two times, but Bush signed it even though it contained no provision to protect women's health. In 2000, when the Supreme Court deliberated on a state law prohibiting the procedure, the justices had determined that a women's health should be the main concern of her doctor rather than politicians, and they'd ruled against it. But with the new makeup of the court and with indifference, even contempt, for women rife in society, that caution was completely ignored. And in a 5–4 decision, the Supreme Court ruling in *Gozales v. Carhart* upheld the ban, signaling a reversed course on abortion and gutting that critical requirement—going back to the 1973 ruling of *Roe*—"all abortion regulations must have an exception to protect a woman's health."

This punitive decision showed a callous disregard of women and profoundly diminished the constitutional respect given to them in the decisions they make about pregnancies and childbearing. Justice Kennedy could hardly have been more paternalistic and patronizing in his rendering of the majority decision. As the *New York Times* wrote, "[He] actually reasoned that banning the procedure was good for women in that it would protect them from a procedure they might not fully understand in advance and would probably come to regret."

"This way of thinking, that women are flighty creatures who must be protected by men reflects notions of a woman's place in the family and under the Constitution that have long been discredited," said Ruth Bader Ginsburg in the dissenting opinion. Equally significant is the way the ruling, emphasizing "ethical and moral concerns," shifts the abortion debate from the rights of women to the rights of the fetus.

"I'm afraid the Supreme Court has just opened the door to an all-out assault on *Roe*," said Dr. LeRoy H. Carhart, the Nebraska physician who brought the case. "The women in my practice may soon experience life without access to safe, legal abortions." Dr. Carhart, who spent twenty-one years in the air force, is a lifelong Republican, a churchgoing Methodist, and a deeply committed family man. He became interested in reproductive medicine after his medical training, when he saw dozens of women suffering from "infections after abortions, usually a self-induced, desperate act. Some died, others were left sterile. It was horrible, worse than watching people die in a war," Carhart said.

When "pro-lifers" set fire to Dr. Carhart's horse farm where he and his family lived, destroying their home and killing seventeen horses and their pet dogs and cat, Carhart decided he would never be deterred and women's health would become his prime focus. Yet Dr. Carhart and other physicians will have to face up to two years in jail if they perform the outlawed procedure.

"[E]ssentially they've taken out of our armamentarium a procedure that for some women is the safest and best course," said Nancy Stanwood, an assistant ob/gyn professor at the University of Rochester. In many ways, she said, "Congress and the court are practicing medicine without a license. And that's against the law."

At greatest risk are young women, likely to delay coming to terms with a pregnancy and making a decision about it, older women who won't have the results of their amniocentesis tests before well into the middle trimester, and poorer women whose access to safe abortion since President Reagan has become increasingly problematic.

The Supreme Court ruling, in effect, drew together three main thrusts of the antiabortion movement. The first is to make it harder and more dangerous for women to terminate their pregnancies, with the ultimate goal of making it impossible; the second is to bombard women with misleading information in the hopes of scaring them away; the third is the movement to give fetuses personhood.

FOR MANY WOMEN the promise of a so-called abortion pill, RU-486, would allow them to avoid navigating the increasingly difficult maze of finding a provider, but the application to approve it has been withdrawn pending a review of the comptroller general of the United States. Unlike Plan B (the "morning-after pill"), which is a higher dose of a common contraception to be taken within seventy-two hours of unprotected sex, RU-486, an artificial steroid, actually ends an established pregnancy. Deb Berry of Orlando, Florida, is one woman who would have benefited from the availability of RU-486 but instead found herself trampled by the right's bait-'n'-switch tactics.

Deb did not plan to become pregnant. She was terrified to tell her boyfriend, who was physically and mentally abusive. Her doctor knew this but still refused to perform an abortion. Deb had been taking birth-control pills, but apparently they'd been rendered ineffective by antibiotics her gynecologist had prescribed for a bladder infection, never telling her to use a back-up contraceptive.

Looking in the phone book under *abortion*, Deb felt relieved to read an ad from a so-called pregnancy crisis center—"Pregnant? Scared? We can help." At the center, Deb wept as she described her situation; the "counselor" handed her tissues, then advised her to "put her faith in God."

When Deb asked about scheduling an abortion, all she got was a gory photograph of an aborted fetus. At first, in her distraught state, she didn't quite get what was going on. But finally she realized—the pregnancy crisis center was really a front for a Christian antiabortion organization.

An increasing number of states are using tax dollars to subsidize antiabortion programs and centers. They make no bones about deliberately deceiving women like Deb Berry; their supporters actually revel in the trickery and public funding. Nancy McDonald, who runs five of them in south Florida, said, "It's a subtle thing . . . but people seem to think if you're affiliated with the state, you must be good." But other women, like Vicki Saporta, president of the National Abortion Federation, disagree. "It's reprehensible that taxpayer dollars are going to organizations that regularly and deliberately deceive women."

At present at least eight states are using public money to finance these pregnancy crisis centers, numbering between two and three thousand nationwide, and tens of millions in federal funding are also going to them for their role in abstinence education.

It took Deb Berry several weeks before she was able to find a doctor to end her pregnancy—precious weeks that could have grave consequences for many young women. And more restrictions are on the way. A bill already passed the House Judiciary Committee on December 30, 2008, making it a federal crime to transport a pregnant woman under eighteen across state lines to circumvent state parental notification laws, even if the parents are abusive or insistent that their daughters unwillingly carry to term. Earlier versions of this bill contained no exception for those whose health is in danger; it remains to be seen what shape its final form will take.

If this measure becomes law, young women will be forced either to involve their parents in their decision, to drive themselves back and forth to abortion clinics that are far from their homes, or perhaps, in desperation, to abort the fetuses themselves.

DR. BARNETT SLEPIAN was one of many. His photograph, name, and address were posted by a fanatic antiabortion organization on their Nuremberg Files Web site. The ob/gyn, who worked at a women's reproductive health clinic, was pictured in an Old West–style "Wanted" ad, slating him for execution. One Friday night as he was preparing soup in the kitchen of his upstate New York home, his wife and children nearby, a so-called pro-lifer shot through the window and murdered him. The next day, his face was x-ed out on the Web site.

In an attempt to avoid negative publicity, the creators of the Nuremberg Files no longer post pictures of targeted doctors, but they ask for help in preparing dossiers with personal information on abortion providers, nurses, and women's health center managers. Bombings of clinics, acid attacks, shootings, and murders, going on for years, have locked those who provide *legal* abortion services in a dungeon of fear. Many have hired bodyguards, some wear bulletproof vests. Rarely have these measures saved their lives.

The terrorizing has paid off for antichoice zealots. Slowly and without fanfare, medical schools have stopped teaching students how to perform abortions, and doctors who know how are refusing to do them. A startling 87 percent of counties in the United States have no abortion provider, and 34 percent of women live in those counties. Entire states have no physicians willing to terminate an unwanted pregnancy. North Dakota is one of these. For women who decide they cannot go through with having a baby, the Red River Women's Clinic in Fargo is their *only* source of information and help.

"Two female physicians fly in from Texas and Minnesota to perform abortions on two patient days," Tammy Kromenaker, who runs the clinic, told me. "Some women drive over five hours to get there, then there are the additional hurdles of parental consent and a twenty-four-hour waiting period."

A nurse practitioner at the clinic does gynecological exams and pap tests and discusses birth control. The clinic sees thirteen hundred patients per year. Many of their patients don't have medical coverage, but they "all leave with a form of birth control in their hands."

Tammy is matter-of-fact about how heroic her work is. Her voice stays calm even when she tells me she takes a different route home each day, how she always checks her rear-view mirror, how her children don't use her last name. She even stays calm when she tells me about the time she had to frighten off an intruder with a stun gun. But she becomes passionate when she says, "Reproductive health care is failing young women today. They're trying to be responsible and do what they need to, but our society fails them."

And we continue to fail them by sinking to dirty-trick scare tactics based on the right's patriarchal assumption that it knows what's best for women. Starting in November 2002 the Web site of the National Cancer Institute, in "an egregious distortion of the evidence," posted a statement strongly suggesting a link between abortion and breast cancer.

Women's groups pressured Congress to act. It insisted the NCI hold a three-day conference with experts in the field to review all the data on any possible connections. The result was *unequivocal*. None exists.

"This issue has been resolved scientifically," said the director of epidemiology research for the American Cancer Society. "This is essentially a political debate." The NCI was forced to change the Web site in accordance with this conclusion, but all over the country—at pregnancy crisis centers, at antiabortion rallies—women are still being subjected to this misleading and frightening claim.

Another tactic similarly manipulating women is the newly discovered "postabortion syndrome." Always looking for fresh angles, the abortion-recovery movement, with heavy religious financial backing, scares women into believing they cannot end their pregnancies without, as a South Dakota task force claims, "suffering significant psychological trauma and distress [because] to do so is beyond the normal, natural and healthy capability of a woman whose natural instincts are to protect and nurture her child." Publicizing this kind of thinking traps women into looking to their abortions to explain any feelings of depression and grief they might someday experience.

Before this movement became a big business, with chapters and recovery counselors across the country, a series of highly respected psychological and medical studies concluded: "There is no evidence of an abortion-trauma syndrome." Overwhelmingly, 76 percent of the women actually reported feelings of relief after an abortion, with only 17 percent saying they felt guilty.

Rhonda Arias, an abortion-recovery counselor who works at Plane State Jail in Houston, says a revelation from God showed her how much her "own pain and unhappiness" came from her abortions. At the prison she helps women who have had abortions "understand how that procedure has stained them, and how it explains what has gone wrong in their lives."

But when you hear Rhonda's own story of a sexually abusive step-brother; a beloved father who died at work after falling from a scaffold; a rape when she was fourteen years old; her longtime bouts with depression, drinking, and freebasing cocaine; a terrible marriage; and a suicide attempt, it's inconceivable to blame *all* her unhappiness on her first early abortion. And why, if that one was so distressful, making her "feel like a piece of evil had entered [her]," did she go on to have three more? If anything, you'd think the initial experience would have encouraged her to campaign for effective, available birth control.

"The main problem with the abortion-recovery movement," Dr. Alvin Blaustein, a New York psychiatrist, told me, "is that it totally ignores the woman's psychological and medical history. Was she depressed? Guilt-ridden? Suicidal before having an abortion? No studies are being done, so no one knows."

Abortion is a difficult decision for the majority of women, some of whom will be left with complex feelings afterward. They may feel lingering sadness and even guilt. "But," even Francis Beckwith, a professor of church-state studies at Baylor University who opposes abortion, admits, "for every woman who has suffered a trauma as a result of an abortion, I bet you could find a half dozen who would say it was the best decision they ever made."

Beckwith disagrees with the abortion-recovery movement because of their "questionable interpretation of social-science data." South Dakota, for example, makes a woman and her doctor certify that she has read and understands the existence of a link between abortion and a higher rate of suicide, although no connection has been established. For Beckwith the real problem with the recovery movement is how it moves the discussion to the well-being of women and away from the "traditional fetus-centered focus," that is, the issue of the life of the unborn.

THE FATE OF the fetus, taking precedence over the rights of women as articulated in the Supreme Court ruling of *Gozales v. Carhart*, is the anti-abortion movement's third line of attack. When I asked Justice Ruth Bader Ginsburg about the prospects for keeping abortion legal, she suggested we concentrate on the state level and what is happening there.

The campaign to protect the fetus and give it personhood is being carried on through a series of state legislative initiatives and laws, many of them completely below the radar. But everyone needs to be aware of this insidious threat, because it carries devastating implications.

Take the case of Regina McKnight. In May 2001, as McKnight grieved over the stillborn death of her third daughter, Mercedes, I'm sure she didn't imagine that she'd end up in prison. But she was soon put on trial for the death of her baby. After deliberating for fifteen minutes the jury reached a verdict. McKnight, a homeless, seasonal tobacco-farm worker with a tenth-grade education and no criminal record, addicted to drugs after her mother was run over by a truck and killed, became the first woman in America convicted of murder for using cocaine while pregnant. She was sentenced to twenty years imprisonment, reduced to twelve.

South Carolina prosecutors were gung ho on making an example out of this poor African American girl who'd spent her schooling in classes for the mentally impaired. No link between cocaine use and stillbirths has been scientifically established. Even the state admitted that she had not deliberately harmed her baby, and if she had—by an illegal third-term abortion—her sentence would have been only two years.

Doctors were appalled at the charges. Deborah A. Frank, M.D., at Boston University's School of Medicine, challenging the alleged connection between cocaine use and the stillbirth, wrote, "It is medically impossible in an individual case of stillbirth to pinpoint a single cause." It's "an outrage," said Robert G. Newman, director of the Edmond de Rothschild Foundation Chemical Dependency Institute, Beth Israel Medical Center. "This case seriously undermines the legitimate societal goal of insuring the best maternal and child health."

Public health and medical communities across the country over-whelmingly supported Regina. The American Public Health Association, the American Nurses Association, the Association of Reproductive Health Professionals, and the South Carolina Medical Association were all part of a long list joining in the amicus curiae effort on her behalf. But the Supreme Court decided not to review the case, ending Regina's hopes of being released.

Pregnant women with addiction problems may well be deterred from getting prenatal care, a critical component in achieving a healthy preg-nancy and baby, say the medical experts. But state officials don't seem to care. If the real issue were the well-being of the fetus, wouldn't we see more substance-abuse programs for these women? South Carolina, leading the nation in arrests of pregnant women, also leads in spending the *least* of its state dollars on drug treatment and the most on building correctional facilities.

Since the McKnight case, increasing numbers of pregnant women in South Carolina have been arrested for "unlawful child neglect." And the practice is spreading to at least eight other states. Most, but not all, of the "crimes" relate to alcohol or drug use.

Lynn Paltrow, an attorney and executive director of the National Advo-cates for Pregnant Women, told me, "What South Carolina has done, in effect, is to make pregnancy a crime waiting to happen."

When the prosecution of pregnant women began during the 1980s with Reagan's War on Drugs, expectant women who tested positive for drugs at their doctors' offices were shackled, with chains around their bel-lies, and thrown into jail. And this happened even if they admitted having an addiction problem and asked for help. All this is part of the right wing's ongoing plan to grant fetuses personhood. And not coincidentally, South Carolina is at the forefront of this movement.

Many of us can still remember our horror over the 2004 murder of the pregnant Laci Peterson, but we might be equally horrified if we knew how the Bush administration manipulated public sentiment over this highly publicized tragedy to gain adherents for Bush's pet Unborn Victim of Violence Act (UVVA). Laci's mother and stepfather's emotional support for this bill, also known as the the Laci and Connor Act, helped to get it passed. Before this, the "child in utero" was, as a general rule, not recognized as a victim of a federal crime of violence.

Now it is a separate crime to harm a fetus at any stage of development—even a fertilized egg—during the commission of some sixty-eight crimes. While the right wing claims the intent of this act is to protect women from violence, we've seen how Team Bush shamelessly eviscerated the Violence Against Women Act, resulting in increased risk for women all over the country. The Unborn Victim of Violence Act is nothing but a deceptive ruse in granting a fetus personhood with the ultimate goal of making all forms of abortion illegal in America. Thirty-four states already recognize the fetus as a crime victim for purposes of homicide or feticide.

Tennessee has introduced a bill requiring death certificates for aborted fetuses. There's one being debated in Kentucky that mandates women wanting abortions to undergo ultrasound and review the pictures before the procedure. And conservatives in the U.S. Congress keep pushing the "Unborn Child Pain Awareness Act," compelling a physician to give a woman seeking an abortion at twenty weeks or more a brochure describing the pain her "unborn child" will endure and offer her a painkilling drug to be administered directly to the fetus. This, in spite of a review of several hundred scientific papers published in the *Journal of the American Medical Association* finding that fetuses are unlikely to feel pain before twenty-nine weeks.

The cost of extra pain medication, locating a doctor trained to administer it, and evaluating its effect on the woman would all limit access to abortion. But the real risk, according to NOW president Kim Gandy, is that the act is another way of establishing fetal personhood.

If *Roe* is overturned, abortion would still be legal in some states. But, cautions Gandy, once the fetus is considered a "person" under the U.S. Constitution, abortion will be considered murder throughout the land.

THE ANTIABORTION PLATFORM has moved from politics to infiltrate popular culture, where it's taken a remarkable hold. Three recent popular films portray female characters whose lives are thrown off balance by unintended pregnancies, and not one seriously thinks about abortion.

In *Knocked-Up* (2007), Alison (Katherine Heigl), a rising television personality, becomes pregnant after a one-night drunken fling with Ben (Seth Rogen), who does his best to show her—and us—that he hasn't progressed far from his frat-boy days. Although one of Ben's buddies talks about Alison having something that rhymes with "shamashmortion"—the word is evidently too odious to utter—she doesn't even consider it.

The plot of the movie revolves around the smart, sophisticated Alison and the well-meaning but boorish Ben trying to make it as a couple, a premise every young woman I spoke to found "beyond implausible." Don't get me wrong, most thought the movie was funny, but "Have Ben as the father of my child? Someone who'd always be in my life? I'd rather shoot myself," a thirty-two-year-old fashion executive told me.

Jenna (Keri Russell), the talented pie-making lead in *Waitress* (2007), is horrified to find she's pregnant. She only slept with her controlling, physically abusive husband because he got her too drunk to resist. All she wants to do is get away from him and has been stashing small amounts of money all over the house, saving up for her big escape. She hates her husband, hates her pregnancy, hates the fetus . . . but never thinks of having an abortion.

Ending her pregnancy is something sixteen-year-old Juno (Ellen Page) in the 2007 movie by that name *does* think about, if only briefly. But the "Women *Now*" clinic she visits is so appalling and unrealistic (and the cheap shot at NOW totally unnecessary) she runs from it, never to rethink her decision. Benefiting from amazingly supportive parents and friends, including Paulie Bleeker (Michael Cera), the baby's father, Juno sails through the nine months with an uncanny wit and ease. Sure there are rough spots—the adoptive parents don't turn out exactly as she hoped—but nothing to warn other teens away from her decision. She continues with school, has the baby, and realizes Paulie, her best bud, is really the love of her life.

Many conservative bloggers have applauded *Knocked Up* for being antichoice, and it's not surprising. As a group, these movies, with their fairy tale endings, simultaneously endorse and ennoble women carrying their unwanted pregnancies to term. Commenting on the lack of discussion about abortion in Hollywood movies, the *New York Times*'s Mireya Navarro wrote, "Perhaps directors of feel-good movies don't want to risk portraying their heroines as *unsympathetic*." (emphasis added)

I'm not sure when having an abortion made a woman unsympathetic, just as I'm not sure when the topic became taboo. Certainly it wasn't in *Dirty Dancing* (1987), *The Cider House Rules* (1999), or *Vera Drake* (2004). But now antiabortion activists are flexing their muscles, and the movie industry is running scared.

There is one exception, but then again, it's not American. The 2007 Romanian film *4 Months, 3 Weeks and 2 Days* is about a university student in the 1980s who helps her friend get an abortion—illegal during the time of Ceausescu's reign. Although the film won an award at the Cannes Film Festival, it wasn't even considered for an Academy Award here. That's too bad, because it would have given the movie a wide audience, enabling Americans to take a good look at the horrifying, bloody world of illegal abortion.

15

TROUBLE@EDU

Sociology professor Rona Fields taught more for less pay than men ranked below her at Clark University. On top of that, when she rebuked the sexual advances of a senior male colleague, she was told, "This is no way to get tenure." Sure enough, her tenure was refused. This story, distressing in itself, is even more alarming when we realize it wasn't culled from the archives of the women's movement. It's current news.

The 1970s, as we've seen, pulsated with wonderful possibilities for girls and young women as feminists exposed the veiled antifemale bias in American education. Sweeping changes followed. But given the scope of second-wavers' work and the hefty resistance they faced, it's not surprising much still needed to be done. A "take back the campus" drive, supported by conservative ideologues who want to erase women's educational opportunities and ensure male domination of our institutes of learning, has been brewing in America since the 1980s. But it took the emboldened sexism of our post-9/11 world to transform it into national policies aimed at reconstructing traditional gender roles.

A 1992 REPORT by the Association of University Women, *Failing at Fairness: How Schools Short-Change Girls*, documented continuing large disparities in achievement between girls and boys in a number of subjects and on standardized tests; teachers who favored and called on boys far more than on girls in the classroom; materials using gender stereotypes; and sports programs, clubs, and student newspapers dominated by and geared to male students. These inequalities, the study said, can bring about lower self-esteem for girls and lead to such destructive behaviors as eating disorders, cutting, and promiscuity.

Eyes popped open all over the country. Schools evaluated the extent to which they'd achieved gender equity; most found they fell far short of the mark. Boys still ruled—in the classrooms, on playing fields, and in extracurricular activities.

Training sessions and workshops, Herculean efforts by administrators, teachers, coaches, and deans—ten years' worth—produced positive changes in how girls were educated and encouraged. And "girl power," the movement to give girls and young women self-reliance and confidence, really took off.

Then came the incendiary blowback, as the "boy crisis" exploded in the media. Suddenly girls had gotten too much attention. Major publications scolded educators for expending too many resources on girls when clearly boys were suffering. "Save our sons" from feisty girls, town criers intoned. And, in a return to the cold war, Philip Wylie mentality, women, be they female school teachers or feminists, were indicted for destroying boykind.

Immediately we were deluged by a genre of books with such red-alert titles as *Hear Our Cry: Boys in Crisis* by Dr. Paul D. Slocumb, and Harvey Mansfield's *Manliness*. And, of course, the leader of the pack, *The War Against Boys*—a book receiving financial support from the conservative think tank American Enterprise Institute, where the author, Christina Hoff Sommers, was a fellow. Like the others, she based her thesis on boys in special-ed classes—their drinking problems and lagging academic performances.

But behind the screaming headlines lay a more nuanced story. Sara Mead, until recently a senior policy analyst at Education Sector, reviewed all the literature on the topic and found, with few exceptions, "American boys [to be] scoring higher and achieving more than they ever had before." The real divide is not gender, but race and class. Poverty, poorly equipped schools, troubled home lives, and a distorted definition of manliness— these inclined boys to drop out. "Focusing on gender may, in fact, take attention and resources away from the populations that need them the most," Mead concluded. But critics on the right insisted on holding female achievement responsible for male malfunction. In their biased math, girls getting more equals boys getting less.

That's not how we should look at it, said David Von Drehle in the 2007 *Time* magazine cover story "The Myth About Boys."

"[Girls'] successes in no way diminish the progress of the boys." Actually, today's boys look good compared to their fathers and uncles. A new report from the American Association of University Women (AAUW) supports Von Drehle's claim. When girls do better academically, so do boys. "A rising tide lifts all boats," says AAUW executive director Linda Hallman.

"[M]uch of the pessimism about young males seems to derive from inadequate research [and] sloppy analysis," said a study by the Washington-based National Assessment of Educational Progress. "The boy crisis has been used by conservative authors who accuse 'misguided feminists' of lavishing resources on female students at the expense of males." *Feminized* schooling is forcing boys to conform to a poorly suited learning style, causing them to lose interest and drop out, claim the sideliners. Since all education—until some forty years ago—was completely male-oriented, and boys now are excelling compared to their past performances, this line of reasoning makes no sense.

Still, the "we're hurting our boys" theme has achieved remarkable tenacity, supported by a renewed round of literature proving the existence of so-called innate and rigid gender differences, and calling for separate boy/girl roles and schools. We wrestled with these damaging theories in the 1970s. Most educators thought decades of female achievement in schools across the nation would have finally banished these ideas to the history books. But they've returned: old myths packaged as "new science."

Gender Difference Goes to School

The absolutist thinking that's taken hold in our nation, the "us versus them," "self versus other" mentality, the bifurcation of our thinking, has encouraged the "boy versus girl" gender-difference reincarnation. It is part of the new misogyny, obliterating years of women's progress. This kind of thinking has permeated both academic and popular thinking.

The female brain is hardwired for empathy, and the male brain is predominantly hardwired for understanding and building systems, asserted Simon Baron-Cohen in his recent book, *The Essential Brain*. The journal *Intelligence* claimed in 2006 that men have higher IQs than women—a dubious finding but one used nonetheless to explain the greater numbers of men achieving distinctions of various kinds for which a high IQ is required—medalists for mathematics, superlative chess players, Nobel prize winners, and the like.

Then there's Louann Brizendine, M.D., whose *The Female Brain* says that because the teen brain undergoes major changes, especially in areas that are particularly sensitive to shifts in hormones, puberty can be an outrageously impulsive time for many girls. While with no stress, on a good menstrual week, the teen girl's prefrontal cortex may function normally, and she may have good judgment, under some stress, like getting a poor grade, on a PMS day, it can cause an exaggerated emotional response and out-of-control behavior.

Studies on brain differences like the above have been subjected to multiple peer reviews and charged with flawed analyses. But, reaping the benefits of an eager-to-hype press, they've flooded public consciousness, used to bolster suggestions of innate biological differences keeping women from excelling in science, engineering, and math made by such luminaries as former Harvard president Larry Summers.

But if it *were* a question of biology, then how can we explain the performance of foreign-born girls who win the extraordinarily difficult International Mathematical Olympiad? asks Sharon Begley in *Newsweek* magazine (October 27, 2008). Gender researchers Rosalind Barnett and Caryl Rivers pose the same question about the high numbers of women working in technology in many parts of the world, especially Eastern Europe. Their book *Same Difference*, a detailed analysis and critique of every leading "innate gender difference" theory, is so thoroughly researched it should have put the entire subject to rest. So should an investigation of the gender theories over the past twenty years, resulting in an extensive meta-analysis of forty-six research studies conducted by all different psychologists, published in the *American Psychologist* in September 2005. Janet Shibley Hyde, Ph.D., the author of the report, found vast *similarities* between the sexes, rather than differences. "One's sex has little or no bearing on personality, cognition, and leadership," Hyde and her colleagues concluded, hoping their work will eliminate "misunderstanding and correct unequal treatment."

When we begin to explore why girls don't take more science, math, and computer courses, the reasons are obvious enough: "The culture has convinced girls they don't belong in these fields," say the experts, even though new studies are showing girls to perform as well as boys on standardized tests. Girls are still unlikely to see themselves on television science shows except in subordinate positions like lab technicians. And parents eagerly encouraging their math-able sons with books and math games tend to ignore equally talented daughters. Add to this the startling 34 percent of female high school seniors who say faculty members told them not to take math, and it results in a lot of math-shy girls. Those who do buck the trend often find the atmosphere so inhospitable they abandon the subject entirely.

"I was always good with numbers and did very well in my high school math classes," Samantha, then a senior at a top New England prep school, told me. "I really saw no reason why that wouldn't continue, so I took the most advanced math class the school offered—Calculus BC." But within weeks Samantha became distraught. "The teacher totally favored the eleven boys in the class and ignored the six girls," she said. "He called on them way more than on us, and after class always engaged them in conversation." One girl dropped out, then another. Soon there were only two girls left in the class. "We complained to our Dean, who spoke to him, but after that things just got worse, and we both ended up leaving also."

For Bernardine Davis, being the only female computer science major in her undergraduate class at Hamilton College was also a pretty lonely experience. She vividly remembers "an abrupt change in the atmosphere and conversation" when she entered a computer lab and had to deal with all the "half-joking comments" from her male classmates about "her intruding on their fun." By teachers' admissions, "testosterone rules computer labs. . . . There are often lots of off-color jokes and comments." Then, too, many girls are turned off computers because they associate them with the violent video games they've watched their brothers play.

Computer science is the only major in which women's participation has actually *decreased* over the years—a drop of almost 10 percent of the degrees awarded between 1984 and 2003. Girls who are not exposed to computers by age twelve are effectively locked out of 90 percent of all future jobs. "[It's] a troubling indicator for American computer science generally—and for the economic competitiveness that depends on it," said a professional in the field.

Carefully planned outreach can reverse the downward trend. At Carnegie Mellon, in 2004, 37 percent of the freshman computer science majors were women—a big improvement for them. University officials attribute this to the effort the school has made to help high school teachers encourage more girls to take computer science. As Lenore Blum, a distinguished service professor of computer science at Carnegie Mellon, said, "It's not going to happen until people actually start doing something."

And yet—there's a lot of opposition to doing *anything* to improve the numbers. It would be pointless: women don't like science, math, and engineering, claims Steven Pinker in his popular book *The Blank Slate*. "They don't have the 'risk-taking impetus and tolerance' for the 'physical discomfort required,'" he writes, as if everyone going into a technological field would be "working on oil rigs and jack-hammering sludge" like those who laid the Alaska pipelines. Pinker even argues against a plan by the presidents of nine top universities to make a concerted effort to recruit women for fellowships and faculty positions in math and science.

And when Senator Ron Wyden, along with a group of more than two hundred concerned scientists, mathematicians, and engineers, asked the Office of Civil Rights (OCR) at the Department of Education to investigate whether the gender inequities in their respective disciplines were the result of discrimination, the OCR defied its legal obligation and refused. And it refused again to look into glaring disparities in vocational education, documented in a comprehensive report by the National Women's Law Center.

Blatant sexism bounces off the pages of the report. Sexual harassment goes on unchecked; teachers tell girls not to take certain courses because they rightfully belong to boys, leaving "young women . . . clustered in 'traditionally female programs' that prepare them for low-wage careers . . .

[while young men] fill the vast majority of slots in programs leading to higher-wage careers that can provide true economic self-sufficiency."

All these infractions have been allowed to stand, in part because half the states across the country *still* haven't met their legal obligation to designate a Title IX coordinator to comply and carry out its responsibilities under the law. What's more, sexual harassment guidelines have "mysteriously" disappeared from the Department of Education guidelines and Web site. Parents, students, and teachers in need of a critical authoritative source are left completely in the dark.

But rather than enforce the regulations, investigate charges of discrimination, and encourage schools to follow Carnegie Mellon's example, our misogynist society came up with the ideal solution: separate schools. This way "system-building boys" won't have to be in the same class as "empathetic, emotional girls." Separation allows, as one teacher put it, "boys to be boys and girls to be girls."

Separate but (Almost) Equal Is OK for Girls

From the get-go, the sidelining right wing set the stage for a major change in education. Conservative periodicals such as the *Women's Quarterly*, a publication of the Independent Women's Forum, attacked the Women's Educational Equity Act (which promotes equality in education for women and girls) as a "sop to feminists," and in 2004, President Bush began to eliminate its funding. Just two years later, in what the *New York Times* (October 25, 2006) said was generally considered the "most significant policy change on the issue since a landmark federal law barring sex discrimination in education, more than thirty years ago, the Bush administration gave public school districts broad new latitude to expand the number of single-sex classes and schools." The move, long sought by conservatives, was finally made possible by ambiguous wording in the No Child Left Behind Act.

"It's really a serious green light from the Department of Education to reinstitute official discrimination in schools around the country," said Marcia Greenberger, a copresident of the National Women's Law Center. An umbrella organization representing about two hundred civil rights groups issued a statement saying the ruling violated both Title IX and the equal protection clause under the Constitution. "Segregation is totally unacceptable in the context of race. Why in the world in the context of gender would it be acceptable?"

And this regulation is even worse than *Plessy v. Ferguson* (1896), which established the basis for "separate but equal" education and was finally overturned in *Brown v. Board of Education* (1954). Now all the schools need to do is show that they are "substantially equal," an ambivalent phrase accepting classic stereotypes, traditionally disadvantaging girls and allotting fewer resources and opportunities to them.

Proponents of this ruling feign concern about girls, pushing a hackneyed claim: girls learn better on their own. But there's no real evidence to support this. In places such as the computer labs, where girls are made to feel uncomfortable, dealing with negative male behavior and attitudes is a better solution in the long run than separating out the girls. What works—and this has been shown time and time again—is individual attention and a belief in a student's potential.

Eleven years ago, when Gregory Hodge became principal at the Frederick Douglass Academy, a public school in Harlem, the student body comprised 80 percent girls and was doing spectacularly well. He immediately began recruiting boys, almost all poor and minority, to this combined middle and high school. Today, boys make up 50 percent of the school's students. Did these rowdy and often troubled boys bring a downturn to the school? Absolutely not! The dropout rate is virtually zero, and just about every year all of the academy's 1,450 students are college bound. Hodge's magic? Validate every student. He tells them, "You are important. You *will* be successful."

I found the same emphasis on achievement when I visited the Bronx Academy of Letters, a coed public school, also in New York City, and also with a rigorous college-preparatory program. Defying the born-again saw that boys aren't interested in reading unless you give them—as *New York Times* columnist David Brooks suggests—manly works like Hemingway and Tolstoy (because of the differing male/female biological factors), the students at this school are assigned the same books regardless of gender. Their journals—which I was privileged to read—show boys and girls often drawing on identical literary sources in their writing, and form a strong argument against pigeonholing the sexes into so-called gender-appropriate education.

Still, advocates of gender-specific instruction are eagerly writing up their lesson plans: "Girls would receive character education. On the other hand, boys' teachers would teach and discuss 'heroic behavior and ideas' and demonstrate what it means to 'be a man,'" said one Louisiana educator. And Regina Choi, a teacher from Los Angeles, explained, "it is sometimes more effective posing problems for girls using shopping examples and for boys using sports."

Title IX was enacted to eliminate this kind of gender stereotyping, but it has been battered and weakened by the Republican right, catering to those who would return us to the bad old days before the women's movement.

The Unequal Playing Field on the Field

"Like my two older brothers, my life has been centered around sports. It is where I met my closest friends and shaped the values that have made me a successful athlete, student, and role model," said Jennie Finch, a member of the National Pro Fastpitch Chicago Bandits.

"Girls who participate in sports are less likely to smoke, use drugs, or engage in other kinds of high-risk behavior and, when they're older, not as likely to develop heart disease, osteoporosis, and other physical ailments. And, in general, they perform better in the classroom," she added. Because of Title IX, increasing numbers of young women have had the benefits Jennie describes. In 1971 fewer than three hundred thousand high school girls participated in interscholastic sports; by 1997 that number had grown to over 2.4 million.

But those gains are waning. The Bush administration chipped away at Title IX, allowing schools to skirt the requirement of providing equal funding and opportunity for their female athletes. And the conservative *National Review* in 2005 took aim at feminists who were critical of these moves by likening them to . . . what else? The axis of evil.

Renewed attacks on Title IX include rulings that allow schools to assess female enthusiasm for sports—a key to determining compliance—

by sending around a *flawed* e-mail survey. Not only is the methodology of the questionnaire unsound, but a nonresponse to the e-mail is construed as the recipient's lacking an interest in athletic programs. Male students don't have to prove their interest, it's a given.

"Not many people open e-mail surveys, let alone take the time to respond to them," said Finch. "As a student I was preoccupied with classes and practice. I doubt I would have paid attention to such a survey."

And that would have been a real loss. Finch might never have had the chance to play softball at the University of Arizona and probably wouldn't have been a pitcher for the gold medal–winning 2004 U.S. women's Olympic softball team. But many men, *New York Times* columnist John Tierney among them, feel the need to show their macho mettle with an over-the-top reaction to modest gains in female collegiate athletic programs. Women "have better things to do, like study or work on other extracurricular activities that will be more useful to their careers," he says.

In a 2006 piece with the provocative title "Let the Guys Win One," Tierney argues: "On or off campus, men play more team sports and watch more team sports. Besides enjoying the testosterone rush, they have a better chance of glory. . . . College football," he goes on, "is such a mass spectacle that it can't really be compared with other sports. It's more of a war rally or religious revival."

"[Women] don't need special federal protection in the one area that men excel. This playing field doesn't need to be leveled," is Tierney's grand—and depressing—conclusion. It shows how much ground women have lost. In the first decade of the new millennium, a columnist at one of the nation's most prestigious and progressive newspapers can wholeheartedly promote a retreat from the commitment to women's equality.

The Unequal Playing Field in Academies

"You should be given this opportunity to drive yourself forward," said one student. "And just because you're Hispanic and low-income or a woman you can still do it. . . . You can go to a really awesome university and you can graduate, and you can go to another awesome university and get your doctorate."

For decades students like this one have benefited from Pell grants, the primary source of federal aid for low-income students, the majority of them women. But slash-and-burn Republicans have reduced the stipends dramatically.

Today the grants cover only 33 percent of the average cost of tuition, fees, and room and board at a public college or university. Twenty years ago, the maximum Pell grant covered nearly 60 percent of that cost. "As a freshman, Temple University student Arsema Solomon needed to borrow just $5,000 to cover college expenses that were not met by grants, some limited family help, and a part-time job. Three years later, in 2005, Solomon has added a night shift as a bank teller; [the reduced grant] and mounting costs have forced her to double her student-loan load to $10,000 a year," reported Patrick Kerkstra, staff writer for the Knight Ridder papers, in 2008.

Our nation's policies enforce class boundaries by effectively shutting out thousands of students from getting a college education. And the same holds true for talented and creative faculty who, because of discrimination, are relegated to secondary status in our institutions of higher learning.

Without doubt, women are a greater presence on college campuses than they were forty years ago, but we need to look at the positions they hold and the pay they receive before we can applaud the numbers. It's tempting to point to Susan Hockfield, president of MIT, and Harvard's Drew G. Faust as signs of major progress, but these are high-profile exceptions, good for PR but not so much for other women. Even the universities these women head admit gender bias. MIT and Harvard were among the nine elite schools issuing a joint statement admitting the "barriers still exist" preventing progress for female academics and committing themselves to change institutional policies.

But rhetoric and reality are worlds apart when it comes to the practices of our most prestigious institutions. While mission statements declare their commitment to diversity, "the workforces of Ivy League universities are starkly stratified by race and gender," with white males dominating the highest-ranking, best-paid, most secure academic positions, reveals *The (Un)Changing Face of the Ivy League*, a 2005 report of the Graduate Teachers and Researchers Union.

A caste system in higher learning is particularly worrisome. "Education and work are the levers to uplift a people," W. E. B. DuBois wrote in 1903, and I think most of us would agree. We look to education to expand the opportunities of the poor and disenfranchised, to be a touchstone for the rest of society. That's why we back colleges and universities with public funding and tax exemptions. We trust our schools not only to teach the intrinsic worth of every human being but also to model that belief in their own practices and composition.

A two-tiered university perpetuates the dangerous stereotypes of a bygone era. It informs the future of our society economically, socially, politically, and culturally. And it raises questions about who controls the knowledge our children receive and how that control affects its content. Are universities simply preserving white male privilege? Or are they—to use a current political term—agents of change? And if they aren't, then how has the extraordinary discrimination gone unnoticed?

By and large, universities and colleges have been able to skirt around the issues of equity by boasting the large numbers of women and people of color on their faculties. What they've failed to mention is how these groups are relegated to the lowest-status and lowest-paying jobs they offer. And low-level jobs have exploded in volume over the past twenty years.

"Nonladder [not on a tenure track] faculty members make significant contributions to the scholarship of this university," said Dr. Connie Allen, former lecturer in the department of chemistry at Yale University. "We are often excellent, dedicated teachers and mentors. . . . Our contributions are acknowledged and celebrated by those who benefit directly, namely the undergraduate students. Yet, often I have found that we . . . are undervalued and exploited by the university administration and serve as window dressing in the institutions' commitment to diversity."

Faculty members without tenure serve as handmaidens to the established faculty. They teach the large lecture classes, often do departmental scut work, and have little recourse against unfair treatment. "Try protesting if you think your ideas are being ripped off by senior faculty," one young woman who teaches American studies at a midwestern university told me. "You'll see how quickly you're out the ivy-covered door."

Widespread, persistent, and insidious discrimination, say a wealth of studies, is keeping women in vulnerable and poorly paid academic positions. Women are held to a higher standard and judged by different, frequently harsher criteria than their male colleagues. Male students and faculty get better recommendations. For the same performance, a man might be described as brilliant and original, a woman as meticulous and reliable. In a catch-22 bind, women quickly pick up the reverse logic: if you want to succeed, you have to tamp down your achievements.

"MEN CAN TOLERATE a woman in physics as long as she is in a subordinate position, but many cannot tolerate a woman above them," said Dr. Gail G. Hanson, distinguished professor of physics at the University of California, Riverside. Even though Dr. Hanson discovered quark jets when she was a postdoctoral fellow, throughout her research career she has been treated like "a junior colleague, instead of a foremost researcher."

Dr. Hanson has finally gotten recognition; in 2006 she received the Panofsky Prize in physics, the only woman ever to do so. Marie Curie is still the only female to be honored with the Nobel Prize in science, and that was in 1903. Since then, one other woman, in 1963, shared the award with male colleagues. The Field's Medal, math's version of the Nobel, has remained totally in the hands of men.

"I thought these kinds of things only happened in the 1950s. It's appalling that women still confront these hurdles," said Dr. Hanson.

Serving coffee at department meetings, volunteering to take the notes, deferring to male colleagues on administrative and scholarly matters—behaviors academic women thought they'd chucked along with their electric Smith Coronas—are now de rigueur.

And those women who won't or can't play these mandated parts are being denied tenure. The official reason—they lack "congeniality." Legal experts delving into what exactly this term meant made a startling discovery: it refers to women who don't accept the traditional female role of making the male faculty feel comfortable.

The label is "a new wild card for discrimination" because it is so subjective, said Leslie Annexstein, director of the AAUW Legal Advocacy Fund. "The discrimination [today] is more subtle and often harder to identify in the legal sense, making it more difficult than ever to prove. Most faculty sexual-discrimination cases filed with the EEOC have not been successful."

Tenure Denied, a report prepared by the AAUW in 2004, is a stinging indictment of academia. Women make up about half the instructors and lecturers and almost half the assistant professors but only 27 percent of the tenured positions in four-year colleges. A thorough, case-by-case investigation of women who were denied tenure—a veritable death blow generally forcing them to leave the school and try to restart the five- to seven-year process at another institution—shows the decisions to be rife with discrimination, manifesting as "tokenism, hostility, backlash, invisibility, and role stereotyping."

One common strategy is denying tenure after women complain about sexual harassment directed at them or their students. This ploy can be used to control students and young faculty and derail those more senior who might become competitors.

A Lab Where the Women Are the Guinea Pigs

He was a married man having affairs with two young women. Everyone in his group knew about his trysts; they were expected to watch passionate kissing, massaging, and fondling. But here's the rub: he was a professor, the young women were his students, the group was the lab he coheaded at the University of Missouri Kansas City.

For years stories had been circulating about Drs. Haddock and Poston of the psychology department. The two men, both bringing in a lot of grant money for the institution, ran a research lab in which the most egregious behavior was tolerated, even rewarded.

In their isolated fiefdom they officially supervised graduate students and research assistants and helped with the publication of papers and the awarding of grants. But that's not all they did. According to the charges filed by graduate student Megan Pinkston-Camp and professor Linda

Garavalia, the lab was an outrageously sexual environment where sadism, intimidation, and threats were employed to keep ten students and two faculty members in positions of subservience and fear.

From the start, Pinkston-Camp, who arrived in 2003 to work with Dr. Poston on obesity research for her doctoral dissertation, realized how many perks Haddock's lovers were getting, like "authorship" of papers they never even contributed to, much less wrote.

"Students were told they had to please Haddock and Poston in order to get into graduate school, obtain funding and other support for research." And pleasing them meant doing their bidding *and* keeping quiet about it. The men directed one of the women to pull up her blouse and let her classmates fondle her breasts. Others, like Pinkston-Camp, were pressured to show their "asses."

The voyeuristic pair hounded the female students for graphic details about each other's bodies. And they didn't refrain from discussing their own, comparing their penises to bananas and rulers. Penis size was a big topic. So was oral sex. All sex, in fact.

When Poston started to grope Pinkston-Camp and insist she accompany him on out-of-town trips, she became increasingly anxious. If she resisted, she thought, it would be the end of her dissertation and maybe her career. She tried to withdraw from him, but strange things began to happen. A Barbie doll she kept on her desk had the limbs cut off and fake blood smeared all over it; another time a noose was put around its neck and a picture of it was shown on her computer screen. (Haddock and Poston had access to the passwords of everyone in the lab's computers.)

Pinkston-Camp began to confide in her husband and some of her friends, but not in Linda Garavalia, who, as a professor, was on a different level and had made an effort to keep to herself and concentrate on her work.

"It was a horrible and busy time," Garavalia told me recently. "My mother was dying of cancer so I was flying to Charlotte to take care of her every third week and preparing for my tenure review at the same time. Both Haddock and Poston wanted me to postpone going before the committee—I think because they thought they'd have more power over me if I didn't have tenure."

But Garavalia saw what was going on in the lab. She saw the videos of animals being tortured, of naked actresses and porn that Haddock and Poston put on their computer screens and coerced the students into watching. And she saw the weapons.

"There were always weapons in the lab and lots of military jargon. A favorite activity was opening a switch blade and flicking it back and forth in front of one of our faces. Then there were choke holds. They'd say, 'Look, I can kill you in two seconds, while holding a thumb against your windpipe.' They did this to almost all the women in the lab," explained Pinkston-Camp. Both men talked constantly about "killin,'" and Haddock boasted that he knew a guy in the air force who could "make someone disappear."

Finally Pinkston-Camp, unable to contain her anxieties any longer, blurted out the whole story to her new department head, who immediately contacted Garavalia.

Once Garavalia attained tenure she left the lab, resigning from a lucrative grant just to get away. But after hearing from the department head, she called Pinkston-Camp. The two women decided to press forward and file a grievance.

The school made its reluctance to investigate obvious. "We did not trust the university, at this point, to protect us," Pinkston-Camp wrote in her statement. "They never said anything about keeping us safe from reprisals."

Finally, feeling they had no alternative, they hired private attorneys and sued the university. "The $1.1 million settlement—the largest in a sexual-harassment suit ever in the whole MU system—was because of the substantial evidence to support the allegations of sexual harassment and abundant examples of bureaucratic bumbling," said professor Miriam Forman-Brunell, a faculty member close to the case. "The university failed to respond to the EEOC complaint even though they had 180 days to do it, failed to seek depositions, and never requested documents," she said.

All the time they were in the lab, neither Pinkston-Camp nor Garavalia realized that a hostile environment was a form of sexual harassment. Under Title IX of the Education Amendments of 1972, all schools receiving federal funds are mandated to have policies and procedures defining sexual harassment and to outline the proper protocol for reporting it. If the school had such a policy in place, students and faculty were not aware of it.

What went on at UMKC was hideous and extreme, but sexual harassment, long considered taboo, is pervasive again. Of the five hundred women whose stories inform my study, a significant majority said they've experienced some form of sexual harassment at school or at work.

Humiliating women, regarding them as sex toys, is a standard feature in the lexicon of masculine control. And slowly, we're internalizing this treatment and becoming inured to it. How could we not when it's so widespread and seemingly accepted? Only a few decades ago, women, secure in the support of their respective institutions, would have unleashed a firestorm of protest against such flagrantly degrading, dangerous, and *illegal* conduct.

But when news of the reprehensible doings in the UMKC lab hit the local papers, there was no outrage on the campus, no cries from the student body for an investigation or change in policy. "Everyone has been cowed into passivity by an administration that has taken every opportunity to promote the party line," said Forman-Brunell.

As for professors Haddock and Poston?

Haddock's annual salary jumped from $75,876 to $93,373, Poston's from $76,707 to $101,707. They've been promoted and moved to the School of Medicine, where they're protected and can keep on truckin'.

16

THE CAMPAIGN AGAINST WORKING WOMEN

"**R**espect for stay-at-home moms has been poisoned by . . . radical feminists' misogynistic crusade to make work outside the homes the only source of . . . social value," writes Rick Santorum in his popular book, *It Takes a Family: Conservatism and the Common Good.* Santorum, the third-ranking senator when the book was published in 2005, believes the traditional, or what he calls the *natural* family, is being undermined by the selfishness of mothers who hold paying jobs. Women may *claim* they're helping support the family, he charges "[b]ut this provides a convenient rationalization for pursuing a gratifying career outside the home." Conservative commentators like Danielle Crittenden have happily spread his message, adding their own spin. "Women themselves say they should stay home," reports Crittenden, failing to tell us who exactly these women are.

The new mantra—"what women really want is a husband and kids"—is being foisted upon us. Here's Lori Gottlieb, arguing in *The Atlantic* that behind the lip service to feminism, the guise of self-sufficiency, and interest in having a career, what unmarried women really long for is a "traditional family." Gottlieb, unwed at forty, offers advice to the single set: Compromise. Settle for Mr. Not-Quite-So-Right. You'll be happier by far. Gottlieb, who had a baby on her own through artificial insemination, has come to regret her go-it-alone decision. As a memoir, this would be a poignant story; as an authoritative discourse on the true and secret yearnings of every unhitched fortysomething female, it sets off lots of alarm bells.

Lots of women I know went Gottlieb's route and are absolutely delighted with their lives; others are "eternally grateful not to be bogged down with a husband or kids." Of course there are plenty of women desperately seeking love. Some of these, by the way, are married.

When I wrote *Crisis of the Working Mother* I was struck by how husbands—in many instances—were the most "peel-off-able" of the whole equation. There were women who for the life of them wouldn't have traded in their children or their jobs but could see themselves—or so they said—living without their mates. So much depends upon circumstances—family, friends, income, job, personality, background, geographic area, ethnicity, religion, and the dominant social values. The variables are endless. But blanket statements about "what women want" when they're not based on careful and thorough research are presumptuous and have repercussive effects, unwittingly hurting women in the workplace.

The magnitude of difficulties working women currently face is nearly incomprehensible. Although the women I interviewed overwhelmingly have encountered workplace discrimination and gender bias (in addition to sexual harassment), they tended to see this bias as an individual occurrence. And that's not in the least bit surprising. Although numerous nationwide studies coming out of our most prestigious universities and respected organizations have documented widespread inequities, the reports have been all but ignored by the press. What the media has given us instead is the self-righteous "opting-out" story and the surly face of the mommy wars—both staple features of the sidelining strategy. But there's no doubt we're in the midst of a full-fledged assault on working women, impractical as it is shameful.

Impractical because baby boomers—over seventy-eight million Americans making up 40 percent of today's workforce—are fast approaching retirement. This, according to 150 senior executives with our nation's one thousand largest companies, will have the most profound impact on the workplace in the next generation. One concern is that even when the economy recovers, the brain drain of older employees who've gained experience and knowledge from careers spent in one industry will hurt us.

Another is the reduction of the labor force, which has to grow proportionally with the scale of global production requirements. Projections of the U.S. Bureau of Labor Statistics warn of a drop-off in the prime labor force projected to continue for the next two decades.

The likely impact on the revitalization of our economy is obvious: "slower workforce growth mean[s] sluggish growth of the economy." And that has potential geopolitical implications, accelerating the relative decline of the United States as compared to China and India. The social consequences are also worrisome. Historically periods of economic stagnation have brought forth the mean-spiritedness of intolerance: more racism, more sexism, more anti-immigration feelings.

Crucial business sectors—education, the energy and aerospace industries, defense, and health care are already being threatened by boomer labor shortages. Experts looking at this problem suggest coming up with "solutions to attract, interest, and educate younger workers into these fields." And they're not talking about attracting only male workers. For a nation committed to remaining globally competitive, discouraging the participation in the labor force of more than half the population makes absolutely no sense. "[D]iscrimination against women and minorities is putting the U.S. at a disadvantage in technology innovation," said Robert J. Birgeneau, chancellor of the University of California at Berkeley.

And it is shameful. The obstacles hurled at working women—bogus studies "proving" our incompetence, the paucity of affordable, quality child care, subtle deterrents right up to blatant discrimination—are unethical, unjust, and in many instances, outright illegal.

We've seen how Reagan launched an attack on women's progress in the workplace. Now those weapons, updated and retooled, are taking aim at women from all classes, backgrounds, and positions. The "women haven't got the right stuff" narrative is the flip side of the post-9/11 machoization of American culture.

Masculine identity in this country has always been bolstered, even established, by the male provider role. In this security-mad time, with the economy and our world image spiraling downward, an addled, feminine dependency becomes ever more crucial to fractured manhood. The greater the male insecurity, the more women are sidelined.

But, ironically, several new reports posit a link between testosterone and risk taking, subtly suggesting that the presence of more women on Wall Street could have muted the current fiscal crisis. The journal *Evolution and Human Behavior*, for example, in 2008 published a study revealing that males tend to make high-risk bets when they feel under financial pressure and are with other males of similar status. Discussing this finding and a number of similar ones in the *New York Times* on February 8, 2009, Nicholas D. Kristoff writes, "Banks around the world desperately want bailouts of billions of dollars but they also have another need they're unaware of: women, women and women."

Gender Difference Goes to Work

Long-discredited notions of innate gender difference theories have, as we've seen, been used to justify separate schools for girls and boys. Now different aspects of these theories are bolstering workplace inequalities.

> Once upon a time . . . men and women lived happily together and worked in harmony. The man would venture out each day into a hostile and dangerous world to risk his life as a hunter to bring food back to his woman and their children. He developed long-distance navigational skills and excellent marksmanship skills.
>
> Women, who stayed tucked away in their cozy caves, never built up an aptitude for many professions like engineer, air traffic controller, architect, actuary. . . . While men play chess, women dance and decorate.

Few ideas are more deeply lodged in our popular imagination than the one expressed in the above quote from Barbara and Alan Pease's international bestseller, *Why Men Don't Listen and Women Can't Read Maps*. The Peases' analysis fits perfectly with the "women prefer low-level jobs in air-conditioned offices because they do best in 'noncompetitive situations'" thesis woven into scores of articles in the popular press. These works all take their cue from what I call Stone Age ideology—a return of the "man the hunter" argument.

The man-the-hunter theory, used to explain Homo sapiens' big win in the evolutionary sweepstakes, first became popular in the 1950s. Back then, scholarship, inevitably reflecting the male dominance of the professions that produced it, looked for and found distinct gender roles rooted in prehistory and in nature. With its constraints upon women, we shouldn't be surprised that this premise has gotten a lot of ink recently, even in the mainstream press.

But new studies using the electron microscope, carbon dating, and DNA technology are challenging the notion of the strutting, spear-throwing male schlepping home a six-thousand-pound creature for the little lady to serve. "[T]he development of male dominance as a genetic adaptation to the hunting life represents an unacceptable distortion of the available data—or at best, pure speculation," said Liverpool anthropologist Robin Compton. And renowned paleontologist Richard Leakey concurred. "There is absolutely no evidence we became human through hunting," he said. "Up until recent times, there's no record at all of human aggression. If you can't find it in the prehistoric record, why claim it's there?"

Cutting-edge research is focusing on cooperative efforts between the sexes of our prehistoric ancestors. Food supplies were probably provided by everyone. Fred and Wilma Flintstone and their children all went after the woolly mammoth together. Brains, rather than brawn, are what scientists now say gave us the advantage over the doomed Neanderthals. As Barnett and Rivers wrote, "[since] hunting is a relatively 'new' phenomenon, we're evidentially not hard-wired for one ability or another."

But none of this has halted the sideliners from lobbing verbal prehistoric stone after stone at working women. Giving a "word of advice" to the guys, *Forbes*'s Michael Noer says, "Marry pretty women or ugly ones. Short ones or tall ones. Blondes or brunettes. Just, whatever you do, don't marry a woman with a career."

"Men just want mommy," puts in Maureen Dowd. When it comes to tying the knot, the new millennium man is choosing his underling: administrative assistants, not the office superstars. And John Tierney, quoting just one study, reached the conclusion that the happiest women want breadwinner husbands who bring in at least two-thirds of the income.

Women aren't willing to "limit their ambitions to make life more congenial for men" and "play a subordinate role," observes economist Andrew Hacker, making the reader wonder if he spent the last fifty years stranded in the Chuuk Islands. In his book *Mismatch: The Growing Gulf Between Women and Men*, Hacker blames competition between marital partners for the growing divorce rate. And who is at fault? Working women, of course, for encroaching on the male terrain.

"Power: Do Women Really Want It?" headlines *Fortune*. The magazine condescendingly asks, "Do women lack power in business because they just don't want it enough?" "It's a turn-off," say unidentified women. The authors themselves admit that the question, even the word, is loaded, but they steer clear of any discussion of the opprobrium and discrimination heaped on professional women. "There's no doubt that unbridled ambition is less acceptable in women than in men," they admit, but even that's our fault. "One reason may be that we've seen some women who push too hard."

The *Fortune* piece had it down: either we push too hard, or we don't push hard enough. "Apparently it's not that women can't get high-level jobs. Rather, they're choosing not to." The article exposes "The dirty little secret [that] women demand more satisfaction in their lives than men." But if that's true then why can't some of that satisfaction come from professional success for women the way it does for men? And if women are finding work unsatisfactory, isn't it as reasonable to ask what's wrong with *work* as it is to ask what's wrong with women?

The authors point to academia, where they say women have made the most gains compared to government and business. But academia is "becoming more competitive. . . . People are working harder than ever . . . [m]any women decide that there are too many compromises they have to make," the authors say, patronizingly.

We've seen how women's progress in the academies is being poisoned by the toxic sexism of our campuses, and *not* because women aren't able to go with the flow. Partisan journalism like *Fortune*'s does us all a disservice by distorting reality. Women are not a bunch of nervous Nellies, afraid to compete and compromise. All our achievements have come from struggle and our willingness to adjust. And adjust again. The editors of *Fortune* could use a crash course on the prejudice rife in academia. Maybe then they'd write a piece titled "Power: Do Men Really Want to *Share* It?"

Copycat Crimes

In many ways the campaign against working women is similar to the drive for single-sex schools. First there's the case of suspiciously disappearing information. The Bureau of Labor Statistics in 2005 stopped collecting data on women workers. What had been a valuable source for tracking women's wage, employment, and job-loss patterns in America has vanished. "It will be almost impossible to gauge how women workers are being treated in this country and formulate strategies for eliminating discrimination and improving their economic status," says NOW.

Other important material went missing. More than thirty publications on the Women's Bureau of the Department of Labor Web site—the only federal organization devoted to the needs of wage-earning women—were there in 1999 and went AWOL in 2004. A catalog of the titles, including *Earning Differences Between Women and Men*, *Black Women in the Labor Force*, and *Don't Work in the Dark: Know Your Rights*, makes it easy to understand why the political right doesn't want women to have this vital information.

The Women's Bureau was formed to empower working women. In 1999 its mission statement committed the bureau to alerting women to their workplace rights and ensuring that the voices of working women were heard. Now that mission has been diluted merely to "enhance [women's] potential for securing more satisfying employment as they seek to balance their work-life needs."

The Bush administration repeatedly attempted to close the ten regional offices of the bureau—a move many feared would be the first step toward abolishing or defunding governmental agencies devoted to women's issues. Only concerted efforts of numerous women's and labor organizations have so far stalled these attempts, but there's been less success in other areas. W.'s scorched-earth policies destroyed the White House

Office for Women's Initiatives and Outreach, the Equal Pay Matters Initiative, the Paycheck Fairness Act, and the Equal Opportunity Survey—a tool to detect and deter discrimination by some one hundred thousand federal contractors.

"The government says it champions women, but it continues to lock us out," said Margot Dorfman, CEO of the Women's Chamber of Commerce. Women small-business owners have long been pushing for a bigger share of government contracts. But the Small Business Administration's new rules—which took it seven years to develop after being ordered by Congress to do so—listed only 4 industries out of 140 in which female-owned businesses could have an advantage for contracts. This was hardly what women had hoped for after a report showed them to be "underrepresented in 87 percent of all industries where the government awards contracts."

What's more, the Department of Justice (DOJ) has weakened its enforcement of the laws against workplace discrimination—in hiring, promotions, harassment, issues surrounding pregnancy, and the like. And it's refused to hear many well-documented complaints, even abandoning pending high-profile sex discrimination cases. That many experienced employment discrimination attorneys have been forced from their jobs only further compounds the problem.

None of this—stereotyping and denigrating our qualities and interests, eliminating crucial information, assaulting our rights—happens without consequence. These retrogressive changes affect how we think about ourselves and how the men in our lives, be they our boyfriends, husbands, doctors, teachers, clients, or employers, think about and treat us.

"Let me be frank with you," the CEO of a major company recently told me. "Without any teeth in the regulations, we don't feel the same level of concern with EEOC-related issues. For us it means a cutback in how much we're willing to spend on those areas, like human resources and bolstering us up against lawsuits. There's a huge ripple-down effect from these policies that'll be felt in future generations."

We do have to worry about the future, but we're in the midst of the fallout right now. Judged by every standard, working women, whether they're childless, married with children, single moms, professionals, or hourly wage earners, are all hurt by the current hostile climate. But they're hurt in different ways.

The majority of women in this country still work in service positions. And those who labor in the lower economic strata, in general, have fewer job options, less flexibility at work and at home, and fewer resources to help them achieve a life/work balance than professionals. But this doesn't mean there isn't plenty of common ground. There are more issues uniting us than separating us—issues all working women can fight for: the ability to care for children and sick family members; the end of gender discrimination; sexual harassment, and the gender pay gap; and paid sick days and family leaves.

Equal Pay for Equal Work? Don't Bet on It

"I don't think anyone would ever say I couldn't do the job as well as a man," Christine Kwapnoski, a manager at a Sam's Club in northern California, said. And yet, the forty-two-year-old Kwapnoski earned less than the man she oversaw when she was a dock supervisor. She received a promotion, but no raise came with it, although men with the same promotions got increases. She complained, but "[b]asically I was told it was none of my business, that there was nothing I could do about it."

"Throughout the 1980s and early 1990s, women of all economic levels—poor, middle class, and rich—were steadily gaining ground on their male counterparts in the work force," reported David Leonhardt for the *New York Times* in 2006. "By the mid-90s, women earned more than 75 cents for every dollar in hourly pay that men did, up from 65 cents just 15 years earlier." Back then it was possible to believe that the gap was closing. Today it seems unlikely.

The gender pay gap is actually widening for those with four-year college degrees. And it's not—as so many argue—because we're taking time off to be with our children. A new report by the AAUW finds that the gap in pay starts immediately after graduation and only increases over time. As Catherine Hill, research director of the study, explained to me, "Right out of school there should be a fairly level playing field, but surprisingly women are already earning 20 percent less, even when they have the same major and occupation as their male counterparts. This, although women earn slightly higher GPAs than men in every college major including science and mathematics."

Women who attended elite colleges earned about the same as men from minimally selective colleges, the report found. And the pay gap is the widest for women in the top professions. They lose about $1.2 million over the course of a lifetime; for the average worker it's about $700,000.

Women employed full-time make an average of seventy-seven cents for every dollar men are paid. The ratio is worse for women of color. African American women get only seventy-one cents and Latinas fifty-eight cents. And this includes women in academia.

Kwapnoski is now part of a class-action lawsuit against Wal-Mart, owner of Sam's Club. "[But] government's efforts to reduce sex discrimination have ebbed over the period that the pay gap has stagnated. In the 1960s and 1970s laws like Title VII and Title IX prohibited discrimination at work and in school and may have helped close the pay gap in subsequent years," wrote Leonhardt. These laws are still in existence, of course; they're just not being enforced.

The 2007 Supreme Court ruling in *Ledbetter v. Goodyear* made it harder for workers to sue for pay discrimination. Lilly Ledbetter, the only female among sixteen men at the Gadsden, Alabama, tire plant, discovered, when she was close to retirement, that for years she'd been paid less than her male colleagues, including those with less seniority.

Always clear about its priorities, the Bush administration filed a brief on the side of Goodyear. And in a five-to-four decision the court ruled against Ledbetter, maintaining that because she failed to file within 180 days after "the alleged unlawful employment practice occurred [the time period mandated by the original Title VII law in 1964], she wasn't entitled to redress." But, as Ruth Bader Ginsburg pointed out in her dissenting opinion, workplaces are notoriously secret about salaries. Most employees have no idea what their coworkers earn. Ledbetter was only tipped off by an anonymous letter telling her of the disparities. Before this ruling, many lower courts allowed employees to sue years after the onset of the discrimination, considering each unequal paycheck "a new discriminatory act."

Fortunately the Lilly Ledbetter Fair Pay Act, signed by President Obama, will allow charges to be filed after any paycheck affected by discrimination, rather than only after the initial discriminatory decision, but what's really needed is a law to end wage discrimination from the start. In this current economic crisis women workers may be reluctant to speak out, and unless we're vigilant, there may be retaliations against those who do bring a suit.

I remember Gloria Steinem once advising women to turn to their male coworkers doing the same job and ask what they're earning. The truth is, we simply don't know. Most female physicians were surprised to hear they were "making 22 percent less than their male counterparts, even after adjusting for differences in practice and personal characteristics." And that figure is up from 16 percent in 1995.

"It is something that seems so untenable," ob-gyn Erin Tracy said, commenting on the wage disparity, "that people assume it's not the situation at their institution, but when they pull the data, it may show otherwise."

"[M]any women still do not realize that they are affected by the gender wage gap," says Diane K. Danielson, who conducted a three-generation survey for the Downtown Women's Club in New York. Despite differences in age and career level, baby boomers, Generation X, and Generation Y businesswomen have one thing in common: most don't know they're being paid less than their male colleagues. Danielson urges women to work collectively to tackle workplace issues. "Fighting battles individually rarely works to change corporate America." Her words ring particularly true as we begin to consider all we're up against.

Right before the 2004 presidential election, Bush announced sweeping changes to the Fair Standards Act, denying overtime pay to millions of workers and potentially widening the gender pay gap. And he chose Paul De Camp, an attorney whose career has been dedicated to stopping legal remedies for women, to head the Department of Labor's Wage and Hour Division.

"I depend on my overtime pay to help with my tuition," Casey, a paralegal who goes to law school at night, told me. Many female-dominated positions, such as nurses, retail clerks, computer operators, secretaries, and nonunionized support workers, have, like Casey's, been recategorized and now are ineligible for overtime pay. "But," added Casey, "this doesn't mean I won't have to work overtime, I just won't get paid appropriately for it."

"All families are struggling to make ends meet in this poor economy—especially single mothers. What happens when she has to work several hours of overtime a week in her so-called management position but doesn't receive proper compensation to pay for her babysitter?" asked NOW's Kim Gandy.

How Are We Discriminated Against? Let Me Count the Ways

Gender discrimination pervades the workplace. Inroads we made years ago in the professions and corporations are being ploughed over into oblivion. And it didn't help that Bush appointed right-winger Diana Furchtgott-Roth to the Council of Economic Advisers. Furchtgott-Roth, who'd been a fellow at the American Enterprise Institute, is the coauthor of a book denying the existence of a wage gap and a glass ceiling. To her, workplace discrimination against women is one big myth.

But this "myth" is threatening the jobs of millions of older women.

"I felt that I had learned a tremendous amount, not only about advertising but how to relate to my clients after being in the business twenty-five years," Pam, a fifty-six-year-old account executive with a large New York advertising firm, said. "But then I noticed increasing demands being made on me—to travel, to put in lots of overtime—that weren't being made on my male colleagues. And when I complained, I was told the company needed to 'project an image of vigor and enthusiasm.' After that, my evaluations tanked."

Facing the dual blades of age and sex discrimination, older women may not get the same opportunities because men doing the hiring often look for younger, more attractive women; they don't get into training programs and have little chance of upward mobility as they approach retirement. Like Pam, they may be subjected to particular burdens that either force them to leave or result in fewer raises. And getting fewer merit increases means they get lower pension benefits. "Job and wage discrimination can have devastating effects on their retirement." For the majority of women over sixty-five, social security is their sole source of income.

"ONE TREND I'M noticing," said AAUW's Catherine Hill, "is the 'feminization' of certain professions and specialties, resulting in lowering their status and salaries," a subtle but definite form of discrimination. Historically, the so-called female jobs—teaching, nursing, and secretarial and administrative positions—garnered lower wages and prestige. Now, with women able to expand their choice of occupation, the same phenomenon is occurring in other fields. Whatever the area, when a critical mass of women moves in, men move out.

Women now constitute over 80 percent of the previously male-dominated veterinary college student population in the United States. Men are reluctant to enter a profession they see as bulging with women because of the presumed decline in stature and salaries. While one report claims that female vets will accept less money than male vets, this doesn't entirely address the issue. "It's what we're offered," one young woman, an attending veterinarian at an animal hospital in New York, told me. "When we first finish our training, many of us with debts, we're happy for the income and just starting our real careers; we're not in a position to argue."

In the broader world of medicine, women get pigeonholed into certain medical specialties. "I'm often asked by male physicians if I am going into pediatrics before I ever tell them anything about myself," Kate Young, then in her third year at the University of Nevada School of Medicine, recalled. Pediatrics is considered by many to be an extension of the mothering-caring role and an "acceptable" field for women.

Jen, a fourth-year resident in reconstructive surgery, told me how the female residents at her hospital were never questioned on rounds as rigorously as the male ones were. "At first I thought the doctors were just being nice to us, then, as I saw the pattern continue, I realized it was a form of subtle discrimination. We weren't being taken as seriously."

"I remember a [male] professor in medical school telling me no one would think badly of me if I just quit the program, went home, and had babies," said Dr. Kathie Horrace-Voighm, an intern from Corpus Christi, Texas. "He didn't realize I already had two children."

Data gathered in 2005 from the American Medical Association (AMA) found that pediatrics, ob-gyn, and dermatology have the greatest percentage of women residents. The fewest are in orthopedic surgery, urology, and otolaryngology. These choices are dictated by many reasons, but high among them are gender stereotypes and discrimination.

When women do enter traditionally male specialties, they're not always welcomed. Bonnie, a resident who chose orthopedic surgery, complained to me of being singled out by the attending physician to transfer surgery patients from the gurney to the operating room table. "There were always aides and orderlies in the OR who should have been asked to do it, but I was always given the task. I'm sure it was a way of making me feel uncomfortable and unwelcome."

"You're such a girl, are you sure you can do that?" Arthur Day, the chief of neurosurgery at Brigham and Women's Hospital in Boston, asked Sagun Tuli, an assistant professor of surgery, while she was in the midst of an operation. And on the night of a hospital dinner, Dr. Day asked Tuli to "get up on the table and dance for us to show the female residents how to behave."

When Tuli complained, she found her pay and research time cut. Her application to be promoted as "director of spine" at the hospital was also turned down, she says, in retaliation for going public against Dr. Day, who reportedly told her, "I want you to continue to be a slave for the department."

Even though increasing numbers of women are enrolling in medical school, it's hard for women to see a future for themselves when only 15 percent of the full professors and only 12 of the 125 deans in U.S. medical schools are women.

"I'D HIRE YOU," numerous photographers told Debi Field, a young photographer based in Montana, "except my clients wouldn't like to see a woman toting around all that heavy equipment."

"I heard this time and time again," said Field. "Photography is overwhelmingly a male world, and they will use just about any excuse they can to keep women out."

"Art is a luxury artists pay for," the sculptor David Smith is reputed to have said. If that's so, then being an artist is an even greater luxury for women.

As art critic Jerry Saltz noted in *New York* magazine (March 2008):

In 1972 it was hard for women to get their work into galleries and museums. Yet it was impossible to be in the art world then and not be totally aware of the form-changing dynamism of women's art. Today, museums love the art of the period. They do massive survey exhibitions of [Richard] Smithson and [Robert] Serra. Where are the surveys of Lynda Benglis, Dorothea Rockburne, Adrian Piper, and Sturtevant? By my count, totaling up the shows and projects at the Guggenheim since 2000, only 24 percent are women. MoMA and the Whitney are a few percent better. The gallery scene is even worse; one Saturday three weeks ago, I checked out every show in every ground-floor gallery in Chelsea, from Eighteenth Street to Twenty-Sixth Street. Of seventy-four solo shows, only 16 percent were by women.

"In art, as in every other field, there is a glass ceiling. While we may dream that the ivory tower of the museum is a refuge from the racial [and] gender issues that impact our society, alas, it is not so," wrote one art critic, commenting on the underrepresentation of women artists at the San Francisco MOMA. Of the museum's entire permanent collection, only one out of twelve works is by a woman, and pieces by women of color—such as Betye Saar, Inez Storer, and Mildred Howard—are entirely absent.

We haven't made much progress from the 1950s, when Hans Hofman told his promising but not yet famous abstract-expressionist student Lee Krasner that her work was "so good, you would not believe it was done by a woman." Even so, Hofman refused to help her get a gallery show.

A survey of a recent contemporary art auctions held at Christie's, Sotheby's, and Phillips de Pury & Company found 13 percent of the paintings to be by women. "There is a vast discrepancy between what the men get and what the women get at [auction]," art historian Irving Sandler said.

"[I]n almost every other field where money changes hands in society, women's production has been and continues to be valued below that of men, except in this field, the difference is sometimes tenfold or more," art expert Greg Allen said. There'll be many excuses for the discrepancy, Allen knows, "[b]ut there is also a short and simple if unpopular answer that none of these explanations can trump. Women's art sells for less because it is made by women."

Although women outnumber men as dance students and teachers, more men are in positions of making decisions about the presentation and creation of dance. Dance companies such as American Dance Festival, American Ballet Theater, New York City Ballet, and Brooklyn Academy Next Wave Festival—performing at prestigious theaters in New York— are headed by men. Men also receive the lion's share (72 percent) of NEA grants for choreography and twice the stipend awarded to women (ten thousand versus five thousand dollars).

And women in the world of music fare no better. Conductors and their orchestras are overwhelmingly male. But, says Anna Fels, author of *Necessary Dreams: Ambition in Women's Changing Lives*, when scrims were used at auditions to conceal the gender of the applicant, the numbers of female applicants accepted into major companies increased dramatically.

The lack of women at the top in just about all professions has barely gotten the attention it deserves. We're 51 percent of the population and almost half of the workforce. Shouldn't we be way past the time of tokenism?

"There have been women in the pipeline for twenty to twenty-five years; progress has been slower than anybody thought it ever would be," said Julie H. Daum of the large executive search firm Spencer Stuart. And Daum doesn't expect the situation to change any time in the near future. "I think we're still way far removed from where we should be and from where women would like to be."

One of the biggest obstacles to women getting the vaunted corner office is the pile of men blocking the doorway. "The men in the boardroom and men at the top are choosing and tend to choose who they are comfortable with: other men," said Carol Bartz, who recently resigned as Autodesk's CEO.

"Corporate boards remain, for the most part, clubby and male-dominated worlds where members have attended many of the same schools, dress the same, and represent a single social class," said Douglas M. Branson, a professor at the University of Pittsburgh School of Law and author of *No Seat at the Table: How Corporate Governance and Law Keep Women Out of the Boardroom*. A Catalyst survey looking at boards of the Fortune 500 companies found only seventy-six of the boards to have three or four women on them; many have no women at all.

This in part explains why women, who hold more than 50 percent of management and professional positions, make up only 15 percent of the officers and 2 percent of Fortune 500 CEOs. For women of color, the situation is far worse: only 5 percent of all managers and professionals are African American women; Latinas are at 3.3 percent; Asian woman at 2.6 percent.

"[G]oing strictly by the numbers it would seem that something akin to the Bermuda Triangle is causing women with architecture degrees to mysteriously vanish before making it into the professional arena," one reporter remarked. Across the country, women account for nearly half of the graduates of university architecture programs, yet they make up only 13 percent of the licensed professionals working at American Institute of Architect member firms.

Stories of women in other fields follow the same arc. "When I was a physics major in the late 1970s, my very few fellow female students and I had high hopes that women would soon stand equal with men in science, but progress has proved slower than many of us imagined," wrote Margaret Wertheim in 2006.

"Encountering another woman working in technology was a rare event for me when I started out in IT many years ago," said Maggie Biggs. "In the years since [then] women have made significant strides, sometimes against great odds, proving their mettle as both tech execs and engineers. Despite these well-earned gains . . . the percentage of young women embracing IT has been in steady decline for some time. So much so that women make up a quarter of today's U.S. IT workforce, down from 37 percent in the mid-1980s. Collaborating with women on a technical project has once again become a rare occurrence."

Explaining the disconnect between the numbers of highly qualified, educated women and their ability to fulfill their professional aspirations has become the work of several organizations, university conferences, and governmental agencies. A major study sponsored by the National Academy of Sciences found pervasive bias, "arbitrary and subjective evaluation processes," and a work environment in which "anyone lacking the work and family support traditionally provided by a 'wife' is at a serious disadvantage." The report also specifically dismisses the contention that women are unproductive and noncompetitive because their real priorities are family time.

What women lack—say a variety of experts—are mentors, access to business networks that could plug them into corporate decision-makers, support for their research, and acknowledgment that their work has value. Marsha Simms, a partner at the New York law firm Weil, Gotshal & Manges, told a story at a conference on Women and Ambition, immediately winning nods of recognition from the audience. When Simms was elected president of the American Council of Trial Lawyers, "it was no big deal at the office. The only comment I heard was from a partner who hoped it wouldn't cut into my work at the firm. But a few years later when a male colleague got the same position, there was a companywide announcement and huge fuss honoring him."

Sugar and Spice—or Else! Gender Stereotyping at Work

Just for a moment, close your eyes and picture an executive. What do you see?

If you're like most of the country, you've probably either just imagined a man or a woman dressed like a man. Despite years of women's achievement in the workplace, our conceptions of authority remain male.

The "think leader, think male" mind-set continues to dominate America, and "this narrows the range of effective behaviors [for women] within the workplace," according to a new report by Catalyst. Women are faced with a dilemma: you're damned if you do try to act like men, doomed if you don't.

Years of study producing three significant research reports have confirmed the persistent prejudice of gender stereotyping in the world of work, forming a "powerful yet invisible threat" to women's progress. Analyzing data from more than twelve hundred leaders, Catalyst documents the ways in which stereotypes or "cognitive shortcuts" have been used to create different standards to judge women. "As prototypical leaders, male potential to lead and, in particular, to lead effectively, is rarely questioned *a priori*: As unnatural leaders women must prove themselves over and over again and are held to higher standards."

"Whenever I exhibited perfectly normal assertiveness traits I got penalized for it, because it was considered a male trait," wrote Daryl Cohen on my survey. Although treated like a child and kept at department administrator level, it didn't stop male bosses from "sucking my brains out and present[ing] the ideas as their own."

Women are assumed to be nurturers and caregivers, but when they exhibit these qualities at work, they are considered "too soft"—likable, but definitely not leadership material. And since men are presumed to have the monopoly on "taking charge" skills, when women initiate and assume control, they are judged to be "too tough" and not likable enough to be elevated to the top.

"Aggressive and blunt," Morgan Stanley's Zoe Cruz, once considered to be the most powerful woman on Wall Street, "didn't act like a typical female pioneer in a masculine world," said Joe Hagan, whose piece about Cruz's spectacular fall ran in *New York* magazine. "And that rubbed a lot of men, who later got her fired, the wrong way."

Cruz had played by the rules and at age fifty-two was one of the highest-paid people, male or female, in finance. At Morgan Stanley her entire professional life, she'd made billions of dollars for the company. Her boss, sixty-three-year-old chairman and CEO John Mack, had slated her to be his replacement when he retired. Three weeks after making that decision, he fired her.

Shocked at the news, Cruz left the building ten minutes later, never to return. She was spared seeing her former male colleagues erupting with glee at the news. The woman they called the "wicked witch" got canned.

Cruz has a family and seemed to be of that rare breed able to give her "all" to both realms. No one could accuse her of sacrificing work to children or of being a soft touch. She even took thorny business calls in the midst of labor while giving birth to her daughter. But when her voice cracked during a particularly contentious meeting, the men in the room ridiculed her. And when she made tough decisions, they referred to her as "Cruz missile"—a term that stuck.

Some insiders think Morgan Stanley was not ready to be headed by a woman. Others, like Wall Street recruiter Linda Bailecki, saw it as a function of tough financial times. Women are the first to go. Women got "slaughtered" during the dot-com bust in 2001, and it's happening again, she said.

But Joe Hagan, who aptly called his article about Cruz "Only the Men Survive," explained it this way: "The real problem is that the proverbial glass ceiling is reinforcing. The traits that a woman must develop to duke it out on the trading floor will come back to haunt her as she ascends the ranks of management."

HOLDING WOMEN TO impossible standards, finding fault no matter what we do, makes me wonder if, when all is said, behind all the excuses about why women aren't getting ahead, the real reason is that men simply don't want to give up their hold on power. How else can we explain the obdurate refusal of our policymakers and employers to accept the obvious—we are no longer a country of breadwinner dads and bread-maker moms—an arrangement true for only 30 percent of the workforce and 16 percent of working families? The convenient falsehood that we all have a spouse at home to tend to domestic and family concerns is putting double-duty hardships on women in the workplace.

Family Affairs

"It's wonderful to see her face light up when she sees me. She might not know who I am, but she knows I'm family," said Arabella Dorth about her eighty-six-year-old mother, who is in the advanced stages of Alzheimer's disease. For three years, Dorth, a paralegal with a San Francisco law firm, traveled to her mother's home in San Diego. Then, as her mother grew sicker, she moved her into a nursing home.

Now Dorth spends about fifteen hours a week paying her mother's bills, doing her laundry, and the like. All her sick and vacation days are used up, and she still spends evenings and part of her weekends caring for her mother.

Andrea Dorth is among the disproportionate numbers of working women caring for elderly relatives. Seventy-one percent of them spend forty hours or more at this "second job," so many, in fact, that sociologists are calling it the "daughter track" (and sometimes it's the daughter-in-law track) because it can totally derail a woman's career.

"It's a safe assumption . . . that women are more likely to put their careers on hold or end them because of caregiving responsibilities," said Carol Levin, an adviser to the National Alliance for Caregiving.

For Rikki Grub, a fifty-eight-year-old, Harvard-educated attorney, the imperative of caring for her father's illnesses and then her mother's resulted in her turning down a partnership at her San Francisco law firm. The pull of parents, work, and her own family was just too much.

With her father now deceased and her mother in a nursing home, Grub is working again, part-time as a consultant. She's off the fast track, grateful for having money saved from her twenty-year legal career and getting benefits from her husband's position as a university professor. But how many women taking care of aging relatives are in her secure situation?

Advances in medical technology enable more people to live long enough to suffer from multiple chronic illnesses, disabilities, and dependency. The majority of these will be women, and because of earlier discrimination and budgetary cuts in available services, they will have limited economic resources.

Their caregivers will also most likely be women. And however much they may find satisfaction in giving back to their ill parents, many will be sacrificing their careers and their own family lives and sometimes their own health. Recent studies document that caregiving can result in increased incidence of physical and emotional illnesses. The difficulties facing both generations of women have been exacerbated by wrongheaded policies, and they call for attention and remediation.

It's a crisis waiting to happen, say experts in elder care. "We haven't really begun to grapple with these issues of what the aging of America is going to mean," said Gail Gibson Hunt, president of the National Alliance for Caregiving. Who will care for them? How will they be paid? How will we compensate them for their career and personal sacrifices? Where will the infirm elderly live? How will they be transported to their treatments?

Instead of leading the nation to address the imperatives of our aging population, the Bush administration buried its head in the sand. At the White House Conference on Aging, policymakers and advocates for the elderly had reason to be pessimistic. President Bush signaled his lack of interest by skipping the four-day meeting—the first time, said John Rother, director of policy at AAPR, "that a president has not addressed his own White House conference."

"Mommy, there's this guy hanging around in front of the house looking in the windows, and it's really creeping us out," Katy's seven-year-old whispered into the phone. Katy Walker, thirty years old, living in Kansas City, Missouri, will never forget the feeling of dread and helplessness washing over her.

Katy was working at her job cleaning houses when the call came. Recently divorced, she could no longer afford to put her children in day care; they were home alone. Finally Katy reached a neighbor, who rushed to her house, but the man had already fled.

Such horror stories are legion among mothers forced to leave young children by themselves. That their children are well cared for is critical to the emotional and physical well-being of working mothers. But, for the most part, we still have a school day ending at three or three thirty, leaving working parents desperate to patch together hours of care for their young children and terribly worried when they can't.

And yet, the past several years have witnessed cutbacks in the highly successful Head Start program and in the major federal programs supporting after-school programs, leaving behind 1.4 million children who depend upon these services. Unfortunately Obama's stimulus package will do little to reverse the downward funding.

Under Bush's administration, reductions in the child-care tax credit removed some 6.5 million families from eligibility for public day care, and federal budget cuts resulted in the loss of child care for some three hundred thousand young children. All this done by those who preach family values and morality to our nation.

These moves have been supported by sensationalized reports critical of group care, like the one hitting the presses in 2007 with an alarming claim:

"keeping a preschooler in a day care center for a year or more increased the likelihood that the child would become [later] disruptive in class."

The author of the study, Jay Belsky, initially in favor of group care, has been opposed to it for a long time. He skyrocketed to fame with a paper appearing in 1986, based on only four studies, warning of insecure attachment to the mother in infants placed in day care. His work has been discredited by years of longitudinal research showing that when all other things are equal, differences between children in and out of group care are minimal. But he's back, the new darling of the right, eagerly cited by those who want to "restore full-time mothering as a social norm." The study was "a blow to feminists, who defend dumping their children in a day-care center," crowed conservative pundit Robert Novak, then at CNN.

What got buried in all the negative spin about group care were several salient facts. Even if—and it's a big "if"—these children (17 percent of them) are more disruptive, the margin is slight and well within the normal range. And, say numerous authorities, parental guidance and genes have been shown to have had a far bigger impact on how the children behaved than time in day care.

In what should have been a caution to the hyperventilating media, Belsky's study had no control group and failed to take into account employee turnover at a center—a key element in how children adjust. It also ignored the role of individual problems and difficult family situations children bring with them when entering care. Even a key member of Belsky's research team, Sarah Friedman, admitted there was no way to know or determine cause and effect.

"I can usually spot children who've been in group care," Ilene Lewis, director of Little Scholars in Washington, D.C., told me. "They have more highly developed social skills and better vocabulary than those who've been home-cared." Lewis discounted the sweeping generalization of Belsky's study. "In my eleven years as a director here, I haven't seen evidence of aggressive behavior in those who've spent years in group care."

Little Scholars, operated by the Library of Congress and open to members of the Senate and House, is by all accounts a model program with a high staff-to-child ratio and educational, imaginative programs. "What we should be looking at are the places low-income families have to leave their little ones," Lewis said. "That's where the attention should be directed."

And she's right. With some 2.3 million children in day care centers, many beginning as early as infants and continuing until kindergarten, we need thorough evaluations of its impact on all our nation's children. (Only 2 percent of companies nationwide have on-site child care.) The answer is not to construe this issue so that it feeds the conservative political agenda. The answer is to make our child care the best that it can be.

When I toured a variety of centers in different parts of the country some years ago, I found an array of conditions—some wonderful, some nothing short of appalling—places so dirty, so smelly, with so few caregivers, most of us would think twice about leaving our pets there, let alone our children. But these were the only alternatives for many working families.

With no federal standards regulating child care facilities, the standards are set by states. They differ widely in provider-child ratio, provider training and assessment, and quality of the programs and supervision. What's needed is access to affordable, available, high-quality child care that is employer, community, and governmentally based.

Mothers are in the workforce to stay. Peggy Sradnick, director of Basic Trust, a highly regarded center in New York City, put it this way: "Bad care is bad for kids, and good care is good for kids."

But as historian Ruth Rosen and others have noted, the issue of child care has simply dropped from view. The lack of concern and support for families is part of a disturbing trend becoming increasingly evident over the past few years—outright discrimination against mothers in the workforce.

17

MOTHERS MATTER(S)

"She should be barefoot, pregnant, and at home!" Andrea Wolff-Yakubovich's boss admonished her husband after firing Andrea from her position as finance director for a Denver-based John Elway AutoNation dealership when she disclosed she was expecting.

Similarly, the Berge Ford auto dealership dismissed twenty-three-year-old Marilyn Pickler a week after she informed the Arizona company she was pregnant.

"I burst into tears," Pickler said. "They thought I was not going to be able to do my job. They thought I would throw up or have a cramp. But pregnant women work every day, it just wasn't fair."

"You can't be pregnant, you just can't." Not if you're looking for a job in academia, is the advice mentors routinely give their female students. Don't disclose pregnancies, an interest in having children, or the presence of children at home during a job interview, suggested one young woman in Joan Williams's study *Beyond the "Chilly Climate": Eliminating Bias Against Women and Fathers in Academe.*

"I was going to put you in charge of the office, but look at you now," Debbie Moore's boss said after denying her a promotion in the admissions department at the University of Alabama when she was eight months pregnant.

And in the northeast, Tanys Lancaster, a top executive at Bloomberg L.P., said, When "[I] informed [the company] that I had become pregnant in September of 2004, almost immediately I began to suffer demotions, decreases in compensation, and retaliation after I complained to human resources." Like other high-salaried pregnant women at Bloomberg,

Lancaster, who is now part of a class-action lawsuit, was replaced by more junior male employees, excluded from management meetings, and subjected to such comments as "You're not committed" and "You don't want to be here."

These stories and hundreds of others are fueling the dramatic explosion in pregnancy discrimination charges over the past decade, making it one of the fastest-growing employment discrimination complaints filed with the government.

"The kind of cases we're seeing are very blatant," said Mary Jo O'Neill, a regional lawyer with the EEOC, "cases where managers say, 'We don't want pregnant women working here.' Employers have even gone as far as urging their employees to 'get rid of it,' 'get an abortion.'"

Firing pregnant women is another tactic in the ongoing effort to push women out of the workplace. Employers I've spoken to have come up with a self-serving explanation: their pregnant employees, they worry, will be less productive because of divided attention and limited performance capacity.

"That's just a lot of b——," Jocelyn, one of my former colleagues, said. Jocelyn stayed at her job during the first several hours of her labor. "I went straight from work to the hospital," she said. "It's so unfair to assume pregnancy is a distraction. I felt great and had more energy than usual. And don't men get distracted also?" She began to reel off a list: "They break up with their girlfriend, their parents are sick, they have a torn tendon in their knee, their golf games tank. But no one suggests they're not effective employees; they're not fired over these things."

The notion of pregnancy as a time of diminished capability is pure contrivance, born out of the mix between animosity against working mothers and the terrible economy. It's the old Victorian idea taken out of mothballs for the new millennium. When society wanted pregnant women to work, it forced them to. I can't imagine too many southern overseers telling their seven-months-pregnant field workers to take time off—even though the humane thing would have been to do just that.

And when it hasn't suited our "needs" to have women in the workforce, the "best" male minds came out against it. The arguments of today merely mirror the "position papers" of the past.

"Women's reproductive organs are pre-eminent," one prominent physician wrote in 1854, expressing the traditional views of his profession. "They exercise a controlling influence upon her entire system." From puberty onward, ovaries were said to dominate a woman's being, affecting her mind, her ability to concentrate, and her physical stamina.

Hysteria, the ailment presumably incapacitating educated, middle-class Victorian women, comes from the Greek word *hystera*, for womb. Our capacity to have children rendered us unreliable and unstable. Only at menopause did a woman find release from the wily dictates of her body, but by then she was an "exhausted and diseased" shell of her former self.

History hasn't been kind to womb-bearing people. The authorities—Puritan preachers of colonial days, physicians in the nineteenth century, Freudians of the cold war era—have changed, but the core of their diatribe against women who tried to expand their roles remained intact until the 1970s, when feminists battled against biology as destiny. Now we're corkscrewing back to a time when women's choices were severely limited: either be childless and have a career or be a mother without one.

Most of us don't realize that it's illegal—a stark violation of the Civil Rights Act of 1964—to be fired for becoming pregnant. But of the women who know about the law, most don't file complaints. Some are discouraged by the EEOC's lackadaisical pursuit of these cases, others are afraid of the repercussions. And in the cult of domesticity redux, taking maternity leave has also become a career killer. In a ten-year study at Penn State, five hundred faculty members became parents, and only seven—all women—took parental leaves. "Those who utilize the policies may be viewed as uncommitted and, at worst, experience the ultimate failure for an academic in the denial of tenure."

Actually, fewer than one in ten women born after 1956 leave the workforce for a year or more during their prime childbearing years, says a recent study published by the *American Sociological Review*, but even those who take minileaves are often punished for them.

Sarah Clarke, who works in finance, couldn't mistake her employer's attitude about her maternity leave. "I said I wanted to work from home [during my leave] . . . [but] they wouldn't allow me to call into meetings. And when I came back to work, I didn't have a desk."

Janet Loures's duties and staff as a senior manager in the company Global Data Consulting, a job she held in 2001, "were reduced after she took a maternity leave for a first and then a second child." Today she has essentially entry-level clerical duties, and no one reports to her.

A manager of interior design at a very busy architecture firm in Boston tried especially hard to show that being pregnant wasn't going to interfere with her productivity. Before taking her maternity leave she put in months of sixty-hour weeks to complete all her assignments. She'd originally planned to return to work full time, but her boss encouraged her to come back as a consultant, taking off Fridays.

After her twelve-week unpaid leave, she had day care all set up and was ready to resume working. That's when things started to get strange. First her boss told her there wasn't enough for her to do (everyone was swamped), then he told her that her performance had been "abysmal" (she'd had great reviews and client feedback). Finally they did take her back, but she was given menial assignments—a total waste of her master's degree in architecture and years of experience.

"I felt like [my boss's] plan was to bore me to death until I eventually quit. Well—they won, and I took the unemployment package. . . . I ended up staying home . . . and having a total identity crisis and depression."

Another woman trained a single, inexperienced man to take her job while she was on leave. When she returned, she had to share her job with this "temporary" replacement. Soon she was told there wasn't enough work for both of them and that *she* was being laid off. And still another woman whose postpregnancy responsibilities were seriously curtailed said, "I had a baby, not a lobotomy."

All over the country women report similar scenarios, and many of the offenders were among the thirty companies routinely designated by *Working Mother* magazine as the country's "Best Companies to Work For."

I asked David Larker, a partner at a major New York law firm, why so many women encounter hostility when they return from having a baby. His answer was telling.

"We give them training, we give them a leave and they don't appreciate it, and when they come back they still ask for time off for one thing or another. At this point, in a choice between hiring a man or a woman, hands down, I'd definitely go with the man. Sooner or later the women are going to leave."

Larker's attitude—which he claimed was becoming universal—is very troubling, especially because it's a self-fulfilling prophecy. As Sarah Clarke explained, "This kind of inequitable treatment forces many women to leave." Mothers in the workforce are demoted and in other ways dealt with unfairly, and when work is too stressful and pays too little, some women decide to call it quits. Then the men say, "See, it's what we've always expected."

"What do you do to try to retain your female employees?" I asked Larker. He shook his head. "Nothing." A minute passed. "Nothing at all." And apparently he's not alone. Bill Amlong, an employee discrimination attorney in Florida, confirmed that some of the worst offenders are big law firms.

And as for Larker's not understanding that family leave wasn't a give-me but something mandated by law, that's not unusual either, according to HR experts.

"It wasn't always this way," Barbara Stoller, an executive recruiter, told me. "There used to be a lot of buzz about leaves, flex-time, job sharing, but no one talks about it anymore, because employees know they're viewed as not serious enough if they take advantage of these policies. In the current climate most employers think that family leave is something they're doing out of the goodness of their hearts."

And the leave itself is constantly under attack by conservatives who'd like to get rid of it entirely. As it is, the United States is one out of only two industrialized nations that doesn't offer *paid* family leave. A joint study conducted by Harvard and McGill universities puts us in the company of Liberia and Papua New Guinea. Our retrogressive policies are really hurting working families, 78 percent of whom say they can't afford to take unpaid family leave. And now, because of a poorly conceived law prohibiting states from using their unemployment funds to compensate workers taking leave for the birth or adoption of a child, their lives will only become harder.

So prevalent is the discrimination against mothers it's earned its own name: the maternal wall. One of its more insidious forms is not providing nursing mothers a quiet, private place to pump breast milk. Given the high infant mortality rate in the United States and studies finding a one and a half to five times lower relative risk of mortality among breastfed children, it's astonishing that, unlike some 107 countries that protect a working woman's right to breastfeed, the United States doesn't.

The American Academy of Pediatrics "urges women to breastfeed exclusively for six months and to continue until the child turns one." But for working women, particularly those in lower-echelon jobs, pumping their milk while at work is often an invitation to discomfort and ridicule.

When Laura Walker returned to her waitress job at a Red Lobster restaurant, she showed her supervisor a note from her nurse explaining her need to pump. But according to a complaint Walker filed with the EEOC, the manager reduced her hours, gave her the worst tables, and made fun of her—"jiggling the restaurant's milk containers and joking that they were for her." Her inability to pump her breasts resulted in clogged ducts, forcing her to be hospitalized with mastitis.

Marlene Warfield, a dental hygienist in Tacoma, Washington, also faced harassing behavior. Her boss, the dentist, thought her pumping on the job was worthy of his wearing a Halloween costume, a big silver version of a pump with Put Breasts Here written on it, to the office. After he told her she had to leave her pump at home, she quit and reported the incident to the local human rights commission, "which found nothing illegal about the dentist's actions."

And Stacey Wexler, an attorney in a small office, had to pump in a communal washroom. "I'd lock the door, but sometimes there'd be so much rattling and banging I'd become so uncomfortable, I'd have to stop before I finished."

Carolyn Malony, representative from New York, has introduced legislation for a federal law to protect mothers who express milk at work. "I can't understand why this doesn't move," she said. "This is pro-family, prohealth, proeconomy." But, unfortunately, the reason her bill is stagnant isn't hard to discern.

"We are coming close to wiping mothers out of the work pool," said distinguished professor and director of the Center for Work/Life Studies

Joan Williams. "There are virtually no mothers in high positions—and that sure as heck is bias."

"Women who have children within the first five years of teaching are more likely than others to become part of the 'nontenured academic second tier' of lecturers and adjuncts," report University of California's May Ann Mason and Marc Goulden. In their study *Do Babies Matter?* they found that "the majority of women who achieve tenure have no children in the household at any time after their Ph.D."

"People actually have underlying stereotypes in which they think of mothers as very nice people, but they don't think of them as competent people," said professor Faye Crosby of the psychology department at the University of California, Santa Cruz, discussing her research.

A recent study coming out of Cornell University confirms both professors Williams and Crosby's work. "We created two applicant profiles that were functionally equivalent," Shelley J. Correll, the author of the study, said. "Their resumes were very strong: they were very successful in their last job. In pretesting no one preferred one applicant over the other; they were seen as equally qualified." Then. They added a memo to one of the profiles that the applicant was a mother of two children; the memo to the other made no mention of children.

When the group was asked if they would hire these applicants, the different responses were striking. The 192 participants in the study said they'd hire almost all of the women *without* children and less than half of those with children. The mothers were assigned an average salary of eleven thousand dollars less and were given fewer vacation days and less leniency over lateness than the nonmothers.

"[W]omen who have children are held to a higher performance standard than women who do not," said Correll, an associate professor of sociology. Interestingly, fatherhood wasn't found to carry the same "liabilities." "We found fathers were in no way disadvantaged. And on several measures they are actually advantaged, such as being seen as more committed to their jobs than nonfathers."

The bias against working mothers falls with particular severity on those in lower-level jobs. Sheila Giles was just about to leave for work when Davohn, her three-year-old son, started vomiting and struggling to breathe. She realized, to her horror, that he'd swallowed a quarter and it had stuck.

Sheila, employed for four years loading semi trucks in Oakland, California, did the only possible thing: she rushed him to the hospital, where he had to undergo surgery to have the coin removed from his esophagus. She did phone her employer, but with two young children at home, family health emergencies had conflicted with work before. When she got back to her job, she discovered that she'd been suspended, then, a short time later, she was fired.

Margo worked for a large Chicago company, cleaning offices at night. When her mom, who usually watches her daughter, fell and needed to go to the emergency room, Margo took her six-year-old with her to work, letting her sleep on various office sofas. The next morning she, too, was fired.

Jeanine, a corrections officer, kept her job, but at a cost. With her husband out on disability, and not sure when he could go back to work, she was afraid to put her position in jeopardy. "But that means never taking off to see my kid in school. Not any of his plays, recitals, nothing. I can't even get to any parent-teacher meetings except the big group one at night where you really can't talk much about your own child," she told me.

Stories like these are rampant among working-class employees—bus drivers, nurse's aides, telephone workers, supermarket cashiers. It's common knowledge: employers who want to support working families should allow for reduced or flexible hours, and—as Joan Williams has suggested—make vacation or personal leave available in increments by the hour to help deal with short-term family emergencies and needs.

And we have to provide our workers with paid sick leave. Barely half of all workers (51 percent) have paid sick days, and only 30 percent have sick days to care for sick children, and they're often penalized for taking them. At least 145 other countries provide paid sick days for short- or long-term illness, recognizing the human and public health costs of forcing sick employees to come to work or to bring their ailing, usually contagious, children to group-care facilities.

"[M]ost companies would be shocked that their policies run counter to the value of family commitment," said professor Williams.

But if that is so, then they have to be told.

Inside Opting Out

Remarkably, none of the hundreds of cases of the early 2000s document-ing outright workplace discrimination against mothers made the head-lines. Our ongoing search for Saddam Hussein, hiding somewhere in Iraq, occupied the news. But one big domestic story did jump off the presses: "The Opting Out Revolution," with the intriguing banner: "Why don't women run the world? Maybe, it's because they don't want to."

The article, written by Lisa Belkin, appeared in the *New York Times Magazine* (October 2003) heralding breaking news: women were ditch-ing their careers to become full-time mothers. Belkin had uncovered an escalating trend. The real *new* normal. The neotraditionalist, stay-at-home mom.

The piece, and the media blitzkrieg it brought, came as a shock to me as well as a lot of my colleagues and friends, especially those who taught and wrote about women's issues and closely followed their employment trends. "How could we have been so wrong?" we asked each other. None of us had picked up on this development. Our research had shown that the major-ity of women, mothers or not, were in the workplace because they *needed* their jobs. Very few had a real choice about whether to quit or stay.

But looking back on the enticing headlines, we shouldn't have been so surprised. The story, filtered through the prism of ideology, followed other major news events of our times—the slim, flawed evidence being seized upon as gospel, anecdotes trumping science, the immediate, uncritical media validation, the undertones of biological predeterminism arguing for traditional gender roles, the gratuitous and inaccurate put-down of femi-nism, and the back-paging of reports and studies disputing its premise.

The Atlanta women, all eight of them who formed the core of Belkin's thesis—"women are rejecting the workplace"—graduated from Princeton, as she did, and had left their high-profile jobs, many of them in tradi-tionally male arenas, so they could take care of their children and stay at home. While Belkin did acknowledge her "elite, successful sample," she argued: "these are the very women who were supposed to be the profes-sional equals of men right now . . . the fact that so many are choosing oth-erwise is explosive."

But the reality is they're *not* choosing otherwise, say economists who've studied the question carefully. Heather Boushey, an economist at the Center for Economic Policy Research, in a study titled "Are Women Opting Out? Debunking the Myth," found a drop in women's—mothers and nonmothers—workforce participation rates between 2001 and 2005 mostly due to a weak labor market. Men's labor rates also dropped during this period. Boushey said, "Mothers today are only half as likely to leave the workforce because of their children than they were in 1984."

"The data stands in opposition to the media frenzy on this topic," said Boushey. Referring to Belkin and others, she said, "Such news stories may lead people to believe that there is a growing trend toward this sort of 'opt out' by highly educated mothers. However, economic data provides no evidence to support these anecdotal accounts."

"The long-term trend," said Heidi Hartmann, MacArthur scholar and founder of the Institute for Women's Policy Research, is "for married women to work more, not less; for women to work more the better educated they are; for women to work more the more they earn." To look at it another way, at the time of Belkin's piece, 63 percent of mothers with preschool-aged children and 78 percent of those with children aged six to seventeen were in the labor force. And the percent of mothers in the workforce was increasing among both groups. In 2005, 42 percent of women said they'd prefer to work outside the home, three years later that number was up to 50 percent.

To bolster her opt-out argument, Belkin quoted a 2003 Catalyst study finding that 26 percent of women in Fortune 500 companies don't yearn to be CEOs. "But," corrected Ilene H. Lang, president of Catalyst, in a letter to the *New York Times*, "in the same study 55 percent of the women *do* want to be CEOs and another 9 percent are undecided. Fifty-one percent of these women have children under the age of eighteen."

The inaccuracies, the scant evidence, the highly selective, unrepresentative population—none of these dimmed the glow of the mom-choosing-home storyline. You couldn't open a paper or journal or turn on a TV without seeing or hearing first-person testimonies of women who'd seen the light. It was "opting out," all the time. *Newsweek*, *Business Week*, *Fortune*, *Time*, and *CBS News* all carried similar stories of career-chucking mothers. Ditto for promising fashion designers who are leaving their jobs to raise children, said *Harper's Bazaar.*

The vote of approval conferred upon the "opting outers" could have gained them a place on the "most popular" page in America's yearbook. Whatever Linda Hardin's daughter decides to do with her life, her mother would support. "But," she admits, "I would be disappointed if she didn't chose to be a stay-at-home mom. . . . I just feel like it's the noblest calling," reported the *Houston Chronicle.* And in an article from Raleigh, North Carolina's, *News and Observer,* a stay-at-home mom is quoted as saying, "I might not get a paycheck, but I get hugs and kisses," as if working mothers aren't immersed in their children's affection.

Not to be outdone by other news outlets, the *New York Times* continued to push versions of the story in what syndicated columnist Bonnie Erbe has called a "bizarre and suspiciously predetermined editorial effort to talk women out of working." In their haste to publish, editors gave front-page status to such pieces as the one by novice reporter Louise Story claiming that many undergraduate women at Yale and other elite colleges say they had already—even as freshmen—decided to pass over their careers in favor of raising children. The article was roundly criticized as being one-sided and based on faulty evidence.

A more recent study conducted at Yale contradicted Story's findings: most young women had the same career expectations as men, but that didn't make it into the *Times.* What did get published was "Stretched to the Limit: Women Stall March to Work," implying that the gender revolution in the workplace had finished, as well as an op-ed for the 2005 Labor Day issue by antifeminist Warren Farrell attributing women's secondary status in the workplace to their own choices rather than to discrimination or the wage gap.

Joan Williams, who has closely followed the press and the opt-out story, said it has been the interpretation "of choice" at the *Times* for decades. And *Nation* columnist Katha Pollitt pointed to the tendency of the *Times* "to write about women dropping out of the workplace without sufficient data to support it."

If the face of Helen of Troy launched a thousand ships, then this story has launched a thousand myths. The opt-out tale became an incontrovertible truth, spawning a cottage industry of publications and seminars dealing with its implications. Books poured forth on teaching women how to transition effectively from work to home and how to help businesses prepare for the exodus of women.

As editor after editor glommed onto this story, it morphed into the master narrative of the new millennium, undermining women who stayed in the workforce. There are a lot of things to be said about the central premise. And one is—we've heard it before. The cover story of *New York* magazine of July 15, 1985, "Second Thoughts on Having It All," opens with Rebecca Murray, a young mother, leaving a great job to stay home with her five-year-old. "So Long Super Mom" and "The End of Razzle-Dazzle Careerism," in other publications, had the same basic message. A coincidence? Not likely, especially when we remember that during the Reagan 1980s attacking working mothers was the new blood sport.

The present-day opt-out stories, whether purposefully or unwittingly, also serve a political agenda. We might not have been able to get our minds around it at the time, but these tales—of the noncompetitive woman, cocooning at home—perfectly express the masculine insecurity of our times.

By focusing on relatively few high-profile women, married to husbands with good if not great salaries, health insurance, and other benefits, the media framed the discussion of women and work with the comforting fiction that women were affirmatively choosing to stay home. The feel-good message—this is a matter of personal will—fit perfectly with the cynical individualism of the Bush years. The *pull* of motherhood, rather than the *push* of employment, left everyone—government, corporations—off the hook.

Recently another interpretation of women's declining employment rates has gained attention. *Equality in Job Loss*, a congressional study released in July 2008, says that women are now in the same boat (sinking though it is) with men. The report documents women's vulnerability to layoffs during the current economic downturn. Women employed in manufacturing and services industries such as transportation and retail, hard hit by the recession of 2001, had a difficult time regaining their positions during the recovery, say the economists. And they're predicting the same will happen in 2009.

With the economy in such terrible shape, it's too soon to speculate whether this will become the new go-to explanation for women's current loss in paid employment. But like the opt-out story, this one also ignores the gale force of discriminatory policies battering women in the labor force. Women "didn't see their employment rates recover to their prerecession peak" in the early 2000s as they had in the recessions of the previous two decades. Why not? Men recovered nicely. The study doesn't explain the difference. But the answer very likely is entwined with the overpowering and underacknowledged workplace bias against women.

When Hunter College sociologist Pamela Stone interviewed stay-at-home moms across the country for a book on professional women who reluctantly "dropped out," she found "many of the women I talked to have tried to work part-time or put forth job-sharing plans, and they're shot down. Work is the real culprit here." In another study, 86 percent of women cite workplace pushes like employers' inflexibility as the reason they stopped working, according to Joan Williams.

Until we recognize and start talking about the harsh, steely tongs of discrimination, inflexibility, and lack of child care and paid sick day leaves—our outmoded and unenlightened corporate and public polices—squeezing mothers out of the workplace, we can't hope to tackle these problems. Also on our agenda should be addressing the unconscionable nonstop demands made on workers of both sexes.

Quality time, considered in the 1980s as the sacred hours carved out of the work day and reserved for children, has become a false idol in the new millennium. Laptops, Blackberries, e-mail—all with great promise of making jobs more flexible, have turned into the technovasion of today, virtually eliminating any ability to shield family life from the intrusive reach of the office.

"For me the idea of being able to take care of my dad in Florida and telecommunicate to my job sounded wonderful a few years ago," Rosalind, a systems engineer at Met Life, told me. "But now the long electronic arm of the office grabs me on weekends and vacations. There's never a break, never the feeling you have any free time. We're on call. Always, every day. We all talk about a life/work balance, but the scales are loaded on one side. And they're not leaning toward making Play-Doh pies."

The excruciatingly real conflict between round-the-clock work and the increasingly isolated, privatized family went a long way toward making the opting-out story so dangerously compelling. From my research I know of hundreds of women across the country—and there are no doubt millions of them—who'd love to be like the women Belkin writes about: to have more time for their children and for themselves, time for book clubs and for midmorning lingering over lattes at Starbucks in "lycra gym clothes" with their friends. But they don't have the option. Opt-out stories very likely made them feel guilty and even resentful that they don't have the choices enjoyed by others.

As for the women who stay home, I think they, too, were done a disservice by the way the narrative was constructed, allowing for a too-optimistic picture of reentry into the workplace and not enough realism about life's uncertainties that might require them to do so. Numerous studies have shown the difficulties women face when they try to restart dormant careers. "Stepping off the career fast track is easy. What's hard is getting back on," notes the *Harvard Business Review*. "Across sectors, women lose a staggering 37 percent of their earning power when they spend three or more years out of the workforce."

Equally problematic, the opt-out story, while placing all the responsibility for taking care of the children and home with the mother, romanticized the "pull" of raising children, often evoking biological predetermination. "It's all in the MRI," one of Belkin's women said, referring to male and female brain differences. Another, Jeannie Tarkenton, who'd just left her job with the Atlanta Girls' School, believes women are born with feelings pulling them to the "stereotypical role of female/mother/caregiver." And Vicky McElhaney Benedict, who left her law firm to care for her children, said, "This is what I was meant to do. I know that's very un-p.c., but I like life's rhythms when I'm nurturing a child."

Writing an editorial about the story in *Time*, one writer waxed euphoric over "these mothers [who] *want* to devote themselves to the raising of their children. They do not want to miss the irreplaceable joys of motherhood.

Work and professional satisfaction may have been their primary concern at some point, but the arrival of children refocuses priorities and raises the largest questions about meaning in life."

The *Time* article quoted Daphne de Marneffe's 2004 book, *Maternal Desire*: "Feminists and American society at large have ignored that basic urge that most mothers feel to spend meaningful time with their children."

A major premise of the mom-choosing-home storyline, winning it needling applause from the right, is the idea that feminism has failed. "Opting out is feminism mugged by reality," brayed Phyllis Schlafly. To which I'd reply, the muggers are really the authors of these opt-out pieces, spreading false and stereotypical opinions. Writes Belkin, "The women's movement was largely about grabbing a fair share of power—making equal money, standing at the helm in the macho realms of business and government and law . . . success required becoming a man. Remember those awful padded-shoulder suits and floppy ties? Success was about the male definition of money and power."

First—and I think it's important to be clear about this—swipes at feminists aren't only against those who define themselves that way, even though that's bad enough. They're against all those who believe in women's autonomy and equality.

And second, as we've seen, the women's movement of the 1970s was about changing every aspect of society that relegated women to inferior status. It called for women to control their own destinies and not to be appendages of men. To the extent that entering the workplace on an equal footing with men empowered women, we fought for it. But to say that all feminists were about is grabbing a piece of the money-pie is reductionism and just plain wrong.

What's also off point is the notion that somehow feminism and motherhood are in opposition. It bears repeating: there is no one-size-fits-all feminism. There are dedicated feminists who have children and dedicated feminists who do not. But I can say this with absolute conviction. Every feminist I know who's a mother cares as deeply and completely about her children as mothers who aren't feminists. And to suggest otherwise—"Soldiers of feminism take only the shortest of maternity leaves"—is harmful and splinters women into adversarial positions.

These stories also perpetuate the impression of a deep generational divide—a fault line separating boomers from generations X and Y. "I don't want to take on the mantle of all womanhood and fight a fight for some sister who isn't really my sister because I don't even know her," said one of Belkin's women, dovetailing with the views of the college students in the Louise Story piece.

As women's studies professor Heather Hewett points out, there's a danger that these women will be seen as representative of Generation X or Y, ignoring the abundant evidence of third-wavers eager to advocate for family-friendly public policy changes.

And it's sheer mythology to suggest, as author Claudia Wallis did in the *Time* piece, that women today stay home because their mothers didn't. "While boomer women sought career opportunities that were unavailable to the mostly stay-at-home moms, Gen Xers were the latchkey kids and the children of divorce."

My research shows little connection between whether mothers worked or not and what their daughters do. And where there was a correlation, it was mostly positive on the side of those with careers. Having a working mother "was a wonderful role model. She was always home in the evenings and morning, which is when we were home. I will always work!" explained one woman, presently getting her master's degree in London.

"It made me work very hard at what I do," a pastry chef in Boston wrote, "to make sure I have something successful to fall back on if something were to happen to my husband." Michelle from New Jersey said, "I grew up knowing that work is something that you need to do, and I have a strong work ethic because of it." Another woman, a sixty-three-year-old from New England, said, "The independence I gained from being raised by a single mother gave me a head start on feminism before we had a name for it."

There were also women like Maggie, an advertising executive in Houston, Texas, who plans to stop working when she has children because she remembers her own working mom was "always too tired at the end of the day" to spend time with her. Some, like Denise, who recently left her corporate job to be with her children, grew up in a household with a mom who didn't work, but was "an ardent feminist and fabulous mother."

For many women, having a stay-at-home mom was ideal, for others, not so much. Susan, a professor of English literature, wrote that she "had a housewife, bored mother and made sure I did not go that route ... though committed to being a primary caretaker of my children, too," while Rosalie, a cancer researcher from Washington, had a stay-at-home mom. "However," Rosalie said, "she was not particularly nurturing, and I and my siblings grew up lonely."

In short, it's the quality of mothering that matters, and this can take many forms. One sixty-seven-year-old who taught figurative sculpture at the U.S. Merchant Marine Academy, the mother of three and one of eight children herself, wrote, "I have seen many different ways of being with children, and what is great for one child is not always great for another."

As the authors of an important study on this subject coming out of the Rochester Mental Health Center have said, "The happier you are with the overall shape of your life, the better parent you will be whether you're home from nine to five or not."

My survey reveals a rich mosaic of women whose decisions about work—whether forced or freely made—are the result of many complex and often intangible factors. But anger and resentment over fast-tracking moms wasn't one of them. In fact I didn't find a lot of generational anger and resentment at all. We've heard so much about second-wavers feeling betrayed by their daughters who aren't embracing the good fight, and about younger women who find our issues irrelevant and outmoded, that it's become a cliché.

Sure, there were those who worried about Generation X and Y women being so blasé about their rights that they'd lose them, and those who thought the boomers were "too judgmental" or some version of that. But mostly what I heard expressed was a great deal of empathy. A thirty-seven-year-old who left a job as corporate director of international employee relations at Dow Jones wrote, "I feel like I set the women's movement back thirty years by stopping work. I have to believe [second-wavers] feel like we have wasted our potential."

And a twenty-eight-year-old single teacher from Vermont wrote, "Based on talking to my mom I think we [young women] take way for granted our starting place in the whole process. I think we're less conscious of how the war is not yet won. And on a positive note, my mom notices that my female friends and I just have the expectation that we can do whatever we want."

Holly, a fifty-year-old CEO of a small nursing home, thought that the different "generations were working to understand one another," and a fifty-seven-year-old retired physician likes "the confidence of the younger women, but worries that so much more is expected of them than was of my cohorts."

When I asked younger women about similarities between "the generation of women responsible for the women's movement of the 1970s and younger women today," I got fairly consistent answers. The young women were "still fighting discrimination, how women are portrayed in media, and even more importantly, treated in society." "Still want equality," one said, and "All want the best for their families and need to fight for it." "Still a man's world. Still unfair!"

Ironically the throttle grip the right has had on the nation possibly has done *some* good, bringing women together again to a renewed understanding: we're all in this together. But whatever the reason, these congruent feelings were, I have to admit, a welcome and surprising discovery.

What didn't surprise me was finding more mommy *accords* than mommy wars. This media-manufactured battle has been around for years, based on the specious notion that most women have a choice about whether or not to work. Its latest incarnation is a result of the equally phony opt-out pandemonium. If the return to full-time mothering is the gold standard, then those who need or want to stay in the workforce aren't making the mark. And nothing gets to mothers more than the suggestion that they're shortchanging their children. It makes working moms feel superguilty and stay-at-home-moms feel superdefensive. And in these seemingly impossible times of the new normal, these feelings have given way to the revved-up, all-encompassing "ultramom." We all know her, she's our daughter, our niece, our friend, ourselves. Overscheduling, overworrying, overinvolved. The consummate micromanager.

As we feel our lives are slipping from our control, when we feel bombarded by overwhelming economic and foreign threats coupled with our own diminishing agency, we become more deeply invested in controlling our children's lives. And this is true whether we work or not. That's why the so-called mommy war is so damaging. It turns women into circular firing squads, taking shots at one another, expending our precious and limited time and energy on such a contrived topic instead of on what's really important.

In 1985, when I called for an end to the first round of mommy wars during the Reagan years, I wrote:

> Working and at-home mothers want the same things for their children: a warm, nurturing environment and quality care. . . . The homemaker knows how easily she can be displaced, and how difficult it might be for her to find a job if she is. The professional must deal with inadequate maternity leaves and the problems of child care. If, however, women accept one another as allies instead of as adversaries, we can try to bring about the changes that will enhance all our lives.

Often, when I reread earlier articles, they sound expectedly dated. This one, unfortunately, has never seemed more relevant.

18

UNPOPULAR CULTURE

Popular culture is our shared social reality, communicating stories, images, and ideas about who we are and how we should feel, think, and act. It powerfully reflects the most salient features of our society. But the images women see of themselves are as distorted as those in funhouse mirrors. Instead of realistic portrayals we're barraged with minimizing deviations—the sultry schoolgirl, the consumerist chick, the militant manhunter, the cold-hearted careerist. Shaped and dominated by a mass media overwhelmingly in the hands of men, popular culture has engaged in years of misogynist maligning, embracing and perpetuating sidelining strategies.

As it simultaneously authenticates and reinforces male fantasies, biases, and fears, popular culture sabotages our value as human beings and gives tacit permission, if not outright encouragement, to women's degradation, browbeating us into hypercritical ways of seeing our accomplishments.

Whatever its source—movies, television shows, video games, advertisements—the cumulative weight of our popular culture exercises an effective form of control. It tells us in so many ways: forget how much you bring to your family and to society, how hard you work, how much you've achieved, how good a person/friend you are—what matters is your six-year-old's soccer scores and the shape of your thighs.

Even as adults, we get sucked into this way of thinking. Imagine how the peddling of stereotypical portrayals affects our daughters, who are constantly assaulted by damaging cultural imperatives.

233

The New Bullies on the Block

"Haven't I told you girls are evil?" says author Rosalind Wiseman, after giving a recent workshop at the all-female National Cathedral school in Washington, D.C.

Cyberslamming. Verbal grenades. Exclusion. Humiliation.

These pejorative terms, and more, are being lavishly applied to the behavior of adolescent girls. How did the radical shift in our thinking about girls come about? Why did girls suddenly change from a population we were afraid *for* to one we're afraid *of*?

A fast rewind to the 1992 report published by the American Association of University Women, *How Schools Shortchange Girls*, provides some clues. Remember how that study and similar ones motivated a renewed commitment to gender equity in education, leading to a blossoming of "girl power"? And how the backlash against giving girls attention materialized into the largely bogus "boy crisis"?

But when poverty, oversized classes, too few books, frustrated teachers, unhappy home lives, and a damaging conception of manliness were proven to be the real villains, and the boy crisis couldn't be pinned on audacious girls, another line of attack was launched to keep girls down.

Reports of malicious middleschoolers flew off the presses, and a new term—"relational aggression"—was interjected into our vocabulary by a determined army of mental health experts.

"Feminists have done too good a job empowering girls," so the new spin said, allegedly resulting in a generation of "manipulative, subversive and aggressive girls," wrote Jessica Ringrose in *Feminism and Psychology*. For all our good intentions, it seemed we had created a generation of minimonsters.

The "new bully" in the schoolyard is no longer the big kid with the football sweatshirt. Today she's thin and pretty, wearing Seven jeans and dashing off for weekly manicures. And she's high-tech. Using the Internet and instant messaging, this tyrant of the middle school controls her underlings through gossip, rumor, and backstabbing.

Starting in the early 2000s, our popular culture was afire with news of a massive upsurge in girl-to-girl cruelty. Windows letting us peer into the darkly vicious world of girldom came from a rash of books: Rachel Simmons's *Odd Girl Out*, Emily White's *Fast Girls*, Rosalind Wiseman's *Queen Bees and Wannabes*, Hayley DiMarco's *Mean Girls* and *Mean Girls Gone*.

Some of the books—*Odd Girl Out*, for example—also advise girls how to develop their own identities, but that message got buried underneath the meanness hype. "Adolescent bitchery" made for major coverage. A few of the authors appeared on *The Oprah Winfrey Show* and saw their works win spots on bestseller lists. The most popular purveyors of this new genre have fully booked calendars of training sessions, workshops, and conferences. The Ophelia Project is a national organization formed to eradicate relational aggression and bullying. The name, taken from Mary Piper's *Reviving Ophelia*, a book dedicated to giving adolescent girls a voice, is now being used by the movement to stifle it.

"Girls Just Want to Be Mean," declared the *New York Times Magazine* and other mainstream media that peddled their own mean-girl exposés. Among the most ornery of the breed were depicted in the 2004 movie *Mean Girls*. In this over-the-top parody, Cady (Lindsay Lohan), who'd been home-taught in Africa, enters a public high school where she faces the do-or-die task of navigating her way around the ice queens, called plastics, the clique of choice, curiously referred to in the *New Yorker* review as "the second wave."

As Cady first rejects then accepts the "in" group, led by the vindictive Regina George (Rachel McAdams), who's fully capable of stomping out anyone trying to bring her down with the heel of her Jimmy Choo, the audience gets to see a bunch of girls in tank tops embracing their inner nazism—a theme played out every week on network TV in the wildly popular show *Gossip Girl* (*GG*). By the time they reach high school, the rival *GG* queen bees Serena and Blair presumably have had plenty of years to perfect their cunning manipulation. Girls start on the path to meanness as early as three years old, reports a study conducted at Brigham Young University.

Girls *and* boys can be pretty nasty to one another at times, as anyone who has children or has worked with them knows. And cruelty and ostracism should be dealt with at once. But, as one woman said, "This has been going on for years. I am fifty-eight years old, and girls were mean back in the 1950s when I was in grade school and junior high." The question is, why is it all over the news now?

We have to wonder about the timing—why something endemic to growing up has suddenly become such a big topic and big business? Why not celebrate girls' capacity for friendship and loyalty—traits most of us who've worked with differing populations of teens find much more compelling and prevalent than their capacity for competitive backstabbing.

Rachel Simmons, the guru of female meanness, thinks we've all become attuned to the dangers of bullying because of the Columbine shootings. But since the perpetrators in all the school massacres have been male, and the victims in many cases exclusively female, this doesn't really explain what researchers and feminist scholars like Dawn Currie and Deirdre M. Kelly are calling "a moral panic over female meanness."

Could it be because this moral panic, like the others before it, is being used to serve a distinct social purpose? Could it be because focusing on meanness provides an excuse to cut back on programs supporting the newly self-reliant adolescent girls our present society finds so threatening?

If we follow the transition from girls at risk to fears of female power by pathologizing assertiveness and aggression, we'll see how the next step—reducing girls to passive sex objects—follows logically in this cycle of marginalization.

From Middle School Meanies to Tween Temptresses

"I want it, Mommy, puhleeze . . . puhleeze!"

A little girl no older than six was sprawled across the aisle, clinging to a Halloween costume and screaming in a voice high pitched enough to break glass. Shoppers bunched up around her, my daughter, Ali, and I among them. There were a few irritated murmurs and groans of exasperation.

It was one of those please-let-me-vanish-into-thin-air mothering moments. I could see the effort the mom was making to stay calm, bending over her daughter, reasoning quietly. But everything she did only resulted in more shrieking. "I want it! I want it!"

The man next to me covered his ears. Finally the mother, flushing with humiliation, peeled her daughter off the large plastic bag. Now we got to see what all the fuss was about.

I couldn't believe it. A Naughty Nurse costume!

It was impossible not to stare. The large picture showed a young girl dressed in white fishnet stockings, high heels, and a satiny candy-stripper mini with a matching bustier. One hand was at her thrust-out hip, the other holding a syringe as if it were a sex toy.

I directed my gaze to the bottom row and took in the other costumes— Transylvania Temptress, Frisky French Maid, and Little Miss Handy Candy—all with shiny bright fabrics, lots of sparkles, knee-high boots, plunging necklines, and fluffy boas. How could these be for the six-year-old set? But there they were, and all in easy reach of little hands. A clash of parent-child wills just waiting to happen.

Meanwhile the situation on the ground rapidly deteriorated. The little girl was writhing on the floor staging a level-five hissy fit. You could almost see the flashing words in the bubble over her mom's head: "I'm not a bad mother. Really I'm not." I watched her expression go from horrified to resigned. With rapid-fire motion, she yanked a fresh Naughty Nurse off the hook and scooped up her daughter. I gave her a sympathetic smile, but she'd already turned her head, anxiously looking for the checkout counter.

"I WONDERED IF I'd accidentally wandered into 'Sluts R Us,'" Rachel Mosteller wrote on Blogging Baby about her search for her children's Halloween costumes. She hoped her little ones would have no idea about the meaning behind names like Handy Candy—a sentiment widely shared by other moms who'd had similar experiences.

While Halloween for boys hasn't changed much—the same blood-dripping masks and ghoulish garb—"costumes for girls have traded silly and sweet for skimpy and sexy," reported James Fussell in the *Kansas City Star* (October 29, 2006). "It's a strange time we live in when half the doctors are women, and half the lawyers are women, and all the little girls are prancing around in sexy costumes," said Albany family therapist Lindy Guttman. Her comment is right on target. Precisely because of the anxiety over women's achievements, marketers are pushing marginalizing costumes on our daughters.

"The real horror on Halloween is that on the one night when girls could let their imaginations run wild, they're encouraged to be sexy divas or French maids," Guttman says.

"In effect, we're telling girls to dream small and dream sexy. And that's wrong," adds Sharon Lamb, author of *Packaging Girlhood: Rescuing our Daughters from Marketers' Schemes.*

And it's not only on Halloween. From all around the country, women wrote to me of their difficulties in finding everyday clothes for their daughters "that don't make them look like tramps."

"Tell me," one asked, "why are stores displaying padded bras for six- and seven-year-olds? Is this so they'll look like Paris or Britney? We need help!"

"Low-rise jeans for nine-year-olds are a really bad idea; they make girls think the only way to attract attention is by exposing their bodies," said another; and a third woman worried about the "message we're giving our kindergartners when we buy them microminis and black lace camis."

Few topics inspired more universal outrage among these mothers than hypersexualized clothing, especially those women who have older daughters and have seen a dramatic change in what's now being marketed to their younger ones.

It's called age compression—a term used by advertising companies to push adult products to younger and younger children, pandering to the idea that kids equate being "grown up" and "cool" with sexy. Research shows that eleven-year-olds don't consider themselves children anymore. "Children always have liked to emulate older kids . . . [and] being more grown-up in a society that is highly sexualized means being sexual," said professor and author Gary Cross.

Our culture is so saturated with sexual imagery that many parents aren't even aware of how inappropriate some of the clothing is. "Even if adults object in the beginning, they can become desensitized if exposed to a product long enough," points out Diane Levin, author of *So Sexy So Soon.*

"It's advertisers who create the demand," said Shari Graydon, an expert on beauty stereotypes and advertising. "And it's very difficult to be alone in your stance against that." You get pressure "from your kid, who feels pressured by . . . peers who feel themselves driven by media ideals—there's a whole system behind it."

"It's also a matter of buying what is being offered, especially at affordable prices," Levin noted. Chain stores like Target and the Gap are loaded with racks of what one journalist called "tarts-in-training" clothing—bikinis, leather pants, spandex shorts, cropped tops, even thongs for seven-year-olds being sold with a picture of a cherry and the words EAT ME or WINK WINK on them.

Licensing and branding have become the way to market directly to girls and young women, undermining parental authority, said Diane Levin. Marketers see a demographic ripe for takeover, spending upward of twelve billion dollars a year targeting girls. Some companies even hire "cool hunters" and "cultural spies" to infiltrate the teen world and help spot the latest trends. Teens (defined as those aged twelve to nineteen), usually unencumbered by the need to pay rent or health insurance, shop an average of fifty-four times per year. The most popular novels for girls reveal an "incessant litany of brand names." One study of the Gossip Girl, Clique, and A-List series of books found an average of one brand mentioned per page. Consumption, more than romance, is the newly minted key to an adolescent girl's heart.

It's an open secret that corporations play on the insecurities of teens by making them believe that to be really "in" they must have their product. This strategy is put to good use in the proliferating teen and 'tween magazines. For years *Seventeen*, *Teen*, and *YM* dominated the market. Now a complete list would reach the hundreds. "Magazines . . . promote sexy images and then encourage girls to buy makeup and clothing to look like the models and celebrities they feature," observed Sharon Lamb.

I'm Too Sexy for My . . . Own Well-Being

"[T]here's definitely a disturbing emergence over the past two decades of highly eroticized images of young women, and they're getting younger and younger," says media expert Jane Tallim. It's in the shows they watch, the magazines they read, the ads they see, the Web they surf. One study found an average twelve-year-old is exposed to 280 sexy images on a normal day.

To sell its clothes, American Apparel uses nonmodels like prepubescent "Lynanne," "Abrielle," or "Jessica" in highly suggestive, often topless poses. Calvin Klein, Guess, and Abercrombie and Fitch all have sexualized advertising campaigns, and Target stores recently captured attention with billboards of a young girl lying spread-eagle, a large bull's eye painted over her crotch.

"A patty with two flat buns!" A seductive teacher dancing on a desktop is trying to interest her students in that delicious combo from Tennessee's Carl's Jr. restaurant. Even Clearasil, the tried-and-true acne medicine, is getting sexy, showing a boy sitting between his girlfriend and her mother looking at naked baby pictures of the daughter. "You should see me now," the girl says provocatively to her boyfriend. And in an ad for the popular Juicy brand, a girl no more than ten years old looks fetchingly over her shoulder, the word JUICY stamped across her bottom.

Sex sells. There's nothing new in that. But what's new is the ads aimed at girls as young as eight years old featuring masturbation, dismembered bodies, fetishism, domination, and control—material so frankly erotic it borders on the pornographic. Fifteen years ago, we would have been shocked to see these images in adult fashion magazines. Now they're ubiquitous in our daughters' world.

While we can all agree that toys and video games promoting violence in little boys are bad—even, as Diane Levin points out, when we're not doing a good job of controlling it—we certainly don't want to condemn sex. What we want is for our children to learn about sex gradually, in a healthy, age-appropriate way so they'll feel comfortable with their bodies and sexuality. This is the key to developing sound, mutually respectful relationships later on. But, say the experts, everything about today's popular culture conflicts with those goals.

Girls are being inundated with sexual messages they can't understand and might find frightening. Unlike healthy sexuality, the *sexualization* of girls provides a very narrow definition of femaleness with a focus exclusively on appearance. This constricted identity "leads to a host of negative emotional consequences such as shame, anxiety, and even self-disgust," says a recent report released by the American Psychological Association (APA).

When sexual allure becomes girls' only path to power and self-worth, the roles of achievement, talent, and being a decent person are diminished. Reduced concentration at school might be the first sign of difficulty. Eating disorders, depression, and unsafe and early sex often follow. The onslaught of sexual images is encouraging a whole generation of girls to think about and treat their bodies as sexual objects, *things* for others' use.

This lack of self-regard is behind what many educators see as "rampant oral sex." At one posh private school the girls engaging in this practice are known as the "senior tools."

"We're called that," said the eighth-grader, blushing slightly, "because it means we 'service' older boys with blow jobs."

"But why do you do it?" I asked.

"Because it makes me feel like I'm popular, and the senior boys talk to me when they pass me in the hall."

IN IDENTIFYING HARMFUL influences on girls such as clothing styles, celebrity antics, and music videos, the APA report singled out one toy—the Bratz doll. With her sloe eyes, pillowy lips, black leather jacket, and red crocodile boots, this self-proclaimed fashion fiend is marketed to girls as young as four. Wearing thick eye makeup and lipstick, with the requisite mobile phones and coarse jewelry, Bratz dolls are more lap dancer than little girl. Their adventures, described in their "sold separately books," include all-night parties and holidays in Las Vegas. Bratz represents the new trend among toy marketers: kids getting older younger, or KGOY.

On a shopping trip to a Maryland Toys R Us, one father likened the Wicked Twin Bratz dolls to streetwalkers. Spunky "always causes trouble," Sparkly was "in love with her reflection." Both were clad in black chokers, tight black T-shirts with BAD GIRL written across them, low-slung skirts—one chartreuse, one hot pink—and one bare-legged, the other in fishnet stockings and lace-up high-heeled boots.

Approximately two billion dollars' worth of Bratz are sold each year, and while that's still less than half of Barbie's numbers, she makes the blond bombshell, who in her heyday pursued careers as a business exec and surgeon, seem as staid as our great-aunt Mildred and as old-fashioned as Betsy-Wetsy dolls.

"When Barbie was in her prime, girls were taught to be career women, to be men's equals," said Bratz product designer Paula Treantafelles. "Today, yes, career and education matter, but it's also 'express yourself, have your own identity, girl power.'"

But there's nothing powerful about a doll that promotes only "fashion and fantasy" and calls herself "boy crazy," say those concerned about girls' development. These experts put Bratz in the same category as underage cigarette smoking or drinking alcohol—activities that might make youngsters feel important and powerful but actually have a "toxic impact."

Competing with Bratz for the six-year-old soul and a share of the profits is the princess. Like Bratz, it too is a marketer's dream come true. Disney's scheme to market all eight Disney princess characters together is fast becoming the "most successful marketing venture ever."

"Your hair is, like, so princess today!" girls say to one another, using the word as a noun-adjective.

"My daughter, April, has all the costumes," Becka, an employment lawyer, told me. "Every day before I leave we decide which character she's going to be that night. It's really something," Becka said with an ironic smile, "to see this little African American girl dressed up as Ariel in a red wig and asking 'Do I look beautiful?'"

Princess birthday parties, sleepovers, dinners—the variety of princess events is seemingly limitless. The appeal to consumerism is limitless as well. Each princess has her "must have" accessories: music videos, storybooks, bedding, wallpaper, party supplies, and of course the tiaras, plastic high heels, wands, wigs, and long gowns in pastel colors.

Costumes differ with the characters, but their backstories are strikingly similar. The princesses are "beautiful," possessing all the traditional feminine qualities: "soft-spoken," "gentle ways," "kindness and patience." Even those who are feisty, like mermaid Ariel, come to realize "there is something to be gained from a father's wisdom."

Whatever adventures the princesses embark upon, they quickly find they need protection and rescuing by dwarfs, fairy godmothers, and the ultimate savior—the handsome prince. "By the time Sleeping Beauty [Aurora] is awakened from her slumber by the Prince, she has been transformed from a sheltered girl into a mature young woman ready to become a bride." Love and marriage are the ultimate and only goals worthy of a princess.

During a recent family trip to Disney World, the princess phenomenon was inescapable. Everywhere we turned in that ninety-degree heat, little girls, tottering on heels and encased in fitted satiny affairs over rustling crinolines, paraded off to princess breakfasts and banquets. Mothers told me they paid upward of four hundred dollars for the gowns and makeup. But, once dressed up, the little girls were stuck in the princess mode, unable to go on any of the rides, some barely able to walk. They became identical to the rarified creatures implied by their costumes—inanimate, decorative objects to be assisted and admired.

The princess/Bratz split is simply an expression of the classic madonna/whore syndrome projected onto young girls: the good girl versus the bad girl, saintly versus sexy, idealization versus denigration: a facet of being rather than a human being. Both extremes place limitations on little girls' abilities to dream big, to see themselves as architects of their own lives. To imagine the unimaginable for themselves. And then when they're older, to make it happen.

With apologies to Robert Browning, a girl's reach should exceed her grasp, or what else is girlhood for?

19

MISSING AT THE MULTIPLEX

"Where are all the girls?" actress Geena Davis kept asking herself as she watched videos of children's movies and television shows with her preschool-age daughter. Where were the girl ninjas, the girl puppy dogs, the animated adventuresome little girls? Why did male characters dominate the speaking parts?

Davis, whose parts in *Thelma & Louise*, *A League of Their Own*, and the television series about the first female president, *Commander in Chief*, challenged and transformed our thinking about women's roles in motion pictures and in society, had hit upon something vastly important.

How young girls, adolescents, and adult women are portrayed on screen—ditsy, uncertain, passive, and sacrificing all for love, or strong, confident, and high achieving—deeply affects how we see ourselves. And, unfortunately, there are far more of the former depictions than the latter.

"We know that kids learn their value by seeing themselves reflected in the culture," said Davis. "They say, 'I see myself! I must matter. I must count. There I am.'" But the message we're sending our children is that girls and women are worth less and that their worth is different from boys and men. "[B]oys are the norms, girls the variation: boys are central, girls peripheral; boys are individuals, girls types. Boys define the group, its story, and its code of values. Girls exist only in relation to boys."

This is damaging for girls, but it also is for boys. They're seeing a world in which females are devalued, and they're learning to take this same worldview into their future relationships. Gender stereotyping poses a severe threat to the equality of the sexes. But when Davis tried to talk about gender with a Hollywood mogul whose studio does a lot of family films, he balked. "No, no, not *us*! We're all over this issue."

What he meant, Davis said, is we have *one* female in each of our movies. The only way to persuade the power brokers, she realized, was to get data. She founded the nonprofit Geena Davis Institute on Gender and Children in the Media (GDIGM) with that goal in mind. Davis, working with professor Stacy Smith of the University of Southern California Annenberg School of Journalism, began to look at gender depictions in the media. Their discovery—gender imbalance reigns across the media—has been confirmed by numerous other studies and researchers.

"No Room for a Womb!" Stereotyped, Hypersexualized, and Silent

That's the lot of women in movies today. In looking at four thousand female film characters from talking turtles to suburban moms, studies showed women much more likely than men to be in decorative or sexually alluring positions, to exhibit traditional behavior (no jobs, no adventures), and to see romance as their purpose in life and have improbably perfect bodies.

"They have no room for a womb!" Amy Pascal, cochair of Sony Pictures, exclaimed, commenting on the ridiculous way animated female characters' bodies are anatomically contrived.

What's really surprising is that the disparities between male and female characters are vast in the movies parents think are the safest and best for their children—the G-rated. Over the past fifteen years, a study of the 101 top-grossing G-rated movies, made for children under the age of eleven, revealed upward of 75 percent of all the characters to be male; these characters, not surprisingly, dominated the speaking roles.

As one father noted of *Toy Story* (1995), "It's a marvelous movie, funny, clever . . . but Bo Peep is the only female toy with a speaking part." The popular *Bee Movie* (2007) also has far fewer girl bees than boy bees in talking roles. The mother (Kathy Bates) of the star, Barry B. Benson (Jerry Seinfeld), is a prototype of the nagging, complaining woman. Barry's friend, the human florist Vanessa Bloom (Renée Zellweger), is a much nicer character, but not a very effective one. Although Vanessa is physically bigger and more savvy, it is Barry who is in charge. He's smarter and more capable, devising the scheme to save the world's flowers when they're on the verge of extinction. To accomplish this, Barry and Vanessa have to fly an airplane by themselves. Vanessa takes the controls, but she quickly becomes flustered. Barry slaps her face, presumably to get her to focus, but it is an inexcusable act, trivializing, even normalizing violence toward women. While clearly this wasn't the intended message, movie producers need to pay close attention to what is conveyed by their work.

G-rated movies deliver a pernicious message to our children: girls' contributions, perspectives, and voices are not as important as boys'. And because children have access to a lot of videos and DVDs at home—most have at least twenty, according to one survey—and usually watch the same videos multiple times, these lessons are constantly reinforced.

Even movies in which girls are the main characters, such as *The Princess Diaries* (2001) and *What a Girl Wants* (2003), don't portray them as complex, fully developed people. Mia Thermopolis (Anne Hathaway) and Daphne Reynolds (Amanda Bynes), both unhappy commoners from America, get to travel abroad and find themselves transformed into royalty in one movie and quasi-royalty in the other. There's lots of time spent getting made up and made over, dressing in gowns and going to balls. If this reminds you of Cinderella, it's supposed to. *What a Girl Wants* even mentions the fairy tale in case we didn't get the connection. In these and similar genre movies, the female roles are as light and narrow as a glass slipper, and just as transparent. What a girl wants turns out to be glamour and romance. Who would have guessed?

Adult movie plots are iterations of the same neutralizing theme, often presented in far worse plots. In the opening minutes of *Touristas* (2006) we see a doctor reflected in the pupil of a young woman strapped to an operating table in the jungles of Brazil. There are enough terrible instruments around for us to know right off the bat that we're not on the set of *ER*. It looks more like a medieval torture chamber, and this patient is in for some terrible punishment. What has she done? Well, actually, nothing. As the doctor performs his anesthesia-less surgery, he rants about all the

United States has taken from his country: sugar, land, sexual innocence. And a woman, any woman, must pay for our nation's rapaciousness. But we can hardly follow the doctor's tirade. We're simultaneously riveted and revolted by the close-ups of him extracting the woman's organs one by one.

Touristas is symbolic of how women are treated in recent movies. Most, of course, are not torture-porn, although *Hostel* (2005) and *Hostel II* (2007) are two popular examples. (*Hostel* earned nineteen million dollars on its first weekend and snagged the number one spot for a week.) But in even those films attempting to be lighthearted and funny, vital parts of women have been *figuratively* removed, leaving us eviscerated and empty shells.

Some of these identity-searing films are lumped together as chick flicks—one of the best ways "to dismiss a movie so sappy or saccharine only a girl could like it, it has [become] . . . the dread communist or terrorist of cinematic allegations—one random accusation and it's all over," one critic said.

Terms such as *chick flick* and *chick lit* categorize and diminish women. The word *chick* has become OK-speak for a whole generation who use it liberally to describe themselves and their friends. But just as the use of *boy* for an adult male African American was rightly considered deliberately demeaning, so the word *chick* for a woman is freighted with negative connotations. It conjures up a person who is flighty, vacuous, passive, overly emotional, and dedicated to finding romance at all costs. And the fact that women, along with men, have embraced this term doesn't make it any less derogatory, only more worrisome.

The movie *13 Going on 30* (2004) is advertised as a feel-good chick flick. But it only feels good to those who think a high-powered career is synonymous with bitchiness and a miserable life. In this movie spanning adolescent and adult worlds—and audiences—Jenna Rink (Jennifer Garner), a nerdy, MTV-watching girl, longs to be part of the "six chicks," the supermean, fashion-obsessed in-group. After a horrendous thirteenth birthday party, Jenna has two wishes: to be accepted by the bossy babes at her school and to be thirty years old.

Thanks to some magical dust, she's catapulted forward seventeen years and wakes up to her future life as a beautiful and sexy editor at a top fashion magazine with a Fifth Avenue apartment, closets stuffed with designer clothing, and a hockey player boyfriend. Her dream has come true. She has everything the "six chicks" had.

But, to her horror, she's turning into one of them—malicious, competitive, and sniping at other women. Her coworkers are no better—teenage nasties in grown-up clothes. (Won't someone please do a movie about women supporting one another on the job?) And Jenna's personal life is the pits. She's not close to her family and yearns to reconnect with her best male friend. Fortunately, *she* can go back again. And—no surprise here—she does.

A cautionary tale, *13 Going on 30* is a warning to all those cold-hearted career women who have frozen out their "natural yearnings" for husband and family. So many executive emotional wrecks (EEWs) march across the silver screen I checked the credits to make sure the Independent Women's Forum didn't have a hand in their production.

In *Sweet Home Alabama* (2002) Melanie Carmichael (Reese Witherspoon), a successful and troubled New York fashion designer engaged to the mayor's (Candice Bergen) son (Patrick Dempsey), is ready to toss her simple southern life and estranged husband aside like an old hoop skirt until she literally has to don one again and discovers the joys of being an unemployed, old-fashioned southern belle. But then again, having the uptight, elitist mayor as mother-in-law might make any girl want to drown herself in a punch bowl of mint juleps to escape from marrying her son.

Similarly the roles of art dealer Madeleine (Embeth Davidtz) in *Junebug* (2005), work-obsessed Meredith (Sarah Jessica Parker) in *The Family Stone* (2006), and the explosive owner of a California ad agency, Amanda (Cameron Diaz), of *Holiday* (2007) all popularize the "career stifles personal happiness" ethos.

"The one thing she was successful at was business," Sarah Jessica Parker said in an interview about her character. "I think she thought she could apply that same theory to human beings. . . . She's not a murderer, she's just someone who is not great with interpersonal relationships."

Many EEWs are able to spin their lives back into the traditional line before the reel ends. Their aha moments are usually brought to them by children, either those they'll never have (childlessness is now the de facto fate of a woman with a career) or those they suddenly acquire.

Lanie Kerrigan (Angelina Jolie) of *Life or Something Like It* (2002) is a hard-driving Seattle television reporter who has her eye on making it to the big time. She has all the accoutrements of the good life, the (requisite) shallow—in this case baseball-playing—boyfriend and a great apartment and career. But when a homeless psychic tells her she has only one week left on earth, she is shocked into a total life makeover. Suddenly she realizes how meaningless all her accomplishments are; she marries her loyal, good-hearted cameraman with the young son, and scales back her professionalism.

When her job takes her to New York to interview her role model, the famous, tough-edged journalist Deborah Connors (Stockard Channing), she has an epiphany. Asking Connors if she has any regrets about her life—"for instance you have no children?"—she sends the paragon of the icy interview into a meltdown, filled with tears and regrets. This scene perfectly conveys what author Eric Hoffer called "the temper of the times." We have the older woman (second-waver?) who sacrificed family and happiness for a career, and the younger woman who will make more life-enhancing choices.

Raising Helen (2004) and *No Reservations* (2007) are both essentially updated versions of *Baby Boom*. In each, a self-centered, self-indulgent careerist has the proverbial "everything in life" except, of course, love. But when a sister dies, Helen (Kate Hudson) and Kate (Catherine Zeta-Jones) suddenly become mommies with a capital M. As these characters undergo a baptism-by-fire initiation into the unpredictable young world of homework and sniffles, their careers—one is a modeling agent with a major firm, the other top chef at a plush New York restaurant—fall apart. Watching the inevitable, you have to wonder why these young women, clearly talented, creative, and resourceful, don't seek help from the experts—other single mothers (most with a lot less at their disposal than these two). The simple question—how do you arrange for after-school care?—would have kept them from being so overwhelmed and defeated. But being defeated by attempting to have it all is exactly the point these movies are making.

The new arrivals in the women's lives change them into the women they were meant to be: kinder, softer, more caring adaptations of themselves who are now ripe for romance. Helen finds love only after she renounces her career entirely, while Kate follows her chef/boyfriend's dream to open his own restaurant, now a family affair.

These movies are vehicles for cultural harrying; each one delivers a sidelining version of retro-womanhood. Whether it's Renée Zellweger as Bridget Jones, Diane Keaton the interfering mother, Daphne in *Because I Said So*, or J-Lo as Mary Fiore in *The Wedding Planner*, our popular movies encourage women to see themselves as empty vessels of longing, demeaning and compromising themselves to find the perfect man.

Movies featuring black women reveal a different kind of stereotype. "Her onscreen presence takes on many variations," wrote Jeremy W. Peters for the *New York Times*, "but she is easily recognizable by a few defining traits. In addition to her size" she "typically finds herself in an exchange that is either confrontational or embarrassing." There's nothing wrong with depicting large-sized women, but if a character can only accept her body because—as in *Phat Girlz*—three doctors from Nigeria are attracted to the curvy, would-be fashion-designer character, Jazmin (Mo'Nique), and her equally zaftig friend, then these are just more stereotypes aimed at narrowing rather than expanding the possibilities for women.

When women try to transcend the sexual barriers keeping them benched, as Maggie Fitzgerald (Hilary Swank) does in the award-winning *Million Dollar Baby* (2004), they find themselves down for the count. Maggie is determined and feisty. She works hard to get the disillusioned Frankie Dunn (Clint Eastwood) to overcome his prejudices about women boxers and agree to train her. At first Maggie seems destined for stardom, duking it out in the ring with the best of them. But there are no soft landings here.

Maggie quickly becomes a stand-in for Frankie's estranged daughter, and when she fails to follow her "father's" advice to "always protect yourself," she ends up a quadriplegic whose legs must be amputated if she's to survive. The film makes us think about euthanasia, loss, and redemption, but it pulls no punches about its meaning: when women enter the male arena, they're going to be cut to pieces.

This hacking away at women has continued to the point where there's nothing left of them in movies today. For thirty years Hollywood watchers have complained about a dearth of leading female roles in major motion pictures, and the numbers now are dwindling down to practically zero. The overall scene is bad for white women; for black women it's even worse. When Halle Berry received the Oscar for *Monster's Ball* (2001), she became the first African American woman to win in the Best Actress category. (Whoopi Goldberg in *Ghost* [1990] and Hattie McDaniel in *Gone with the Wind* [1939] had already broken the barrier for Best Supporting Actress.)

What's of specific concern to women in Hollywood is the "disappearance of many of the movie world's most visible female power brokers," wrote Sharon Waxman in the *New York Times* (April 26, 2007). While women made some modest gains during the 1990s, there's been a decrease from 19 percent of women holding decision-making roles in these industries to less than 16 percent today, where one insider said, "sexism . . . is not seen as a negative but a badge of honor."

Within the span of little more than a year, three of the four women at top positions at major studios have left. Nina Jacobson, president of Disney, Gail Berman, head of Paramount, and Stacey Snider, chairwoman of Universal Pictures, have all been replaced by men.

Whether or not Warner Brothers' president, Jeff Robinov, really said, "We're no longer doing movies with women in the lead," as has been widely reported, it's becoming painfully obvious that women are being pushed aside in movies today. By one count of the thirty top-earning films released in 2007, not one had a female lead character. A review of *There Will Be Blood*, nominated for an Oscar as the best motion picture, noted, "Like most of the finest American directors working now, Mr. Anderson makes little onscreen time for women."

"I feel like it's a different time; it's not the time that it was," said Lynda Obst, the producer of several popular films including *How to Lose a Guy in 10 Days*. Now she has to fight to get her work in production. While she didn't feel specific prejudice directed against her, she said, "It's not like the heyday, either. It's a boy's era. And the market is driving that."

"In general, female markets have been underserved, and the over-twenty-five female audience is one that's dramatically underserved, said Lionsgate's Tom Ortenberg. "You could speculate that it's because this is a male-driven world with people green-lighting the movies they feel more close to," he observed.

"You don't see companies saying 'More than half of this population is women, we should design a slate to [reflect that],'" said Lindsay Doran, an independent producer and former head of United Artists. In her review of the 2009 movie *He's Just Not That into You*, noted film critic Manohla Dargis wrote, "To judge by the recent crop of what are often sneeringly referred to as chick flicks, today's woman wants designer threads, extravagant weddings and a generous helping of public humiliation served up with a laugh mostly at her expense."

Not much has changed. Two years earlier, Dargis wrote, "All you have to do is to look at the movies themselves, at the decorative blondes and brunettes smiling and simpering at the edge of the frame, to see just how irrelevant we have become."

Women's absences are particularly evident in the new wave of fast-flying, incredible-feat-performing superhero movies. *Iron Man, The Incredible Hulk, Indiana Jones, Ant-Man, Thor, Kung Fu Panda, Hellboy II, Batman*—a whole battalion of superbly endowed creatures have landed in our post-9/11 society on a collective rescue mission of the American male.

Spider-Man, the first of this genre, achieved popularity in fall 2001, giving a reassuring shot of testosterone to a nation of uncertainty. We projected our fears and anxieties on his larger-than-life battles. To a society cut to the core, threatened by new and unfamiliar foes and deeply worried about its ability to vanquish them, *Spider-Man* allowed the comforting belief in someone who could conquer the forces of darkness and return justice to the world.

In the years since the terrorist attacks, traditional sources of manliness have been pummeled even further. Invincible anti-evil crusaders provide the perfect fantasy for insecure masculinity. And if the box office is any indication, they'll be flying across the silver screen for some time to come.

The one notable exception to the hailing males of Hollywood is the movie *Sex and the City* (*SATC*), a smash hit racking up fifty-seven million dollars on its opening weekend. Just about every reviewer mentioned the gal pals responsible for this spectacular success, just as they made much of male absence (except for gay men, who are presumably big fans).

Of course, there's the old adage in Tinsel Town that women will see a "male" movie, but not vice versa. Still, the way men dissed *SATC* (most without having seen it) hints at something deeper going on. Perfectly wonderful men shuddered in horror at the very mention of the movie. They seemed absolutely phobic, as though watching a movie about four devoted friends who together wielded power and authority was an affront to their manhood.

"In an Internet Movie Database poll, 7,197 men voted to give *SATC* an average score of 3.8—that puts it among the worst movies of the year," reported Ramin Setoodeh in *Newsweek* (June 16, 2008). Male reviewers were particularly nasty. Anthony Lane wrote in *The New Yorker* that the movie "was more like a TV show on steroids. . . . All the film lacks is a subtitle, 'The Lying, the Bitch and the Wardrobe.' David Poland at Hot Button said, "The only genuinely emotional moment I experienced in this film came to pass in a moment where the characters actually shut up for a moment."

SATC is the first movie in a long time to reverse the formula and put women, not men, at center stage. Is it a big surprise that many males immediately called for them to be silenced? Maybe they're just pissed that *SATC* scored more at the box office than their favorite "dick flick," *Indiana Jones*.

WHEN IT COMES to television, producers are upfront about catering to a young male market. "The entire industry these days is obsessed with the pursuit of young male viewers, trying to woo them away from their iPods, and video games," *Washington Post* reporter Lisa de Moraes concluded after interviewing several producers of new series whose sole purpose appears to be slicing and dicing up women (or, in one case, impaling them on the ceiling where they spontaneously combust). Shows like *Criminal Minds, Killer Instinct, Supernatural*, and *The Invasion* seem to be competing with the top-billing *CSI* and with one another in coming up with ever more grotesque ways of slaughtering women.

In the pilot episode of *Killer Instinct*, poisonous spiders are sent crawling under a woman's door so she can be paralyzed by their bites, before the real "bad guys" rape and murder her. "When they're looking to sell the show, they always put the women in chains," said Florida TV critic Tom Jicha, commenting on what insiders call the "Die, Women, Die!" television series.

Why should this be? What is it about mutilating women that's so compelling to young men? Is it because our society is teaching them to see women as threats to their ego and manhood? Is it because the entire thrust of our culture is that the weaker and more defenseless women are, the stronger, braver, and more macho men will appear to be, making domination, aggression, and violence the embodiment of authentic masculinity?

Plenty of shows, of course, don't feature pregnant women pulled out of the shower by huge creatures who rip the fetuses out of their wombs, but television for the most part delivers a different, albeit more tasteful, version of the same antiwoman enterprise.

Gilmore Girls used to be a big favorite in our household. Ali and I always tried to watch it together and deconstruct the poignant, humorous, and dangerously intimate mother/daughter relationship. Lorelai (Lauren Graham) and Rory (Alexis Bledel) formed an indomitable duo. Unapologetically single, they were confident and savvy, their everyday speech dotted with SAT-level words. Then came the change. Lorelai reunited with Rory's father, the dialogue slowed, and the edgy brainiacs became duller, their witty energies directed toward romance; they became, in a word, conventional. We stopped watching.

But what wasn't immediately apparent to either of us is that women "dumbing down with self-doubt," especially when it comes to their relationships with men, has evolved into the new must-watch TV. Female characters today are distinguished by their talk about the men in their lives, or the lack of them, said *New York Times* critic Alessandra Stanley. And this talk goes on all the time, especially at work.

The Marriage Mart

In *Women's Murder Club*, the female detectives, dressed in low-cut blouses and spike-heeled boots (outfits the no-nonsense gumshoes Cagney and Lacey of the 1982 series by the same name wouldn't have been caught dead in) ignore a bloodied woman's corpse while they're busy chatting away about wrecked marriages.

And in *Private Practice*, a show about seven women doctors, love relationships are always on the table. These man-needing physicians are so desperate and neurotic they require healing far more than their patients. Dr. Violet Turner (Amy Brenneman), a psychiatrist, spends her free time stalking her former boyfriend, now married to someone else. And a fertility specialist whose husband has moved out apparently has no other way to express her feelings than to lock herself in the bathroom and binge on an entire cake.

On the surface, these shows seem harmless enough. Bubble gum for the mind, one of my friends calls them. But encoded in the various episodes is the now familiar theme: no matter what she achieves or where she works, at heart a woman is more girlie girl than professional, incomplete on her own. And wherever she is—in the operating room or the police station—it's all one big dating game to her.

Television series in which professional women bond over their broken hearts (or the hearts they break) are modeled after cable TV's amazingly successful *Sex and the City*. As they did with the *SATC* movie, women across the country connected to the characters, their capacity to care deeply about one another, their intelligence and vulnerability, and, of course, their knockout outfits. Many viewers enjoyed seeing the tables turned and men, for once, be objectified and ridiculed.

"We've all been there," Haley, a thirty-three-year-old accountant with Citibank, told me. "We've had relationships come together and fall disastrously apart. And to see how the characters deal with something as awful as a break-up scrawled on a Post-It helps us cope."

Because the fab foursome—Carrie, Samantha, Miranda, and Charlotte—are heralded as smashing the mold of traditional sitcom women, it's important to take a closer, more critical look. The women might, in fact, succeed in establishing, once and for all, the worth of the single life. And at first glance they seem to be uniquely free.

But are they?

Although Charlotte sometimes yearns for a beautiful home, the others are as far from domestic goddesses as a Jimmy Choo is from a Ked.

Neither spatulas nor spray starch ever chip their French manicures. They run from Fantastik as if it were bird flu.

Their sex talk is frank and open and often funny. Samantha reports that James is an inadequate lover, so small he's like a "gherkin," while Charlotte's first encounter with an uncircumcised male makes her think of a wrinkled shar-pei. The women can be voracious and bawdy, flaunting their sexual appetites, and as discriminating in boyfriends as an Ivy League school is in acceptances.

They're all affluent and white, living in glitzy, ritzy A-list New York, where parties at Lotus and Pastis never cost too much in time or money. Their bona fides—Smith College–educated Charlotte, Harvard Law graduate Miranda—are enviable. So are their careers as journalist, PR executive, corporate attorney, and art dealer. But their good education and jobs don't translate into anything other than providing the means for these women to pursue their product lust, be it the latest must-have Chanel tote or the perfect male specimen.

They can be hedonistic and often irresponsible. When Carrie, realizing that she's spent forty thousand dollars on shoes and can't afford to buy her apartment, quips, "I'll really be the little old lady who lives in her shoe," it's as close to a reality-check moment as the show gets. By and large, these women are unstoppable partygoers.

Because, for most of the series anyway, the friends remain single, *Sex and the City* was viewed as a celebration of truly liberated women, unencumbered by bugaboo strollers and bathroom-hogging mates. That their pleasure-seeking existence bears no resemblance to the lives of most single working women was probably part of its escapist appeal. But even as savvy, sassy urbanites, the women are more caricature than real.

When we compare Carrie with Mary of the *Mary Tyler Moore Show* (debuting in 1970), who's also a reporter, the differences are striking. Mary and her best friend, Rhoda, had enviable wardrobes and did zany things to meet men—they pretend to be divorced and join the Better Luck Next Time Club—but they had lives infused with a feminist sensibility. Mary's job with the *Six O'Clock News* at WJM-TV held real significance for her. She supported her coworkers, ran the studio herself when needed, received awards for excellence, dealt with her crabby boss, and confronted sexism whenever she saw it. And of course there was the brilliant and tough TV journalist at the fictional Washington-based *FYI*, Murphy Brown, a recovering alcoholic whose decision to become a single mom so infuriated Dan Quayle.

The *Sex and the City* foursome may appear cosmopolitan, but, in comparison to these earlier TV women, their cosmos are watered down and weak. Where is the thrill of traveling alone, of pursuing a solitary interest or hobby, of finding meaning and fulfillment in a job or cause or political campaign? Their brash, locker-room-level talk gives them the facade of power and independence, of being something really different. But the characters are as conventional as the traditional mold they're trying to break. The would-be joys of independence are stifled in the hunt for the ideal mate. Even the epitome of the have-it-all career woman, Enid (Candice Bergen), Carrie's fictionalized editor at *Vogue*, is reduced to tears when she spots her man with a younger woman at a book party for Carrie. She comes apart, screaming and hiding behind other guests before sneaking out the door.

When asked, "Who was that?" Carrie answers wryly, "My role model."

For all her droll insight, Carrie isn't free from the Jane Austen angst of singledom. She is perennially chasing after Mr. Big, who won't let her leave even a toothbrush at his apartment because it's too much of a commitment. When she finds out he's moving to Napa Valley she wonders, somewhat pathetically, if she can have sex with him one more time, and then she embarks on a series of doomed affairs. And even Samantha, the most sexually aggressive of the group, allows herself to be taken in by a man who stands her up on a second date because, as she puts it, "sometimes you need to hear a 'we.'"

The strongest and really wonderful part of the series is its depiction of female friendship *sans* the jealousy and backbiting that the media always insists is inevitable among women. But their capacity to bond with one another doesn't make them autonomous.

"How does it happen that four such women have nothing to talk about other than boyfriends?" Miranda asks. Exactly! At the end of the day, as at the end of the series (with Mr. Big finally ensnared), Carrie & Co. turn out to be delightfully wisecracking, but not really earth-shattering.

The final episode of *SATC* aired in 2004, but if it were still on today, chances are the four women would now be called *fembots* (female robots), the derogatory new term playing on old stereotypes of single, working women, ousting them from the realm of acceptability. A fembot, according to a 2007 article in *Marie Claire*, is a woman who's had her sensitivity chips removed. Her creed—"You don't have to—can't really—think about last night's spat with the boyfriend, just focus on work instead. Disengage, hold your shit together, keep your cards close to your chest, and you'll get ahead"—paints her as an "executive emotional wreck" if ever there was one. "Fembots have mastered these lessons and can apply them just as easily outside the office." They're cold and unfeeling—"emotional anorexics."

In a recent *Today Show* segment, *Marie Claire* editor Joanna Coles was one of two experts brought on to discuss the alarming trend of fembotism. "The fembot is putting off getting married, she's putting off having children, and she may have several relationships before she does eventually get married. And I think that changes the way she interacts with other women. . . . She's the girl in the office that isn't interested when the colleague brings in her new baby. She doesn't want a cupcake with her friends to celebrate her birthday, she wants to get on with life, she wants to explore and she wants to be about 'me,'" offered Coles.

"I think that's a little sad," interjected the host.

"It's a woman who doesn't want to be held to the stereotype of women as nurturers and caregivers who sit and talk about their feelings all the time . . . it's a different kind of woman. It's not the kind of woman who's sitting at home worrying about, is she having her periods at the same time as her friends." Huh? As if this is what noncareer women, or any real women, ever do!

"[Nurturing] is *not* a stereotype," corrected another guest on the show, psychologist Janet Taylor. "Our brains are wired to be nurturers, but when we're emotionally unavailable [because we don't want cupcakes?] it can affect our decision making, our ability to enhance a relationship."

The segment ends with warning signs: how to tell if you or your friends are affected by fembotism—evidently the new disease rampant among professional women.

Being called an android is one thing, at least, the female contestants on reality TV will probably avoid. Tune in to any one of the marriage-market shows, *Joe Millionaire*, *Average Joe*, *Bachelor*, or *Meet My Folks*, and you'll find young women overflowing with emotion. From their giddy highs at staying in the competition to their sobbing lows—"I'm a joke," "I'm a loser"—when they're sent home, each episode reinforces the idea that catching a man is the most important thing a woman can do. "You always hear those horror stories: forty and single! I don't want that!" moaned one expelled bachelorette.

These shows are part of the sidelining pattern to revive the cultural coercion of the 1950s-style marriage, feeding the huge wedding business in this country. "[The] producers construct these shows to drive home the notion that no emotional, professional or political accomplishment can possibly compare with the twin vocations beauty and marriage," explained media expert Jennifer L. Pozner.

Hopefuls are "decked out in expensive gowns, ferried about in horse-drawn carriages and festooned with Harry Winston diamonds." But, objects Pozner, "[t]here's something ridiculous about watching grown women masquerading as would-be Cinderellas hoping to snag some sub-urban Prince Charming" who appears on a white horse or in an expensive sports car.

The dynamic behind these so-called reality shows is the notion that "beautiful women are lured to compete for riches through marriage," an idea equally demeaning to women and men. The women all have to be young, hot, and generally white; the men are all rich or seemingly so. In general, say psychology professors and authors Sharon Lamb and Lyn Mikel Brown, "women of color fare badly in these shows; the few that appear are made to seem hypersexual or hyperbitchy and controlling."

There are no scripts for these series, but it's easy to spot the one recurring theme: the humiliation of women, whether they're referred to as "money-grubbing, gold-digging whores" or "beavers." Upon his second meeting with his potential fiancées, Evan Wallace Marriott (*Joe Millionaire*) makes his dates, teetering in high-heeled boots, shovel fetid horse manure out of the stalls before going on a ride through the French countryside. And in *For Love or Money*, Rob Campos, who was thrown out of the Marines for molesting a female officer while he was intoxicated, gets drunk and makes a woman remove his boots, then sends her sprawling with a kick.

"The real concern," said Pozner, "is the millions of viewers, scores of whom are young girls who take in these misogynistic spectacles uncritically, learning that only the most stereotypically beautiful, least independent woman with the lowest-carb diet will be rewarded with love, financial security and the ultimate prize of male validation."

Mirror Mirror on the Wall

The other colossally popular form of reality TV is a variation on the beauty contest—shows like *America's Next Top Model*, *Search for the Next Pussy Cat Doll* (the burlesque dance team), *Beauty and the Geek*, and *Crowned: Mother of All Pageants*, which pits one mother-daughter duo against another.

Each of these shows does its part to hawk poisonous, stereotypical views of women. When we meet the "brainless beauties" who are paired with socially inept "geeks," they tell us of their interests: getting manicures and pedicures (Jennylee), talking on the phone (Tori), going shopping on Rodeo Drive (Cecille). The geeks include a double major in finance and entrepreneurship with a minor in philosophy (Drew), an electrical engineering major with a perfect SAT score (Neils), and a medical student with a specialty in computer engineering and biology (Sanjay). When one woman, asked in 2006 when the next presidential election would be held, shrugged, the guys laughed at her. I'm sure right now any one of us could come up with a list of smart, capable women who could refute the dumb-broad stereotype. But then, what would the men find to ridicule?

Lots of women I interviewed started out intrigued by *America's Next Top Model*. They liked the glamour, watching contestants create their own outfits, the inside look at the photo shoots and industry workings. But most of them, except the real diehards, are now switching the channel. Tyra Banks, the megamodel, started the series supporting the contestants. Episodes showed her concerned about their well-being. She sat with the women and discussed their dieting habits and boyfriend angst. The summary scenes, where she and the other judges gave their assessments of the would-be models, were usually more constructive than critical. But that's changed.

Now Tyra stands before them like a hanging judge, issuing harsh comments about their "lumpy butt" and "weird hair." Body parts are disparaged and even mocked. While the girls under scrutiny bite their lips and hold back tears like chastised children, she makes short shrift of them. Autonomy and identity vanish as fast as the click of a camera.

Recent shows have stooped to new lows in dehumanizing women. In the dead model episode, the girls pose as various murder victims—shot, beaten, stabbed, even beheaded, surrounded by filth, metal pipes, and plastic wrap. That the contestants were presumably murdered by other models adds another debasing touch to this already disgusting concept. (Maybe this is what Banks means when she says her show empowers women. It turns them from victims of violence into perpetrators of it.)

In another photo shoot the contestants pose in personas and positions already chosen for them: the "drug-addicted" model who looks slightly beaten up and about to overdose, the "dumb blond," the anorexic, the bulimic sitting on the toilet with vomit on her face and hands, the jealous girl who pulls the hair of another. Maybe I missed the memo, but when did it become cool to glamorize harmful, self-destructive behavior?

Model, *Crowned*, and *Pussycat Dolls* are contests, and on each, only one of the women (or girl and mom) will make it to the finish line. But competitions don't have to be mean-spirited. These are. The girls casually refer to one another as "bitch," "ho," and "slut" and are encouraged by a voyeuristic newscaster to dish dirt on the others. To some extent these shows are a product of our winner-take-all culture, but the spectacle of catty women who'll trample each other when it suits them is a standard feature of our popular culture.

The most intriguing part of these shows is how they reinforce and ritualize the boundaries between acceptable and unacceptable definitions of womanhood. Each show exiles those who don't conform to the standard markers of patriarchy—sexy, skinny, passive. Following a tense and tearful public humiliation in which contestants' deficiencies are broadcast—

in deeply somber tones—to the assembled troupe, those singled out for expulsion must perform the rites of separation.

In *Pussy Cat Dolls*, they have to "hang up their boas"; the mothers and daughters of *Crowned* "de-sash," cutting off their ribbons. And in *Model* the expelled girl returns alone to her hotel room like the pariah she's become, packs her bags, and leaves at once.

We've already seen how ousting members of a community can define boundaries and solidify the values of a dominant group. Conservatives use this device to demonize feminists and other progressive-minded Americans; men use it to marginalize women. We've become so accustomed to this tactic that it's hard to recognize when we do it to ourselves. To some extent, it's a safe vehicle for our anger: we don't often get the opportunity to sit in judgment of men, but we *can* judge other women. Given the world we're living in, it wasn't all that surprising to read reports of the Delta Zeta sorority at DePauw University evicting twenty-three members for no apparent reason other than their appearance. All of the overweight and sisters of color were told to leave. Those allowed to remain were conventionally pretty, slender, white, and popular with fraternity men.

Night after night, week after week, as we watch girls banished from the Eden where only the thin, toned, young, and hot are allowed, we internalize and accept the rigid, unattainable standards of beauty, along with the vulnerability of those left standing. Little wonder we identify with Tyra or Robin or Carson—they're the only ones with power and control.

"All of a sudden, we're really regressing. TV doesn't live in a vacuum," communications professor Martha Lauzen reminds us. "These portrayals of women are reflecting what is going on in our society. . . . On television feminism has become the other F-word."

20

THE DISAPPEARING GIRL

"**A**re you OK?" I asked.

"Sure, fine. Don't worry about me."

But I was worried. *Very.* Everyday I watched Rachel, a high school senior in my American history class, with a growing sense of alarm. She'd always been a good student, at times almost too driven to do well. And like so many of her classmates, her day extended well beyond school hours. Track and field, her special passion and talent, took a demanding toll in both time and energy. A big competition was coming up in a few weeks, and so were college admissions letters. There was no shortage of things to worry about.

But senior stress couldn't be the only explanation for why Rachel seemed to be vanishing before my eyes. It wasn't just her weight; she didn't seem healthy anymore. She'd stopped participating in class, her once boundless energy seemed diminished, and her hair hung lank and thin, her eyes dull.

I spoke with the school nurse, psychologist, and track coach. We asked Rachel's mom to meet with us, and she confirmed what we'd suspected. "Rachel isn't really eating much, hardly at all," she said, and broaching the subject had proved futile. Rachel would become angry, burst into tears, then storm off to her room. And—she still refused to eat.

With Rachel's knees wider than her thighs and her arms the diameter of pipe cleaners, her coach wouldn't let her train unless a doctor certified that she was strong enough to run. That decision probably saved her life. As soon as the doctor saw Rachel—at five-foot-seven and ninety-two pounds—he hospitalized her, straight from his office, and kept her there for the remainder of the semester.

Dangerous dieting, obsession with food, and dislike of our bodies—I heard about this from women all over the country, as we trade being strong and striving for the fragile silhouette of passivity.

"My seven-year-old niece called me," Kari, an executive assistant said, "and she was crying because her friends told her she's fat. Now all she wants to do is jump rope in the basement so she'll lose weight. She doesn't want to play with her friends or go out to dinner."

"There was so much bulimia," the president of a sorority at Cornell University said, "the pipes in the bathroom were all corroding, and we had to have them completely replaced. After that, the girls vomited into plastic bags."

"I'm not what you'd call heavy, but I'd like to get rid of at least ten pounds," said an eighteen-year-old from Wisconsin. "I have calves only a mother cow would love," said a Boston mom. And a middle schooler from Florida complained, "Everyone at my school is so skinny, they look great in leggings. Next to them, I feel like a freak."

A thirty-eight-year-old nurse from Virginia said, "When I told my grandmother that I'd finally gotten pregnant, I thought she'd be over-joyed." Instead the grandmother's response was "I just hope you don't use this as an excuse to gain weight."

Any time my conversation with women and girls veered toward appearance, I heard a litany of dissatisfactions. No body part escaped criticism, but nothing matched concern about weight. "It's a tyranny," a college freshman said. "No matter what else we do, how much we achieve, we can't escape the pressure to be thin."

Skeletal female forms clothed in Dolce & Gabbana, Marc Jacobs, and Burberry fill our most popular fashion magazines and saunter down the runway. There's no escaping them. We're in an era of ad overload. Thirty years ago, most of us saw about two thousand ad messages a day. Now it's up to five thousand. "Ubiquity is the new exclusivity," said a chief executive at a New York ad agency. The idea is to catch the consumer at every turn. Digital-screen billboards, bus stops, ads for gyms, posters around schools, the Internet, and magazines all reinforce unattainable and unhealthy beauty ideals.

"Anne Frank girls" is what James Scully, one of the fashion industry's most sought-after casting directors, calls the emaciated models. And they're in great demand. Not until the twenty-two-year-old Uruguayan model Luisel Ramos collapsed on the catwalk and died after a three-month starvation diet, followed by Ana Carolina Reston, the Brazilian model who was five-foot-eight and weighed eighty pounds when she succumbed to complications from anorexia, did the call go out to ban underweight models. But a virtual Yalta Summit of the fashion world failed to produce uniform or lasting results. Initially Madrid and Milan agreed to keep young women with a body mass index (BMI) below 18 from participating in their shows. (BMI is calculated by height and weight. The NIH says that 18.5 to 24 is normal.) But Milan later joined with France, Great Britain, and the United States and refused to abide by any formal regulations. Designers prefer ultrathin models, they say, because they believe the small form shows off their fashions better.

"I thought that subzero was just a kind of refrigerator, until I looked around some trendy boutiques and discovered it's a coveted clothing size," one woman I interviewed joked. Marc Jacobs, who doesn't cut in larger sizes, sells more of size 0 than any other size in his collection. And Lela Rose, Banana Republic, and Nicole Miller are offering size 00, or subzero, clothing.

"Part of it is really a status thing," a buyer at Bergdorf Goodman's department store told me. "It's called vanity sizing. Putting a lower number like a 4 on items that a few seasons back would have been a 6. I remember when a 6 used to be a small size," she said. "Today the girls are only interested in 0 and 00." As one writer put it, "Skinny is the new fat. . . . [The m]ost famous, recognizable women today are famous primarily for being thin and pretty."

"Girls today, even very young ones, are being bombarded with the message that they need to be superskinny to be sexy," said author Sharon Lamb. And the media, more than their parents, more than their peers, is responsible, according to Nada Stotland, a psychiatry professor and vice president of the American Psychiatric Association.

"Six Ways to Easy Thin: Diets That Really Work" (*Allure*), "Get the Body You Want" (*Seventeen*), "Get a Bikini Body by Spring" (*Shape*), "Lose 20 lbs in 30 Days" (*Star*), "Be Thin by Memorial Day" (*InTouch*). The words scream at us from the magazine racks. *Vogue*, for years, has chronicled the weight losses of its staff. And Oprah recently revealed her promise to lose twenty pounds before she could appear on *Vogue*'s cover.

This constant reading about dieting, a theme in most teen magazines, says a recent study in *Pediatrics*, the journal of the American Academy of Pediatrics, can have an unhealthy impact on girls and adolescents. "Some are trying to emulate the girls they see on the covers," explained Ed Bucciarelli, CEO of Henri Bendel. And that's got a lot of health experts worried. "The promotion of the thin, sexy ideal in our culture has created a situation where the majority of girls and women don't like their bodies," said body image researcher Sarah Murnen, a professor of psychology at Kenyon College. "And if you don't feel good in your body, you don't feel good," added psychologist Daniel Rothstein.

When young women were given pictures of skinny or "ideal-thin" models, they reported greater unhappiness with their own weight, an obsession with dieting and exercise, and generalized negative feelings. Those—like the majority of us—who already had concerns about their bodies typically felt the worst, often experiencing "shame, guilt, and stress." And the responses become more intense as girls get older.

A striking 80 percent of ten-year-old girls are on diets, because dieting, the girls say, makes them feel better about themselves. And adolescent girls (eleven to seventeen years old) list dropping ten to fifteen pounds as a more important goal than future success in love or work. They actually fear getting fat more than nuclear war or losing their parents. So great is the pressure to achieve a certain look, the percentage of girls in the United States who are "happy with the way I am" drops from 60 percent in elementary school to 29 percent during high school because of the pressure to achieve a certain look.

"Body dissatisfaction can lead girls to participate in very unhealthy behaviors to try and control weight," said Murnen, who has studied this topic for fifteen years. At least one out of three "normal dieters" progress to pathological dieting. Half of our teenage girls are already skipping meals, fasting, smoking cigarettes, using laxatives, and vomiting so that they can lose weight.

Approximately ten million girls and women in this country are struggling with an eating disorder. But, say the experts, that's probably a low estimate because so many cases go undiagnosed and unreported. Anorexia nervosa is crippling, often killing, with the highest premature fatality rate of any mental illness, and yet there's little support for studying it. In 2005 the NIH gave $12 million for research on eating disorders. Alzheimer's, affecting 4.5 million of the population, got $647 million in funding; and schizophrenia, with 2.2 million sufferers, received $350 million.

Girls are preoccupied with dieting well before they get to drug and alcohol use, but while schools have educational programs on the dangers of substance abuse, "weight abuse" is hardly every discussed. There's no handy explanation as to why eating disorders are the orphans of education and health care, but maybe it's because the disorder affects girls and women ten times more than boys and men, or that body dissatisfaction revs up enough insecurity to support a huge beauty and diet industry. But even more to the point, the attenuated female form is the perfect complement to our hypermasculine society.

The Shape of the Month

Women's ideal body size and shape has changed dramatically over time, very much products of the culture that created them. During the 1950s curvaceous women were "in." The exaggerated feminine form—large hips and breasts, symbolizing nurturing and motherhood—emerged as the perfect shape for a war-weary society whose prodigious nesting produced the famous baby boom. Marilyn Monroe, probably the most photographed woman of the time, wore a size 14.

A decade later the 1960s generation rejected stereotypical gender roles with a new icon: Twiggy. The slight, round-eyed British model encapsulated the era's celebration of androgyny. Her prepubescent body also spoke to the freedom of the sexual revolution—the ability (because of the birth-control pill) to make love without risking pregnancy.

By the 1970s and 1980s the fashionable figure had done a complete 360. Out with the tiny, in with the large. New "supermodels" Cheryl Tiegs, Claudia Schiffer, and Cindy Crawford very much embodied the vision of the women's movement—strong, healthy, and capable. They were thin, but not excruciatingly so. Crawford at the peak of her career was a "slender size 8." These women prided themselves in being toned and fit. But they were quickly eclipsed by the waif, the antithesis of strength and vigor.

In 1993 Kate Moss put her stamp on the look with her Calvin Klein ads. But in an impressive show of independence, most magazine readers and store customers rejected "gaunt" and its implication of fragility. Women had achieved too much, had too much self-esteem to allow themselves to be represented by someone who looked so insubstantial.

By May 1994 *Vogue* anointed the full-figured, blond German Nadja Auermann as the body of the future. "Strong and sexy." "Steely femininity." The editorial accompanying her photographs told readers that women were opting for the "timeless sleek cut of a masculine pantsuit, circa 1975 . . . and the gusto (but not the shoulder pads) of the 80s working woman." The following year, when stunningly muscular Gabrielle Reece, a top model turned professional volleyball player, appeared on the cover of *Outside* magazine, the caption read, "Meet the Ubergirls: The New Female Ideal Is Big and Beautiful. And She Can Mop the Floor with You. Got a Problem with That?"

Apparently a lot of men answered yes. No sooner you could say *ubergirls* than they were gone—replaced by the new breed of threadlike models.

Moss, at five-foot-seven and one hundred pounds, was considered very thin; today's models are, on average, three or four inches taller and don't weigh much more. Their emaciated bodies convey dependence and passivity, a crying out to be fed, to be taken care of. The whole package is one of powerlessness. Childlike and unassuming, these young women don't appear strong enough to drive a car, let alone hold a job or command respect. Next to them, any man will feel more capable and macho.

Advertisers tell us that thinness sells, but a batch of new studies throws that premise into doubt. Average-size models are actually equally effective as the ultrathin ones in selling a range of consumer goods including food and health and beauty products, according to new research. And looking at slightly larger models improves girls' self-esteem. So, we need to ask, why stick with the skinny?

"I can understand why the fashion industry may want women to look a certain way, but what I don't understand is why we 'buy' into it," a woman from Akron, Ohio, wrote in my online survey. "We're so obsessed with appearance," a twenty-six-year-old from North Carolina suggested, "because while we're told we can be anything we want, what a lot of us are realizing is that it translates into: we can *look* any way we want to look. So we're focusing on that, instead of what in our hearts and minds we want to become."

Women of all ages are embracing the constricting image. Turning upside down the feminist imperative to think for ourselves, we're allowing others to decree what we should look like, how much we should weigh. And our value to society and to ourselves is measured accordingly.

Why do we feel we have to conform to manipulating "images yo-yoing over time?" Why don't we say "Enough!" as women did decades ago? Just think about how ridiculous it is that there's even such a concept as a "right" shape. There's nothing comparable for men, except, maybe, the movement toward healthier, fitter bodies.

It's very likely that women submit to the harsh, critical gaze because we no longer have the self-reliance to refuse it. For years we've seen our rights and opportunities slowly diminishing, our intellect, our attributes, and our effectiveness disparaged, strong women ridiculed and maligned. We've lost our sense of identity, that core of confidence that would enable us to resist the pernicious dictates of an external, artificial ideal.

Here a Nip, There a Tuck

We need only look at the soaring plastic surgery industry—raking in fifteen billion dollars a year and counting—to see how completely we've bought into that ideal. Thinness may not sell better, but body anxiety does. Redoing our bodies has become the new growth industry. Once the province of the aging and rich, plastic surgery is now commonplace. Reality television shows like *The Swan*, *Extreme Makeover*, and *I Want a Famous Face* have pulled the veil off the once-secret process, making it "fun and exciting."

There used to be a time, not so long ago, when women who had "work done" stayed hidden in their homes, venturing out only under large Jackie O–style glasses. Now the bruises are paraded openly, even proudly, battle wounds in our fight to stop the clocks and make our bodies into temples of perfection. Proudly, competitively, we soldier on searching for the deepening laugh line, the slightest sag in our chin.

Liposuction, breast implants, eyebrow lifts, tummy tucks, Botox, and Restylane shape and mold our offending parts until . . . until we end up looking like one another! Where once women celebrated our diversity, our uniqueness, and our inner beauty (yes, we really believed it), today we're opting for sameness. There's a plastic surgeon on the Upper East Side of Manhattan who's known for his signature noses. No matter what the women look like—tall or petite, oval-faced or round—they get the standard-issue nose. One woman told me that when she's at a tony restaurant she and her friends count noses by Dr. Q.

Alex Kuczynski, author of *Beauty Junkies*, told the story of a Beverly Hills party where a group of surgically enhanced thirtysomethings so strongly resembled each other that one of their husbands actually mistook the wrong woman for his wife. And on *The Swan*, the contestants are all "ugly ducklings" who undergo multiple procedures and compete with one another for the chance to participate in a beauty pageant in the last episode. I don't know how anyone could select a winner, since they all wind up looking remarkably the same, like Dallas Cowboys cheerleaders. Even beautiful trademark signs of ethnicity are cut and whittled away. On *Extreme Makeover*, a black woman's lips were made smaller, and the doctors on *The Swan* "softened" the eyes of an Asian woman. "The media pressures every woman—regardless of class, age or ethnicity—to modify herself in order to feel 'normal,'" says *Ms.* magazine.

Of the shows dealing with cosmetic makeovers, *The Swan* is premised on the worst (ugliest) concept. It plays upon our insecurities, each week subjecting two women to a panel of experts who critique their appearance and then perform the requisite procedures with amazingly little input from the contestants themselves. When they emerge, fully Stepfordized, only one is deemed beautiful enough for the next level. The other—for all the pain she's gone through—is still considered more duckling than swan, and may require more "renovation" in the future.

The producers of the show have skillfully tapped into a central component of the cosmetic surgery mania: you're never quite finished with it. One woman wrote about how she couldn't get an appointment for a skin cancer body check with her Chicago dermatologist after May because all the women were going for pre-vacation Botox injections. Another told of her friends "talking about touch-ups of Restylane the way we used to describe getting our roots done."

It's easy to see why the lure of continued "improvement" is so seductive. If your eyes look good after surgery, why not get rid of the flaps under your arms? Your saddlebags? Your turkey wattle? Bra fat? Back fat? The "doughnut" around the belly button? It all adds up to serial surgeries. And, since—when I last checked—we are still getting older, the list of parts needing correction multiplies over time, while those parts already fixed require fine-tuning. As for those who have been plastic surgery abstainers—will they be the lone holdouts in our new bulgeless society? Or will they too succumb to the pressure to be forever young?

None of this, of course, is making the case for aging gracefully. I'm not even certain we still think of that as a worthy goal. After all, didn't Rush Limbaugh say the problem with Hillary Clinton's candidacy was that no one wants to watch a woman getting older in the White House? I suppose that was in contrast to John McCain, who is old to begin with.

"All the styles in the stores are for younger women," one fifty-eight-year-old complained. "It makes you look in the mirror, pull your skin up, and wonder what it would be like to have your twenty-year-old face back. . . . I wish our society would make us feel better about getting older instead of glamorizing youth, which is a very short period." The problem, to put it succinctly, is that women simply aren't meant to grow up.

"I think it's because women feel they get their power from their sexuality," a small business owner from New York wrote. "As they age, they lose it, so they decide to have plastic surgery."

Some 11.7 million plastic surgery procedures were done in the United States during 2007. Since 1997 surgeries increased by 114 percent;

noninvasive procedures skyrocketed 754 percent. This surge has been helped by new marketing and advertising techniques, along with increased accessibility. Stop-and-shop mini–treatment centers are even popping up at our nation's malls. With their no-fuss approach to a bit of Botox or lasering, they've become a huge retail business. Andrew Rudnick, owner of Sleek MedSpa, with seven locations in upscale shopping centers along the East Coast, plans to offer his quick-fix services in forty more locations in twenty-five cities, joining the estimated 2,000 to 2,500 MedSpas nationwide. In 2002 there were twenty-five.

"I can be in and out in a half hour," said Kim Wanderley, a thirty-nine-year-old mother from Parkland, Florida. "It gives me an excuse to go to the mall afterward to do a little shopping," she said, admitting being drawn to the convenience and speed of these facilities.

Doctors in a wide array of fields are cashing in on the plastic surgery phenomenon, attaching medi-spas to their offices. The mix-and-match of cosmetics with medical treatment began to take off in 2001. Gynecologists, dentists, oncologists, and urologists are among the growing list of specialists who see the beauty business as a lucrative, pay-as-you-go adjunct to their traditional practices. Plastic surgeons and dermatologists resent this encroachment into their fields and claim the short-shrift training the noncore physicians (those not specialized in cosmetic surgery) received amounts to what one dermatologist I spoke to called "plastic surgery for dummies."

Just about every specialist has a story of the "do-over" patient he or she has treated after a noncore botched the job. Cases of poorly aligned eyebrows, facial paralysis, drooping noses, and severe skin ulcerations all get sent their way. But there are other, even more worrisome complications. Some patients end up with disfiguring infections, serious blood clots, and severe and lasting pain.

Less common but not unheard of are patients dying during cosmetic procedures. And this can happen even with board-certified surgeons doing the work. "We should concentrate on the *surgery*, not the *cosmetic* part of the term," one doctor cautioned after the recent death of a Florida cheerleader from a rare reaction to anesthesia during a breast augmentation to correct asymmetry.

There's also concern that in the rush to capture an increasingly eager consumer base, new, uncertain procedures, such as the "antifat shot," are taking hold.

"Dissolve to your beautiful shape" beckon the advertisements for centers in Missouri and Kansas that inject lipodissolve into the skin. Although it's vigorously advertised on television and in magazines, some researchers worry about the liquidized fat roaming around the body and possibly causing heart disease. Others say it's not at all effective. But even if it's simply another version of snake oil, it translates into a profitable business in our beauty-obsessed society.

The demand for more methods of turning back the clock and new doctors to deliver them has resulted in an explosion of students opting to go into cosmetic surgery. So many seniors in our top medical schools are looking to dermatology and plastic surgery residences that fields like family medicine are being shortchanged. "It is an unfortunate circumstance that you can spend an hour with a patient treating them for diabetes and hypertension and make one hundred dollars, or you can do Botox and make two thousand dollars in the same amount of time," said Eric C. Parlette, a Massachusetts dermatologist. In 2007, 383 people competed for six slots in Harvard's dermatology program, which breaks down to sixty-four applicants per place. Compare this to the eleven applications per each admissions spot for Harvard College's class of 2010.

"Everyone wants to have a designer body and wear the newest fashions," one makeover aficionado told me, detailing the shortening, lengthening, even amputation of toes to fit into pointed shoes, injecting fat into the ball of the foot to make standing in stilettos easier, liposuctioning the pubic area to look better in bikinis, and butt reshaping. By the time she finished, I was beginning to think that Scarlett O' Hara, painfully laced into a whalebone corset, had nothing to complain about.

The combined effects of television, advertising, and bare-your-body clothing have sparked the increase in plastic surgery among teens and young women. One quarter of the procedures performed today are on women under thirty.

Rhinoplasty—the one plastic surgery some adolescents wanted in the past—is getting swift competition. Doctors have reported a huge uptick in breast augmentation, tummy tucks, and liposuction on girls as young as fourteen. Sometimes they perform several procedures at once.

Breast implants are particularly popular. Within one year's time the number of girls eighteen and younger who received them nearly tripled. Mothers sometimes give their daughters "new breasts" as birthday or graduation presents, and make appointments to have theirs enlarged at the same time.

While there's no regulation prohibiting girls under eighteen from having breast augmentation, many doctors share the concerns of Scott L. Spear, chief of plastic surgery at Georgetown University Hospital. Younger teens aren't sufficiently mature to understand that there is more to the procedure "than just having your ears pierced," he explained. Some come in so eager to look like Britney Spears or Pamela Anderson that they don't really hear the risks. But the risks are plentiful, including permanent scarring, pain, hardening, the possibility of rupture leading to future surgeries, and the potential to hinder breastfeeding and mammograms. Silicone implants taken off the market for safety concerns are now back again, even with open-ended questions about their link to arthritis, lupus, and other systematic diseases.

Psychologist Ann Kearney-Cooke, an expert in girls and body image, believes the "increase in cosmetic surgery among adolescents reflects a pernicious trend that pervades popular culture: the glorification of rail-thin, large-breasted women—an unnatural body type rarely achievable without surgery."

If media bombardment is responsible for skyrocketing breast augmentation surgeries, then the proliferation of pornography is leading to another fast-growing procedure—vaginal rejuvenation. Once confined to sex workers, nude entertainers, and nude models, doctors report that women from all backgrounds are asking for labiaplasty, the reshaping of the female external genitals.

Very few women get the idea to have their inner labia shortened on their own. Generally women traipse into the surgeon's office in response to some negative comment made by a guy, said Dr. Pamela Loftus, a Florida doctor.

"There's often pressure from a man who tells them they need it. I assume that their standards of labial beauty were set by a combination of the porn industry, sex-oriented magazines, and the Internet," said Dr. V. Leroy Young, who, as chair of a task force looking into emerging trends in plastic surgery, has identified labiaplasty as one of the fastest growing.

Ileana Vasquez, a twenty-nine-year-old mother of four in southern California, had the surgery after her husband told her that she was looser now after having the children and didn't satisfy him sexually.

Vasquez said that the procedure did improve their love life. "But," she added, "there are times when I still can't forgive him for how he made me feel. Sometimes I get so mad, so hurt. I mean, I had the kids, he should have understood."

But women are under increasing pressure to wipe out signs of their pregnancies. For the past several years the media has created huge excitement over pregnant celebrities featured in the gossip weeklies. Intended to activate our internal thin-o-monitors are celebrity photos taken before and after their babies are born, meant to show off their new, svelte forms. As we look at these pictures we know in our hearts that these women have spent huge amounts of money and time working out with trainers and nutritionists to become hot mamas. But theirs is the must-have look that we, with far fewer resources, are supposed to achieve.

Keri Russell, only two months after giving birth, was already down to a size 0! (The rest of us be shamed.) Even Nicole Richie, rumored to have been anorexic, is being touted as an icon of the postpregnancy slimdown. *Us Weekly*, conducting an online poll, asked readers to vote on the best postbaby bod. "It's only been a few months since they gave birth, but as these photos show, Katie Holmes, Angelina Jolie, and Gwyneth Paltrow have already bounced back to their formerly skinny selves," the Web site proclaimed.

And now there's an additional form of persuasion. The "mommy makeover," a trio of procedures including breast lifting (with or without augmentation), tummy tuck, and liposuction, has become as popular among elite new mothers as the Prada diaper bag.

"The severe physical trauma of pregnancy, childbirth, and breastfeeding can have profound negative effects that cause women to lose their hourglass figures," said plastic surgeon David A. Stoker. "Twenty years ago, a woman did not think she could do something about it and she covered up with discreet clothing. But now women don't have to go on feeling self-conscious or resentful about their appearance."

Could we just all wait a minute! Since when are pregnancy and birth "severe physical traumas"? And why should we be resentful or self-conscious about our postpartum bodies, unless it's being drilled into our heads that we're supposed to be?

The advertisements and doctors pushing for multiple, potentially risky, even life-threatening procedures are engaging in nothing more than crass marketing ploys. And they come at a time when we're feeling vulnerable, sleep-deprived, and on a hormonal roller coaster, trying to adjust to the major changes in our lives and alterations—usually short term—in our bodies.

But the idea that mothers need to be remodeled degrades our bodies as if they're so flawed only cutting and suctioning can return us to "normal." It goes without saying this makes us feel bad about ourselves, but it also reinforces the idea of pregnancy as a disability, supporting special constraints on pregnant workers.

The women's movement struggled hard to make pregnancy accepted as another part of a woman's life, like the onset of menstruation and menopause, rather than as a frailty or disease. Now we're urged to embrace motherhood and simultaneously told we'll become undesirable hags when we do. No wonder so many women feel lost.

The worst thing about the mommy makeover (aside from its deceivingly appealing name) is that it negates the value of our life experiences. I remember how miffed my graduate school friend Sherry became when people complimented her by saying, "You don't look like you had a baby." Sherry, who finished her doctorate in history and then went to law school and became a judge, wondered, "Why would I want to look like I never was pregnant? Having a baby was one of the most wonderful things in my life."

Along similar lines, Gerda Lerner, my department chair and a pioneer scholar who fought to establish the first M.A. program in women's history in the country at Sarah Lawrence College, stopped coloring her hair over one summer. When we returned to school in the fall, she announced to us, "I felt, as a feminist, I wasn't setting the right example to my students. Besides," she said, running her fingers through her short gray crop, "I've earned every one of these."

Narrow, conforming beauty standards destructively erase the landscape of our lives. When the physical signs of our accomplishments—wrought with hard work, patience, joy, and pain—are whittled and filled and planed down because they don't correspond to some external ideal, then we are, in effect, trivializing them. We're buying into the notion that how we look is more important than who we are and what we do. "[As a society] we know more about women who look good than we know about women who do good," former teen model and author Audrey Brashich said.

We're living at a time when so much—the economy, our social and foreign policies, women's progress—is veering dangerously off course. Perhaps we're obsessing about our laugh lines and love handles because they give us something we are able to "repair."

Lots of women who've had quick zaps of Botox or Restylane say the procedures made them feel better about themselves. I couldn't (and wouldn't) argue with these assessments. But I do think when we ask to have "a J-Lo butt" or "Angelina Jolie lips," we're opting for someone else's persona and sacrificing some of our own.

Our bodies have become undertakings, parts for us to work on, not parts that work for us. Attaining the body beautiful becomes the ultimate purpose, a consuming endeavor worthy of our time, energy, and money. But while we're busily fixing ourselves rather than society, we risk becoming ever more self-absorbed, competitive, and insular. And less effective.

21

TOXIC MALES AND TARTY FEMALES

"SEX! SLEAZE! VIOLENCE! New York's infamous grind-house culture comes back from the dead" headlines a recent issue of *TimeOut* in what might be an apt description of our current state of society. "Boys are being socialized to be more violent and girls to be more sexual," author Diane Levin told me, and it affects the way they think about themselves and interact with one another.

The machoization of our society has resulted in an extreme and increasingly toxic brand of manhood. The stereotypical male, at his default setting, is brawny and tough. Now he's on steroids, literally and metaphorically. Aggression, dominance, and control taint our cultural terrain. Belligerent masculinity can take many forms: gang violence, bench-emptying playing-field brawls, or hostile corporate takeovers. But however furious the warring male camps, it's nothing compared to the wrath those camps unleash on women—the universal scapegoats.

"SHOW US YOUR breasts, you slut!" Within minutes a ferocious mix of chants and banging can be heard coming from the spiral ramp at Giants Stadium's gate D. Men are wedged together, hot and sweaty, in the cold November afternoon, their faces contorted with rapacious sneers, pounding, yelling, "Boobies! Boobies! We want boobies!"

A raw display of male domination, the stuff of the gladiator, the toreador, is the halftime norm for Jets fans at gate D, where harassment is ritualized and made popular. Women and girls who find themselves caught on the spiral are groped indiscriminately while security guards look on, smoking cigarettes. "This *is* the game," twenty-year-old Patrick Scofield, a two-season ticket holder, said of the spectacle.

"All men must cope with the complications of feminism," wrote Richard Goldstein in *The Nation*. "I would argue that the demand for sexual equality is a major reason for the global rise of fundamentalism." Whether or not we agree with Goldstein's assessment, it certainly demonstrates the extent to which issues of gender equality can generate anxiety.

Traditional masculinity has always been uneasy about social and sexual change, but in its compensatory hypermacho form, it's taken "booting out the bitches" as an anthem. The worst insult you can give a man, author and scholar Robert Jensen observed, is the accusation that he's like a woman. And this is true whether it's corporate players in the boardroom or kids playing the schoolyard. Or politicians. When pundits wanted to put down Barack Obama during his presidential run, they called him a "sissy" and a "priss."

For a man to feel like a "real man" he must be aggressive and competitive. Of course not every man feels this way, Jensen added, but it's the prevailing view, reinforced in the mass media and sanctioned by our major institutions and activities—the military, business, and athletics. "Men are defined by how tough we are, and the best way to prove it is by trumping any 'female-like softness.'"

It was exactly this high-octane testosterone flowing freely in her son's Manhattan all-boys school that finally convinced Teresa to move Kevin to "a kinder environment." It wasn't an easy decision. The reputation of the place is stellar, and selective. Even mothers who want to serve on school committees can't just volunteer, they have to be invited. The roster of fathers and alums fills the boardrooms of Wall Street. Extraordinary wealth is assumed.

"The school puts a premium on the boys acting like men," Teresa said, but in the six years Kevin was there, his parents saw a ruthless masculinity begin to take hold. The school's idea of manhood was the worst of the stereotypes. "It was like we were in the midst of *Lord of the Flies*. And that atmosphere permeated the athletic fields, the classroom, and out-of-school trips. Kids got away with being vicious to one another, even physically abusive, and the teachers did nothing. When Kevin complained, he was chided with being a "candy ass." And this was from the headmaster.

No one would call the men who are "hunting Bambi" candy asses. They're dressed in full-fledged combat gear, roaming the terrain in military-style jeeps. The Bambis they're after are women, naked except for running shoes. The videos of the action, selling for twenty dollars apiece, are being advertised as "one of the sickest and most shocking videos ever made."

Controversy exists as to whether these hunts are real or just staged and filmed to attract visits to the Web site and sell videos. But Michael Burdick, creator of the concept, claims to be holding live hunts for men from around the world who pay ten thousand dollars to act out the fantasy of shooting a woman (with paint balls, reportedly reaching two hundred miles an hour) then dragging her off, presumably for sex. On his Web site he urges men to come out and "shoot one of these nagging whiny bitches where it hurts and shut her the fuck up. Then mount her like a 'Real Man.'"

In covering the story, the media asked if it was an example of shocking degradation of women or just a big put-on. But this question misses the point. Even if the hunts are a hoax, isn't a video of men stalking and "shooting" naked women as if they were animals in itself degrading? Or have we so lost our perspective as to think that it's acceptable?

BACK IN THE 1960s, men justified their grasp on power as a privilege, a responsibility to do good. Now no explanations are given or needed. Power exists to generate power, creating a world of restless violence. And as the sources of male authority slip away—America's impotence abroad, the endless wars in Iraq and Afghanistan, homes snatched as easily as Monopoly markers, jobs imploding and lifetime savings disappearing overnight—the threat to manhood grows greater, the perceived need to control those "threats" fiercer.

Images of men dominating women—abusing, battering, raping, and murdering—saturate our culture. Dolce & Gabbana made fashionable the gang rape with its "gorgeous" picture of a woman being held to the floor by one man while sneering onlookers wait their turn. Cesare Paciotti tapped into another flourishing image: the woman-assaulted ad, with the model sprawled out helplessly, her head lolling off to the side, her legs askew. She joins a parade of surrendering women. Gucci does a good job showing us a woman's place—where else but flat on the ground at a man's (Gucci-clad) feet? Manufacturers of men's fragrances such as Tag and Unforgivable promise to make their users so virile they'll have multiple women flopping all over their beds. And in one ad for Tom Ford for Men, the fragrance bottle is jammed between a woman's glistening, ready-for-action thighs, barely covering the woman's naked genitalia.

Ownerless feet, legs, breasts, torsos, and butts are plastered across glossy fashion pages and on billboards. Dismembered women in films and in life are symbols of misogynist rage; when they're clad in Calvins they're less frightening and definitely more palatable, but they're all part of the same dehumanization of women.

Men look at the ads; so do women. And in their eyes and ours, we cease to be autonomous beings with unique minds and emotions integrally connected to our bodies. In this new calculus we're not greater than the sum of our parts. We're much, much less.

Rap—In Need of Serious Revision

In April 2007, when Don Imus called the young members of the Rutgers' women's basketball team a bunch of "nappy-headed hos," the demands for *his* head were immediate and unremitting. Even the shock jock's knee-capping, take-no-prisoners style couldn't excuse this gratuitous verbal attack. As the show's sponsors jumped ship one by one and various civil rights groups condemned the racism, and to a much lesser extent, the sexism of Imus's remark, CBS president Leslie Moonves yielded to the growing pressure and fired the radio icon.

The Imus brouhaha, effectively eclipsing news of what was turning into the deadliest month to date in the Iraq war, put into bold relief the language of hip-hop spewed out by our most popular rappers—language that has become so mainstream, Imus's supporters argued, it was absurd to punish him.

Suddenly stories about hip-hop culture dominated the news. Hip-hop began with deejaying, break dancing, and graffiti-writing among black and Latino teens in New York City; it has expanded to fashion, nightclubs, and commercials. But its most recognizable and popular expression is rap: "a form of poetry said over musical instrumentation," much of it violent and demeaning to women.

Network news teams immediately descended on high schools and college campuses to poll the women students. "Do you ever call your friends *hos*?" "Would you be offended to be called one?" "What about *bitch*?"

The answers were ambivalent, hesitant, and mixed. Few adolescents wanted to be branded as prisses or prudes, and many talked about the ubiquity of these words in our culture. A lot, of course, depends on the context, but name-calling at its core dehumanizes and dishonors women. Ayanna, on the Web site My Sistahs, writes, "If a man labels a woman with any of these names, he may feel justified in committing physical or psychological violence against her."

The media, after ever-so-briefly pointing its moral compass at racist and sexist language, moved on and applauded Don Imus's quick return to the radio. But looking at the offending words dominating hip-hop culture is only a start. It's the stories the rappers tell that advance a brutal misogyny.

Their lyrics turn women into nothing but receptacles of sadistic male behavior. In "Low Down Dirty," Eminem "killed the bitch and did her," announcing he "support[s] domestic violence, Beat your bitches asses while your kids stare in silence . . . " And in "Just the Two of Us," he gives a detailed description of a man slitting his wife's throat. It's nothing more than ketchup on her shirt, he tells his son, before asking the boy for help in carrying this dead mother: "Because Da-da made a nice bed for mommy at the bottom of the lake."

The blue-eyed rapper's woman-hating music struck a responsive chord in macho America, gaining him three Grammy nominations in 2001. Academy Award–winning songwriter Randy Newman dismissed Eminem's misogyny, calling him "funny," while Madonna defended the twenty-eight-year-old singer as "just a boy," adding that "he's reflecting what's going on in society right now." It's not clear exactly what part of society the Material Girl was referring to? Domestic violence? Murder? Misogyny?

In our new gender politics, "[w]omen are disposable, exchangeable, throwaway commodities to charismatic males who bond around keeping them 'down' or in their place," says T. Denean Sharpley-Whiting, a professor of African American studies at Vanderbilt University.

The most common way that men relate to women in rap is as pimp and whore. Women are slapped, abused, and killed for disobeying, for getting in the way, for being women.

> *Punch the bitch in the eye / then the ho will fall to the ground*
> *Then you open up her mouth / put your dick in, move the shit around*

This—the recommended way to attack a fourteen-year-old—comes from the popular rap group N.W.A. In "One Less Bitch" they boast of tying a woman to a bed, raping, then shooting her. In "Too Much Trouble" a rapist kills his victim when she crawls for the phone. The hero of "Too $hort" slaps a young girl until she has oral sex with him, but she dies, choking on the semen in her windpipe.

Not all rap music urges men to "control 'their' women and define their own pleasure in that control," but a good amount of it regards women, especially black women, as degraded sex objects.

The exaggerated image of male aggression in rap, say the experts, "actually reflects male insecurity and long-standing powerlessness." The exploitation of women is a vehicle through which some young black men, seeing few healthy alternatives for themselves, express their manliness. It's not surprising—given the racism and classism of society—that inside these hypermasculine men are feelings of utter fragility. But finding empowerment through debasing and hurting others offers a very skewed and damaging view of masculinity. When you get your sense of self from violating and dominating others, you are trapped in an endless struggle for mastery. And its impact on women, "especially black women, who have less access to power, wealth and protection," and may come to see sex as "'the bartering chip,' the way to gain access," can be devastating.

Nikki, a thirty-year-old woman whose lovers read like a "Who's Who of Rap" list, explained it this way to *Vibe* magazine: "I've got nothing to offer. . . . No education, no good job, no nothing. So why would a man want me other than sex? I felt I had to give, so I used myself."

As the notion that our value equates with our sexuality embeds itself into our psyches, some women become complicit in patriarchy's use of them. It can be as consumers of the multibillion-dollar hip-hop industry, as one of the hundreds of flimsily dressed women who show up begging to be unpaid extras in rap videos, or as participants in a host of other male-controlled behaviors.

And while numerous new studies document how listening to rap music reviling women can prime or bring out sexist attitudes and tendencies, hip-hop is neither the cause of misogyny in America nor its only expression.

Sex, Death, and Video Games

"It's awesome," said James Parker, a Washington computer network administrator. "You can carjack any car, go to the seedy part of the town, beep the horn and pick up a prostitute. Then you take her to a dark street. . . . When the prostitute jumps out, your money is down, but your energy is full," so you get your cash back by killing the hooker.

Poor Pac-Man. If the 1980 icon of the arcade who looked like a pizza minus a slice found himself in one of today's video games, he'd be shot to smithereens. As for Mario, the famous plumber from Nintendo who uses superhuman jumping power to rescue Pauline and Princesses Peach and Daisy from the clutches of evil, he's probably labeled a wuss.

Thirty years ago the heroes of video games saved stereotypically weak women cast as damsels in distress. Now the most popular games are about raping and murdering highly sexualized women. The methods of killing are varied—knives, guns, poison, drowning—but overwhelmingly, vicious assaults on women are celebrated as the vital ingredient in electronic gaming, the second most popular form of entertainment in America.

Native American women are raped in Custer's Revenge, women fighters are brutally beaten to death in Mortal Kombat, and elderly women are battered with pipes in Road-Rash 3D. And instead of being punished for their deadly deeds, the perps are rewarded.

The most troubling of the games are known as "first-person shooters," in which the player advances by killing. In Duke Nukem, the gamer (Duke) goes into strip clubs and porn theaters where naked women are tied up to poles, pleading with Duke, "Kill me, kill me." And in the Grand Theft Auto games, the decapitated, mangled bodies left by the hero, a petty criminal making his way up the ranks to become an A-list killer, are often those of his female victims, whose pleas for mercy go unheeded.

"The level of brutality and violence in these games is disgusting, at best," admitted one of its fans, who is nonetheless hooked on the realism: the fast-moving cars, the gang wars, the ringing telephones, and the detail and accuracy of Liberty City where it all goes down. The graphic resolution of the games and use of 3-D give them an unprecedented authenticity, make for more excitement, and blur the line between fantasy and reality. As one seasoned player observed, "They're less like games and more like experiences."

The gaming industry is both extraordinarily profitable and savvy, using age compression to get kids as young as eight to buy "teen" videos and those of twelve to want those rated "Mature." One way is to market action figures, like killer-Duke, to those ten years old and up. But most preteens don't play with action figures anymore. Little boys do, and when they bond with Duke, they get sold on the brand at a very young age.

A lot of us don't really know the content of the games our kids play. In a survey of over six hundred parents and teachers, less than 3 percent knew about the antifemale content of Grand Theft Auto (GTA). More than 70 percent of American preteen and teenage boys have played the Grand Theft Auto videos even though they're labeled M (Mature—not recommended for anyone under twenty-five). "[E]very day millions of boys and young men are entertaining themselves with a game that denigrates women and glamorizes violence against them," wrote the nonpartisan MediaWise Video Game Report Card. Overall, they said, the gaming industry showed "an increasingly appalling attitude toward women."

Although critics have noted the general violence in Grand Theft Auto IV, there's been little talk in the mainstream press about its misogyny.

One reviewer, defending GTA, said that the games don't *create* violent sex, they only tap into a prevailing male fantasy. But even if that were true, why should boys as young as ten play games glorifying and normalizing thoughts that sometimes lead to destructive behavior against women?

Plenty of evidence links exposure to media violence with aggressive behavior and shows how video games, because of their interactive nature, can have an even greater impact, imprinting violence in the minds of their players.

Video games also may play a part in the psychological process known as desensitization. Over a period of time, contact with screen violence will weaken feelings of concern and empathy toward victims of real violence. Participants in several experiments exposed to media violence demonstrated far less sympathy for rape and domestic violence victims and rated their injuries less severe than those in the control group.

Porn Goes Mainstream

Electronic gaming is a younger brother to the pornography industry. The resemblance is striking in terms of porn's online accessibility, its soaring popularity, and the male and female roles it glorifies. Pornography shames, abuses, and demeans women while exalting male violence and control. Maintaining hegemony over women, pornography makes female subordination appear erotic, sexy, and thrilling. Its message to women is: do whatever your man tells you, be the hot, grateful girlfriend, the patient, adoring wife. Expect to be hurt, want it, ask for it. You deserve it. You even enjoy it. Your subjugation and pain are a major turn-on. The more powerless you are, the more attractive you become.

Use of pornography in this country stretches back to our nation's earliest days. Although the word didn't enter the English language until the 1850s, "ribald" or "bawdy" images meant to incite sexual desire beyond the norms of propriety were available during the colonial period, especially to the elite, who could afford to import them clandestinely from Europe. It wasn't until the mid-nineteenth century, spurred on by photography and commercial printing, that erotica became mass produced, although still consumed stealthily in controlled settings.

Over the past thirty years the industry's change has been more dramatic than anything preceding it. Once "raincoaters" (as the industry calls them) peeked at porn in the darkened corners of society; now they boast their interest. Porn has gone mainstream—part of pop culture, widely available, and increasingly accepted.

During the 1980s, with the VCR sweeping America at the same time as the AIDS epidemic, wary sexual explorers found cause to stay at home. Before long, lewd magazine pictures and seedy porn theaters were eclipsed by DVDs, VHS, our own home computers. Add to these the pay-per-view movies available on cable, satellite, and in motel rooms, paid phone sex, and sex toys, and it comes to a whopping ten-billion-dollar business, bigger than professional baseball, basketball, and football combined. We have more outlets for hard-core porn in America than we do McDonald's restaurants.

"Porn doesn't have a demographic—it goes across demographics," Paul Fishbein, the founder of *Adult Video News*, a journal rating adult videos, says. Some twenty years after he began his business, this compact forty-nine-year-old commands an empire with trade shows, its own awards dinners, ten Web sites, and AVN Online.

Fishbein is "proud of what he does." His mother comes to his awards table every year, watching as the girls get honored for oral sex. Porn, to him, is just another form of sex. "Sex . . . drives the media," he says. "Billboards, movies, ads, commercials. It's what we're thinking about all times of the day."

"It still amazes me," said Dr. Jane Brickman, chair of the humanities department at the Merchant Marine Academy, "when I walk over to cadets looking at porn online in the library, they don't even bother to switch their screens."

Maybe they've been emboldened by supreme court justice Clarence Thomas's long attachment to pornography—a topic aired at his confirmation hearings in 1991. Yale classmate Don Johnson recalls Thomas's saying, "My favorite movie of all time is [the porn flick] *Deep Throat*. I've seen that motherfucker six times." How much more mainstream can you get than that? An endorsement by someone who serves on the highest court in the country.

The combination of Britney Spears's breakthrough videos orchestrated by a porn director, with stars like Jenna Jameson giving away trade secrets in *How to Make Love Like a Porn Star* and becoming the public face of the multibillion-dollar industry and making non–X-rated appearances on TV, could lead us to imagine that porn has started preaching the gospel of nonviolent sex.

But nothing could be further from the truth. The panelists at the 2007 National Feminist Conference on Pornography and Popular Culture held in Boston made it clear just how far. A team of experts analyzed *Adult Video News*'s top picks for a period of six months and chose 250 to study. The films contained a total of thirty-three hundred acts of aggression, approximately one per every minute and a half, overwhelmingly male toward female. When women did aggress (which was rare), it was to other women, not men. Verbal aggression, hurling out words like *bitch*, *slut*, and *whore*, were usually combined with slapping, gagging, choking, biting, kicking, and the use of weapons. Violence, in general, came after some form of extreme sex, like anal penetration followed by fellatio, known in the industry as ATM (ass-to-mouth). As one member of the panel put it, "The women are literally forced to eat their own shit."

Kissing, usually associated with affection, was present in less than 10 percent of the scenes, condom use only in 11 percent. In almost every scene in which a woman was abused, she either stayed silent or cooed her approval with a whispered "This feels great" or "I love this." "The distorted message is that women are choosing this kind of treatment," said panelist Ana Bridges, who's done exhaustive work on the subject. "In most instances vicious behavior was rewarded, in no case was the aggressor punished."

The main consumers of pornography are male, so it's no real surprise that male desires and sexual practices are overrepresented in porn and women's are grossly underrepresented. This is so even in the less than 7 percent of videos directed by women. One difference was more woman-to-woman sex.

"Look, I think there's tons of research linking porn to increased real-life violence," says Kim Cho, a young woman leading a discussion for a New York–based prisoners' rights organization. She rifles through her briefcase and hands out stapled packets with the results of several meta-analyses looking at the effects of pornography on sexual aggression. In a few hours the group is heading upstate to visit two correctional facilities. Violence is very much on their minds.

One study, conducted by University of Texas's Robert Jensen, considered an expert on pornography, is based on interviews with sex offenders and pornography users and concludes that the use of pornography can initiate victims, break down their resistance to unwanted sexual activity, and contribute to the user's difficulty in separating sexual fantasy and reality. Other research posits a relationship between viewing dehumanizing materials and a greater likelihood of "engaging in rape or other coercive sex acts than in the control group."

"I don't buy this," says twenty-eight-year-old Jody, who works with formerly incarcerated women. She points to another article on how the use of porn affects a couple's bed. For a moment everyone looks over the piece. "First, many women believed they were no longer sexually attractive to their partners, and this was the reason why sexual relations had diminished. Secondly, in relationships where sexual relations had continued despite the partner's pornography use, women believed they were viewed more as sexual objects than real people in the relationship."

"I don't know who they interviewed," Jody says. "My boyfriend and I look at porn together once or twice a week, and it helps our relationship. As a sex-positive feminist, I enjoy porn and find it empowering."

THE TERMS *SEX-POSITIVE* or *prosex feminist* arose in opposition to anti-porn feminists of the 1980s. The latter, best embodied by the writings of Catharine MacKinnon and Andrea Dworkin, condemned pornography for its dehumanization of women and advocated a civil rights approach that enabled women to sue in civil court. Some of their opponents accused them of calling for a ban. MacKinnon and Dworkin did a real service to women—and to men—by opening our eyes to the violence and domination inherent in the porn industry. But however brilliant many of their insights, their legacy has been haunted by critics linking them to the extreme right. As it happens, Dworkin wrote a book critiquing right-wing women and their support of patriarchy. But for the many

First Amendment freaks like me, anything that might lead to censorship is a major red flag.

Of course the press, typically eager to fan the flames of differences among women, jumped into the dispute and proclaimed the "Feminist Sex Wars." Reductionist as always, the hyped-up media coverage drew a bright line separating one group from the other. Antiporn feminists immediately became synonymous with an angry, repressive hostility to men, denying a woman's right to enjoy sex or her own sexual agency. In short, being opposed to pornography became conflated with being sex-negative, or antisex. Anyone who didn't find it a major turn-on to see a woman in chains, with a knife at her throat, being screwed by two men at a time, was a tight-laced Victorian killjoy.

As for sex-positive feminists, well, they were a wild group of kinky, self-indulgent girls, far younger and prettier than the bad-haired man-haters before them. Do-me feminists, as the *Wall Street Journal* dubbed them, got lots of acclaim. Many men applauded the advent of the new feminatrix. After all, men had long suspected what conservative writer Christine Hoff Sommers came right out and said: women become feminists because they're ugly. "They go around preaching antisex, antimale sermons [because] they're just mad at the beautiful girls."

So has the younger generation of women finally realized that the panty is mightier than the pen?

Hardly.

In reality both sides urgently believe they're fighting for what's in the best interest of women. And both points of view are shaded by nuances and areas of agreement not obvious from the way the topic has been reported.

Dana Clark, a sex-positive sex educator from Olympia, Washington, teaches workshops at colleges and private parties. "Being sex-positive," she said, "means that you have personally abandoned shame about sex and that you're open to all possibilities that sex brings to your life."

As opposed to whom?

Certainly not the second-wavers, who wrote and devoured *Our Bodies, Ourselves*, the book that sent thousands of college girls into the bathroom with mirrors between their legs so they could examine their genitals. That told us "[m]asturbation is a special way of enjoying ourselves" and then gave us instructions on how to do it.

Shame? I don't think so.

As for Susan Brison, the prosex, proerotica Dartmouth professor who makes a point of saying she's "anti–violence against women and anti–sexual torture and sexual murder as entertainment"—her views sound pretty much like those of most of the antiporn crowd.

And what about the late, sex-loathing Andrea Dworkin? Here's what she had to say when asked directly what sex is: "I think of sexual contact and sexual intimacy as pleasure. . . . And as a way of experiencing freedom."

Here's the thing: you can be prosex and antiporn, and proporn and anti–sexual intimacy.

The fact is feminists understand that the issues surrounding pornography are complex and entangled with aspects of femininity, masculinity, sexuality, and the distribution of power in this country. We see how our arguments have been oversimplified and polarized. You don't have to support censorship to protest the objectification of women. And it isn't denying women their sexual agency or being prudes if we condemn those who do violence to women's bodies.

What I hear from both sides is the hope that sex will only be engaged in freely by consenting adults with the expectation that it will be mutually pleasurable and fulfilling. From this point of concurrence we should look to establish middle ground with women whose views differ from our own. To paraphrase one of the panelists at a Boston conference, we should try to find a way to piss off both Jerry Falwell and Larry Flynt.

MEANWHILE, AT THE prisoners' rights meeting, Jody's comment has unwittingly sparked a deeply felt conversation about the morality of supporting pornography.

"Are you saying the girls who act in the porn flicks don't have the right to do it?" Jody asks, her voice rising.

No one has suggested that. But several in the group have noted that most young women who get drawn into the pornography industry either have histories of sexual abuse or very few other economic options. And even if you could point to one, let's say Jenna Jameson, who has achieved stardom and a certain amount of control over her life, when you consume pornography you're supporting an industry where women most assuredly will be hurt, physically battered, and emotionally scarred in the future.

"But that's still their choice," Jody said, ending the discussion.

"Choice"—Suddenly Turned Against Us

Over the past decade the concept of choice has become a verbal sledge-hammer used to silence complex explanations for women's decisions. Not too long ago, being pro-choice meant you supported reproductive justice. Now the word has been appropriated and turned against women. Choosing is seen as something happening in a vacuum, disassociated from constraining circumstances, without any consideration of the possible pushes and pressures during this time of cultural undertow. It's the perfect expression of our individualistic, dog-eat-dog times. Personal responsibility has become code for "society is not accountable."

Few would say Katrina flood victims *chose* to flee their homes, but we shrug our shoulders about a working mom who routinely puts in heavy overtime because she needs the money with a dismissive "Well, that's her choice." In the same way, one commentator, describing porn actresses and prostitutes, punned, "These girls made their beds, now they have to lie in them."

When the news broke about former New York governor Eliot Spitzer's involvement with the Emperors Club, a pricey prostitution ring, Harvard law professor Alan M. Dershowitz declared on MSNBC that it was no big deal. Based on the "it's her choice" argument, Dershowitz, a noted civil rights activist, famously declared "prostitution is a victimless crime."

John Stossel expressed the same view on ABC. "Don't prostitutes own their bodies? Shouldn't they be able to freely contract to use their bodies as they wish? Who was hurt here?" He reiterated, "This is a victimless crime."

To be fair these men and all the others who ascribe to the doctrine of free choice probably weren't thinking about sex trafficking. Most of us are horrified about the young girls disappearing from Thailand, Cambodia, and Eastern Europe, a good number of them actually brought to the United States through New York City and San Francisco and kept in inhumane, unimaginable conditions. And girls are being snatched off streets here too, in shocking numbers. More than one hundred thousand children and young women, ranging in age from nine to nineteen, are currently trafficked in America. Malls, beaches, ski slopes, even local streets are hunted by procurers looking for young prey.

Some girls are runaways from terrible family situations. But increasingly, the FBI says, they're like Debbie—the fifteen-year-old straight-A student from a close-knit air force family in suburban Phoenix, kidnapped right in front of her home. Debbie was held captive at gunpoint, periodically gang-raped, forced to have sex with approximately fifty different men, and kept locked in a dog crate until she was rescued forty days after her abduction.

But even if we put sex trafficking in a special category of horrors, devastating similarities afflict the lives of all prostitutes.

"It's the men who buy prostitutes who spew the myth that women choose prostitution, that they get rich, that it's glamorous and turns women on," says Melissa Farley, author of *Prostitution and Trafficking in Nevada*.

The women who worked for the Emperors Club had to have sex as often as twice an hour; the pimps kept half of what they made. Ashley Alexandra Dupré, otherwise known as Kristen, Spitzer's "date," said she'd been abused, homeless for a time, and a drug user, but still she's far better off than most in the trade.

Those who work with street prostitutes paint a very different picture from wine-sipping trysts at four-star hotels. In this dark, unsafe world of garbage-strewn rooms and fetid alleys, pimps exercise total control. To prove ownership, in an act reminiscent of slavery, a pimp may insist that "his girls" have his name tattooed on their thigh. He may give them some presents as a way of cementing loyalty, but most often they are chained to their miserable lives by fear.

In one study of 114 prostitutes, "82 percent had been victimized by physical violence, 78 percent threatened with a weapon, 48 percent had been raped more than five times." The *American Journal of Epidemiology* (*AJE*) reported that the "workplace homicide rate for prostitutes is 51 times that of working in a liquor store, the second most dangerous place for women."

Typically girls, especially the runaways, get into "the life" at thirteen or fourteen years old. They don't last long. The *AJE* study found the average age of death for the prostitutes studied to be thirty-four. And as for enjoying their lives, 81 percent of the women Melissa Farley interviewed desperately wanted to escape.

Under the constant threat of violence, girls turn tricks all night until they reach their quotas. But the pimps pocket all the cash. "I have a really good pimp—he beats me only with an open hand," one young woman told Rachel Lloyd, the founder of a program for teenage prostitutes in New York City. Any infraction of the "rules"—not bringing in your allocated amount of cash, looking your pimp in the eye, calling him by name—can result in a beating, or it can rain down completely unexpectedly with terrifying force.

Because most prostitutes are not high-priced call girls but more often poor women and women of color, what Rachel Lloyd, herself a former prostitute, calls "throwaways," they're invisible to society. Not one of the 250 young women she's worked with has ever been deemed "worthy" of an amber alert, the urgent communitywide bulletin issued when a child has been abducted.

Women become prostitutes for a variety of reasons, but usually it's to escape from poverty, from a dangerous domestic situation, or both. That young women actively choose the life is simply one more fiction justifying our nation's laissez-faire approach to social and economic problems we'd rather ignore than fix.

Most Americans get their ideas about prostitution from Hollywood rather than experience. And sex workers in films tend to be a type: smart, witty, beautiful, and wealthy (or certain to be before your popcorn runs out). The heroines in *Irma la Douce* (*The Sweet*), *Pretty Woman*, *Klute*, and *Mayflower Madam* are likable, independent, and goodheartedly generous. Belle Watling, the "painted lady" of *Gone with the Wind* who gives her wages to the Confederate cause, is a far more honorable soul than the proper women who shun her. (Belle Brezling, the prostitute on whom Watling's character was based, actually died a morphine-addicted pauper.) And *Klute*'s Bree Daniels (Jane Fonda), stalked by a killer, puts her life in danger because she won't disappoint an old man whose only happiness comes from sitting off to the side, watching her undress.

Misleading and highly romanticized as these portrayals are, they at least exhibit a modicum of sympathy for their subjects, a sympathy that's entirely absent in the present mainstream media take on the topic.

"Bad Girl" blasted the *New York Post* in March 2008, giving us a full frontal shot of "Kristen," wearing nothing on top except her hands, followed by inside spreads of salacious photographs. Other media heavies like *Us Weekly* ran a series of seminude pictures called Portraits of a Prostitute. "Boo-Hoo! Don't Shed Any Tears for This Busty Brat," screamed another headline, blaming the call girl for Spitzer's jarring lapses.

The Right Amount of Sexy

Whatever Eliot Spitzer's transgressions, the chattering crowd, including some of his loudest critics, such as MSNBC's Tucker Carlson, made excuses for his behavior. "[M]en are pretty dumb when it comes to stuff like that. It's kind of who they are," said Carlson.

Maybe talking about powerful males with zipper problems is too 1990s. In our present misogynist society, macho men naturally have robust carnal appetites. It's not their fault if they're lured astray by the true transgressors—seductive women. It's a lesson many boys get in school. *Reasonable Reasons to Wait*, an abstinence-only workbook, preaches that "girls' attire can rouse sexual feelings in boys. . . . A boy can get the wrong message from what a girl might wear." Another workbook, *Sex Respect*, says, "Deep down, you know that your friend's plunging necklines and short skirts are getting the guys to talk about her. Is that what you want? To see girls drive guys' hormones when a guy is trying to see her as a friend? . . . Is it fair that guys are turned on by their senses?"

On LoveMatters.com, evangelical Mike Mathews, commenting on how sexy fashions inflame male passion, asks, "Why do men react this way, and why don't women always realize it?" and answers, "Because men and women are 'wired' differently when it comes to the human body." Mathews urges us to "remember, the sight of a woman's body is so powerful for men, that unless men are well trained and highly disciplined," just about anything can happen.

A dangerous contradiction exists in our consumerist culture. Everywhere women and girls turn, 24/7, we're exhorted to be sexier, younger, hotter versions of ourselves. And when we comply? Bingo! We're damned as temptresses.

"Figuring out the right amount of sexy is the biggest obstacle women face today," a twenty-six-year-old responded on my survey. With every aspect of popular culture pressing us to be objects ripe for male consumption, where do we draw the line? Certainly not as we age. In "The Graying of Naughty," the *New York Times* introduced us to De' Bella, a fifty-year-old clad in a black chiffon and pink satin nightie sheer enough to show off her matching thong. "I love sex," gushes this administrative assistant who dreams of making it big as a porn star.

And *Tech Digest* announced the new gaming concept the Peekaboo Pole in response to the new pole dancing craze hitting America. "Pole Dancing Parties Catch On in Book Club Country" we're told, the teachers hawking the promise to "unleash that sexual kitten" within us all.

"Be a Sex Genius," advises *Cosmopolitan*, while *Glamour* gives us the "Orgasm Q&A" and as an add-on provides "Men's Advice About Sex." *Cosmo* also boosts the authoritative male voice with "What Men Want You to Know About Sex." *W*'s cover says "Sexy" in bold letters, referring to Cameron Diaz, and *Vogue* wants us to be "Sexy Comme Kate Moss." The power of seduction is showcased by Victoria's Secret, featuring nubile models strutting and posing in the scantiest of undergarments on huge screens all over their midtown stores.

No one—except those on the far right—would cheer the return of docile, sequestered womanhood, but trading girdles for garter belts in the name of liberation carries its own risks.

Self-objectification. That's what happens, psychologists say, when we see ourselves only through the eyes of others. Instead of refusing the one-size-fits-all prefabricated image, we become unquestioning and self-critical, monitoring our actions and appearances to satisfy the critical male gaze.

We dress for the supermarket as if we're heading to a strip club. Younger women proudly wear T-shirts with WHY DO I NEED BRAINS WHEN I HAVE THESE? written across the chest, and FUCK FOREPLAY scrawled over a tube of KY Jelly, broadcasting the message that women will be ready to open their legs on demand.

The pressure to accede to these demeaning images is enormous. In my online survey one of the most surprising responses I received was to a set of questions about equality: Do the women you know think of themselves as equal to men? Most answered yes. But then to the follow-up question, Do they *act* as though they are equal to men? astonishingly, a huge number said no:

"All around me I see women being controlled by a bizarre set of ideas that we have to act submissive . . . to be counted."

"I don't think the women's rights movement worked out for American women under a certain age. Young women seem to think that sex is their only power."

"We still live in a world totally controlled by men. Women do what they must and act as they must to get ahead."

"Men make the rules, women play by them, even if it means playing the sex kitten."

By allowing others to define who we are and how we behave, we sacrifice our identity and autonomy. A striking example of self-abnegation forms the subtext of bestselling author Stephenie Meyer's young adult series. Starting with *Twilight*, these books feature smart, capable high schooler Bella Swan, who falls in love with her mysterious classmate Edward Cullen. Everything about Edward is appealing, even the fact that he's a vampire. In the course of their relationship, he rescues Bella from numerous accidents and mishaps, but Edward himself is actually the greatest threat. "As if I needed another motive to kill you," he bursts out on one occasion.

The risks Edward poses to Bella's life are plentiful, but these perils are portrayed as exciting and sexy, and sometimes as a cause for sympathy. Bella finds herself filled with compassion for Edward, "even now, as he confessed his craving to take my life." Encouraging the idea that young women are (or should be) drawn to dangerous men, these books give us a heroine who is willing and eager to give up everything, even her life, to be completely subsumed by her lover.

Lesser forms of female self-forfeiture are apparent among Bella's human counterparts. Author Jackson Katz, in his outstanding work with boys and young men, recently noted, "Many young women now engage in sex acts with men that prioritize the man's pleasure with little or no expectation of reciprocity."

Particularly worrisome, some girls and women see objectification as a kind of empowerment. There's a faux feminism permeating the atmosphere masquerading as hip and sophisticated. Even the most degrading acts, as long as they're seemingly your choice, are considered liberating. This way of thinking puts women in the company of such seedy manipulators as Joe Francis, the producer of the Girls Gone Wild (GGW) videos.

When asked why college girls, some underage, most who have had *many* too many drinks, dance on bars, flash their breasts, and French kiss one another, Francis says, "It's empowering, it's freedom."

With his camera crew, Francis stalks college towns and spring break haunts—Cancun, South Beach, Padre Island—to film women who'll take it all off for the camera, offer their shaved genitals up for inspection, and fondle their breasts. If there's liberation here, it belongs to Francis, who'll never have to hold a nine-to-five job again in his life. He's making a veritable fortune with GGW, broadening his brand to include an apparel line, restaurants, and cruises. Referred to in the tabloids as the new Hugh Hefner, Francis has no illusions about his purpose: "Everything that gets covered in my name drives the business."

A few decades ago, women's groups and individual women would have castigated Francis and his cynical use of young women, many of whom are too drunk to resist pressure from the six-foot-two video producer. Now, to criticize GGW is to be considered uncool, retro, or worse. Far better to stay quiet than to risk ridicule by bucking the trends. But it is a peculiarity of our consumer-obsessed society that we've come to equate commercialization with freedom. In reality we're encouraged to desire consumer products along with the images used to sell them and, finally, to become these images ourselves.

Understandably young women accustomed to Facebook, MySpace, and YouTube have a sense of privacy different from those who hid the keys to their diaries, but even so it's hard to see "going wild" for the camera as anything but reinforcing women's subjugated status. In one spring break video, one of Joe's girls boasts, "I'm ready and willing, and I'm a dirty slut."

"Anybody enjoys the attention. T-shirts, hats—we got all the accessories. It's almost like your fifteen minutes of fame," said twenty-one-year-old Jillian Vangeerty. Kaitlyn Bultema, who planned on going wild the moment she turned eighteen, earning the camera men who found her an extra thousand, said, "I want everyone to see me because I'm hot. If you do this, you might get noticed by somebody [and become] an actress or model. Getting famous will get me anything I want."

For some young women it's a way of drawing attention and feeling important. For others, "going wild" is a symbol of the "if you can't beat 'em, join 'em" philosophy—a sense that you can do whatever men can. But freedom, as Janis Joplin sang, may be "just another word for nothing left to lose." Being free isn't the same thing as being equal, the harsh lesson quickly learned by postemancipation African Americans in the United States.

It isn't a question of whether or not young women have the right to participate in GGW. What is in question is that being a sexual object affords sexual agency or any agency whatsoever. Actually it's a contradiction in terms. An object is a thing, a commodity. It has no force or authority of its own. It is the recipient of action, in this case, the action and authority of a group of dominating men.

I know I'm not the only one who finds it surprising and disturbing that young women are embracing objectification as a kind of might, as a way of having control. But how could they not when they've been sexualized since childhood?

What I'm coming to think is that women of all ages carry around in their heads a longing to be autonomous, independent, to feel that they matter. In a society exalting hypermasculinity it may well be that they're searching for something, *anything* to give them a sense of power because they feel threatened by the culture's insistence on their deficiencies and deviancies. That women would use their sexuality may strike some as sad, but it really isn't surprising—it's what we've always fallen back on when we've seen no other options, no other paths to finding an identity.

22

DESPERATELY SEEKING SELF

"We may not (all) aspire to be bitches, but it's a step in the right direction to see women celebrated for something other than young, delicate, quiet and pretty," writes author Ariel Levy in a recent article on the new "bitch culture." So we can be either Dracula or a lifeless doll—what options! This dichotomy is yet another version of the diminishing madonna/whore split gaining currency in society.

I'm certainly not welcoming a new age of bitchiness, but part of me can understand where Levy is coming from. It's been a long time since any of us have seen women celebrated for being smart, kind, talented, athletic, adventurous, stoic, or creative. And this omission, simultaneously a cause and a result of the marginalization of women, has a profound effect. Over the past few decades, we've lost our sense of self, our confidence in our inner worth and purpose.

Women are facing an identity void, and one place we look to find it is in our passionate devotion to celebrity culture. "My parents' generation had the sixties and seventies, women's rights and the Beatles. What do we have? Paris Hilton," one young woman said, accurately summing up the situation.

Larger-than-life personalities—Marilyn Monroe, Grace Kelly, Princess Diana—have always captured our collective imagination, but nothing approaches the current starstruck mania. Graydon Carter, editor of *Vanity Fair* since 1992, sees Americans as "more 'obsessed' than ever by celebrity culture." To some extent, it's a distraction from the hideous realities of our post-9/11 world, but there's a deeper dynamic drawing young women into the glittery celebrity stratosphere.

"We want to live their lives," said La Toya Taylor, a college sophomore. When Jake Halpern, author of *Fame Junkies*, interviewed 650 middle school kids from Rochester, New York, the girls he spoke to chose being famous over being smart. And given the option of numerous professions—college presidents, doctors, U.S. senators, and the like—they yearned to be celebrities and even celebrity assistants—underpaid and unappreciated as they are—more than any other job.

Celebrity news and gossip come at us from every direction. Originally media junk food, they're fast becoming our steady diet, often eclipsing real news stories. The day Britney Spears lost custody of her children, the *Larry King Live*, *Anderson Cooper 360*, and *Nancy Grace* shows all headlined the "breaking story" on CNN.

Back in 2004 the major news networks—ABC, CBS, NBC—spent a combined 130 minutes on Martha Stewart's legal woes and devoted just twenty-six minutes to the tragedy in Darfur.

At a time when newsmagazines and newspapers are seeing dwindling numbers of readers, celebrity weeklies are growing. "In the first half of 2005 *Us Weekly*'s paid circulation shot up by 24 percent to 1.7 million, *Star*'s increased 21 percent to 1.4 million, while *People* led the pack at 3.7 million." VH1, formerly a music video channel, is now host to *Celebrity Showdown 2* and *40 Greatest Celebrity Feuds*. And *Entertainment Tonight* and *Access Hollywood* dish up their own tasty bits for prime-time viewing.

All day every day, Web sites such as E! Online, TMZ, Hollyscoop, Celebrity Gossip Twitter, Celebrity Gossip, Gossip Blog Coverage, and Celebrity Baby Blog get hits from young women addicted to Jennifer Aniston's latest romance and Lindsay Lohan's drinking problems. Mario Lavandeira Jr., whose blog PerezHilton.com won him acclaim from the *New York Times*, says he gets about six million visits a day. One woman told National Public Radio host Tom Ashbrook she checks PerezHilton.com twelve times a day from her office computer.

On an average morning at a New York sports club in Manhattan, at 5:45 A.M. all of the fifty machines are already taking a pounding by twenty- or thirtysomethings who need to be in early at work. Most of the multitaskers (reading and exercising) are young women. One or two have newspapers, the others—twenty-eight, in fact—are scanning shiny-paged star tabloids: *US Weekly, Star, OK, Globe, People.*

In 2006 eight of Yahoo's top ten search terms were the names of celebrities. Typing in *celebrity gossip* on Google brings up 377,000 sites. By comparison *equal pay for women* gets you 187,000 and *abortion rights* 144,000.

It's a feeding frenzy. And it's self-fulfilling. As the number of media outlets multiplies, they generate the need for a constant supply of telegenic stars to fill the ever-expanding celebrity slots. Suddenly the word *celebrity* has become attached to trainers, chefs, stylists, doctors, and designers, pole-vaulting the newly anointed into superstars with their own television shows and bestselling books.

We devour the tidbits they throw our way. Who's in love? Who's in rehab? Who's in over her head? How did Miley Cyrus fix her crooked teeth? Are Natalie Portman and Devendra Banhart really a pair? What diet helped Christina shed her pregnancy pounds? We call them by their first names—Katie, Paris, Angelina—and debate their behavior as if they were family. Our need to feel close to these women, to nurture the illusion of intimacy, to slip into their personas, is palpable. That's why knock-offs of red carpet gowns sell so spectacularly and a celebrity endorsement of a product—Cameron Diaz wearing J & Co. jeans—sets off a spike in sales. And now girls have found a new way to imitate their idols. "Hair stylists have become skilled in giving a twelve-year-old Paris Hilton's blonde tresses, Vanessa Hudgens' black curls, and even differentiate between the Ashley Tisdale of *High School Musical* and Ashlee Simpson, the singer," writes Camille Sweeney in the *New York Times.*

"Stars—they're just like US!" proclaims *US Weekly,* feeding our false sense of intimacy with them. They wait in line to use the restroom, their kids knock their glasses, they lick sprinkles off their ice-cream cones. We can relate to them! And if they only knew us—they'd feel the same. As the new generation of publicity-seeking stars invites us to look at the messy, off-limits aspects of their lives, the lines between us blur. We feel we know them as well as we know our friends.

Of course a lot of young women scoff at the obvious attention-grabbing stunts and say they're sick of hearing about Katie and Tom's marital problems. But, as one wrote, "I think our fascination with celebrities makes us think of their shallow accomplishments as worthy, but that said, I can't get enough of it."

"It's the Warholian phenomenon," media watcher Ronna Reich said. In her years of studying what motivates girls and young women, she's seen a dramatic increase in their attachment to celebrities. Reich, who owns the PR firm Ink and Roses, said, "For many girls it represents a way of feeling affirmed, of gaining status, as though they, too, are bathed in the stars' aura."

It's hard to resist the gravitational pull of the star-studded pages. Perhaps our attachment to celebrities confers a sense of belonging and significance that feels all the more important because our connections to other people, organizations, and social causes are declining. Many young women I interviewed, even those with families, spoke of feeling lonely. "I'm not certain how to describe it," said a mother of three from Chicago. "I see a lot of people during the day because of my kids, but I still feel this kind of isolation."

In my survey very few respondents wrote that they "participate in any community activities and organizations." Fewer still—and this was a surprise—responded to questions about the women they admire by talking about their friends. And when they wrote about what in life brought them happiness, only a handful mentioned their friendships.

These anecdotal findings are consistent with a recent study in the *American Sociological Review* reporting a drop over the past two decades in the friends and confidants we have outside of our immediate families. Increasing numbers of Americans (double what it was in 1985) say they have no one to turn to or talk to about serious matters. For women, who have traditionally found support and affirmation from their close friendships, the sense of loss is acute, especially because few of us these days are walking around with Helen Reddy's encouraging words in our heads: "I am strong. I am invincible. I am woman." Instead we hear the droning buzz saw of criticism, undermining our choices whether we stay home or work, pitting us against one another, trivializing our achievements, and deriding, even ridiculing, feminist beliefs. No wonder we don't confide in each other. No wonder we want to identify with those who seem so powerful, so secure, so established. We're pulled into their orbit and believe—and are encouraged to believe—that we're part of their community, sharing their values and ideals.

But what a pernicious, antiwoman community it is! On the surface it appears otherwise. The glamorous lifestyles, the exciting getaways, the coupling and uncoupling at will all wow us into believing the stars are independent and autonomous. But they're more like schoolgirls monitored by the toughest of ruler-wielding headmistresses. Some commentators have noticed a double standard in play, with women stars getting what publicist-to-the-celebs Ken Sunshine calls "rougher treatment, less sensitive treatment, more outrageous treatment" than their male counterparts.

Week after week the glossy pages scream at the famous to lose weight, shape up, buy more flattering clothes. Bodies of rail-thin actresses are mercilessly scrutinized for signs of cellulite, making its comeback as public enemy number one. And we are unwittingly entrapped into becoming participants in this sexist world by sitting in judgment: Who has the best bikini body? (*Star*); Who has the best "Body After Baby"? (*US Weekly*); "Who Wore It Better?" (*In Touch*). Everything is a vote, everything a contest.

It's the age-old competitive game, divide and conquer. Jess is jealous of Ashlee's baby news, Kate Hudson and Anne Hathaway are warring, and Paris Hilton is at odds with reality-show star Kim Kardashian—presumably jealous of the actress's butt! And on it goes.

Author and feminist-slammer Camille Paglia loves celebrity culture, especially its acknowledgment that beauty matters above all else. But it's a good bet she also applauds its insidious marginalizing message. Celebrity tabloids don't celebrate anything the women do except exercise, party, and shop. Oh, and have babies.

Not since the Victorian glory days has motherhood been so deified. Jennifer Lopez sold photographs of her infant twins to *People* for six million dollars, and pictures of Brad Pitt and Angelina Jolie's tiny twosome fetched fifteen million. The weeklies go after "baby bumps" with the determination of truffle-sniffing hogs. "The one thing that *US Weekly* has done, that's a great boost to the nation is, they've probably increased the birthrate," social critic Tom Wolfe commented. Within the glossy pages pregnant stars look gorgeous as ever, showing off their tummies. Morning sickness, bone-tired fatigue, varicose veins, and stretch marks have no place in this pixie-dust world. Halle Berry is "all aglow," "Nicole Richie never looked better than when she was preggers," and Gwen Stefani's baby turned her album *No Doubt* into "the most inspired record so far."

If there's trouble in paradise, it's not looking pregnant *enough*. *Star* magazine gasps, "[S]kinny-minny Nicole Kidman, who is having her first baby at 40 . . . barely looks like she's expecting! The dress is definitely hiding something, but 20 weeks?" The tabloid goes on to give her an ignominious "last in the race for the most prominent baby belly."

If *looking* pregnant is important, than loving every minute of motherhood is next to godliness. "My passion is my family," gushes model Claudia Schiffer, while Marcia Cross of *Desperate Housewives* claims, "My life is centered around home now." And Gwyneth Paltrow told *Entertainment Weekly* after her daughter Apple was born, "I can't imagine going back to shoot a movie."

Celebrity moms are dishing out retrograde fare. Their proclamations are powerful and subtle endorsements of a romantic dream we should have awakened from decades ago. Maternal bliss is real, but nonstop maternal bliss is a fairy tale, a story foisted upon us by magazine mothers and the artificial world they represent, making the rest of us feel guilty as hell.

Just about all moms adore their babies, and many would love to be home with them, at least for a time. But few of us have the options or ease of these A-listers who—I'm only guessing here—haven't spent too many nights pacing the floors with a crying infant, dashing out at 6:00 A.M. to buy diapers and then rushing home to sort through piles of laundry searching for the one blouse that doesn't have spit-up on it to wear to work. But we're supposed to forget all that, forget that they have entourages of help: nannies, cooks, housekeepers, stylists, and personal trainers on call 24/7. We're supposed to think they're just like us. So if Julia and Gwyneth and Angelina aren't complaining, then how can we?

Celebrity culture rigorously defines its boundaries by public outings of the "deviants"—Ashlee Simpson for drinking while pregnant, Britney

Spears for . . . just about everything. The media hypes these stories, giving the impression that it cares deeply about unborn babies and child welfare while totally ignoring the profiles of poor women who can't afford decent prenatal care or lose custody of their babies because they can't support them. But hey—it's much more fun to sigh over the spectacular mishaps of the it girls while insidiously strengthening the celebrity community's core values—beauty, youth, and airbrushed motherhood.

Because it's silly and trivial and even fun, celebrity culture feels deceptively harmless. But we shouldn't be fooled. The seductive, picturesque landscape of Hollywood is a minefield for feminism and the rights women struggled to secure.

23

MORE THAN A FEW GOOD WOMEN

From what we read and see today, it would be hard to imagine there are any estimable women out there, the kinds of women we used to call role models. When asked in my questionnaire which women they admired, most of the respondents wrote, "my mom," "my nana," sometimes a teacher or coach. But even those who said "women who've overcome great adversity to excel" or "women who've paved a path for others" didn't name (with the exception of Oprah and the occasional Hillary) specific women.

The annals of women's achievement are plentiful. Madeleine Albright, Maya Angelou, Ruth Bader Ginsburg, Denise Chavez, Mary Crow Dog, Major Tammy Duckworth, Tina Fey, Billie Jean King, Susan G. Komen, Jennifer Lopez, Wangari Maathal, Margaret Mead, Toni Morrison, Rachel Maddow, Michelle Obama, Suze Orman, Tracy Reese, Hilda Solis, Gloria Steinem, Amy Tan, Kara Walker, Vera Wang, Venus and Serena Williams—any of these and so many more might have been cited as admirable contemporary women. But it isn't surprising that most of us don't think of them. Few in the press commit their intellect and talent to spreading the word that there are countless women worth emulating.

In 2006, when Betty Friedan died, the *New York Times Magazine* included her obituary in its "How They Lived" section. I had to read it twice to make sure I hadn't missed what they so glaringly did: any mention of her earth-shattering book *The Feminine Mystique*, as relevant now as it was fifty years ago.

The piece claims it doesn't want to "whitewash" Freidan, so instead it airs a lot of dirty laundry, some of it unnecessarily heaped on the pile. First there's a discussion of the conflict between older feminists, called "hopelessly bourgeois" by younger women, who in turn presumably were dubbed "crazies" by Friedan's faction. Then there are the antagonisms of her three children, whose parents had split at the time of their mother's activism. Her daughter Emily, now a pediatrician, recalls how she felt at fourteen years old: "It wasn't her fame I resented . . . [i]t was her as a mother." This leads to the obit writer's gratuitously sneering rhetoric at the end of her article: "What does it mean that the mother of feminism was . . . not necessarily a good mother to all of her children?"

What is this public drubbing supposed to mean? That Betty Friedan was a failure in her most important role? That feminism is incompatible with good mothering? Or should we see it as part and parcel of a culture denigrating women who fought for our rights?

DURING THE HARD, frustrating years of feminism's second wave, we searched for inspiration in the lives of other women, many from the civil rights movement, many excavated from the rich yet untapped soil of women's recorded past. The Boston ladies who slipped coins to streetwalkers in dark alleys, the abolitionists hiding runaways in their homes, the slave women enduring the lash so they could feed their children, the suffragists taunted and force-fed in prison. Crippling restraints and staunched dreams carved inner beings of indomitable strength. Connecting to them urged us to continue fighting for equal footing in a soul-deflating society systematically forcing women into second place. They gave us an emotional fulcrum when we most needed it.

We called these women role models. Our icons. We memorialized them in adult and children's books, in speeches and seminars. Their stories served as both life raft and compass in the perilous, uncharted seas of sexism. Not because they were perfect, but because they weren't, they empowered us. We believed it was important for men and boys, nurtured on masculine superiority, to realize the sweeping range of women's accomplishments and to know that our successes would enhance rather than subtract from their own. Today we need role models as much as we did in the 1970s to remind ourselves and our children what gender equality looks like.

Unfortunately the media has unleashed a flood of negativity washing women's achievements from view. Sexist media content is the result of both changes in the industry, creating bloated supermonopolies, and decades of right-wing manipulation of media messaging and perspective. According to *Out of the Picture: Minority and Female TV Station Ownership in the United States* by S. Derek Turner, women own less than 5 percent of commercial broadcast television stations and 6 percent of full-power radio stations. Little wonder the press has become a publicist for the sidelining strategy.

Like other male-controlled industries, the media had to be pressured to treat women fairly. Marlene Sanders, a pioneer in broadcasting, was the first woman sent by her television station to report on the war in Vietnam. "Even though I was married with a family when WNEW asked me to go, I went," she recently told me. "It was 1966 and very risky, but I did very important stories. When I got back to the U.S., though, I found out that none of them aired at night."

It took the lawsuits of the 1970s to force television networks and newspapers to stop discriminating against women in hiring and promotion. As a result of one of these class actions, Anna Quindlen secured a position on the *New York Times* op-ed page, and for the decade of her tenure she wrote about issues of gender, race, and class in a deeply thoughtful way. But the enthusiasm for advancing women in journalism, very high in the 1980s, has definitely faded, said Sheila Gibbons, editor of *Media Report to Women*.

The conservative, hypermasculine climate in the media has been chilly for progressive men, but it has frozen out women nearly completely. Over the past few decades, women's presence in television has declined. Women currently make up just 21.3 percent of news directors at U.S. television stations. And we've remained stuck at 37 percent of the newsroom staff since the start of the twenty-first century.

We've seen how women's already small representation in the press dwindled after 9/11. But years after the terror attacks, women are still conveniently assumed to be reliable only on such topics as child care, health, nannies, dance, and so on. Our expertise and experience qualify us to report on every imaginable topic (with the possible exception of erectile dysfunction). Just to take a few examples, women account for 90 percent of the world's sweatshop workers; they're a huge majority in the environmental movement; they're extremely active in criminal justice reform. And, yet, rarely are women considered as sources or authorities on stories about any of these or countless other "nonfeminine" topics.

Down for the Count

A simple count tells the story. When Ruth Davis Konigsberg, an associate editor at *Glamour*, first noticed the lack of women in such general interest magazines as *Vanity Fair* and *The Atlantic*, it was just a "pet peeve." Now it has become a work of conviction. Her tallies have nailed a male-to-female ratio of writers of 525:170. And if you look at the "heavy stories," those are *all* given to the guys; women's numbers drop to zero.

Another counting project compared the fifty-one front-page stories in one week published in the *New York Times* written by men to the seven bylined by women. And the Pew Trust, in examining newspapers, cable and network shows, and several Web sites for nine months, found that "three-quarters of all stories studied contained at least one male source, but just a third contained a female source."

Women have a lot to say, and they want to be heard. They "write about half of all 96 million blogs," Ellen Goodman, a syndicated columnist for the *Boston Globe*, noted in August 2007. "[But among the] top 90 political, a full 42 percent were edited and written by men-only, while seven percent were by women-only. The 45 percent 'coed' mix was overwhelmingly male." The reason for this imbalance may well be harassment, Goodman suggests, citing instances in which female bloggers have been threatened into silence.

Not surprisingly women bloggers are neither taken as seriously as men nor are they making as much money, according to new evidence. As a *New York Times* article in July 2008 noted, when TechCult, a technology Web site, named one hundred top "Web celebrities," only eleven women made the cut.

And the bad news continues. Just seven women were among the "50 Top Journalists" singled out in 2007 by *Washingtonian* magazine. In its list of journalists on the rise, only two of twelve were women.

Because of the media's power to shape society's attitudes, when women are underrepresented in the industry, it has far-reaching consequences. Those who tell the news also, to a very large extent, make the news, says Jennifer L. Pozner, executive director of Women in Media and News. What's reported on, discussed, editorialized, and *spun* sets the agenda of *what* we think about and *how*. The amount of time afforded an issue or a person can either make it an important part of our consciousness or not.

When women journalists are given positions of importance, women and women's issues are taken more seriously. The reverse is also proving true. With few women in decision-making roles, 96 percent of news stories worldwide say little about issues of gender inequality.

When the esteemed late columnist Judy Mann—the first to apply the term *gender gap* to the media—retired in 2001 after twenty-three years at the *Washington Post*, she used her bully pulpit to run the final piece "A Farewell Wish: That Women Will Be Heard," noting "a society in which women are invisible in the media is one in which they're invisible period."

Those invested in keeping the status quo used to point to Katie Couric as a sign of women taking the media by storm. But the amount of publicity given to Couric's position as anchor for *CBS Evening News* was itself evidence of her being an anomaly. Something so novel, so experimental was being tried you'd think the network chose one of those savvy chimpanzees to deliver the news through sign language rather than a smart, competent woman with years of television experience. Then there was all the heavy-duty gendered criticism about everything from her "too dark eyeliner" to her overly long sit-down conversations with newsbreakers. Her extreme makeover, turning her into a muted version of her former self with boring jackets, a somber tone, and eyes fixed on the monitor, apparently didn't produce the hoped-for butterfly.

Before her game-changing interviews with Sarah Palin, reports were all over the news that Couric would soon be throwing in her computer.

Discussing her poor ratings, Sean McManus, president of CBS News, said in 2007, "For certain people in America, they're not used to getting their news from a woman. . . . There's an automatic assumption . . . that they would rather get news from a man."

What McManus was actually saying is: our society doesn't see women as authoritative enough to be communicators of important information. But ironically he only has his own industry to blame. The way women seeking leadership roles, particularly in politics, are treated in the American media provides a clear picture of woman-bashing at work.

"Why aren't we shocked?" *New York Times* columnist Bob Herbert asked, referring to the unbridled misogyny sweeping our society. One answer is because our newscasters have made sexism so much a part of their everyday rant, we've become completely inured to it.

The press—especially cable—made their dislike of Hillary Clinton palpable during her run for the Democratic nomination for president. "She's gotten the worst coverage of any candidate in our history," said Rita Henley Jensen, founder and editor in chief of Women's eNews. Her competence was attacked and her appearance dissected—a particularly effective ploy used by commentators to trivialize a woman's accomplishments.

Some of the worst offenders have argued that sour-grape feminists only cried "sexism" after Senator Clinton lost her bid. But that simply isn't true. Media watchers commented and complained about the misogyny expressed throughout her campaign, pointing to the following (a small sample of the very many).

From Bill Kristol:

Look, the only people for Hillary Clinton are the Democratic establishment and white women. . . . White women are a problem . . . we all live with that.

And from Maureen Dowd:

It's odd that the first woman with a shot at becoming president is so openly dependent on her husband to drag her over the finish line.

These gems are all from Chris Matthews:

The only reason women are voting for Hillary is because they feel sorry for her.

The men who support her are [castratos] in the eunuch chorus.

Modern women like Clinton are unacceptable to Midwest guys.

[T]he reason she may be a front-runner is her husband messed around.

From Mike Barnicle on *Morning Joe*:

She look[s] like everyone's first wife standing outside a probate court.

From Ken Rudin of National Public Radio:

She's like Glenn Close in *Fatal Attraction*, she keeps coming back."

You don't have to ascribe to Freudian psychiatry to figure out what these statements from Tucker Carlson are about:

[Hillary] is tough [b]ut the one thing we learned from the Lorena Bobbitt case is there's a great deal of resentment among women aimed at men.

[W]hen she comes on television, I involuntarily cross my legs.

And she was called a bitch far too many ways to count.

Even a supposedly neutral front-page news story appearing on March 4, 2008, in the *New York Times* revealed subtle bias, calling Clinton "the first woman to be a serious contender for president" while describing Obama as "the charismatic young black man who has packed arenas across the country and overtaken Mrs. Clinton in many polls and the delegate count." And of course there's the accepted patronizing way Senator Clinton was always referred to by her first name and all other candidates by their last.

The 2008 Democratic primaries, the historic contest between a black man and a white woman, inevitably prompted a lot of talk about racism and sexism in this country, and speculation about which is more deeply ingrained in our society. Shirley Chisholm, who in 1968 became the first African American woman elected to Congress, representing New York's twelfth congressional district, said she encountered far more discrimination as a woman than as a black person. She urged "[w]omen in this country to become revolutionaries. . . . We must refuse to accept the old, the traditional roles and stereotypes."

In the years since Chisholm was elected, numerous studies show racism to be more easily overcome than sexism. "We can make categorization by race go away, but we could never make gender categorization go away," said the University of California's John Tooby, who has conducted in-depth experiments on this topic. Discussing the obstacles faced by female and black candidates, he said, "Based on the underlying psychology and anthropology, I think it's more difficult for a woman."

"In general, gender trumps race," agreed Alice Eagly, a psychology professor at Northwestern University. "Race may be easier to overcome."

Prejudice—whether because of the color of your skin or your gender or sexual preference—is unacceptable, or should be. But if you transform the comments made about Clinton's sex to Obama's race, it would be unimaginable for anyone in the media to utter them without serious repercussions. The fact is, while racism certainly exists in America, it's considered hideous and shameful. If you're a racist, you keep quiet about it or risk a tongue-lashing.

But sexism has become camp. It's riotous and cool. It's chest-thumping fun, powerful and self-reinforcing. The media exhibits all the heady recklessness of the old boys' club, dumping over women to make men feel strong and in control.

A strange facet of our times is how bountiful antiwoman sentiments have become the ticket to fame, according to Eric Boehlert of the nonprofit organization Media Matters for America. Chris Matthews's intense dislike of then-Senator Clinton dripped so venomously from his tongue that women's groups protested outside MSNBC studios, forcing him to make a quasi-apology to her. But rather than being called to task for his offensive comments, he was rewarded just three months later with a laudatory eight-thousand-word cover story—a length usually granted to a head of state—in the April 2008 *New York Times Magazine*.

It's tempting to think that Clinton evokes a special kind of pillorying. There are whole clubs of Hillary haters. And for sure a lot of people see her "as the poster girl of everything they hate about the women's movement," as one commentator suggested. But in today's media environment, women in leadership roles all come in for their own share of "Hillarying."

In the weeks immediately following Nancy Pelosi's election as Speaker of the House, the media labeled her "Nancy Shrew," "a caricature of the shrill, petty woman boss," and the "Wicked Witch of the West." Fox contributor Dennis Miller called her "a nimrod, a C-minus, D-plus applicant . . . who no doubt would have been drummed out of the Mary Kay corps after an initial four-week evaluation period." *Washington Times* editor in chief Wesley Pruden said her election was a "triumph of feminism and estrogen . . . more powerful than strontium-90, deadlier than polonium-210 [the substance used to kill the former Soviet spy Alexander Litvinenko]." And numerous pundits wondered aloud if she was going to "castrate Steny Hoyer if he was elected majority leader in the 110th Congress."

Tucker Carlson thought that Michelle Obama "sounded like she's got a log-sized chip on her shoulder from lucking into Princeton due to affirmative action." Maureen Dowd called her to task for infantilizing and emasculating her husband, and Fox News dubbed her Obama's "Baby Mama."

And it's not just female Democrats who are demeaned. When Condoleezza Rice visited Wiesbaden, Germany, a *Washington Post* reporter couldn't stop fussing over her military-style coat and her knee-high black boots with the slender heel—boots so "sexy" they made Rice looked like a "Dominatrix!"

Harriet Miers, the scorned nominee to the Supreme Court, also came in for some powerful scrutiny. Poor Harriet, with her "clumsy merger of Washington's particular brand of stodgy power-dressing and with one of the iconic markers of gender: dark-rimmed look-at-me eyes," wrote Robin Givhan. What Miers needed, according to the press, was an "aesthetic fairy godmother to explain that dark eyeliner can make one look harsh." A page and a half of an article in the *Washington Post* was devoted to a discussion of Miers's appearance, "her hair—clipped in short layers and a curtain of bangs . . . the blue suit with gold buttons the diameter of an espresso cup . . ." Miers may have been unqualified for the Supreme Court, but reading this piece you'd think the nomination failed because of her fashion faux pas.

Verbal assaults are millstones to the determination of those who dare to break tradition. How many more times must women be told, by such nationally known media personalities as Michael Savage, that "[the U.S. Congress has become] more vicious and more histrionic than ever, specifically because women have been injected into [it]," without becoming discouraged? Such remarks and the deep wellspring of sexism they represent go a long way toward explaining why the United States ranks seventy-first in the world for representation of women in government, even after the Democratic sweep in 2008.

With the high-profile candidacies of senators Obama and Clinton and Governor Palin, media coverage became increasingly diverse. More women, along with black and Hispanic reporters, were added to the news desk. "[But] with few exceptions, like Donna Brazile, the Democratic strategist on CNN, almost all the new additions either [spoke] . . . from the Republican or Conservative point of view, and for the most part, they comment[ed] on race or gender," wrote Felicia R. Lee in the *New York Times* on April 2, 2008. Michelle Bernard, for example, a regular on MSNBC, is CEO of the ultraconservative Independent Women's Forum, but she's never identified as representing the views of the antifeminist organization.

But there's been some progress. Although Katie Couric's calm but probing and persistent interviews with Sarah Palin—largely responsible for revealing how spectacularly unprepared Palin was for the VP spot—haven't exactly broken down all resistance to a woman's delivering serious news, she's garnered respect for her journalism skills and has recently received positive press for her special one-time, prime-time edition of *CBS Evening News*.

Campbell Brown of CNN now has a show of her own, *No Bias No Bull*, and Rachel Maddow's smart, iconoclastic hourlong MSNBC news program is getting rave reviews. Some of CNN's female political correspondents—Candy Crowley, Dana Bash, Suzanne Malveaux, Elaine Quijano— have remained visible even after the election, as have women reporters at other stations.

Without a doubt, having more female candidates in the 2008 elections translated into putting more women in front of the camera, but only enough for some mild celebration. As Lee points out in her *New York Times* piece, "The most prominent positions on television remain overwhelmingly with those who are white and male."

CONCLUSION

THE CHANGE WE NEED

A society delegitimizing women's accomplishments is one putting its future at risk. We are robbing ourselves of the creativity, intelligence, resourcefulness, and vision of more than half our population. There's no acceptable reason for this. And it makes no sense. Not economically, politically, or socially. Maintaining our ballast amid the battering waves of both fiscal and foreign upheavals will be arduous enough. If ever our nation faced an "all hands on deck" moment, this is it. But instead of utilizing all available talent, our culture pounds with distorted values and ideas about human nature, behavior, and interaction, consistently pushing women to the sidelines.

Eighteen Million Cracks Waiting to Be Smashed

During the long, drawn-out 2008 primary season, women's issues hardly got a mention. Not from John McCain, nor from Barack Obama. Only toward the end of Hillary Clinton's campaign did she mine the rich lode of women's support and transform herself into their candidate. It proved to be political gold. Women who for years had been marginalized, who had been cowed and uncomfortable about speaking up, suddenly felt invigorated. They flocked to her side. Even those who weren't big Hillary fans grudgingly admired her pluckiness and smarts. Women of a certain age marveled at her boundless energy and at how good she looked with so little sleep. Her refusal to quit months before the end, when the "big boys" in the party angrily told her to go home, gained her new respect.

Many women saw themselves in her struggles—in her troubled marriage and messy backstory—but mostly in her encounters with male

323

intolerance. When hecklers mocked "Iron my shirts," the female audience heard their own versions of the same.

Whether it was sheer luck or brilliant intuition, Clinton opened a sealed-off chamber within the hearts of women across the nation. Out flowed a mighty unhappiness at lives sculpted by a barely acknowledged gender inequality. She summoned women to a new cognizance of the brambly, still-unfinished path to liberation. Onto her candidacy they projected their previously unidentified grievances and hopes. This, as much as any other factor, explains the fervor and passion of her female supporters. Not because they necessarily liked everything she did or how she'd voted, but because she was them, writ large. Right or wrong, they believed she was fighting their battles. And just at the end, they made her believe it also.

Although Hillary Clinton's "I Am Woman" stance came just a little too late, her achievement validated to millions of women the righteousness of their cause. It's too soon to know how history will judge her failed run for the nomination. In her concession speech she talked about the eighteen million cracks in the glass ceiling. Most likely another woman at another time will smash it entirely, without having to prove over and over again that she's tough enough, man enough, to do it. Sarah Palin, in her speech at the Republican convention, referred to that fractured barrier, anointing herself Clinton's heir apparent.

The Palin Perplexity

Sarah Palin had astonishing appeal. Energetic and articulate, the self-proclaimed hockey mom mobilized the conservative base, turning John McCain's tepid rallies into Angelina Jolie–sized events. Palin knew how to walk the walk and talk the talk, inserting coded pro-life messages into her fiery speeches. In discussing her Down syndrome baby, she told a crowd, "John McCain and I have a vision for America where every innocent life counts." The right went gaga over her. William Kristol praised her to the hilt; Pat Buchanan was adoring; Rush Limbaugh called her a babe. She portrayed herself as a populist, the ultimate maverick, the real deal who scorned pretense and made a virtue out of anti-intellectualism, lack of curiosity, even of ignorance. Any attempt to scrutinize her background or question her readiness for office received vociferous condemnation from her supporters, who cried "Sexism!"

Conservatives probably used that word more often in the three months of Sarah Palin's power trip than they had in the past three decades. Those (including Palin herself) who accused Hillary Clinton of "whining" when the senator complained about unfair press coverage did a whole lot of whining themselves, effectively insulating the governor from media scrutiny.

Women's groups expressed horror and outrage, not at Sarah Palin as a person but as a contender for the vice presidency. The Web site Women Against Sarah Palin went live immediately; e-mails shot around the country asking for comments and signatures. And the press loved it, happily declaring another round of the mommy wars and charging feminists with hypocrisy for not supporting a working mom juggling a demanding job and children. But if there were women who objected to Palin because her family obligations might prevent her from fulfilling the responsibilities of the second-highest office in the land, they were most likely on the right rather than the left.

What feminists criticized were Sarah Palin's policies. When she was mayor of Wasilla, Alaska, Palin forced women who had been raped to pay the cost of their rape kits and considered banning books from the library. She supports the ineffective and dangerous abstinence-only programs, would deny women control over their own reproductive lives, is against same-sex marriage and domestic partner benefits, and opposes both laws mandating equal pay for women and the Family and Medical Leave Act. She advocates small government and cutting back programs to help working poor and impoverished women. She believes in teaching creationism in schools and opposes environmental protection. The list goes on.

As Amanda Marcotte wrote in the *Los Angeles Times*, you can't really be a feminist and a social conservative. Feminists urge gender equality at every level; they advocate progressive policies and using government to promote the common good. Sarah Palin is a throwback to the same old, same old: antigovernment regulation, anti-intervention, and go-it-alone individualism.

Indeed the real hypocrites are not feminists but those on the right, those abstinence-only advocates suddenly applauding the governor's seventeen-year-old daughter Bristol's out-of-wedlock pregnancy. (Can you just imagine what would be said if Obama had an unwed pregnant daughter?) The right saw in Sarah Palin a new Phyllis Schlafly. Ironically, Palin's greatest appeal wasn't to women but to men. In many ways Sarah Palin emerged as the perfect symbol of our times: a gunslinging, sharpshooting macho mom who flirted and "you betcha"-ed her way into the hearts of dudes across the country who no longer felt like First Dudes in their own families. Peppering her speeches with hunting and fishing references, Palin made men, insecure over America's declining status abroad, the imploding economy, and loss of jobs, feel like real men. Even her five children underlined the procreative role of women, enhancing a sense of virility. And she seemed to relish male comments on her looks: the PROUD TO BE VOTING FOR A HOT CHICK buttons and the yells of "You tell 'em, babe," and "Marry Me, Sarah" earned big grins and winks of approval from Palin. But these remarks, like "Iron my shirts," are simply different ways for men to assert their superiority over women.

Palin, clothed and coiffed (we didn't know then at what cost) to look like an ordinary working mom, exploited the class divide in this country and played upon our fears of "otherness." She channeled old-school right-wing tactics of resentment like a pro. Obama represented the elite, the intellectual; he wasn't like the rest of us, he didn't "get" small-town traditions; he palled around with terrorists; he wasn't a real American. In short, he was a deviant.

We've seen how successive Republican administrations since Ronald Reagan have used this demonizing strategy to promote cohesion among their supporters, deflect attention from the nation's real problems, and silence their opponents. That they now used a woman, typically *the* designated symbol of otherness, to deliver their destructive message, was a brilliant ploy.

But—this time it didn't work.

When John Lewis, former civil rights leader and member of Congress, representing Georgia since 1987, spoke out against the frenzied hatemongering going on at Palin's gatherings, warning it could bring tragic consequences, public opinion turned. A string of Republican and conservative notables—Peggy Noonan, David Brooks, Colin Powell, Christopher Buckley—became deeply critical and withdrew support of their party's ticket.

Palin's female supporters backed away in droves. Women throughout the country, who've struggled hard to prove their own competence, weren't going to endorse a candidate so ill prepared for the job.

Fingers Crossed, Eyes Open: Cautiously Optimistic About Obama

Aside from the *very* few Clinton supporters who remained angry at Obama for winning the nomination and then not choosing their candidate as his running mate, women of every demographic supported the Democratic ticket. But the final months of Obama's campaign didn't offer much in the way of support for women. Reproductive rights, once a certain platform for those who wanted to distance our society from the pre–*Roe v. Wade* coat-hanger days, appeared to become political irrelevancies. Although Obama won the support of NARAL, his views on abortion didn't completely mesh with those of the organization. In a July 1, 2008, interview with *Relevant*, a Christian magazine, he made a point distinguishing between physical health and "mental distress," saying the latter would not constitute a reason to perform a late-term abortion. This statement put him at odds with a significantly large number of court decisions clearly considering emotional well-being as important as physical well-being in evaluating a mother's health.

And in the third presidential debate, Obama used the term *partial-birth abortion*—coined by the foes of reproductive rights and despised by supporters of *Roe*, who always refer to the late-term procedure by its medical name: intact dilation and extraction (or evacuation).

Just as surprising, Obama's running mate, Joe Biden, author of the landmark Violence Against Women Act, signed into law in 1994, made no mention of it during his debate with Sarah Palin. And no mentions were made throughout the entire campaign of affordable child care, the rise in heart disease among women, the explosion of workplace discrimination against mothers, the ways in which women are disproportionately affected by the financial disaster, or anything about the revitalizing of agencies, bureaus, and programs dedicated to women's progress and well-being.

But the sizable constituency of newly galvanized female voters pushed the Democratic ticket to acknowledge the importance of extending the

Family Leave Act, ensuring pay equity, and ending the global gag rule as important future goals. As a result, shortly after the Obama/Biden ticket was swept into office—garnering 56 percent of the female vote in general and 70 percent among single women, the most economically vulnerable population—the Lilly Ledbetter Fair Pay Act swept through Congress and was among the first bills our new president signed into law. And to commemorate the anniversary of *Roe v. Wade*, Obama overturned the international gag rule, enabling agencies to discuss a full range of reproductive health services without losing U.S. funding.

Despite these positive steps, several women's rights groups have been disappointed with the number of Obama's female appointments to his cabinet. Out of all the immensely qualified candidates, he initially chose five women, the same number as was in Bill Clinton's first cabinet, four fewer than in his second, and only one more than the cabinet of George W. Bush, who started out with four women. With the confirmation of Kathleen Sebelius as secretary of health and human services in April 2009, Obama added an additional woman to his cabinet, but only because his male nominee dropped out due to ethical concerns.

Even more disappointing was Obama's selection of pastor Rick Warren to deliver the invocation at the inauguration. The choice was particularly hurtful to the gay community, for whom the overall election represented a huge civil rights setback. In four states gays were barred either from marriage or from adoption. Warren goes even further. It's not just that he doesn't allow homosexuals to worship at his California Saddleback Church, he considers gay marriage akin to incest and pedophilia. Women who have abortions are like nazis, according to Warren, who believes marriage is an unequal arrangement in which wives must obey and submit to their husbands on all matters.

Then there was the concern many of us felt over Obama's stimulus package, expressed by Randy Albelda, a senior fellow at the Center for Social Policy at the University of Massachusetts—Boston. Writing in the *Boston Globe* on November 28, 2008, Albelda called Obama to task for only looking to create "male" jobs in his stimulus package by focusing on our *physical* infrastructure. Of course "our crumbling roads and bridges need fixing," but construction jobs go overwhelmingly to men. There's also a need to develop *human* infrastructure, to rebuild health care, our faltering education system, child care, services for the elderly and the disabled, to support women-owned business as well as the inclusion of women in traditional male jobs.

So many women's groups objected that a second proposed package, titled *The Job Impact of the American Recovery and Reinvestment Plan*, specifically addressed our apprehensions and contained a gender component, estimating that 42 percent of the jobs created by the proposal will go to women.

WE HAVE A president who listens. But many voices will be competing for his attention and for the very limited resources at his disposal. Our economy is teetering on the brink of collapse; the nation is saddled with an all-time-high national debt; and we are engaged in two draining, seemingly unwinnable wars. Nuclear weapons in the hands of unstable and hostile nations intensify our persistent worries about terrorist attacks. We cannot wait for our leaders, however well intentioned, to decide it's finally time to attend to women's well-being.

Recent reports are showing a sizable uptick in incidents of domestic violence—a by-product of joblessness and the sinking economy. And while all Americans are being hurt by the financial debacle, single mothers, newly unemployed, who once might have benefited from receiving welfare, are now increasingly facing destitution. Particularly frustrating is the speed with which provisions to expand access to affordable family planning and to provide basic, vital health care, contained in the Medicaid Family Planning State Option, were cut from the economic stimulus bill. This cost-effective legislation would have helped millions of low-income women. The haste with which Obama eliminated this measure must raise questions about the administration's real commitment to it in the first place. Money for school construction, food stamps, and aid to the unemployed were also cut from the original bill.

This Is Where We Come In

We've seen a media and society that applauds the "change" wrought by the 2008 election yet nonetheless remains stuck, postelection, in 1960s mode, starting with the media's obsession over First Lady Michelle Obama's appearance. It's as if her casual style and well-toned arms are the most significant things about this woman with a distinguished career and degrees from Princeton and Harvard. And those of us who watched the 2009 Super Bowl couldn't help but notice the same degrading, misogynist advertisements, as always. Then there's the new television series *Man Caves*, a testosterone-drenched version of *Extreme Makeover: Home Edition* in which decked-out, male-only spaces are built because, as one man put it, "I had to have a little place where I could anchor my manhood." A place, he said, that prevented him from "feeling emasculated." And what about a recent survey published in *Child Development* revealing that 90 percent of adolescent girls experience sexual harassment, including unwanted physical contact and romantic attention, teasing related to their appearance, and demeaning gender-related remarks?

So yes, of course, sexism, like racism, persists in America despite the Obama-era *change* mantra. And yet, after a fleeting acknowledgment of the issue during the primary campaign, the topic has again gone underground, where, if left to fester, it will continue to pollute the soil of our nation. At a recent luncheon celebrating the women whose biographies were included in the book *Feminists Who Changed America*, Gloria Steinem warned against complacency, or "thinking things will simply get better on their own."

A powerful voting bloc of women has emerged. And it doesn't matter which candidate we backed. For the first time in thirty years we have the ability and organization to move beyond the sidelining strategies we've so long endured. We won't always agree, but differences and debates will only enrich and strengthen our work.

I've spoken to hundreds of women from all over the country, and from them I've learned how much we're hungering to connect and *reconnect* with one another. Heather Stone, a thirty-six-year-old social worker, is one of many who said what women need most is a sense of unity, an urgency to join each other in a common cause.

Together, there's no question we can effect positive social change.

The Woolworth's in Greensboro, North Carolina, didn't suddenly, in 1960, decide to invite black students to sit at the counter. And neither did our administration. American Airlines didn't have a *eureka* moment about how unfair it was to force Barbara "Dusty" Roads into retirement at the age of thirty-two. And neither did our administration. It's worth noting, as Gail Collins did in the *New York Times* (January 29, 2009), that the three female flight attendants who behaved so heroically when US Airways flight 1549 went down in the Hudson River were all in their fifties.

The victory in 2008 of the laid-off employees who staged a six-day sit-in at their shuttered Chicago factory until a settlement secured severance pay and two months of continued health coverage for the workers proved again the power of group action.

Throughout our history, the struggles for social justice—for workers, minorities, women, and gays and lesbians—were successful because they were genuine *movements*, made up of outpourings of courageous, committed people determined to make things happen.

Everyone who believes in gender equality—women and girls, men and boys, whether they call themselves feminists or shun the label—must join together to push for progressive policies that will enhance *all* of our lives. Now we know what these are: universal health care, inclusion of women and minorities in medical research and analysis, national standards for affordable child care and elder care, and equal educational opportunities for our children. We must work to rescind the current limitations on Title IX that constrain girls' athletic programs, and to eliminate workplace discrimination, sexual harassment, and outmoded institutional structures that *still* draw from the male wage earner / female homemaker model. We must put in place paid federal family leave and paid sick days in every state, end the gender wage gap and wage penalty women face when they take time off, make flexible and part-time hours more available to all workers, and reinstate the collection of data on women in the labor force.

We can and should protect the rights of lesbians and bisexual women, abolish the Don't Ask, Don't Tell regulation in the military, and bolster programs for protecting our servicewomen from sexual assault and enhancing their medical care. And it's within our power to urge lawmakers to expand funding for prevention and treatment of HIV/AIDS, strengthen the Violence Against Women Act, and increase supports for single mothers.

To ensure the smooth implementation of all these policies and initiatives as well as address additional areas of inequity, nearly fifty different women's groups joined together to urge President Obama to create a cabinet-level Office on Women. He has started instead a White House Council on Women and Girls. With no full-time staff, set meeting schedule, or Cabinet-level leader, the council is not what many women hoped for, but at least it's a start.

Still, government can only do so much. We must also try to counteract the extreme misogyny in our popular culture and find ways to engage and empower young women so that they'll see themselves in a mirror of their own making. Jennifer L. Pozner has urged us to launch a media campaign to ensure that social and political issues are no longer sifted through a male corporate strainer and that women's voices—not just of the few and well placed but of the many—will be heard again.

Making Ourselves Heard

There are those of us who've long been activists. Many others may have become engaged politically during the recent presidential campaigns. Some have never done more than simply vote, and a few not even that. But you don't have to commit to being a full-time activist to get involved.

Sometimes we're impelled to take action by a specific cause. In their book *Grassroots*, Jennifer Baumgardner and Amy Richards give the example of Pat Beninato, a thirty-seven-year-old from Richmond, Virginia, who worked as a customer service representative. Beninato found herself increasingly frustrated at the vitriolic attacks on abortion constantly being broadcast on her local television stations. "Slaughter" and "murder" were the favorite descriptions. Beninato had had an abortion herself, and although the decision was fraught with difficulty, she never regretted it. She decided to start imnotsorry.net, a Web site where other women who felt as she did could tell their stories. Jennifer Baumgardner learned of the site from a piece Katha Pollitt wrote about it in *The Nation*. Working with Beninato and other like-minded feminists, Baumgardner raised money for a documentary in which women discussed their abortion experiences. From the hundreds of women Beninato and Baumgardner spoke to, before selecting twenty for the film, they became aware of the need for postabortion care, so as part of their project they distributed thousands of cards to abortion clinics with resources for aftercare.

Sometimes our activism begins with a simple problem or question. One woman with a four-year-old daughter didn't want her to play with Bratz dolls and wondered how to prevent it. A good first step would be to talk to the mothers of her daughter's friends in the hope that they'll agree not to give the dolls as presents; teachers, relatives, and caregivers should also be told about the objections. Beyond that several mothers *and* fathers could send e-mails and letters to the designers at MGA Entertainment, the manufacturers of Bratz, expressing concern about the dolls' sexually provocative appearance and clothing. Bratz have already been singled out by the APA as harmful to girls; hearing from consumers strengthens that position. (When the toy company Hasbro was going to release a line of Pussycat Dolls, based on the burlesque dancers who now have their own reality show, they encountered so much parental disapproval they withdrew the product.) Another form of action is to organize protests and pickets outside of Toys R Us and other large stores carrying Bratz to increase public awareness about the damaging nature of the doll and the sexualization of girls that it encourages.

There's a great amount you can do as an individual by just being gender conscious, some of it right at your computer. Numerous progressive and women's Web sites (many listed in the resource section) post weekly or even daily news summaries about important issues and include petitions to sign, numbers to call to make your opinions known, and meetings to attend for more information. You can arrange to get these updates sent to you through e-mail and forward them to others who might be interested.

Networking through Facebook, MySpace, and e-mail about feminist issues are all wonderful ways to educate, inform, and form a community of activists. So is using whatever group and neighborhood resources we have available to us. One woman I know suggested her book club read works about women to stimulate discussion and awareness. Toni Morrison's *Beloved*, Rita Mae Brown's *Ruby-Fruit Jungle*, Joan Didion's *The Year of Magical Thinking*, and *Can't Buy My Love*, Jean Kilbourne's classic study about how advertising hurts women, were among the choices. Another woman is working with her children's school to set up a series of evening workshops for parents and teachers on a range of topics including eating disorders, making certain girls' sports receive the same attention as boys', and encouraging girls in technology; and a third is taking a women's history course at her local college. Professional organizations, houses of worship, museums, and community and medical centers can all be asked to sponsor activities to promote gender equality. They can host women's health days, seminars teaching young women to become financially independent, and exhibitions of female artists, and they can spread awareness of sexual assault among teens.

Some women will want to volunteer their time or services at shelters, food banks, or neighborhood health clinics; others prefer to support such organizations through charitable contributions. We can bring our gently used business clothing to Dress for Success, a group providing appropriate attire for job interviews to women who'd been on welfare; we can help formerly incarcerated women fill out college applications; we can become Big Sisters and mentors to young girls. We can write letters protesting women-bashing media and boycott movies that demean women or exalt violence against them; we can do research, write position papers, organize conferences, lobby in Washington, run for office. Our talents are virtually unlimited. So are the ways we can use them.

And we can encourage our daughters to become equally involved—to start women's and girls' issues clubs, journals, healthy-eating groups, and 'zines, and to participate in school government. We should talk with them about the television shows they watch and the magazines they read. And, most important, we can help them see one another as friends, not adversaries and competitors. We can encourage all our children to become active participants in their own lives. And to remember: the narrative of the next decade is yet to be written.

Daunting as all this may be, we're not putting new footprints in the soil. Some paths to equality are still navigable; others will have to be forged again. But now that we see how easily they can be bulldozed over, this time we need to make them permanent.

We all can imagine a better, more equitable society for women and for men, for our daughters and our sons, than the one we're living in.

Now we have to make it happen!

RESOURCES

Education and Sports

American Association of University Women
1111 Sixteenth Street NW
Washington, DC 20036
(202) 785-7700; fax (202) 872-1425
www.aauw.org
e-mail: connect@aauw.org

Gay, Lesbian and Straight Educational Network
121 West 27th Street, Suite 804
New York, NY 10001
(212) 727-0135; fax (212) 727-0254
www.glsen.org
e-mail: glsen@glsen.org

The Mid-Atlantic Equity Consortium, Inc.
5454 Wisconsin Avenue, Suite 1500
Chevy Chase, MD 20815
(301) 657-7741
www.maec.org

The National Women's History Project
3343 Industrial Drive, Suite 4
Santa Rosa, CA 95403
(707) 636-2888; fax (707) 636-2909
www.nwhp.org
e-mail: nwhp@aol.com

National Women's Studies Association
University of Maryland
7100 Baltimore Boulevard, Suite 500
College Park, MD 20740
(301) 403-0525; fax (301) 403-4137
www.nwsa.org
e-mail: nwsaoffice@nwsa.org

Title IX
www.titleix.info

The Women's Campaign School at Yale University
PO Box 3307
New Haven, CT 06515-0407
(800) 353-2878 or (203) 734-7385; fax (203) 734-7547
www.wcsyale.org
e-mail: wcsyale@wcsyale.org

Women's Sports Foundation
Eisenhower Park
East Meadow, NY 11554
(800) 227-3988; fax (516) 542-4716 or (516) 542-4700
www.womenssportsfoundation.org
e-mail: wosport@aol.com

Fighting Rape and Domestic Violence

Laura's House
California Domestic Violence Center
999 Corporate Drive, Ste. 225
Ladera Ranch, CA 92694
(949) 361-3775 or (866) 498-1511;
fax (949) 361-3548
www.laurashouse.org
e-mail: info@laurashouse.org

Men Stopping Violence
533 W. Howard Avenue, Suite C
Decatur, GA 30030
(404) 270-9894
www.menstoppingviolence.org
e-mail: msv@menstoppingviolence.org

**National Coalition Against Domestic
   Violence**
PO Box 18749
Denver, CO 80218
(800) 799-7233 or (303) 839-1852; fax
   (303) 831-9251
www.ncadv.org
e-mail: mainoffice@ncadv.org

**National Organization for Men
   Against Sexism**
PO Box 455
Louisville, CO 80027
(303) 666-7043
www.nomas.org
e-mail: info@nomas.org

Take Back the Night
109 Summer Hill Lane
St. Davids, PA 19087
(610) 989-0651; fax (610) 989-0652
www.campusoutreachservices.com/
   foundation-tbtn.html

For Young Women and Girls

Center for Campus Organizing
165 Friend Street
Boston, MA 02114-2025
(617) 725-2886

GirlsGoTech
Girl Scouts of the USA
420 Fifth Avenue
New York, NY 10018
Phone: (800) GSUSA 4 U
www.girlsgotech.org
e-mail: emailus@girlscouts.org

Girls Inc.
120 Wall Street
New York, NY 10005-3902
(800) 374-4475
www.girlsinc.org
e-mail: communications@girlsinc.org

Girls on the Move / Outward Bound
2582 Riceville Road
Asheville, NC 28805
(800) 437-6071
www.obgotm.org

Girls Speak Out
146 Edinburgh Street
San Francisco, CA 94112
(650) 678-1555
www.girlsspeakout.org
e-mail: gspeakout@aol.com

Home Alive
1400 Eighteenth Street NW
Washington, DC 20007
(202) 720-0606
www.homealive.org

iEmily—health and wellness site for young girls
www.iEmily.com
e-mail: iemilyinfo@yahoo.com

Third Wave Foundation
511 West 25th Street, Suite 301
New York, NY 10001
(212) 675-0700; fax (212) 255-6653
www.thirdwavefoundation.org
e-mail: info@thirdwavefoundation.org

Young Women's Project
1328 Florida Ave. NW, Suite 2000
Washington, DC 20009
(202) 332-3399; fax (202) 332-0066
www.youngwomensproject.org
e-mail: ywp@youngwomensproject.org

YWCA
1015 18th Street NW, Suite 1100
Washington, DC 20036
(202) 467-0801; fax (202) 467-0802
www.ywca.org
e-mail: info@ywca.org

Health Care

Breast Cancer Fund
1388 Sutter Street, Suite 400
San Francisco, CA 94109-5400
(415) 346-8223 or (866) 760-8223
www.breastcancerfund.org
e-mail: info@breastcancerfund.org

Center for Young Women's Health
Children's Hospital
300 Longwood Avenue
Boston, MA 02115
(617) 355-2994
www.youngwomenshealth.org

Disability Project
Director@uppityCo.com
Links to numerous sites for people with disabilties

Eating Disorders Coalition for Research, Policy and Action
611 Pennsylvania Avenue SE, #423
Washington, DC 20003-4303
(202) 543-9570
www.eatingdisorderscoalition.org
e-mail: manager@eatingdisorderscoalition.org

National Asian Women's Health Organization
250 Montgomery Street, Suite 410
San Francisco, CA 94104
(415) 989-9747
www.nawho.org
e-mail: nawho@aol.com

National Black Women's Health Project
600 Pennsylvania Avenue SE, Suite 310
Washington, DC 20003
(202) 543-9311
www.nbwhp.org
e-mail: nbwhp@nbwhp.org

National Breast Cancer Coalition/Fund
1101 17th Street NW, Suite 1300
Washington, DC 20036
(800) 622-2833 or (202) 296-7477; fax (202) 265-6854
www.stopbreastcancer.org

National Latina Institute for Reproductive Health
50 Broad Street, Suite 1825
New York, NY 10004
(212) 422-2553

www.latinainstitute.org
e-mail: nlirg@igc.apc.org

Native American Women's Health Education Resource Center
PO Box 572
Lake Andes, SD 57356-0572
(605) 487-7072
www.nativeshop.org

Our Bodies Ourselves
34 Plympton Street
Boston, MA 02118
(617) 451-3666; fax (617) 451-3664
www.ourbodiesourselves.org
e-mail: office@bwhbc.org

Ovarian Cancer National Alliance
910 17th Street NW, Suite 1190
Washington, DC 20006
(202) 331-1332 or (866) 339-6262; fax
    (202) 331-2992
www.ovariancancer.org

World Institute on Disability
510 16th Street, Suite 1000
Oakland, CA 94612
(510) 763-4100
www.wid.org

Organizations Working for / Doing Research on Women's Equality

Boston Alliance for Gay, Lesbian, Bisexual and Transgendered Youth
BAGLY INC.
PO Box 960814
Boston, MA 02196-0814
(617) 227-4313
www.bagly.org

Catalyst
120 Wall Street
New York, NY 10005
(212) 514-7600
www.catalyst.org
e-mail: info@catalyst.org

Feminist Majority Foundation
1600 Wilson Boulevard, Suite 801
Arlington, VA 22209
(703) 522-2214; fax (703) 522-2219
www.feminist.org

Gay Lesbian and Straight Education Network
GLSEN National Headquarters
90 Broad Street, 2nd Floor
New York, NY 10004
(212) 727-0135; fax (212) 727-0254
www.glsen.org
e-mail: studentpride@glsen.org

National Council for Research on Women
11 Hanover Square
New York, NY 10005
(212) 785-733
www.ncrw.org
e-mail: nrcw@ncrw.org

National Organization for Men Against Sexism (NOMAS)
PO Box 455
Louisville, CO 80027-0455
(303) 666-7043
www.nomas.org
e-mail: info@nomas.org

National Organization for Women
733 15th Street NW, 2nd Floor
Washington, DC 20005
(202) 628-8669; TTY (202) 331-9002;
    fax (202) 785-8576
www.now.org

National Women's Law Center
11 Dupont Circle, Suite 800
Washington, DC 20036
(202) 588-5180
www.nwlc.org

Senior Action in a Gay Environment
305 Seventh Avenue, 16th floor
New York, NY 10001
(212) 741-2247; fax (212) 366-1947
www.sageusa.org
e-mail: sageusa@aol.com

The Wellesley Center for Women
Wellesley College
106 Central Street
Wellesley, MA 02481
(781) 283-2500
www.wellesley.edu/wcw

Political Activism

Center for Third World Organizing
1218 East Twenty-First Street
Oakland, CA 94606
(510) 533-7583
www.ctwo.org

Equality Now
PO Box 20646, Columbus Circle
    Station
New York, NY 10023
www.equalitynow.org
e-mail: info@equalitynow.org

ERA Campaign
www.ERAcampaign.net
e-mail: ERACampaign@aol.com

ERA Summit
PO Box 113
Chatham, NJ 07928
(973) 765-0102; fax (973) 660-0766
www.equalrightsamendment.org
e-mail: era@equalrightsamendment.org

Greenpeace USA
702 H Street NW, Suite 300
Washington, DC 20001
(800) 326-0959
www.greenpeaceusa.org

The League of Women Voters
1730 M Street NW, Suite 1000
Washington, DC 20036-4508
(202) 429-1965; fax (202) 429-0854
www.lwv.org
e-mail: lwv@lwv.org

The Mothers Movement Online
www.mothersmovement.org
e-mail: editor@mothersmovement.org

Reproductive Rights

Abortion Conversation Project, Inc.
908 King Street, Suite 400W
Alexandria, VA 22314
(703) 684-0055; fax (703) 684-5051
www.abortionconversation.com

Catholics for a Free Choice
1436 U Street NW, Suite 301
Washington, DC 20009
(202) 986-6093
www.cath4choice.org
e-mail: cff@igc.apc.org

Center for Reproductive Rights
120 Wall Street
New York, NY 10005
(917) 637-3600; fax (917) 637-3666
www.reproductiverights.org
e-mail: info@reprorights.org

Choice USA
1010 Wisconsin Avenue NW, Suite 410
Washington, DC 20007
(888) 784-4494 or (202) 965-7700; fax
    (202) 965-7701
www.choiceusa.org
e-mail: info@choiceusa.org

Fair Access to Contraception
Cover My Pills
(800) 727-2996
www.covermypills.org
or
www.healthlaw.org
www.imnotsorry.net
A site where women can share abortion
    experiences; links to numerous other
    sites

National Abortion Federation
1755 Massachusetts Avenue NW, Suite
    600
Washington, DC 20036
(202) 667-5881 or (800) 772-9100
www.prochoice.org

New York Abortion Access Fund
PO Box 7569, FDR Station
New York, NY 10150
(212) 252-4757
www.nnaf.org
e-mail: nyaaf@nnaf.org

**Planned Parenthood Federation of
    America**
434 West 33rd Street
New York, NY 10001
(800) 230-7526 or (212) 541-7800; fax
    (212) 245-1845
www.plannedparenthood.org
e-mail: communications@ppfa.org

Planned Parenthood New York City
Margaret Sanger Square
26 Bleecker Street
New York, NY 10012
(212) 274-7200
www.ppnyc.org
e-mail: choicevoice@ppnyc.org

Women and the Arts

The Feminist Art Symposium
Artwomen.org
e-mail: artwomen@artwomen.org

Guerrilla Girls
www.guerrillagirls.com
e-mail: gg@guerrillagirls.com

Ladyslipper, Inc.
PO Box 3124
Durham, NC 27715
(919) 383-8773
www.ladyslipper.org
e-mail: info@ladyslipper.org

Michigan Womyn's Music Festival
PO Box 22
Walhalla, Michigan 49458
(231) 757-4766
www.michfest.com

National Museum of Women in the Arts
1250 New York Avenue NW
Washington, DC 20005-3990
(800) 222-7270 or (202) 783-5000
www.nmwa.org
e-mail: werise@hotmail.com

Women and the Media

About Face (combats sexist advertising)
About-Face/Agape Foundation
PO Box 77665
San Francisco, CA 94107
(415) 436-0212
www.about-face.org

Bitch **Magazine**
4930 NE 29th Avenue
Portland, OR 97211
(877) 21-BITCH
www.bitchmagazine.org

Bust **Magazine**
PO Box 1016, Copper Station
New York, NY 10276
(212) 675-1707
www.bust.com

Colorlines
4096 Piedmont Avenue, PMB 319
Oakland, CA 9411-5221
(510) 653-3415; fax (510) 653-3427
www.colorlines.com

Feminist Majority
The Feminist News Digest
1600 Wilson Boulevard, Suite 801
Arlington, VA 22209
(703) 522-2214; fax (703) 522-2219
www.feminist.org

Mother Jones
731 Market Street, Suite 600
San Francisco, CA 94103
(800) 438-6656
www.motherjones.com

Ms. Foundation for Women
120 Wall Street, 33rd Floor
New York, NY 10005
(212) 742-2300; fax (212) 742-1653
www.ms.foundation.org
e-mail: info@ms.foundation.org

Ms. **Magazine**
433 S. Beverly Drive
Beverly Hills, CA 90212
(310) 556-2515; fax (310) 556-2514
www.msmagazine.com
e-mail: info@msmagazine.com

New Moon Publishing
PO Box 3587
Duluth, MN 55803-3587
(218) 728-5507
www.newmoon.org
e-mail: newmoon@newmoon.org

She **Magazine**
6511 Nova Drive, #173
Davie, FL 33317
(954) 474-0183; fax (954) 474-1641
www.shemag.com

Women on Waves
PO Box 1800
1000 BV Amsterdam, the Netherlands
www.womenonwaves.org

Women's eNews
135 West 29th Street, Suite 1005
New York, NY 10001
(212) 244-1720
www.womensenews.org

The Women's Media Center
350 Fifth Avenue, Suite 901
New York, NY 10118
(212) 563-0680
www.womensmediacenter.com
e-mail: tristein@womensmediacenter.
  com

The Women's Review of Books
Wellesley College
Wellesley, MA 02481
(781) 283-2087
www.wellesley.edu/WomensReview/
e-mail: lardiner@wellesley.edu

Women's Wire
www.womenswire.com
A service providing information about
  women and girls around the world

Working Mother Magazine
60 East 42nd Street, 27th Floor
New York, NY 10165
(212) 351-6400
www.workingmother.com

Working Women: Employ-
ment Equality

Acre Family Day Care Corporation
14 Kirk Street
Lowell, MA 01852
(978) 937-5899
www.acrefamily.org

An Income of Her Own
www.anincomeofherown.com
An organization that encourages girls
  to be entrepreneurs

Dress for Success
32 East 31st Street, Suite 602
New York, NY 10016
(212) 545-3769; fax (212) 684-0021
www.dressforsuccess.org
e-mail: newyork@dressforsuccess.org

**Equal Employment Opportunity
  Commission**
1801 L Street NW
Washington, DC 20507
(202) 663-4900; fax (202) 663-4494
www.eeoc.gov

Legal Momentum
395 Hudson Street
New York, NY 10014
(212) 925-6635; fax (212) 226-1066
www.legalmomentum.org
e-mail: peo@legalmomentum.org

Living Wage Campaign
Living Wage Resource Center
1486 Dorchester Avenue
Boston, MA 02122
(617) 740-9500; fax (617) 436-4878
www.livingwagecampaign.org

National Committee on Pay Equity
1925 K Street NW, Suite 402
Washington, DC 20006-1119
(202) 223-8360 ext. 8; fax (202)
  776-0537
www.pay-equity.org
e-mail: fairpay@patriot.net

9 to 5, National Association of Working Women
152 West Wisconsin Avenue, Suite 408
Milwaukee, WI 53203
(414) 274-0925; fax (414) 272-2870
www.9to5.org
e-mail: 9to5@9to5.org

Organization for Black Career Women
PO Box 19332
Cincinnati, OH 45219-0332
(513) 531-1932; fax (513) 531-2166
www.bcw.org
e-mail: linda.parker@uc.edu

Self Employed Women's Association
SEWA Reception Centre
Opp. Victoria Garden
Bhadra, Ahmedabad 380 001
India
(91-79) 5506444 or 5506477; fax (91-79)
   5506446
www.sewa.org
e-mail: mail@sewa.org

Sexual Harassment Support
No address or telephone provided
www.sexualharassmentsupport.org

Sweatshop Watch
310 Eighth Street, Suite 303
Oakland, CA 94607
(510) 834-8990
www.sweatshopwatch.org
e-mail: sweatinfo@sweatshopwatch.org

Women's Economic Development Organization
355 Lexington Avenue, 3rd Floor
New York, NY 10017
   (212) 973-0325; fax (212) 973-0335
www.wedo.org
e-mail: wedo@wedo.org

NOTES

Chapter 1: The Awakening of American Women

1   *We watch—as*   Lynn Spigel, *Make Room for TV* (Chicago: University of Chicago Press, 1992), 131.

1   *My class is quiet*   For a discussion of this scene, see Gerard Jones, *Honey I'm Home* (New York: St. Martin's Press, 1992), 99.

3   *Uncertain at first*   Susan J. Douglas, *Where the Girls Are: Growing Up Female with the Mass Media* (New York: Three Rivers Press, 1992), 46. For a discussion of women workers during World War II, see Barbara J. Berg, *The Crisis of the Working Mother* (New York: Summit Books, 1986), chapter 3.

3   *Lucy Greenbaum, noting*   Berg, *Crisis of the Working Mother*, 30.

4   *By promoting upwardly*   Ella Taylor, *Prime Time Families* (Berkeley: University of California Press, 1989), 20; Eileen Tyler May, *Homeward Bound: American Families in the Cold War Era* (New York: Basic Books, 1989), 18.

5   *Basements, backyards, garages*   May, *Homeward Bound*, 105.

6   *Throughout the 1950s*   Ibid., 97.

8   *Recalling her own*   Sheila Weller, *Girls Like Us* (New York: Atria, 2008), 154.

8   *The postwar consensus*   By preventing the concentration of workers in the cities and easing them into middle-class home ownership, our government hoped to diffuse a potentially explosive labor movement.

8   *By the mid-1950s*   Stephanie Coontz, *The Way We Never Were* (New York: Basic Books, 2000), 29.

10   *All I ever*   Quoted in Betty Friedan, *The Feminine Mystique* (New York: Laurel, 1983), 17.

10   *I needed a name*   Betty Friedan, "Up from the Kitchen Floor," *New York Times* (March 4, 1973), 12.

11   *Significantly, almost all*   May, *Homeward Bound*, 209–211.

11   *They articulated a sense*   For a full discussion of these early feminists, see Barbara J. Berg, *The Remembered Gate* (New York: Oxford University Press, 1978).

12   *In every southwest*   Sara M. Evans, *Born for Liberty: A History of Women in America* (New York: Free Press, 1989), 270.

12   *The only thing*   Penny Colman, *Fannie Lou Hamer and the Fight for the Vote* (Brookfield, CT: Millbrook Press, 1993), 15.

13   *The attitude around*   Evans, *Born for Liberty*, 68.

13   *[I]n too many*   Flora Davis, *Moving the Mountain: The Women's Movement in America Since 1960* (New York: Simon & Schuster, 1991), 74.

15   *It felt right*   For a fuller discussion of consciousness raising, see Evans, *Born for Liberty*, 282.

Chapter 2: Feminism Takes Flight

18   *In 1998, 72 percent*   Poll taken in *Folio 51* (September 2008).

18   *Like any great*   Quoted in Barbara J. Love, *Feminists Who Changed America 1963–1975* (Chicago: University of Illinois Press, 2006), ix.

19   *Throughout history women*   Barbara J. Berg, *The Remembered Gate* (New York: Oxford University Press, 1978), 245.

19   *It looks forward*   Susan Faludi, *Backlash: The Undeclared War Against American Women* (New York: Anchor, 1991), xxiii.

20   *The Equal Opportunity Commission*   Davis, *Moving the Mountain*, 22.

21   *We wore high heels*   Ibid., 17–20; interview with Barbara "Dusty" Roads, *People's Century*, http://www.pbs.org/wgbh/peoplescentury/episodes/half thepeople/roadtranscript.html.

22   *I was twenty-eight*   Davis, *Moving the Mountain*, 18.

23   *For a great many*   Davis, *Moving the Mountain*, 60–61; Betty Lehan Harragan, "Blasting Out of the Secretarial Trap," *New York Times* (April 24, 1977).

24   *They meandered across*   Enid Nemy, "Sex Stereotyping Persists in the US Classrooms Despite Pressure," *New York Times* (June 12, 1973), 50.

24   *Johnny says: 'Girls*   Judith Stacey (ed.), *And Jill Came Tumbling After: Sexism in American Education* (New York: Dell, 1974), 159.

26   *Role models for girls*   Quoted in Stacey, *And Jill Came Tumbling After*, 214.

26   *Several years into*   Georgia Dullea, "Women in Classrooms: Not the Principal's Office," *New York Times* (July 13, 1975), A15.

26   *In explaining these*   Dullea, "Women in Classrooms."

27   *Her colleague's words*   " 'Too Strong for a Woman'—The Five Words That Created Title IX," Women's Research and Education Institute, http://bernice sandler.com/id44_m.htm.

27   *Soon afterward the organization*   Davis, *Moving the Mountain*, 208–210.

28   *Many departments had*   "Sandler Works to Warm Up 'Chill Classroom Climate,' " *Emory Report* 50 (September 29, 1997), http://www.emory.edu/ EMORY_REPORT/erarchive/1997/September/erseptember.29/9_29_97 Sandler.html; Dena Kleiman, "Academic Women Show Gains in Combating Sex Discrimination," *New York Times* (July 15, 1980), C4.

28   *I think girls*   Davis, *Moving the Mountain*, 215.

28   *There is the possibility*   Ibid.

29   *Las Vegas oddsmakers*   Ibid. 215–216.

Chapter 3: Gender Roles Under Fire

31   *As women's groups*   Sara M. Evans, *Born for Liberty* (New York: Free Press, 1989), 289.

32   *Isn't it funny*   *The Diary of a Mad Housewife* Universal Pictures (1970).

32   *In another take*   See Susan Douglas and Meredith W. Michaels, *The Mommy Myth* (New York: Free Press, 2004), 59.

33   *Obligated to shut off*   Tillie Olsen, *Silences* (New York: Delta, 1979), 252.

33   *Fewer ulcers, fewer*   "All Our Problems Stem from the Same Sex Based Myth," Gloria Steinem's statement before the Subcommittee on Constitutional Amendments of the Committee on the Judiciary, 91st Cong., 2nd session, May 5, 6, and 7, 1970; *History Matters*, The U.S. Survey Course on the Web, http://historymatters.gmu.edu/d/7025/; Gloria Steinem, "Women's Liberation Aims to Free Men, Too," *Washington Post* (June 7, 1970), http:// scritorium.lib.duke.edu/wlm/aims/.

34   *Scholars in every*   For a complete discussion of gender myths, see Rosalind Barnett and Carly Rivers, *Same Difference: How Gender Myths Are Hurting Our Relationships, Our Children, and Our Jobs* (New York: Basic Books, 2004).

35   *Everything for girls*   Sharon Lamb and Lyn Mikel Brown, *Packaging Girlhood: Rescuing Our Daughters from Marketers' Schemes* (New York: St. Martin's, 2000), 213.

35   *In the lab, little*   Barnett and Rivers, *Same Difference*, 225.

36   *Did I wash*   Judith Adler Hennessee and Joan Nicholson, "NOW Says: TV Commercials Insult Women," *New York Times* (May 28, 1972), A15.

36   *Complaints filed with*   Ibid.

37   *Onscreen 1980s fathers*   Gayle Kaufman, "The Portrayal of Men's Family Roles in Television Commercials," *Sex Roles: A Journal of Research* (September 1999), http://findarticles.com/p/articles/mi_m2294/is-1999-Sept/a1-58469479; Sarah Maccarelli, "How Men Are Portrayed on Television." http://www.associatedcontent.com/pop-print.shtml?cotentt-type=article&cotent-type-id (accessed October 4, 2007).

37   *The heroines of*   For a further discussion of these films, see Faludi, *Backlash*, 125–126.

Chapter 4: Do Not Bend, Fold, Spindle, or Mutilate

42   *There are two types*   Quoted in Barbara J. Berg, *Nothing to Cry About* (New York: Seaview Books, 1981), 44.

43   *We will never*   Quoted in Flora Davis, *Moving the Mountain: The Women's Movement in America Since 1960* (New York: Simon & Schuster, 1991), 228.

43   *Sanger was haunted*   Gerda Lerner (ed.), *The Female Experience* (New York: Oxford University Press, 1977), 99–104.

43   *The scandal [of unwed pregnancy]*   Sheila Weller, *Girls Like Us* (New York: Atria, 2007), 131.

44   *It was all shame*   Ibid.

44   *Would the pill*   Rickie Solinger, *Pregnancy and Power* (New York: New York University Press, 2007), 168.

45   *Here and there*   Elizabeth Siegal Watkin, *On the Pill: A Social History of Oral Contraceptives 1950–1970* (Baltimore: Johns Hopkins University Press, 1998), 88–89.

45   *British medical researchers*   Ibid.

45   *We must not*   Ibid., 109–110.

46   *The drive to*   The term is used by Davis, *Moving the Mountain*, 228.

48   *But the book*   Alexander Jacobs, "A Feminist Classic Gets a Makeover," *New York Times* (July 17, 2005), 1, http://www.nytimes.com/2005/07/17books/reviews/17JACOBSL.html?-r+1&adxnnl+0&0 (accessed September 26, 2007).

48   *What's striking about*   James C. Mohr, *Abortion in America* (New York: Oxford University Press, 1978), 5–7.

48   *The demand for*   Ibid., 8–9.

49   *I had treated*   Quoted in Solinger, *Pregnancy and Power*, 120.

50   *Sovereignty over their*   Davis, *Moving the Mountain*, 165–167.

51   *Upon returning home*   Davis, *Moving the Mountain*, 183; "On This Day 1962: Abortion Mother Returns Home," BBC.co.uk, http://news.bbc.co.uk/onthisday/hi/dates/stories/august/26/newsid-3039000/3039322.stm (accessed October 3, 2007).

51   *It made early*   Davis, *Moving the Mountain*, 180–183.

Chapter 5: Reagan and the Great Reality Check

53   *Some of us*   Barbara J. Berg, "End of the Juggler," *Savvy* (February 1986), 36–41.

53   *The worst stereotype*   Ibid.

54   *Every day, no matter*   Ibid.

54   *On-site child care*   Barbara J. Berg, *The Crisis of the Working Mother* (New York: Summit Books, 1986), 68.

54   *As the* New York Times   Jack Rosenthal, "President Vetoes Child Care Plan as Irresponsible," *New York Times* (December 10, 1971), A22.

54   *Through the 1970s*   Arlie Russel Hochschild, *Second Shift* (New York: Penguin Books, 1989).

56   *Over "100 captive*   Lewis H. Lapham, "Tentacles of Rage," *Harper's* magazine 309 (September 2004).

56   *Money poured in*   Lapham, "Tentacles of Rage," 2; Jean Hardisty, *Mobilizing Resentment* (Boston: Beacon Books, 1999), 63.

56   *Television evangelist*   Pat Robertson, fundraising letter (1992).

56   *Of course the GOP*   Tanya Melich, *The Republican War Against Women* (New York: Bantam Books, 1992), 92.

56   *Only twenty years*   Tom Hamburger and Eric Black, "How Did Liberal Get to Be Such a Dirty Word?" (September 30, 1996), *Star Tribune* archives, http://www.startribune.com/blogs/bigquestion/?page-id=359; Lapham, *Harper's*, 1.

57   *But what really*   See Lapham, "Tentacles of Rage."

57   *Discrediting, devaluing, and making*   For a full discussion of this concept, see Kai T. Erikson, *Wayward Puritans: A Study in the Sociology of Deviance* (New York: Macmillan, 1966).

58   *Goodwives gather in homes*   Ibid., 58.

58   *An essentially negative program*   Melich, *The Republican War Against Women*, 171.

59   *The nation needed*   Ronald Reagan, speech to the National Association of Evangelicals (March 8, 1983), especially 1–6, http://www.nationalcetner.org/ReaganEvilEmpire1983.html (accessed November 14, 2007).

59   *These enemies of*   Ibid.

59   *The woman's liberation*   Quoted in Susan Faludi, *Backlash: The Undeclared War Against American Women* (New York: Crown, 1991), 233.

60   *America's decline as*   Ibid., 232.

60   *Hundreds of thousands*   Davis, *Moving the Mountain*, 438–439.

61   *Falwell swore*   Faludi, *Backlash*, 232.

61   *Already the process*   Davis, *Moving the Mountain*, 171.

61   *But Reagan went*   Robert Pear, "Reagan Bars Mention of Abortion at Clinics Receiving US Money," *New York Times* (January 30, 1988), A1.

62   *The 1989 Webster v.*   Judith Warner, *Perfect Madness: Motherhood in the Age of Anxiety* (New York: Penguin Books, 2006), 179.

62   *It's simple—if*   Melich, *The Republican War Against Women*, 90.

Chapter 6: Welfare Queens, Herculean Women, and Sex-Starved Stalkers

63   *President Reagan's vividly*   Franklin D. Gilliam Jr., "The 'Welfare Queen' Experiment," Nieman Foundation for Journalism at Harvard University: 53 (Summer 1999) 1; author interview.

64   *They overwhelmingly portrayed*   See, for example, Martin Gilens, *Why Americans Hate Welfare* (Chicago: University of Chicago Press, 1999). According to an extensive analysis by Yale political scientist Martin Gilens, there was no evidence of a significant problem with welfare cheating and this figure includes errors committed by the agency; Susan Douglas and Meredith W. Michaels, *The Mommy Myth* (New York: Free Press, 2004), 177; U.S. Bureau of Census 1995; Staff House Committee on Ways and Means (1996).

64   *Repeatedly, conservative pundits*   Douglas and Michaels, *The Mommy Myth*, 180.

65   *Wizened old men*   Quoted in Erich Goode and Ben-Yehuda Nachman, *Moral Panics: The Social Construction of Deviance* (Cambridge: Blackwell Publishers, 1995), 216.

65   *Scapegoating is what*   Goode and Nachman, *Moral Panics*, 213.

65   *The number of incarcerated*   "The Population of Women in Prison Increases Rapidly," Women's Prison Association, *Focus on Women and Justice* (August 2003), 1.

65   *Dr. Claire Coles*   Goode and Nachman, *Moral Panics*, 219.

66   *Throughout the 1980s*   Douglas and Michaels, *The Mommy Myth*, 86–88.

66   *Was it because*   J. Larry Brown and Deborah Allen, "Hunger in America: Physician Task Force on Hunger in America," Harvard University School of Public Health, Boston, MA, *Annual Review of Public Health*, www.annual reviews.org/aronline; W. Reed Moran, "Jeff Bridges Cooks Up an End to Hunger in America," *USA Today* (November 20, 2001), http://www.Usato-day.com/news/health/spotlight/2001-11-21-bridges-hunger.htm.

66   *The first heady*   Fern Schummer Chapman, "Executive Guilt: Who's Taking Care of the Children?" *Fortune* (February 16, 1987), 30.

67   *While the article*   Barbara J. Berg, *Crisis of the Working Mother* (New York: Summit Books, 1989), 58–59.

69   *We've all read*   This is an updated version of Ellen Goodman's "Typical Superwoman's Day" in Areva D. Martin, "Hang Up the Superwoman Cape and Build Real Power with Empowerment Circles" (October 2006), www .arevamartin.com.

69   *The implication that*   Laurel Parker West, Marial Center, Emory University Marial working paper 16 (April 2002), 6.

69   *[W]hen asked if*   Quoted in Warner, *Myth*, 90.

70   *This is a pivotal*   Faludi, *Backlash*, 131.

70   *With J.C. nesting*   Ibid.

71   *[It] causes working*   Emanuel Levy, "Film Review," http://emanuellevy .com/Reviews/details.cfm?id=552.

71   *The statistics made*   "Marriage After 40? Not Impossible!" CBS News (May 31, 2006), http://www.cbsnews.com/stories/2006/05/31/earlyshow/ main1671139.shtml?source=search_story.

72   *Writing after the election*   Davis, *Moving the Mountain*, 429.

74   *[T]he anarchy and lack*   Michael Wines, "Views on Single Motherhood Are Multiple at White House," *New York Times* (May 21, 1992), 5.

74   *Quayle's wife, Marilyn*   Alessandra Stanley, "Politics and the Family: Issues: Family Values," *New York Times* (August 21, 1992), http://query .nytimes.com/gst/fullpage.html?res=9eoced8123bf93211a157bcoa964958 (accessed November 1, 2007).

75   *And to prove that*   Bradford Plummer, "Taking Leave," *Mother Jones* (June 7, 2005), www.motherjones.com/commentary/columns/2005/06/ FMLA.html.

76   *NOW's membership, fueled*   Davis, *Moving the Mountain*, 411.

76   *In addition to women*   Ibid., 466.

76   *Looking back on*   Anna Quidlen, "Recalling a Proud Moment for U.S. Women," *Newsweek* (October 15, 2007), www.msnbc.msn.com/id/21162310/ site/newsweek/print/1/displaymode/1089/10/8/2007,5.

77   *Eloquent, often angry*   Carole Ellen DuBois and Lynn Dumneil, *Through Women's Eyes* (New York: St. Martin's Press, 2005), 642.

77   *And while the press*   Faludi, *Backlash*, 316.

77   *Bank tellers from*   Dorothy Sue Cobble, *The Other Women's Movement: Workplace Justice and Social Rights in Modern America* (Princeton, NJ: Princeton University Press, 2005), 214.

Chapter 7: The Mixed Bag of Bill Clinton

79   *More than half*   Carol Ellen DuBois and Lynn Dumneil, *Through Women's Eyes* (New York: St. Martin's Press, 2005), 655.

80   *At forty-one*   Unpublished regional hearings of the American Cancer Society (1990).

81   *Once he signed*   The Personal Responsibility and Work Opportunity Reconciliation Act of 1996.

81   *No one would receive*   Susan Douglas and Meredith W. Michaels, *The Mommy Myth* (New York: Free Press, 2004), 199; "Introduction: Welfare Is Not the Problem—Poverty Is the Problem," Women's Programs Office, APA Online, http://www.apa.org/pi/wpo/; Olivia A. Golden (project director), "Assessing the New Federalism" (Urban Institute, 2005).

81   *NOW activists joined*   "Viewpoint Clinton: Our Option, Not Our Answer" (October 1996), http://www.now.org/nnt/11-96/oped.html.

82   *The press hammered*   "Feminists, Prostitutes and Nazis: Media Labeling in the Lewinsky Story," *Fairness and Accuracy in Reporting* (November/ December 1998), 3.

83   *But many other*   "Women Leaders Take Action to Stop Impeachment," Common Dreams News Wire (September 24, 1998), 1, http://www .commmondreams.org/pressreleases/Sept/98092498b.htm.

84   *The reports of numerous*   David Brock, "The Right Wing Conspiracy," speech at Barnard College (February 2006); David Brock, *Blinded by the*

Right (New York: Three Rivers Press, 2005); Philip Weiss, "The Clinton Haters; Clinton Crazy," *New York Times Magazine* (February 23, 1997), 34; Jean Hardisty, *Mobilizing Resentment* (Boston: Beacon Press, 1999), 63.

85   *Daring to raise*   Richard W. Stevenson, "10-Year Estimate of Budget Surplus Surges Once More," *New York Times* (December 20, 2000), http://query.nytimes.com/gst/fullpage.html?res=980CE3DA163BF93AA15751C1A9669C (accessed November 9, 2007); Paul Krugman, *The Great Unraveling* (New York: Norton, 2004), xxix–xxxi.

85   *For the first time*   Rates fell from 18.3 percent in 1989 to 16.6 in 1999. 1989–1999 U.S. Census Bureau, *Census 2000 Poverty*.

85   *Serious crime, including*   A. Negrusz et al. "Estimate of the Incidence of Drug-Facilitated Sexual Assault in the United States," School of Public Health, University of Illinois at Chicago (June 2, 2005), ncjs.gov/pdffilessi/ni/grants21200pdf.

85   *The death rates*   "Progress Shown in Death Rates from Four Leading Cancers," National Institutes of Health (September 2, 2003), http://www.gov/news/pr/sep/2003/nci-02 htm (accessed November 9, 2007).

86   *Between Clinton's first*   John Santelle et al., "Can Changes in Sexual Behaviors Among High School Students Explain the Decline in Teen Pregnancy Rates in the 1990s?" *Journal of Adolescent Health* 35 (2004); Olenick Iviva, "U.S. Teenagers' Birthrate and Pregnancy Rate Fall During the Mid-1990s," *Family Planning Perspectives* (November/December 1998), http://findarticles.com/p/articles/mi_qa3634/is-199811ai-n8817533.

86   *By the mid-1990s*   "The American Family," Department of State, 3, http://usinfo.state.gov/journals/itsv/0101/ijse/numbers.htm; "Nonmaternal Care and Family Factors in Early Development: An Overview of the NICHD Study of Early Child Care," *Journal of Applied Developmental Psychology* 22 (September–October 2001): 457–492.

86   *A compilation of*   Sharon Jeffcoat Bartley et al., "Antecedents of Marital Happiness and Career Satisfaction: An Empirical Study of Dual-Career Managers," *Journal of Management* 1 (2007): 2–13; Caryl Rivers and Rosalind Barnett, "Women Happier as Homemakers? Time to Recheck Data," Women's eNews (March 22, 2006), 2–5, http://www.womensenews.org/articles.cfm/dyn/aid/2678.

87   *After the feisty detective-friends*   Faludi, *Backlash*, 152.

87   *The show's writer*   "Buffy the Vampire Slayer, the Girl Power Movement and Heroism," AOL Prime Picks, http://hometown.aol.com/mdelar9493; T. L. Stabley, "Buffy to Slay Small Screen," *Mediaweek* (February 17, 1997), 9–10.

87   *In a made-in-heaven*   Gabrielle Moss, "From the Valley to the Hell-mouth: *Buffy*'s Transition from Film to Television," http://slayageonline.com/essays/slayage2/moss.htm.

88   *Film critic*   Hannah Tucker, "High School Confidential," *Entertainment Weekly* (October 1, 1999), 23.

88   *The movement began*   For a discussion of riot grrls, see Leslie Heywood and Jennifer Drake (eds.), *Third Wave Agenda* (Minneapolis: University of Minnesota Press, 1998).

88   *Others wanted to accomplish*   Jennifer Baumgardner and Amy Richards, *Manifesta* (New York: Farrar, Straus & Giroux, 2000), 21.

89   *In much the same*   Ibid., 56.

89   *They remind us*   Lisa Jervis, "The End of Feminism's Third Wave," *Ms.* magazine (Winter 2004), http://www.msmagazine.com/winter2004/third-wave.asp.

Chapter 8: Bushwinked to Bushwhacked

91   *History will decide*   Alan M. Dershowitz, *Supreme Injustice: How the High Court Hijacked the Election of 2000* (New York: Oxford University Press, 2001).

91   *The way the justices'*   "How We Got Here" (December 13, 2000), http://archives.cnn.com/2000/ALLPOLITICS/stories/12/13/got.here/index.html.

92   *The "mediathon" is*   Frank Rich, *The Greatest Story Ever Sold* (New York: Penguin, 2004), 225.

92   *And even though*   Hearusnow.org project at Consumers Union, http://www.hearusnow.org/mediaownership/; Granville Williams, "Bestriding the World, Media Global Giants," MediaChannel.org, http://www.mediachannel.org/ownership/granville.shtml (accessed November 26, 2007); Rich, *The Greatest Story Ever Sold*, 224.

93   *As Gerald Levin*   Williams, "Bestriding the World."

93   *The only security*   "Thomas Jefferson on Politics and Government: Freedom of the Press to Lafayette," 1823; Lipscomb and Bergh (eds.), *The Writings of Thomas Jefferson: Memorial Edition*, 14:491, http://etext.virginia.edu/jefferson/1600.htm.

94   *When during a campaign*   Laura Flanders (ed.), *The W Effect* (New York: Feminist Press, 2004), xiv.

94   *We're sending a*   Grover Norquist, *National Journal* (2002), quoted in David Brock, *The Republican Noise Machine: Right-Wing Media and How It Corrupts Democracy* (New York: Crown, 2004), 50.

94   *Under the right's*   Brock, *The Republican Noise Machine.*

94   *Fictional, nasty, spun*   "The Press vs. Al Gore: How Lazy Reporting, Pack Journalism and GOP Spin Cost Him the Election," http://www.rollingstone .com/news/story/5920188/the-press-vs-al-gore.

95   *You can actually*   Ibid.

95   *In the race*   Bob Herbert, "The Trivial Pursuit," *New York Times* (October 13, 2007), op-ed; PaulWaldman, quoted in *The Daily Howler* (October 19, 2007), http://www.dailyhowler.com/dh101907.shtml.

95   *In his concession*   Al Gore's concession speech, http://www.commondreams. org/21/300-108htm.

95   *We didn't appreciate*   William Einwechter, "The Feminization of the Family," *Vision Forum Ministries* (December 8, 2005), http:www.vision forumministries.org/issues/familt/the_feminization-of-the-family.aspex (accessed November 28, 2007).

96   *Her words were*   David Leonhardt, "He's Happier, She's Less So," *New York Times* (September 26, 2007), A10.

96   *Researchers mulling over*   Ibid.; Betsey Stevenson and Justin Wolfers, "The Paradox of Declining Female Happiness," unpublished paper, http:// bpp.wharton.upenn.edu/beteys.

96   *Not only is this*   "US Slips in Gender Equality Survey," *International Herald Tribune* (November 9, 2007), http://www.iht.com/articles/ap/2007/11/ 09america/Na-Gen-Us-Global-Gender-Gap.php (accessed November 29, 2007).

96   *It's hard to advance*   Jeff Green, "US Has Second Worst Newborn Death Rate in the Modern World, Report Says," CNN.com, www.cnn.com/ HEALTH/parent/05/08/mothers.index (accessed November 11, 2007).

98   *As best-selling*   Nina J. Easton, "The Power and the Glory: Who Needs the Christian Coalition When You've Got the White House? The Religious Right's Covert Crusade," in Laura Flanders (ed.), *W: Bush's War Against Women* (New York: Feminist Press, 2002), 5–10.

98   *From the moment*   Flanders (ed.), *W*, xx.

98   *It signaled Bush's*   Jeff Robinson, "Many Evangelicals Unwittingly Live as Feminists," *Baptist Press* (November 28, 2005).

98   *His administration restricted*   Jane Spencer, "Not Stocked Here," *Newsweek* (June 19, 2001), http://www.newsweek.com/78920.

98   *Then, notably, he asked*   Ashcroft later did provide security at the clinics only because women's groups so vehemently protested his discussion (PAW and *National Journal*).

99   *Similarly, Vice President*   "Rebuilding America's Defenses: Strategies, Forces and Resources for a New Century," *Christian Science Monitor* (September 2000), http://www.csmonitor.com/specials/neocon/index.html.

99   *The Project, officially*   David Armstrong, "Dick Cheney's Song of America: Drafting a Plan for Global Dominance," *Harper's* 305 (October 2001), 6.

100   *Even then, Bush's*   "Bush Unpopular in Europe, Seen as Unilateralist," Pew Research Center (August 15, 2001), http://pewglobal.org/reports/displat .php? Report iD=5.

100   *It was after all*   Armstrong, "Dick Cheney's Song of America."

100   *Lord Guthrie, a former*   Quoted in Francis Shor, "Hypermasculine Warfare: From 9/11 to the War on Iraq," http://www.bad.eserver.org/ reviews/2005/shor.html; "Rebuilding America's Defenses: Strategies, Forces and Resources for a New Century," http://crytome.info/0001/rad/rad.htm.

Chapter 9: 9/11 and Women

101   *That moment and*   Quoted in Bob Deans, "After 9/11, Unity on Bush's Leadership Faded," *Cox Newspapers* Washington Bureau (September 11, 2006), 1.

102   *Whether as damsels*   J. Ann Tickner, "Feminist Perspectives on 9/11," *International Studies Perspectives* 3 (2002), 335.

102   *The Hunk Factor*   "Hunk Factor: Manly Men in Their Uniforms," *USA Today* (November 26, 2001), 1; Patricia Leigh Brown, "Heavy Lifting Required: The Return of Manly Men," *New York Times* (October 28, 2001).

103   *I miss John*   Rosalind Barnett and Caryl Rivers, *Same Difference* (New York: Basic Books, 2004), 60; Maureen Dowd, "Liberties; Hunks and Brutes," *New York Times* (November 28, 2001).

103   *I was immediately struck*   Lt. Brenda Berkman, quoted in Lorraine Dowler, "Women on the Frontlines: Rethinking War Narratives of Heroism Post 9/11," *Geojournal* 58 (2002): 160.

104   *Numerous commentators, the British*   Quoted in Tickner, "Feminist Perspectives on 9/11," 335.

104   *To be sure*   Jennifer Pozner, "The Gender Gap," in Laura Flanders (ed.), *W: Bush's War Against Women* (New York: Feminist Press, 2002), 101.

104   *In print, women's*   Ibid.; Geneva Overholser, "After 9/11: Where Are the Voices of Women?" *Columbia Journalism Review* (March/April 2002), http://cjarchives.org/issues/2002/2/girls-over.asp printerfriendly=yes.

105   *The women we*   Tickner, "Feminist Perspectives on 9/11"; Dowler, "Women on the Frontlines: Rethinking War Narratives of Heroism Post 9/11," *Geojournal* 58 (2002).

105   *And, after Laura*   Tickner, "Feminist Perspectives on 9/11," 340.

105   *Avenging wronged women*   Ibid., 341.

106   *[M]en and women*   Paul Farhi, "The Great Worry Divide," *Washington Post* (November 29, 2001), C01.

106   *But the researchers'*   Patricia Donovan, "Study Finds Gender, Ethnicity Predict 9/11 Response Health Effects," *University of Buffalo Reporter* 38 (December 14, 2006); Thai Q. Chu and Mark D. Seery, "Ethnicity and Gender in the Face of a Terrorist Attack," *Basic and Applied Psychology* 28 (2006): 291–301; Sandra Galea, M.D., et al., "Pyschological Sequalae of the September 11 Terrorist Attack in New York City," *New England Journal of Medicine* 346 (March 28, 2002): 1–3; Sarah Graham, "9/11: The Psychological Aftermath," ScientificAmerican.com (November 12, 2001), http://www.sciam.com/article.cfm?id=911-the-pyschological-aft (accessed July 13, 2007).

106   *In the wake*   Quoted in Barnett and Rivers, *Same Difference*, 60.

106   *And journalist Chris*   Flanders (ed.), *The W Effect*, introduction.

107   *It would be easy*   Matthew B. Stannard, report by Columbia University School of Journalism, "9/11: Five Years Later," *San Francisco Chronicle* (September 6, 2006), http://sfgate.com/911five/.

108   *The appeal of the panic*   Quoted in "Fear Is the Key," *Film and Television After 9/11* (2001).

108   *Today's panic rooms*   http://articles.homesecuritystore.com/articles/1330/Panic-Romm-do-you-Need-a-Panic Room-in-Your homes/Page1.html.

108   *Typically the credible*   Stannard, "9/11: Five Years Later," 6.

109   *In the two years*   Interview with Gertrude Schaffner Goldberg, Ph.D., author of "Assessing the Impact of the Terrorist Attacks of 11 September 2001 on Women's Employment in the United States," for the National Jobs for All Coalition.

109   *As the authors*   Gertrude Schaffner Goldberg and Helen Lachs Ginsburg, "Assessing the Impact of the Attacks of 11 September 2001 on Women's Employment in the United States," 5–12; report of National Jobs for all Coalition.

109   *We were ignored*   Quoted in Linda Varghere, "Post 9/11 The Working Poor Pay the Price," *Ghadar* 5 (July 21, 2002): 5, http://www.proxsa.org/reourcesghadar/v5n2post9-11.html.

109   *As they watched*   Mindy L. Gewirtz, Ph.D., "Coping with the Changing Realities of Work and Life: Impact and Implications for Women in New Economy Companies," presented at the Seventh International Woman's Policy Research Conference (June 2003), 2.

110   *And interestingly, about*   Professor J. Timmons Roberts, Department of Sociology, College of William and Mary, "Newly Hazardous Jobs in a Changed America," http://www.jtrobe.people.wm.edu/Newly-Harardous-Jobs-26Apr3p.htm.

110   *For Kim it was*   Stephanie Armour, "After 9/11 Workers Turn Their Lives Upside Down," *USA Today*; "Press Room Act 1—Talent and Technology," http://www.act1tech.com/pressroom1.

112   *After 9/11 I reconnected*   Gabrielle Gayagoy, "Lasting Changes: Readers Share How the 9/11 Attacks Transformed Their Lives," *Shape* (September 2004), http://findarticles.com/p/articles/mi_ mo_846is_1_24/ai-n6168546.

Chapter 10: 9/11 and Men

113   *And that it*   Osama bin Laden quoted by Tony Judt, "America and the War," *New York Review of Books* (November 15, 2001).

114   Washington Post *columnist*   Dana McGrath, "Gendered Language of War," *The Laughing Medusa* (Washington, DC: George Washington University Press, 2001), http://www.gwu.edu/-medusa/langaugne.html.

114   *We talked of*   Liz Marlantes, "More John Wayne Rhetoric Infuses Politics," *Christian Science Monitor* (July 18, 2003), http://www.cesmonitor.com/2003/07/0718/p02s02-usfp.html.

114   *When "men [become]*   Patricia Leigh Brown, "Heavy Lifting Required: The Return of Manly Men," *New York Times* (October 28, 2001).

114   *Military analysts, especially*   Gerald L. Atkinson, "Women in Combat After the Terrorist Attack on America" (November 11, 2001), http://www.newtotalitarians.com/WomenInCombatAfter9-11.html.

115   *Any alternative to*   Francis Shor, "Hypermasculine Warfare: From 9/11 to the War on Iraq," http://bad.eserver.org/reviews/2005/shor.html.

115   *The assault on*   In the lead-up to the war and war itself there was never any official reference to the United States' role in helping the Taliban get a strong hold in the country.

115   *Men make war*   Quoted in Shor, "Hypermasculine Warfare," 1.

115   *It was pretty*   Frank Rich, *The Greatest Story Ever Sold* (New York: Penguin Books, 2004), 40.

116   *With 80 percent of*   George Lakoff, *Don't Think of an Elephant* (White River Junction, VT: Chelsea Green Publishing, 2004).

116   *Two weeks after*   Ibid.

116   *Fundamentalists believed, as did*   Jeff Sharlet, "Through a Glass Darkly," *Harper's* (December 16, 2006), 33–44.

117   *Now we are engaged*   George W. Bush, White House speech, "National Sanctity of Human Life Day" (January 18, 2002).

117   *It was all*   Gar Smith, "Shock and Awe: Guernica Revisited," AlterNet (January 27, 2003), http://www.alternet.org/story/15027/.

118   *G. Gordon Liddy*   Quoted in Paul Waldman, "Macho, Macho Man," Tom Paine.com (June 28, 2006), http://www.tompaine.com/articles/2006/06/28/macho-macho.man.php.

118   *It showed him*   Ibid.

118   *Thought that showing*   Richard Goldstein, "Bush's Basket: Why Bush Had to Show His Balls," in Laura Flanders (ed.), *W*, 176. For a different discussion of this topic see: Susan Faludi, *The Terror Dream: Fear and Fantasy in Post 9/11 America* (New York: Henery Holt & Co., 2007).

Chapter 11: Military Madness

119   *Some brave souls*   Quoted in John Kampfer, "Saving Private Lynch Story Flawed," BBC News (May 15, 2002), http://news.bbc.co.uk/2/low/programmes/correspondent/3028585.stm.

120   *I went down*   "Jessica Lynch Sets the Record Straight," CBS News (April 23, 2007), http://www.cbsnews.com/stories/2007/04/25earlyshow/main/2725423.shtml; Christopher Hanson, "The Press Finds the War's True Meaning," *Columbia Journalism Review* (August–September 2003).

120   *So if the story*   Kampfer, "Saving Private Lynch Story Flawed."

120   *The confusion of*   David S. Cloud, "Private Gets 3 Years for Iraq Prison Abuse," *New York Times* (September 28, 2005), A10.

121   *Frankly one of*   Quoted in Sara Corbett, "Battle of the Sexes," Times Online, http://www.timesonline.co.uk/tol/news/world/iraq/articles1622986.ece.

121   *Saying something [about abuse]*   Sara Corbett, "The Women's War," *New York Times Magazine* (March 18, 2007), 40–55.

122   *Women are frequently*   Miles Moffeit and Amy Herdy, "Female GIs Report Rapes in Iraq War," *Denver Post* (January 25, 2004).

122   *I feel like*   Christine Hansen, "A Considerable Sacrifice: The Cost of Sexual Violence in the U.S. Armed Forces," *Military Culture and Gender* (September 16, 2005).

122   *There has been*   Helen Benedict, "The Scandal of Military Rape," *Ms.* magazine (Fall 2008), 41.

122   *Why is there*   *Slip Sliding Away: Erosion of Women's Rights*, Women's Law Center (April 2004), 43.

123   *And it's happening*   David Goodman, "Military Recruiters Work Hard to Leave No Child Off Their Lists," *Seattle Times* (October 6, 2006), http://seattletimes.nwsource.com/html/opinion/2003290949_dgoodman06.html

123   *This policy enables*   James A. Gillaspy and Dan McFeely, "Recruiter Accused of Sex Assaults," Inystar.com (March 1, 2005), http://www.ncdsv.org/images/ReecruiterAcssusedofSexAssaultsCountsAgasint.pdf (accessed January 5, 2007).

123   *Regulations to protect*   Ibid., 5.

123   *Part of it*   Lizette Alvarez, "Army Giving More Waivers in Recruiting," *New York Times* (February 14, 2007), A1.

124   *The Pentagon invited*   Jonathan Markovitz, "Reel Terror Post 9/11," in Wheeler Winston Dixon (ed.), *Film and Television After 9/11* (Carbondale: Southern Illinois Press, 2004), 212.

125   *Since Padilla already had*   Ibid., 211.

125   *Through toys, especially*   Nick Turse, "Bringing the War Home: The New Industrial Military Complex at War and Play" (October 16, 2002), http://www.nickturse.com/articles/tom_warhome.html.

126   *This toy states*   Quoted in Petra Bartosiewicz, "From G.I. Joe to Tora Bora Ted," Salon.com (September 11, 2003), http://dir.salon.com/story/mwt/feature/2003/09/11/war_toys/index.html (accessed December 17, 2007).

126   *The new war toys*   James Poniewozik, "That's Militainment!" CNN.com (February 25, 2002), http://www.cnn.com/ALL POLITICS/time/2002/03/04 militanment.html (accessed December 23, 2007).

126   *One, coming out*   Karen Springen, "Teen Brains Changed by Violent Videogames," *Newsweek* (November 28, 2006), http:www.windley.com/archives/2006/11/.

127   *Murder stimulators*   For a further discussion of this topic, see Col. David Grossman, *Stop Teaching Our Kids to Kill* (New York: Crown, 1999).

127   *Does this toy*   Quoted in Bartosiewicz, "From G.I. Joe to Tora Bora Ted."

Chapter 12: Starve the Beast, Sink the Nation

129   *It's virtually unheard*   Paul Krugman, *The Great Unraveling* (New York: Norton, 2004), xix.

129   *The whole idea*   Ibid.

129   *Bush gave a*   Ibid.

130   *Social commentators talked*   Paul Krugman uses this term in *The Conscience of a Liberal* (New York: Norton, 2007).

130   *That's roughly one*   Bob Herbert, "Send in the Clowns," *New York Times* (October 6, 2007), http://www.nytimes.com/2007/10/06opinion/06herbert.html (accessed December 2, 2007).

130   *The poignant struggles*   Bob Herbert, "More than Just Talk," *New York Times* (May 8, 2007), http://select.nytimes.com/2007/05/08opinion/08herbert.html (accessed on January 9, 2008).

130   *Poverty is a kind*   Paul Krugman, "Poverty Is Poison," *New York Times* (February 18, 2008), A22.

130   *It wasn't always*   Paul Krugman, "For Richer," *New York Times* (October 20, 2002), http://www.nytimes.com/202/10/20/,magazine/for-richer.html (accessed January 8, 2008).

131   *Not too long*   Quoted in Paul Krugman, "For Richer."

131   *We need only*   "After Bailout, AIG Executives Head to Resort," *Washingtonpost.com*, http://voices,washingtonpost.com/livecoverage/2008/10/after_bailout_aig_executivesh-.h-html (accessed November 21, 2008).

131   *A report conducted*   "Study: As Banks Failed, Top Executives Earned 1.6B," FOXNews.com, http://www.foxnews.com/plotics/2008/12/21/study-banks-failed-executives-earned/ (accessed January 6, 2009).

131   *Conservative think tanks*   Sam Pizzigati, "Surprise Strike on Stealth Wealth," TomPaine.com (February 16, 2007), http://www.tompaine.com/articles/2007/02/16/surprise_strike_on_stealth_wealth.php (accessed January 4, 2008).

132   *The average single*   "Sacrificing Women's Priorities to Pay for Tax Cuts for the Wealthy Few," National Women's Law Center (May 2006), 1.

132   *Bush's tax policies*   Paula Roberts, quoted in "Critics Say Budget Cuts Hurt Women, Children," Women's eNews (January 2, 2006), http://www.womensenews.org/articles.cfm/dyn/aid/2623/ (accessed January 2, 2008).

133   *How did this*   Krugman, "For Richer"; Bob Herbert, "Sharing the Pain," *New York Times* (March 11, 2008), A23.

133   *When news appeared*   Bob Herbert, "The Divide in Caring for Our Kids," *New York Times* (June 12, 2007), A16.

134   *The subprime mortgage*   "Women Targeted for Subprime Lending," *Ms.* magazine (Winter 2008).

134   *And studies conducted*   Anne Moore Odell, "Subprime Lending Hurts Homeowners," Social Funds, http://www.socialfunds.com/news/article .cgi/2266.html (accessed May 15, 2008).

134   *Elderly women especially are*   Anita F. Hill, "Women and the Subprime Crunch," *Boston Globe* (October 22, 2007), 16.

135   *Twenty years ago*   Steven Greenhouse, "Will the Safety Net Catch the Economy's Casualties?" *New York Times* (November 16, 2008), 3.

135   *Being a good*   Quoted in Shannon Brownless and Matthew Miller, "Lies Parents Tell Themselves About Why They Work," *U.S. News and World Report* (May 12, 1997), 12, http://online.sfsu.edu/-rone/BuddhismFive Precepts/ParentsLies.html (accessed January 8, 2009).

135   *Not surprisingly, violent*   "US: Soaring Rates of Rape and Violence Against Women," Human Rights Watch, http://www.hrw.org/en/news/ 2008/12/18/us-soaring-rates-rape-and-violence-against-women (accessed February 12, 2009).

Chapter 13: Bodily Harm

138   *The American Cancer*   "American Cancer Society Report Finds Breast Cancer Death Rate Continues to Drop," Science Daily (September 26, 2007), http://www.sciencedaily.com/releases/2007/09/070925130014.htm (accessed June 12, 2008).

138   *We're at jeopardy*   Dr. Ben Ho Park, quoted in "Scientists: Cuts Hurt Cancer Research" (January 25, 2007), http://www.cbsnews.com/sto-ries/2007/01/25/eveningnews/main2400032.shtml.

139   *It's men who present*   Rachael Combe, "Unbreak My Heart," *Elle* (January 2007), 198; "Heart Disease and Women," *Medical Encyclopedia*, http://www .nlm.nih.gov/medlineplus/heartdiseaseinwomen.html (accessed September 27, 2007).

139   *Obesity and its twin*   Melissa Temmem, "Obesity Swallowing America," Health A to Z, http://www.healthatoz.com/healthatoz/Atoz/common/ standard/transform.jsp?requestURI=/healthatoz/Atoz/dc/caz/nutr/obes/ alert08032004.jsp (accessed May 14, 2008).

140   *Female cardiac patients*   Roni Caryn Rabin, "More Delays for Women in Emergency Care," *New York Times* (January 27, 2009), D6.

141   *Mama, please help*   Jane Zang, "Amid Fight for Life, Lupus Victim Fights for Insurance," *Post-Gazette* (December 5, 2006), http://www.post-gazette .com/pg/06339/743713-84.stm (accessed February 12, 2009).

141   *As one of*   Paul Krugman, "Health Care Horror Stories," *New York Times* (April 11, 2008), A23.

141   *If her illness*   Doug Trapp, "State-by-State Analysis Ties Lack of Insurance to Earlier Death," *American Medical News* (May 5, 2008), http://www .ama-assn.org/amednews/2008/05/05gvsc0505.htm.

141   *Women without insurance*   "47 Million Americans Lack Health Insurance: Report," (November 1, 2007), Common Dreams, http://www.common dreams.org/archive/2007/11/01/4963 (accessed May 19, 2008); "The Wrong Place to be Chronically Ill," *New York Times* (November 18, 2008), A26.

141   *Holding on to*   "Ask a Working Woman," AFL-CIO survey (August 7, 2006).

142   *This disparity may*   "Women Weighed Down by Health Care Costs, New Study Finds," Commonwealth Fund (April 19, 2007), http://www.common wealthfund.org/Content/News/News-Releases/2007/Apr/Women-Weighed -Down-by-Health-Care-Costs—New-Study-Finds.aspx (accessed January 25, 2008).

142   *I've never been this stressed*   Lisa Girion, "Sick but Insured? Think Again," *Los Angeles Times* (September 17, 2006), http://www .consumerwatchdog.org/search?searchQuery=girion.

142   *Health insurance companies*   Krugman, "Health Care Horror Stories."

143   *They are four*   Cynthia Shoohoo and Katrina Anderson, "The American Health Care System Is Failing Women of Color," AlterNet (March 11, 2008), http://www.alternet.org/healthwellness/79211?pages=entire.

143   *In our nation's capital*   Rogelio Saenz, "The Growing Color Divide in U.S. Infant Mortality," Population Reference Bureau (October 2007), http://www .prb.org/Articles/2007/ColorDivideininfantMortality.aspx?p=.

143   *A cut of more*   David Border, "Stealthy Budget Cuts," *Washington Post* (February 27, 2005), B07.

143   *When President Obama*   David Stout, "Bush Vetoes Children's Health Bill," *New York Times* (October 3, 2007), A10.

143   *Over the course*   Robert Greenstein, "Poor Children First or Last," Center on Budget and Policy Priorities (October 17, 2007); Allison Stevens, "Critics Say Budget Cuts Hurt Women; Children," Women's eNews (February 2,

2006), http://www.womensenews.org/articles.cfm/dyn/aid/2623/; "Children and Low-Income Families Continue to Be Left Behind," Children's Defense Fund (February 15, 2007), http://www.childrensdefense.org./child-research -data-publications/data/2008-Presidents-fy-Buget-Analysis.pdf (accessed April 27, 2007).

144   *Under Bush's administration*   Michael Abramowitz and Lori Montgomery, "Bush Plans to Rein In Domestic Spending," *Washington Post* (February 6, 2007), A01.

144   *It will help*   Tami Luhby, "States Counting on Their Slice of $787B" (February 13, 2009), CNNMoney, http://money.cnn.com/2009/02/13/news/economy/stimulus_states/ (accessed February 15, 2009).

144   *[S]ubstandard care and*   Betty Brink, "Carswell Prison Blues," *Ms.* magazine (Summer 2008), 40–44; author interviews with incarcerated and formerly incarcerated women.

145   *I wish someone*   *My Sister's Keeper* (New York: The Correctional Association, 2008).

145   *Continuity of medical*   *My Sister's Keeper*; Nancy Stoller, "Improving Access to Health Care for California Women Prisoners," California Program on Access to Care (October 2000).

145   *When female veterans return*   "Female Vets Return Home to Find Services Lacking," National Public Radio (July 24, 2007); Anne Hull and Dana Priest, "It Is Not Just Walter Reed," *Washington Post* (March 5, 2007), A1.

145   *But programs to*   Helen Benedict, "For Women Warriors, Deep Wounds Little Care," *New York Times* (May 26, 2008), A15; Pamela Burke, "Female Vets Come Home to Second War on Trauma," Women's eNews (March 28, 2006), http://www.womensenews.org/articles.cfm/dyn/aid/2755.

146   *Some eight hundred*   Erin G. Edwards and Hallie D. Martin, "Will More Women Vets be Homeless?" (March 12, 2008), http://news.medill.northwestern.edu/Chicago/news.aspx?id=83199&print=1 (accessed March 12, 2008).

146   *Women are less likely*   Allison Stevens, "Critics Say Budget Cuts Hurt Women, Children," Women's eNews (February 2, 2006), http://www .womensenews.org/articles.cfm/dyn/aid/2623/; "Children and Low-Income Families Continue to Be Left Behind," Children's Defense Fund (February 15, 2007), http://www.childrensdefense.org/child-research-data-publications/ data/a-look-at-the-presidents.html (accessed April 27, 2007).

146   *Each of the seven*   Henry Waxman (chair), "Private Medicare Drug Plans: Seniors and Taxpayer Hurt by High Expense, Low Rebates," Report by Rules and Jurisdiction Subcommittee (October 15, 2007), http://oversight.house .gov/story.asp?id=1536 (accessed May 20, 2008); "No Bargain: Medicare

Drug Plans Deliver High Prices," report from Families USA, http://www
.familiesusa.org/resources/publications/reports/no-bargain-medicare-drug
.html (accessed January 25, 2008).

146   *What really turns*   Dorothy Rosenbaum, "President's Budget Would Cut
Food for over 420,000 Low-Income Seniors," Center on Budget and Policy
Priorities (February 14, 2006), http://www.cbpp.org/2-6-06fa.htm (accessed
May 20, 2008).

147   *Hunger is a*   "The Consequences of Food Security and Hunger" and "The
Consequences of Hunger and Food Insecurity for Children," Center on
Hunger and Poverty, Brandeis University (June 2002).

148   *The outlook for women's*   Quoted in "50 State Study on Women's Health
Finds Small Gains, Key Setbacks," National Women's Law Center (May
6, 2004), http://www.nwlc.org/details/cfm?id=1863&section=newsroom
(accessed October 23, 2006).

148   *We rank forty-fifth*   Ewen MacAskill, "US Tumbles Down the World Rating for Life Expectancy," Guardian.co.uk (August 13, 2007), http://www
.guardian.co.uk/world/2007/aug/13/usa.ewenmacaskill (accessed December
9, 2008).

148   *And for the first time*   Kevin Sack, "The Short End of the Longer Life,"
New York Times (April 27, 2008), 14.

148   *Dr. Majid Ezzati*   Dr. Ezzati quoted in Kevin Sack, "The Short End of the
Longer Life."

149   *It's a nightmare*   Quoted in Allison Stevens, "Bush's Budget Alarms
Safety Advocates," Women's eNews (February 11, 2007), http://www
.womensenews.org/articles.cfm/dyn/ai/3064/.

150   *It's a band-aid*   Pamela Burke, "Gateways to Safety Scarce for Navajo
Women," Women's eNews (December 12, 2006), http://www.womensenews
.org/article.cfm/dyn/aid/2994 (accessed May 22, 2008).

Chapter 14: Birth-Control Activists, Please Phone Home

151   *How many millions*   Author interview with Dr. Angela Diaz; 90 percent
of young adolescents are sexually active before marriage.

151   *What's more, AO*   Shannon Pettypiece, "Teens Having More Sex and
Using Fewer Condoms, U.S. Study Says," CDC study reported in Bloomberg.
com (June 4, 2008), http://www.bloomberg.com/apps/news?pid=2060114&
refer=home&sid=aRM2TuCBiqJl (accessed June 23, 2008).

152   *The right's faith-based*   Gardiner Harris, "Teenage Birth Rate Rises for the First Time Since '91," *New York Times* (December 6, 2007), A25; Amanda Robb, "Abstinence 1, S-Chip 0," *New York Times* (October 18, 2007), A15; also see *New York Times* (March 12, 2008), A1, 20. As Amanda Robb, who's writing a book about the abstinence-only program, makes clear, "By dropping the financing for abstinence-only sex ed, Congress could save enough money to insure 150,000 children a year."

152   *One out of*   "Study: 1 in 4 Teen Girls Has at least one STD," http://www .msnbc.msn.com/id/23574940/ (accessed March 11, 2008).

152   *The courses exaggerate*   Thomas Frieden, M.D., et al., "Applying Public Health Principles to the Transmission of the HIV Virus," *New England Journal of Medicine* 353 (December 1, 2005): 2397–2402.

152   *And even though*   Ibid.

153   *A baby begins*   Henry Waxman, "The Content of Federally Funded Abstinence-Only Education Programs," United States House of Representative Committee on Government Reform—Minority Staff Special Investigations Division (December 2004), 1–17.

153   *Ten to twelve*   Ibid., 12. When you check out the source, it actually states: "fetuses begin to react to sounds between the fourth and fifth months."

153   *A popular feature*   Quoted in Ibid., 15–17.

153   *It may be*   William Smith, quoted in "The War on Contraception," *New York Times Magazine* (May 7, 2006), 53.

154   *Energized by the*   "Abortion Proposal: Set Condition on Aid," Robert Pear, *New York Times* (July 15, 2008).

154   *Whether it's to*   "Even Grandma Had Premarital Sex, Survey Finds," Associated Press (December 28, 2006); see also Susan Faludi, *Backlash: The Undeclared War Against American Women* (New York: Crown, 1991), 414.

154   *Bayer, the maker*   Department of Health and Human Services correspondence MACMIS ID #11730; Natasha Singer, "The Birth Control Pill That Promised Too Much," *New York Times* (February 11, 2009), B5.

155   *There was Dr. W. David Hager*   "Family Planning Farce," *New York Times* (November 24, 2006), A34.

155   *That something was*   "Food and Drug Administration Decision Process to Deny Initial Application for Over-the-Counter Marketing of the Emergency Contraceptive Drug Plan B Was Unusual," U.S. Government Accountability Office (November 2005).

156   *A new trend*   Rob Stein, "Pro-Life Drugstores Market Beliefs," Washington Post.com (June 16, 2008), http://www.washingtopost.com/wp-dyn/cotent/article/2008/06/15AR20080615021180.html.

157   *Difficulty accessing emergency*   Jeanine Plant, "Planning Ahead Still Advised for Morning After," Women's eNews (November 30, 2006), http://www.womensenews.org/articles.cfm/dyn/aid/2977; Molly Ginty, "Some Hospitals Withhold Plan B After Rape," Women's eNews (February 13, 2007), http://www.womensenews.org/article.cfm/dyn/aid/2584/ (accessed February 13, 2007).

157   *The potential is*   Monica Davey, "Big Rise in Cost of Birth Control Hits Campuses," *New York Times* (November 22, 2007), A1.

157   *Places that outlaw*   Elisabeth Rosenthal, "Legal or Not, Abortion Rates Compare," *New York Times* (October 12, 2007), A9.

158   *This harrowing situation*   Martha Mendoza, "Between a Woman and Her Doctor," *Ms.* magazine (Summer 2004), http://www.msmagazine.com/summer2004/womanandherdoctor.asp.

159   *Amazingly, between March*   Quoted in David Wallis, "Editorial Pages Nix Toons Mimicking Abortion Foes," Women's eNews (March 21, 2007), http://www.womensenews.org/articles.cfm/dyn/aid/3104.

159   *Barely had the*   Kim A. Gandy, "Supreme Court Upholds Abortion Procedure Ban," http://www.now.org/press/04-07/04-18.html (accessed April 19, 2007).

159   *These procedures are*   Quoted in Nina Totenberg, "Supreme Court Considers Abortion-Ban Arguments," National Public Radio (January 22, 2008), http://www.npr.org/templates/story/story.php?storyId=6450160 (accessed December 22, 2008).

160   *As the New York*   "Denying the Right to Choose," *New York Times* (April 19, 2007), A26.

160   *This way of thinking*   Quoted in ibid., 22.

160   *When pro-lifers*   Linda Greenhouse, "Public Lives: Doctor Spurns Euphemism in Pursuing Abortion Rights," *New York Times* (April 8, 2000), http://questia.com/PM.qst?a=o&se=gglsc&d=5001970570 (accessed January 19, 2008); LeRoy Carhart, M.D., quoted in Stevens and Bowen, "Court's Abortion Ruling Undercuts Roe," Women's eNews (April 19, 2007), http://www.womensenews.org/article.cfm./dyn/aid/3154 (accessed April 23, 2007).

161   *[E]ssentially they've taken*   Totenberg, "Supreme Court Considers Abortion-Ban Arguments."

162 *When Deb asked*   Deb Berry, "Choose Lies: One Woman's Experience at a Crisis Pregnancy Center," *Orlando Weekly* (April 17, 2003), http://www .abortion.org.au/chooselie.htm (accessed December 9, 2008).

162 *It's a subtle thing*   Quoted in Stephanie Simon, "Abortion Foes Are Getting Public Funds," *Los Angeles Times* (February 11, 2007), 1.

162 *But other women*   Vicki Saporta, quoted in Toyin Adeyemi, "Portugal May OK Choice; Health Funding Diverted," Women's eNews (February 1, 2007), http://www.womensenews.org/article.cfm/dyn/aid/3070/context/ archive (accessed February 20, 2007).

162 *At least eight states*   Simon, "Abortion Foes Are Getting Public Funds," 1.

162 *If this measure*   Allison Stevens, "Senate Bans Out-of-State Travel for Teens," Women's eNews (July 26, 2006), http://www.womensenews.org/ article.cfm./dyn/aid/2838/context/archive (accessed January 8, 2007).

163 *Two female physicians*   Author interview with Tammy Kromenaker.

164 *Women's groups pressured*   "Delinking Abortion and Breast Cancer," *New York Times* (March 11, 2003), http://query.nytimes.com/gst/fullpage .html?res=9E0DE6DA173EF932A25750C0A9659C8B63&scp=3&sq=%20 abortion%20breast%20cancer&st=cse (accessed January 21, 2008); M. Melby et al., "Induced Abortion and the Risk of Breast Cancer," *New England Journal of Medicine* (January 9, 1997), 81–85.

164 *Always looking for*   Emily Brazelton, "Is There a Post-Abortion Syndrome?" *New York Times Magazine* (January 21, 2007), 43.

165 *Overwhelmingly, 76 percent*   Ibid., 42.

165 *Rhonda Arias*   Quoted in ibid.

165 *And why, if*   Ibid.

165 *The main problem*   Author interview with Dr. Alvin Blaustein.

165 *But "even," Francis*   Brazelton, "Is There a Post-Abortion Syndrome?" 2.

165 *For Beckwith the*   Ibid.

166 *When I asked Justice*   Question asked at a meeting honoring Justice Ginsburg and feminist lawyers sponsored by Veteran Feminists of America.

166 *After deliberating for*   Bob Herbert, "Stillborn Justice," *New York Times* (May 24, 2001), http://www.query.nytimes.com/search/archive.html.

166 *It is medically*   Quoted in Cynthia L. Cooper, "Pregnant and Punished," Ford Foundation Report (Winter 2003), http://realcostofprisonss.org /hardlife.pdf/ (accessed January 22, 2008.

167 *Public health and*   "SC Supreme Court Hears Appeal: Don't Punish Women for Stillbirth," *National Advocates for Pregnant Women* (November 6, 2002), http://www.advocatesforpregnantwomen.org/issues/criminal

_cases_issues/ (accessed December 10, 2008). After serving eight years of her sentence, McKnight was released and (as of March 2009) is currently awaiting a new trial.

167   *Most, but not all*   Adam Nossiter, "Rural Alabama County Cracks Down on Pregnant Drug Users," *New York Times* (March 15, 2008), A10.

167   *What South Carolina*   Author interview with Lynn Paltrow.

168   *Before this, the*   "Senate Passes Unborn Victims of Violence Act," News with Views.com (March 27, 2004), http://www.newswithviews.com/ NWVexclusive/3htm (accessed January 22, 2008).

168   *Thirty-four states*   "Bush's Latest Masquerade Exposed as Attack on Women's Reproductive Health," National Organization for Women (April 1, 2004), http://www.now.org./press/04-04/04-01.html/printable (accessed October 23, 2006).

168   *Tennessee has introduced*   "Tennessee Representative Proposes Death Certificates on Abortions," http://womenshealthnews.blogsot.com/2007/02/ tennessee-representative-proposes-death.html (accessed December 10, 2008); Joe Biesk, "Bill Would Require Pre-Abortion Ultrasound," *Herald Leader* (January 14, 2008), http://www.medicalnewstoday.com/articles/64748.php

168   *This, in spite of*   Denise Grady, "Study Finds 29-Week Fetuses Probably Feel No Pain," *New York Times* (August 24, 2005), http://www.nytimes .com/2005/08/24/health/24fetus.html (accessed January 23, 2008).

168   *But the real risk*   Kim Gandy, "Roe-Be-Gone Effort Focuses on Fetal Personhood," National Organization for Women (December 13, 2006), http:// www.now.org/news/note/121306.html?printable (accessed December 14, 2006).

170   *Commenting on the lack*   Mireya Navarro, "On Abortion, Hollywood Is No-Choice," *New York Times* (June 10, 2007), http://www.nytimes.com/ 2007/06/10fashion/10Knockedup.html (accessed January 17, 2008).

Chapter 15: Trouble@edu

171   *A 1992 report by*   "Failing at Fairness: How the Schools Shortchange Girls" (Washington, DC: American Association of University Women, 1992).

172   *Major publications scolded*   Lyn Mikel Brown et al. "What About the Boys?" *Education Week* (June 7, 2006), http://www.wcwonline.org/content/ view/240/208/ (accessed December 3, 2007); see also David Von Drehle, "The Myth About Boys," *Time* (August 6, 2007).

172   *Focusing on gender*   Sara Mead, "The Truth About Boys and Girls," *Education Sector* (2006), www.educationsector.org.

173   *[Girls'] successes in*   Von Drehle, "The Myth About Boys," 44–45.

173   *When girls do*   "Where the Girls Are," AAUW Report, quoted in Valerie Strauss, "No Crisis for Boys in Schools, Study Says," *Washington Post* (May 20, 2008), A01.

173   *[M]uch of the pessimism*   Quoted in Jay Matthews, "Study Casts Doubt on the 'Boy Crisis,'" *Washington Post* (June 26, 2006), A01.

173   Feminized *schooling is*   For more on this line of reasoning, see Brown, "What About the Boys?"

173   *Since all education*   Von Drehle, "The Myth About Boys."

174   *The female brain*   Studies quoted in Carol Midgely, "Lobal Warfare," Times Online (August 9, 2006), http://www.timesonline.co.uk/tol/life_and_style/article603199.ece.

174   *Because the teen brain*   Louann Brizendine, M.D., in *The Female Brain* (New York: Morgan Road Books, 2005).

174   *But, reaping the benefits*   Larry Summers, remarks at the NBER Task Force on Diversifying Science and Engineering Workforce, Cambridge, MA (January 14, 2005), 5, http://wiseli.engr.wisc.edu/news/Summers.htm.

174   *But if it* were   Sharon Begley, "Math Is Hard, Barbie Said," *Newsweek* (October 27, 2008), 57; Barnett and Rivers, *Same Difference*, 161.

174   *Their book* Same   Rosalind Barnett and Caryl Rivers, *Same Difference* (New York: Basic Books, 2004).

175   *One's sex has*   "Men and Women: No Big Difference," APA Online, http://www.psychologymatters.org/nodifference.html (accessed May 28, 2008).

175   *Girls are still*   Barnett and Rivers, *Same Difference*, 149–152.

175   *By teachers' admissions*   Carmen J. Lee, "Study Finds Girls Are Turned Off by Computers," *Post-Gazette News* (April 11, 2000), http://www.post-gazette.com/regionstate/20000411girls1.asp; Valerie Strauss, "Decoding Why Few Girls Choose Science, Math," *Washington Post* (February 1, 2005), A07.

176   *[It's] a troubling*   Quoted in Lee, "Study Finds Girls Are Turned Off by Computers"; Barnett and Rivers, *Same Difference*, 165.

176   *At Carnegie Mellon, in*   Ed Frauenheim and Alorie Gilbert, "Opening Doors for Women in Computing," *CNET News* (February 7, 2005), http://news.cnet/Opening-doors-2100-1022_3_5557311.html (accessed February 13, 2009).

176   *It would be pointless*   Barnett and Rivers, *Same Difference*, 160.

176   *They don't have*   Ibid.

176   *Pinker even argues*   Ibid., 161.

176   *And when Senator*   *Slip Sliding Away,* National Women's Law Center (April 2004), 17.

176   *Blatant sexism bounces off*   "Title IX and Equal Opportunity in Vocational and Technical Education: A Promise Still Owed to the Nation's Young Women," National Women's Law Center (June 2002).

177   *Separation allows "boys*   Jane Gross, "In a Coed Setting, School Separates the Boys and Girls, Just for the Tougher Years," *New York Times* (May 31, 2004), B4.

177   *Bush, in 2004*   Funding was restored by Congress, then in 2007 completely eliminated.

177   *The move, long*   Diana Jean Schemo, "Change in Federal Rules Back Single-Sex Public Education," *New York Times* (October 25, 2006), A1, 16.

178   *Segregation is totally*   Ibid., A16.

178   *He tells them*   Quoted in Von Drehle, "The Myth About Boys," 46.

178   *Defying the born-again*   David Brooks, "The Gender Gap at School," *New York Times* (June 12, 2006), A15.

179   *And Regina Choi*   "Single-Sex Education and Gender Roles," Feministing (October 26, 2006), http://feministing.com/archives/005936.html (accessed January 28, 2008).

179   *Like my two*   Jennie Finch, "Don't Make Girls Prove They Want to Play," *Arizona Daily Star* (June 28, 2006), http://www.azstarnet.com/allheadlines/135484.php.

179   *And the conservative*   Jessica Gavora, "Girl Power," *National Review* online (January 31, 2005), http://www.nationalreview.com/comment/comment-gavora013103.asp (accessed January 29, 2008).

180   *But many men*   John Tierney, "Let the Guys Win One," *New York Times* (July 11, 2006), A16.

180   *You should be given*   Jennifer Engle et al., "Straight from the Source," *Pell Institute for the Study of Opportunity in Higher Education* (December 2006), 21.

181   *Three years later, in 2005*   Patrick Kerkstra, "Bush's Pell Grant Plan Would Shut Out Thousands," *SouthCoast Today* (January 28, 2008), http://archive.southcoasttoday.com/daily/12-04/12-13-04/a16ed314.htm (accessed January 28, 2008).

181 *It's tempting to point*   "9 University Presidents Issue a Statement on Gender Equity," *Inside Higher Ed* (December 7, 2005), www.insidehighered.com/layout/set/print/news/2005/12/07/gender (accessed February 3, 2008).

181 *But rhetoric and*   *The (Un)Changing Face of the Ivy League*, Graduate Teachers and Researchers Union (February 2005).

182 *Education and work*   Quoted in *The (Un)Changing Face of the Ivy League*, 2.

182 *We trust our*   Ibid., 5.

183 *For the same*   Joan C. Williams et al., *Beyond the "Chilly Climate," Eliminating Bias Against Women and Fathers in Academe, Thought and Action* (Fall 2006).

183 *Men can tolerate*   Margaret Wertheim, "Numbers Are Male, Said Pythagoras, and the Idea Persists," *New York Times* (October 3, 2006), A22.

183 *And those women who*   The new slippery slope for proving sexual discrimination is in part responsible for the low success rate. Approximately 24,000 cases were filed with the EEOC in 2007. Of these, 57 percent were dismissed as having "no reasonable cause." Another 20 percent were closed without resolution.

184 *The discrimination [today]*   Quoted in *Tenure Denied: Cases of Sex Discrimination in Academia*, American Association of University Women (October 2004).

184 *In their isolated*   Ibid.

185 *Students were told*   Based on author interview with professor Linda Garavalia; statement of Megan Pinkston-Camp; letter from Linda S. Garavalia, laying out the charges to Provost Bubacz (September 6, 2005).

185 *It was a horrible*   Garavalia.

186 *Both men talked*   Dan Margolies, "UMKC Settle Sexual Harassment Suit for 1.1 Million," KansasCity.com (July 11, 2007), http://www.broushorn.com/20070712_KC_Star_article.pdf.

186 *The university failed*   Author interview with professor Miriam Forman-Brunell.

187 *Haddock's annual salary*   Margolies, "UMKC Settles Sex-Harassment Suit for 1.1 Million"; Joshua Seiden, "New Investigation Opened Following Settlement," *Campus Confidential* (August 20, 2007), http://meida.www.unews.com/meida/storag/paper274news/2007/98/20/News/CampusC (accessed January 28, 2008).

Chapter 16: The Campaign Against Working Women

189   *Respect for stay*   Rick Santorum, "It Takes a Family," interview on CBN
.com, http://www.cbn.com/cbnnews/news/050811a.aspx?option=print
(accessed May 31, 2008); quoted in Ruth Connif, "Rick Santorum's America,"
The Progressive (October 5, 2005), http://www.progressive.org/?q=mag
_conniff1005 (accessed December 1, 2008).

189   *Women themselves say*   Quoted in Brandeis University, "Work and Parenting: The Debate Goes On" (July 7, 2005), http://my.brandeis.edu/news/
item?news_item_id=103921&show_release_date=1 (accessed December 11,
2008).

189   *Gottlieb, unwed at forty*   Lori Gottlieb, "Marry Him!," *The Atlantic* (February 2008).

190   *This, according to*   "MetLife Study finds Employer/Employee Worry
About Aging" (February 28, 2006), http://hr-topics.com/wire-usa/met-life
.htm.

191   *Slower workforce growth*   Megan McArdel, "No Country for Young Men,"
The Atlantic (January 2008), 80.

191   *Experts looking at*   Lynn A. Karoly and Constantine W. A. Panis, "Forces
Shaping the Future Workforce and Workplace in the United States," U.S.A.
Rand Labor and Population Study, 2004; Kathy Krepcio, "Boomers in Retirement: Implications for the Workforce," John J. Heldrich Center for Workforce Development (December 4, 2006).

191   *[D]iscrimination against women*   Quoted in Lucas Mearian, "US Faces
Competitive Disadvantage from Lack of Women in Tech Jobs," *Computer-
world Careers* (September 25, 2007).

191   *Women haven't got*   Used by Rosalind Barnett and Caryl Rivers, *Same
Difference* (New York: Basic Books, 2004), xii.

192   *Once upon a time*   Ibid., 128, 132.

192   *The Peases' analysis*   Ibid., 132.

193   *[T]he development of*   Ibid.

193   *hunting is a relatively*   Ibid., Caryl Rivers, "Stone Age Had Rocks, Not
June-and-Ward Cleavers," Women's eNews (December 13, 2006), http://www
.womensenews.org/article.org/article.cfm/dym/aid/2995/context/archive
(accessed December 11, 2008); Nicholas Wade, "Neanderthal Women Joined
Men in the Hunt," *New York Times* (December 5, 2006), http://www
.nytimes.com/2006/12/05/science/05nean.html?=r=1&oref=slogin (accessed
February 13, 2008).

193   *Marry pretty women*   Michael Noer, "Point: Don't Marry Career
      Women," *Forbes* (August 23, 2007), http://www.forbes.com/home/2006/08/
      23/Marriage-Career-Divorce-cx-mn-land.html (accessed February 6, 2008).

193   *Men just want*   Maureen Dowd, "Men Just Want Mommy," *New York
      Times* (January 13, 2005), A15.

194   *And John Tierney*   John Tierney, "The Happiest Wives," *New York Times*
      (February 28, 2006), A16.

194   *Women aren't willing*   Carol Tavris, "Women Are from Europe, Men Are
      from America," *New York Times* (March 30, 2003), http://query.nytimes.com/
      gst/fullpage.html?res=9D05E5D61031F933A05750C0A9659C8B63&scp=
      2&sq=women+are+from+europe&st=nyt (accessed February 6, 2008).

194   *Do women lack*   Patricia Sellers, "Power: Do Women Really Want It?
      That's the Surprising Question More of Them Are Asking When They Pon-
      der Top Jobs in Business, Academia and Government," *Fortune* (October 13,
      2002), http://money.cnn.com/magazines/fortune-archive/2003/10/13/350932
      /index.htm (accessed February 1, 2008).

195   *It will be*   "Effort to Reinstate Data Collection on Women Workers
      Stalled," National Organization for Women (December 12, 2005), http://
      www.now.org/issues/economic/121205_bls_stalled.html (accessed February
      14, 2008).

195   *Other important material*   "Missing: Information About Women's Lives,"
      National Council for Research on Women (March 2004); Sarah Stewart Tay-
      lor, "Plan to Close Working Women's Offices Draws Fire," Women's eNews
      (January 9, 2007), http://www.womensenews.org/article.cfm/dyn/aid/762/
      context/archive (accessed January 9, 2007).

195   *The Bush administration*   Letter to Senator Bill Frist in *Women's Preroga-
      tive* (October 18, 2005), http://www.womensprerogative.org/fristletter.cfm
      (accessed January 8, 2007); Stewart Taylor, "Plan to Close Working Women's
      Office Draws Fire."

196   *The government says*   Elizabeth Olson, "Women's Business Owners Dis-
      pute Contracting Rules," *New York Times* (January 16, 2008), C5.

196   *That many experienced*   *Slip Sliding Away*, 13.

197   *I don't think*   David Leonhardt, "Scant Progress in Closing the Pay Gap,"
      New York Times (December 24, 2006), 1.

197   *Back then it*   Ibid.

197   *The gender pay*   Author interview with Catherine Hill.

198   *And the pay*   "Women Lose Millions Due to Wage Gap," National Organization for Women (April 24, 2007), http://www.now.org/press/04-07/04-24.html?printable (accessed December 11, 2008).

198   *In the 1960s*   Leonhardt, "Scant Progress," ibid.

198   *Before this ruling*   "Justices' Ruling Limits Lawsuits on Pay Disparity," *New York Times* (May 30, 2007), 1.

199   *It is something*   Myrle Croasdale, "Women in Primary Care Earn Less than Men," Amednews.com (July 23/30, 2007), http://www.ama-assn.org/amednews/2007/07/23/prsb0723.htm (accessed October 1, 2007).

199   *[M]any women still*   "Women in the Workplace Generationally Speaking," Downtown Women's Club (April 26, 2007), http://womensdish.typepad.com.resource/2007/07/downtown-womens.html.

199   *Right before the*   "Overtime Pay Under Attack," AFL-CIO, http://www.aflico.org/yourjobseconomy/overtimepay/underattack.cfm (accessed December 11, 2008).

200   *All families are*   "NOW Blasts Bush Administration for Leaving Millions of Working Families Behind" (August 23, 2004), http://www.now.org/press/08-04/08-23.html (accessed December 11, 2008).

200   *Gender descrimination pervades*   Michael Selmi and Naomi Cahn, "Women in the Workplace: Which Women, Which Agenda?" *Duke Journal of Law and Policy* 13 (Spring 2006): 1–23.

201   *For the majority*   Jane DeGooyer, "Women, Work and Age Discrimination," Educational Resources Information Center, http://www.eric.ed.gov/ERICWebPortal/recordDetail?accno=ED210496 (accessed March 27, 2008).

201   *Women now constitute*   Jeanne Lofstedt, "Gender and Veterinary Medicine," *Canadian Veterinary Journal* 44 (July 2003): 533–535.

201   *I'm often asked*   Linda Childers, "Female Medical Students Continue to Grapple with Gender Stereotypes," American Medical Student Association (December 2006), http://www.amsa.org/tnp/articles.cfx?id=332 (accessed February 20, 2008).

202   *I remember a [male]*   Ibid.

202   *Data gathered in 2005*   Ibid.

202   *You're such a girl*   Liz Kowalczyk, "Women Surgeons Complain of Bias by Male Chief," *Boston Globe* (December 30, 2007), http://www.boston.com/news/local/articles/2007/12/30 women_surgeons_complain_of_bias_by_male_chief/ (accessed December 30, 2007).

202   *When Tuli complained*   Ibid.

202   *Even though increasing*   Childers, "Female Medical Students Continue to Grapple with Gender Stereotypes."

202   *I'd hire you*   Author interview with Debi Field.

203   *Art is a luxury*   "Where Are the Women? Not at SF Moma," Bay Area Art Quake (December 15, 2007), http://baartquake.blogspot.com/2007/12.

203   *In 1972 it*   Jerry Saltz, "The Venus of Long Island City," *New York* magazine (March 2008).

203   *In art, as*   "Where Are the Women?"; ibid.

204   *A vast discrepancy*   Greg Allen, "The X Factor: Is the Art Market Rational or Biased?" *New York Times* (May 1, 2005), C8.

204   *Although women outnumber*   Angeli R. Rasbury, "Female Choreographers Face Slippery Career Stereotypes," Women's eNews (February 11, 2008); Bay Area Art Quake (December 15, 2007), 3.

204   *There have been women*   Julie Creswell, "How Suite It Isn't: A Dearth of Female Bosses," *New York Times* (December 17, 2006), sec. 3, 1, 9.

205   *A Catalyst survey*   "Critical Mass on Corporate Boards: Why Three or More Women Enhance Governance," Wellesley Centers for Women, http://www.wcwonline./pdf/Critical MasExecSummary.pdf (accessed May 14, 2007).

205   *This in part*   Ibid.

205   *For women of*   Ibid.

205   *[G]oing strictly by*   Susan Deutschle, "Female Architects a Rare Breed, Despite Advances," *Columbus Business First* (October 3, 2003), http://columbusbizjournals.com/columbus/stories/2003/10/06/focus7.html (accessed February 20, 2008).

205   *When I was*   Margaret Wertheim, "Pythagoras Said Numbers Are Male and the Idea Still Persists," *New York Times* (October 3, 2008), A22.

205   *Encountering another woman*   Maggie Biggs, "Activism Provides Competitive Advantage for IT," *InfoWorld* (January 29, 2007), http://www.infoworld.com/article/0701/2905FEwomentechbiggs_1.html? (accessed January 30, 2007).

206   *A major study*   Cornelia Dean, "Bias Is Hurting Women in Science," *New York Times* (September 19, 2006), A22.

206   *Marsha Simms, a*   Marsha Simms, Conference on Women and Ambition, National Council for Research on Women (May 14, 2008).

206   *Despite years of*   "The Double-Bind Dilemma for Women in Leadership: Damned If You Do, Doomed If You Don't," *Catalyst* (July 2007); Christine Frey, "Colleges Push Women to the Top," *Seattle Post-Intelligencer* (Novem-

ber 16, 2006), http://seattlepi.nwsource.com/specials/glassceiling/292482
_glassceiling-college16.html (accessed December 11, 2008).

207   *As unnatural leaders*   Catalyst, "The Double-Bind Dilemma for Women
in Leadership."

207   *Women are assumed*   Ibid.

207   *Aggressive and blunt*   Joe Hagan, "They Fired the Most Powerful Woman
on Wall Street," *New York* magazine (May 5, 2008), 32–37.

208   *Women got "slaughtered"*   Ibid.

208   *The real problem*   Ibid.; see also Lisa Scherzer, "Women on Wall Street
Are Getting Short-Changed," *Smart Money* (August 9, 2007), http://www
.smartmoney.com/investing/economy/Women-on-Wall-Street-Are-Getting
-Short-Changed-21660 (accessed August 13, 2007).

208   *It's wonderful to*   Wendy Fox-Grange, "Caring for the Caregivers,"
National Conference of State Legislatures (The Gale Group, 1998), http://
www.encyclopedia.com/doc/1G1-20852444.html (accessed June 3, 2008).

209   *It'a safe*   Jane Gross, "Forget the Career, My Parents Need Me at Home,"
New York Times (November 24, 2005), A16.

209   *Recent studies document*   "Absent on the Job? Work and Elder Family
Care," Duke Center for Aging, Duke University Medical Center publication.

210   *President Bush signaled*   Janet Kornblum, "Crisis in Elder Care Fore-
seen," *USA Today* (December 11, 2005), http://www.usatoday.com/news/
heatlh/2005-12-11-eldercare-aging_x.htm (accessed June 3, 2008).

210   *And yet the*   Besa Luci, "After School Programs Lose Funds," *Gotham
Gazette* (July 30, 2007), http://www.gothamgazette.com/print/2248
(accessed February 15, 2008).

211   *Under Bush's administration*   Carol Towarnicky, "On Women's Issues,
Bush Going Backward," St. Paul Pioneer Press, (November 1, 2004), 1–2.

211   *These moves have*   Benedict Carey, "Poor Behavior Is Linked to Time
in Day Care," *New York Times* (March 26, 2007), A1. For a review of day
care literature, see Barbara J. Berg, *The Crisis of the Working Mother* (New
York: Summit Books, 1986); Caryl Rivers, "Day Care Report Launches Mis-
informed Hysteria," Women's eNews (April 21, 2001); Cathy Young, "New
Squabble over Day Care," *Reason* magazine (April 25, 2001), http://www
.reason.com/news/show/31912.html (accessed December 11, 2008); Jessica
Garrison, "Researchers in Child-Care Study Claim Study Has Been Misrep-
resented," *Los Angeles Times* (February 15, 2008), A01.

211   *Even a key*   Carey, "Poor Behavior Is Linked to Time in Day Care," A1.

211   *I can usually*   Author interview with Ilene Lewis.

212 *Bad care is*   Quoted in "Day Care Study Raises Hackles, More Questions" (March 2007), http://www.msnbc.msn.com/id/17876040/ (accessed February 15, 2008).

212 *But as historian*   Ruth Rosen, "Why Working Women Are Stuck in the 1950s," AlterNet (February 27, 2007), http://www.alternet.org/story/48370/ (accessed February 28, 2007).

Chapter 17: Mothers Matter(s)

213 *She should be*   Al Lewis, "Pregnancy Shouldn't Cost Women Jobs," Denverpost.com (October 15, 2006), http://www.denverpost.com/business/ci_4494032 (accessed February 23, 2008).

213 *I burst into*   Stephanie Armour, "Pregnant Workers Report Growing Discrimination," *USA Today,* http://usatoday.com/money/workplace/2007-10-24-caregivers-work-discrimination_N.htm (accessed February 5, 2007).

213 *You can't be*   Joan C. Williams et al., *Beyond the "Chilly Climate": Eliminating Bias Against Women and Fathers in Academe, Thought and Action* (Fall 2006).

213 *I was going*   Ibid.

213 *And in the*   Ray Rivera, "Pregnancy Led to Discrimination at Bloomberg L.P., Lawsuit Says," *New York Times* (September 28, 2007), B1, 6.

214 *The kind of cases*   Stephanie Armour, "Pregnant Workers Report Growing Discrimination"; "Pregnancy Discrimination Reports at Record High," Feminist Daily News Wire (March 28, 2008), http://www.feminist.org/news/newsbyte/uswirestory.asp?id=10906 (accessed March 28, 2008). The rise in pregnancy discrimination cases is something we should keep a close eye on because more women of child-bearing age are working outside the home: women make up about half of the total labor force and we're having children at a later age. This puts us having children right at the same time we're trying to build our careers.

215 *Women's reproductive organs*   Carroll Smith Rosenberg, *Disorderly Conduct* (New York: Alfred A. Knopf, 1986), 183.

215 *Some are discouraged*   Hannah Cho, "Pregnant Need Not Apply," Baltimoresun.com (March 28, 2007), http://www.hosted.law.wisc.edu/wjlgs/issues/2007-spring/krugernobanner.pdf.

215 *In a ten-year study*   Williams et al., *Beyond the "Chilly Climate."*

215 *Actually fewer than*   Quoted in the *American Sociological Review* 73, no. 13 (June, 2008): 500.

215   *Sarah Clarke, who*   Kimberly Tso, "Go Home!" The Mothers Movement
Online (April 2005), http://www.mothersmovement.org/features/05/go_
home/k_tso_discrimination.html (accessed December 12, 2008).

216   *Janet Loures's duties*   Ibid.

216   *I felt like*   "Have You Been Discriminated Against Because You're a
Mother?" http://www.momsrising.org/node/577?page=2 (accessed February
17, 2008).

216   *I had a baby*   Janet Wiscombe, "Tearing Down the Maternal Wall," Business Services Industry, http://www.academicworklife.org/search/search
.php?SType=B&Ppage=3&ordering+Date&count+10&keyword=Work/
life%balance (accessed December 12, 2008).

216   *All over the*   Jennifer L. Jackson, "Current Indicators Women Are Still
Not Equals in U.S. Society," http://www.globalpolitician.com/24873
-feminism (accessed June 9, 2008); author's interview.

217   *This kind of*   Tso, "Go Home!"

217   *And apparently he's*   John Pacenti, "Workplace Discrimination: Hitting
the 'Maternal Wall,'" *Daily Business Review* (January 24, 2008), http://www
.law.com/jsp/ihc/PubArticlesIHC.jsp?id=1201255554661 (accessed December
12, 2008).

217   *It wasn't always*   Author interview with Barbara Stoller.

217   *And now, because*   Jody Heyman et al., "The Work, Family and Equity
Index," (Montreal: Institute for Health and Social Policy, 2007).

218   *Given the high*   Ibid.

218   *The American Academy*   Jodi Kantor, "On the Job, Nursing Mothers Are
Finding a 2 Class System," *New York Times* (September 1, 2006), A1, 14.

218   *But according to*   Ibid.

218   *After he told*   Ibid.

218   *I can't understand*   Ibid.

218   *We are coming close*   Wiscombe, "Tearing Down the Maternal Wall."

219   *Women who have*   Williams et al., *Beyond the "Chilly Climate."*

219   *People actually have*   Quoted in Tso, "Go Home!"

219   *Their resumes were*   Daniel Aloi, "Mothers Face Disadvantage in Getting
Hired, Cornell Study Says" (August 4, 2005), http://www.news.cornell.edu/
stories/Aug05/soc.mothers.dea.html (accessed February 18, 2008).

219   *The mothers were*   Ibid.

219   *We found fathers*   Ibid.

219   *The bias against*   Joan Williams, "One Sick Child Away From Being Fired," Bay Area Business Women (June 2006), http://www.babwnews.com/artciles.php?id=606.

220   *When she got*   Ibid.

220   *Barely half of*   "Paid Sick Days Improve Public Health by Reducing the Spread of Disease," Institute for Women's Policy Research (February 2006), www.iwpr.org.

220   *[M]ost companies would*   Wiscombe, "Tearing Down the Maternal Wall."

221   *Belkin had uncovered*   Lisa Belkin, "The Opt-Out Revolution," *New York Times Magazine* (October 26, 2003), http://www.nytimes.com/2003/10/26/magazine/26WOMEN.html?ex=1237262400&en=55f277a4e2d8bf67&ei=5070 (accessed August 15, 2006).

221   *While Belkin did*   Ibid.

222   *Heather Boushey, an economist*   Heather Boushey, "Are Women Opting Out? Debunking the Myth," Washington, D.C., Center for Economic and Policy Research, www.cepr.net.

222   *The long-term trend*   Quoted in Katha Pollitt, "There They Go Again," *The Nation* (November 17, 2003), http://www.thenation.com/doc/20031117/pollitt (accessed August 23, 2006).

222   *And the percent*   "Child Health USA 2004," U.S. Department of Health and Human Services, *US NEWS and World Report* (September 7, 2007); for similar stories see: "Opt-Out Revolution" (Child Health USA) 2004 U.S. Department of Health and Human Services.

222   *"But," corrected Ilene H. Lang*   Belkin, "The Opt-Out Revolution," letter to the editor published in *New York Times* (November 16, 2003).

223   *Ditto for promising*   Claire Cain Miller, "Women's Work: Still Not Done," AlterNet (August 16, 2006), http://www.alternet.org/module/printversion/40384 (accessed August 24, 2006).

223   *Whatever Linda Hardin's*   Quoted in Joan C. Williams et al., "'Opt Out' or Pushed Out?: How the Press Covers Work/Family Conflict" (California: The Center for Work Life Law, 2006), www.worklifelaw.org; "Staying at Home," CBS News (October 10, 2004), http://www.cbsnews.com/stories/2005/07/11/60minutes/main708196.shtml?source=search_story (accessed October 12, 2006).

223   *I might not get*   Quoted in Williams, "'Opt Out' or Pushed Out?" 12–13.

223   *Not to be*   Quoted in Williams, 5.

223   *In their haste*   Louise Story, "Many Women at Elite College Set Career Path to Motherhood," *New York Times* (September 20, 2005), A1.

223 *The article was*   Jack Shafer, "Weasel-Words Rip My Flesh!" Slate (September 20, 2005), http://www.slate.com/id/2126636/.

223 *As well as an op-ed*   "Dueling Data on Women and Work," *Inside Higher Ed*, http://www.insidehighered.com/news/2006/10/04/women (accessed October 9, 2006); Edaurdo Porter, "Stretched to Limit, Women Stall March to Work," *New York Times* (March 2, 2006), D5, quoted in Williams, "'Opt Out' or Pushed Out?"

223 *Joan Williams, who*   Williams, "'Opt Out' or Pushed Out?" 5.

223 *And* Nation *columnist*   Pollitt, "There They Go Again."

224 *The cover story*   Tony Schwartz, "Second Thoughts on Having It All," *New York* magazine (July 15, 1985), 32–48.

224 *The report documents*   Louis Uchitelle, "Women Are Now Equal as Victims of Poor Economy," *New York Times* (July 22, 2008), A1, 17; Senator Charles E. Schumer, chair, and Carolyn B. Maloney, vice chair, "Equality in Job Loss: Women Are Increasingly Vulnerable to Layoff During Recessions," report by the Majority Staff of the Joint Economic Committee.

225 *When Hunter College sociologist*   Quoted in Claudia Wallis, "The Case for Staying Home," *Time* magazine (March 22, 2004), http://www.time.com/time/magazine/article/0,9171,993641,00.html (accessed February 26, 2008); Williams, "'Opt Out' or Pushed Out?" 12.

226 *Stepping off the career*   Sylvia Ann Hewlett and Carolyn Buck Luce, "Off-Ramps and On-Ramps," *Harvard Business Review* (March 2005), 2.

226 *It's all in*   Quoted in Belkin, "The Opt-Out Revolution."

226 *Writing an editorial*   Albert Mohler Jr., "*Time* Magazine and the New Stay-at-Home Moms," (June 7, 2004), www.albertmohler.com.commentary_read.php?cdate=2004-03-24.

227 *The* Time *article*   Quoted in Wallis, "The Case for Staying Home," 6.

227 *Opting out is*   *The Phyllis Schlafly Report* (December 2004), http://www.eagleforum.org/psr/2004/dec04/psrdec04.html (accessed December 13, 2008).

227 *First—and I*   Imelda Whelehan, *Overloaded* (London: Women's Press, 2000). See the introduction for an elaboration of this point.

227 *And to suggest*   Belkin, "The Opt-Out Revolution."

227 *As Women's Studies*   Heather Hewett, "Telling It Like It Is," The Mother's Movement Online (October 2005), http://www.mothersmovement.org/features/05h-hewett-1005-out-print.htm (accessed August 23, 2006); Wallis, "The Case for Staying Home."

231 *Working and at-home*   Quoted in Barbara J. Berg, "Women at Odds," *Savvy* 5 (December 1985): 5.

Chapter 18: *Un*popular Culture

233 *Popular culture is*   See statement of Karen E. Dill, Ph.D., Hearing for the Subcommittee on Commerce, Trade and Consumer Protection, "From Imus to Industry: The Business of Stereotypes and Degrading Images" (September 25, 2007).

234 *Haven't I told*   Margaret Talbot, "Girls Just Want to Be Mean," *New York Times* (February 24, 2002), http://query.nytimes.com/gst/fullpage.html?res=9C05E5D81E3FF937A15751C0A9649C8B63&scp=1&sq=girls%20just%20want%20to%20be%20mean&st=cse (accessed February 28, 2008).

234 *Feminists have done*   Jessica Ringrose, "A New Universal Mean Girl: Examining the Discursive Construction and Social Regulation of a New Feminine Pathology," *Feminism and Psychology* 16 (2006): 405–24.

234 *Starting in the*   For a further discussion, see Nina Shapiro, "Are Girls Mean?" AlterNet (May 30, 2002), http://www.alternet.org/story/13250/?page=entire (accessed March 28, 2007); Dawn Currie and Deirdre M. Kelly, "Mean Girls and Moral Panics: Feminism Awry?" Report Card on Women and Children in B.C. (July 15, 2004), http://www.wmst.ubc.ca/pdfs/fwcbc/FWCBCJul04.pdf (accessed February 21, 2009).

235 *The name, taken*   The Ophelia Project Mission Statement, http://www.opheliaproject.org/main/who_we_are.htm (accessed March 5, 2008).

235 *Girls Just Want*   Talbot, "Girls Just Want to Be Mean"; Gretel C. Kovach and Arian Campo-Flores, "Mean Girls," *Newsweek* (August 21, 2007), http://www.msnbc.msn.com/id/16441559/site/newsweek/ (accessed March 28, 2007); Anthony Lane, "Mean Girls," *The New Yorker* (May 17, 2004), 28.

235 *By the time*   "Study: Mean Girls Start as Tots," CBS News (May 7, 2005), http://www.cbsnews.com/stories/2005/05/07/tech/main693714.shtml (accessed March 3, 2008). As they get older, they presumably hone and refine their vicious skills.

236 *Rachel Simmons, the guru*   Quoted in Shapiro, "Are Girls Mean?"

237 *I wondered if*   Rachel Mosteller, Blogging Baby, http://www.bloggingbaby.com (accessed October 18, 2007). She no longer keeps this blog but her back clips can be obtained by contacting her at: http://www.mosteller.com.

237 *While Halloween for boys*   James Fussell, "Sexy Styles for Girls Frighten Some Parents," *Kansas City Star* (October 29, 2006), http://www.pantagraph

.com/articles/2006/10/29/freetime/doc45428d8e79d16602700507.txt
(accessed December 14, 2008).

237   *It's a strange time*   Kelly Smith, "Sexy Halloween Costumes Rile Parents,"
Albany Times Union (October 16, 2006), http://www.azcentral.com/familes/
articles/1018sexyhalloween1018html (accessed November 22, 2006).

238   *In effect, we're*   Quoted in Fussell, "Sexy Styles for Girls Frighten Some
Parents."

238   *Research shows that*   "Sex Sells: Marketing and 'Age Compression,'" CBS
News (January 9, 2005), http://www.cbc.ca/comsumers/market/files/money/
sexy/marketing.html (accessed March 6, 2008).

238   *Children always have*   Ibid.; Karen MacPherson, "Is Childhood Becoming Oversexed?" *Pittsburgh Post Gazette*, http://www.frankwbaker.com/is
_childhood_becoming_oversexed.htm (accessed January 24, 2007).

238   *Even if adults*   Quoted in Jenny Deam, "Sexy Styles Beckon Little Girl,"
Denver Post (June 24, 2006), http://www.commercialexploitation.org/news/
stylesbeckongirls.htm (accessed March 6, 2008).

238   *It's advertisers who*   Graydon, quoted in "Sex Sells: Marketing and 'Age
Compression.'"

239   *Licensing and branding*   Author interview with Diane Levin.

239   *The most popular*   "Buying into Sexy: The Sexing Up of Tweens," CBS
News (January 9, 2005), http://www.cbc.ca/consumers/market/files/money/
sexy/3/6/2008 (accessed March 6, 2008); "The Tween Market," Media
Awareness Network, http://www.media-awareness.ca/english/parents/
marketing/issues_teen_marketing.cfm (accessed December 7, 2006);
Interview with Diane Levin; Michael Winerip, "In Novels for Girls Fashion
Trumps Romance," *New York Times* (July 13, 2008), LI, Region, C1.

239   *[T]here's definitely a*   Joanne Richard, "Selling Sex to Kids," *Toronto Star*
(July 17, 2005).

239   *One study found*   CBS News, "Buying into Sexy: The Sexing Up of
Tweens."

240   *A patty with*   "Do Racy Ads Aimed at Teens Cross a Line?" ABC
News (September 11, 2007), http://abcnews.go.com/GMA/TurningPoints/
story?id=3585337&page=1 (accessed March 6, 2008).

240   *This constricted identity*   APA Task Force on the Sexualization of Girls
(2007), http://www.apa.org/pi/wpo/sexualizationsum.html (accessed February 26, 2000).

241   *The APA report*   Laurie Meyers, "Dangerous Dolls?" *APA Monitor* (September 2006).

241   *Wearing thick eye makeup*   *Daily Mail*, "Over-Sexed and Over Here: The 'Tarty' Bratz Doll" (January 24, 2007), http://www.dailymail.co.uk/femail/article-411266/Over-sexed-The-tarty-Bratz-Doll.html (accessed January 24, 2007).

241   *Bratz represents the*   Talbot, "Little Hotties."

241   *On a shopping trip*   Margaret Talbot, "Little Hotties," *The New Yorker* (December 4, 2006), 74–79; "Over-Sexed and Over Here: The 'Tarty' Bratz Doll."

241   *Approximately two billion*   Ramin Setoodeh, "Get Ready to Rumble," *Newsweek* (December 11, 2006), 46.

242   *Today, yes, career*   Quoted in "Over-Sexed and Over Here." *Daily Mail*.

242   *These experts put*   Ibid.

242   *Your hair is*   Setoodeh and Yabroff, "Princess Power."

242   *Costumes differ with*   Disney Princess, official Web site, http://disney.go.com/princess/ (accessed March 7, 2008); Ramin Setoodeh and Jennie Yabroff, "Princess Power," *Newsweek* (November 26, 2007), 66–67.

242   *Even those who*   Disney Princess Web site.

Chapter 19: Missing at the Multiplex

245   *Where are all*   Sarah Voorhees, "Where Are All the Girl Ninjas? Sexist Stereotypes Pervade Children's Media," AlterNet (February 22, 2000), http://www.alternet.org/module/printversion/77347 (accessed March 8, 2008).

245   *We know that*   Geena Davis, "Where Are the Girls? It's Time to Take Notice of Gender Imbalance in Films," Common Sense Blog, http://www.commonsenseblog.org/archives/2006/02/where_are_the_g.php (accessed March 8, 2008).

245   *[B]oys are the*   Katha Pollitt, "The Smurfette Principle," *New York Times* (April 7, 1991), 6, 21.

246   *No, no, not us*   Davis, "Where Are the Girls?"

246   *They have no*   Voorhees, "Where Are All the Girl Ninjas?" Quoted in Lynn Ziegler, "On Screen Sex Ratios Add Up to One Big Minus," Women's eNews (April 2, 2008), http://www.womensenews.org./articles.cfm?aid=3550.

246   *Over the past*   Barbara Meltz, "G-Rated Movies Favor Boys, a New Study Says," *Boston Globe* (February 9, 2006), http://www.boston.com/yourlife/family/articles/2006/02/09/g_rated_movies_favor_boys_a_new_study_says/ (accessed February 14, 2009).

247   *G-rated movies*   Nancy Signorelli, Ph.D., "A Content Analysis: Reflections of Girls in the Media," Kaiser Family Foundation (1997).

247   *In the opening*   David Edelstein, "Ugly Disemboweled Americans," *New York* magazine (December 4, 2006), 85.

248   Hostel *earned nineteen*   Rachel Corbett, "Torture Porn Makers Shrug Off the Label," Women's eNews (March 18, 2008), http://www.womensenews.org/article/cfm/dyn/aid/3531.

248   *Some of these*   Quoted in "Giving 'Chick Flicks' Flack," Salon.com, http://www.salon.com/mwt/broadsheet/2005/11/13/chick_flicks/index.html (accessed March 3, 2008).

250   *We have the*   Diane Negra, "Quality Postfeminism?" *Genders* (2004), 4.

251   *Movies featuring black*   Jeremy W. Peters, "An Image Popular in Films Raises Some Eyebrows in Ads," *New York Times* (August 1, 2006), http://www.nytimes.com/2006/08/01/business/media/01adco.html?scp=1&sq=an%20image%20popular%20in%20films&st=cse (accessed January 16, 2007).

252   *When Halle Berry*   "Hattie or Halle...And the Oscar Goes To...?" BlackSeek.com, http://www.blackseek.com/articles/2002/03/mr_halle_berry.htm (accessed March 13, 2008); Stacy L. Smith, Ph.D., "Asymmetrical Academy Awards? A Look at Gender Imbalance in Best Picture Nominated Films from 1977–2006," Annenberg School for Communication (2007).

252   *What's of specific*   Sharon Waxman, "Hollywood's Shortage of Female Power," *New York Times* (April 26, 2007), http://www.nytimes.com/2007/04/26/movies/26wome.html?scp=1&sq=hollywood's%20shortage%20of%20female&st=cse (accessed December 15, 2008); Waxman, "Hollywood's Shortage of Female Power," E1. Amy Pascal is still cochairwoman of Sony.

252   *Whether or not Warner*   Josh Tyler, "Women Kicked Out of the Movies," Cinema Blend (October 11, 2007), http://www.cinemablend.com/new/Women-kicked-outOfMovies-6613.html (accessed March 13, 2008). Although Jeff Robinov denied making the statement, it has been widely accepted and reported.

252   *A review of*   Manohla Dargis, "An American Primitive, Forged in a Crucible of Blood and Oil," *New York Times* (December 26, 2007), http://movies.nytimes.com/2007/12/26/movies/26bloo.html? (accessed Febuary 15, 2008).

252   *I feel like it's*   Waxman, "Hollywood's Shortage of Female Power."

253   *You don't see*   Nancy Vialatte, "As the Ranks of Top Female Execs Dwindle What's to Become of the Chick Flick?" *Hollywood Wire Tap* (April 16, 1997).

253   He's Just Not   Manohla Dargis, "Young Women Forever Stuck at Square One in the Dating Game," *New York Times* (February 6, 2009), C10.

253   *All you have*   Manohla Dargis, "Is There a Real Woman in This Multi-plex?" *New York Times* (May 4, 2008), 3.

253   Spider-Man, *the first*   "Hold On. The Superhero Genre?" Brandweek (June 9, 2008), http://www.brandweek.com/bw/esearch/article_display .jsp?vnu_content_id=1003813659 (accessed June 1, 2008).

254   *In an Internet*   Quoted in Ramin Setoodeh, "Sexism and 'Sex and the City,'" *Newsweek* (June 16, 2008), 46.

254   *Anthony Lane wrote*   Anthony Lane, "Carrie," *The New Yorker* (June 9 and 16, 2008), 112.

254   *The entire industry*   Lisa de Moraes, "Female Characters Made to Suffer for Our Art," *Washington Post* (September 18, 2005), N01.

255   *Lorelai reunited with*   Virginia Heffernan, "A Series Changes Horses and the Ride Gets Bumpy," *New York Times* (November 7, 2006), E1.

255   *In* Women's Murder   Alessandra Stanley, "Homicide and Heels," *New York Times* (October 12, 2007), B1.

256   *And a fertility*   Alessandra Stanley, "New Series: Women Test Mettle and Metal," *New York Times* (September 26, 2007), E1; "Homicide and Heels," E1.

257   *When we compare*   Catherine Orenstein, "What Carrie Could Learn from Mary," *New York Times* (September 5, 2003), http://query.nytimes.com/ gst/fullpage.html?res=9D07E2DB1138F936A3575AC0A9659C8B63&sec= &spon=&&scp=1&sq=what%20carrie%20could%20learn&st=cse (accessed March 10, 2008).

258   *Even the epitome*   Sarah Hepola, "Candice Bergen's Casting Problem," *New York Times* (May 25, 2003), http://query.nytimes.com/gst/fullpage .html?res=9C01EFDC113EF936A15756C0A9659C8B63&scp=1&sq=candice %20bergen's%20casting&st=cse (accessed March 12, 2008).

258   *Carrie isn't free*   A similar point is made by Orenstein, "What Carrie Could Learn from Mary."

258   *And even Samantha*   Diane Negra, "Quality Postfeminism? *Genders Online Journal* (2004), http://www.genders.org/g39/g39_negra.html. For a further discussion of *SATC*, see Wendy Shalit, "Sex, Sadness and the City," *City Journal* (Autumn 1999), http://www.city-journal.org/html/9_4_a4.html (accessed March 10, 2008); see also: Kay S. Hymowitz, "Scoring on Sex and the City," *City Journal* (Autumn 2003), http://www.city.journal.org/html/13 _4_urbanities-scoring.html (accessed March 17, 2008).

259   *In a recent*   Transcript of the *Today Show* (October 5, 2007).

259   *You don't have*   Theresa O'Rourke, "Are You a Fembot?" *Marie Claire* (November 2007), http://www.marieclaire.com/sex-love/relationship-issues/ articles/fembot-woman?click=main_sr (accessed February 14, 2009).

260   *You always hear*   Jennifer L. Pozner, "The Unreal World," *Ms.* magazine (Fall 2004), http://www.msmagazine.com/fall2004/unrealworld.asp.

260   *Hopefuls are "decked*   Ibid.

260   *In general, say*   Quoted in Kristin Dietsche, "Who Will Love Joe Millionaire for Who He Really Is?" *ArtSpike* (March 5, 2003), http://www.artspike.org/publish/public_html/article.php?sid=1750 (accessed March 14, 2008).

261   *And in* For   Dietsche, "Who Will Love Joe Millionaire for Who He Really Is?"; Pozner, "The Unreal World."

261   *The real concern*   Pozner, "The Unreal World."

263   *Those allowed to*   Sam Dillon, "Sorority Evictions Raise Messy Issue of Looks and Bias," *New York Times* (February 25, 2007), A1.

263   *TV doesn't live*   Quoted in Sandra Kobrin, "Prime-Time TV Sweeps Women to All-Time Lows," Women's eNews (April 25, 2007), http://www.womensnews.org/article.cfm/dyn.aid/3145/context/archive (accessed April 27, 2007).

Chapter 20: The Disappearing Girl

266   *Ubiquity is the*   Quoted in Louise Story, "Anywhere the Eye Can See, It's Likely to See an Ad," *New York Times* (January 15, 2007), http://www.nytimes.com/2007/01/15/business/media/15everywhere.html?scp=1&sq=anywhere%20the%20eye%20can%20see&st=cse (accessed January 16, 2007).

267   *Anne Frank girls*   Quoted in Guy Trebay, "Look at Me Please," *New York Times* (September 17, 2006), 1, 6.

267   *Not until the twenty-two-*   Eric Wilson, "When Is Thin Too Thin?" *New York Times* (September 21, 2006), G1, 7; Larry Rohter, "Burst of High-Profile Anorexia Deaths Unsettles Brazil," *New York Times* (December 30, 2006), A4; Eric Wilson, "U.S., Italy Addressing the Health of Models," *New York Times* (September 7, 2006), G5.

267   *And Lela Rose, Banana Republic*   "Zero—The Next New Size," Some Small Sense (October 10, 2006), http://somesmallsense.blogspot.com/2006/10/zero-next-new-size.html (accessed March 24, 2008); Rosemary Feitelberg, "Those Zeros Keep Adding Up," *Women's Wear Daily* (October 10, 2006), http://www.wws.com/issue/article/109843 (accessed December 15, 2008).

267   *[The m]ost famous*   Susanna Schrobsdorff, "Skinny Is the New Fat," *Newsweek* (October 30, 2006), 55; *Ladies' Home Journal*, Valerie Bertinelli, "I Love My New Body!" (April 2008); Nanci Hellmich, "Do Thin Models Warp

Girls' Body Image?" *USA Today* (September 26, 2006), http://www.usatoday
.com/news/health/2006-09-25-thin-models-x.htm (accessed March 21,
2008).

267   *Girls today, even*   Quoted in Hellmich, "Do Thin Models Warp Girls'
Body Image?"

268   *Six Ways to*   Sheila Gibbons, "RX for Teen in Diet Danger: Healthier
Magazines," Women's eNews, http://www.womensenews.org/article.cfm/
dyn/aid/3027 (accessed January 9, 2007).

268   *Oprah recently revealed*   Ibid.

268   *Some are trying*   "Zero—The Next New Size"; Hellmich, "Do Thin Models
Warp Girls' Body Image?"; "Is Dieting Advice from Magazines Helpful
or Harmful? Five-Year Associations with Weight-Control Behaviors and
Psychological Outcomes in Adolescents," *Pediatrics*, http://pediatrics
.aappublications.org/cgi/content/full/119/1/e30?maxtoshow=&HITS=
10&hits=10&RESULTFORMAT=&fulltext=is+dieting+advice+from+
magazines&searchid=1&FIRSTINDEX=0&sortspec=relevance&resource
type=HWCIT; Gibbons, "RX for Teens in Diet Danger."

268   *Those—like the majority*   But computer-altered images of models who
were average or a bit overweight actually led to a rise in body self-esteem.
Beth Krane, "Ultra-Thin Models May Hurt Women's Self-Esteem, Study
Finds," UConn Advance (December 11, 2006), http://advance.unconn
.edu/2006/061211/0612111.htm (accessed March 24, 2008); Liz Dittrich,
Ph.D., "About-Face Facts on the Media," http://www.about-face.org/r/facts/
(accessed December 6, 2006); National Eating Disorders Association, http://
www.nationaleatingdisorderers.org/p.asp?WebPage_ID=294 (accessed
March 21, 2008).

268   *So great is*   Phoebe Cramer, Ph.D., and Tiffany Seinwert, Ph.D., *Journal of
Applied Developmental Psychology* 19, no. 3 (1998): 429–51, http://
Filenames+/published/emeraldfulltest.articles/pdf/1421019501_ref.html;
"The Body Image Project," http://www.etfo.ca/issuesinEducation/Body/
Image/Pages/default.aspx; Dittrich, "About Face Facts on the Media."

268   *At least one out*   Hellmich, "Do Thin Models Warp Girls' Body Image?"

269   *In 2005 the NIH*   "Eating Disorders and Their Precursors," National Eating Disorders Association, http://www.nationaleatingdisorders.org/p.asp
?WebPageID=294&Profile-ID=41138 (accessed March 21, 2008); Council
on Size and Weight Discrimination, http://www.cswd.org/docs/kids.html
(accessed March 24, 2008).

270   *By May 1994*   Amy Spindler, "How Fashion Killed the Unloved Waif,"
New York Times (September 27, 1994), http://query.nytimes.com/gst/

fullpage.html?res=9A03EFD6133AF934A1575AC0A962958260 (accessed August 15, 2006).

271 *And looking at*   "But Thin Doesn't Sell Better: Body Anxiety and the Use of Unhealthy Models in Advertising," press release of the Economic and Social Research Council (October 2006), http://www.esrcsocietytoday.ac.uk/ESRCIntoCenter/PO/releases/2006/october/thin.aspx? (accessed March 24, 2008).

272 *Alex Kuczynski, author*   Alex Kuczynski, "A Woman's Work Is Never Done," *Vanity Fair* (September 2006); Catherine Orenstein, "Stepford Is Us," *New York Times* (June 9, 2004), A23.

272 *And on* The Swan   Jennifer Pozner, "Unreal World," http://www.msmagazine.com/fall/2004/unrealworldasp.

272 *The media pressures*   Jennifer Cognard-Black, Ph.D., "Extreme Make-over: Feminist Edition," *Ms.* magazine (Summer 2007), 47–49.

273 *All the styles*   Natasha Singer, "Is Looking Your Age Now Taboo?" *New York Times* (March 11, 2007), G1, 3.

273 *Some 11.7 million*   "US Use of Cosmetic Surgery Soars in 2007," report by the American Society for Aesthetic Plastic Surgery, *Health* (2008), http://news.xinhuanet.com/english/2008-03/04/content_7716870.htm (accessed March 27, 2008); "Huge Numbers Want Cosmetic Surgery, Study Finds," Science Daily (October 28, 2007), http://www.sciencedaily.com/releases/2007/10/071026162139.htm (accessed March 28, 2008).

274 *Andrew Rudnick, owner*   Jane Morrissey, "Having a Little Work Done (at the Mall)," *New York Times* (January 13, 2008), http://www.nytimes.com/2008/01/13/business/13sleek.html?scp=1&sq=having%20a%20little%20work%20done%20at%20the%20mall&st=cse (accessed March 28, 2008).

274 *I can be*   Ibid.

274 *Doctors in a wide*   Natasha Singer, "More Doctors Turning to the Business of Beauty," *New York Times* (November 30, 2006), A1, 26.

274 *Less common but*   Tanya Rivero and Joann Brady, "Florida Teen Dies After Complications During Breast Surgery," ABC News, http:///www.abcnews.go.com/GMA/PainManagement/story?id=4520099 (accessed March 27, 2008).

275 *Dissolve to your*   Natasha Singer, "Feel Pudgy? There's a Shot for That," *New York Times* (September 20, 2007), http://www.nytimes.com/2007/09/20/fashion/20skin.html?scp=1&sq=feel%20pudgy?%20there's%20a%20shot%20for%20that&st=cse (accessed March 28, 2008).

275 *It is an unfortunate*   Natasha Singer, "For Top Medical Students, an Attractive Field," *New York Times* (March 19, 2008), A1, 12.

275   *One quarter of*   Lesley-Anne Reed, "More Youths Go Under the Knife," *Arkansas Traveler* (October 24, 2003), http://highbeam.com/doc/1P1-68883159.html (accessed March 28, 2008).

276   *Mothers sometimes give*   Ibid.

276   *While there's no regulation*   Scott L. Spear, president of the ASPS, quoted in Sandra G. Boodman, "For More Teenage Girls, Adult Plastic Surgery," *Washington Post* (October 26, 2004), A01.

276   *Silicone implants taken*   Natasha Singer, "Implants Are Back, So Is the Debate," *New York Times* (May 24, 2007), G1, 5.

276   *Psychologist Ann Kearney-Cooke*   Quoted in Boodman, "For More Teenage Girls, Adult Plastic Surgery."

277   *There's often pressure*   Lisa Anderson, "Would You Have Cosmetic Surgery 'Down There'? *Chicago Tribune* (March 20, 2007), http://www.boomergirl.com/stories/2007/jul/20/would_you_have_cosmetic_surgery_down_there/ (accessed March 27, 2008).

277   *"But," she added*   Sandy Kobrin, "More Women Seek Vaginal Plastic Surgery," Women's eNews (November 14, 2004), http://www.womensenews.org/article.cfm/dyn/aid/2067/context/archive.

277   *It's only been*   "Who has the best post-pregnancy bod?," *US Weekly* Online (September 11, 2006), http://www.usmagazine.com/.

278   *The severe physical*   Natasha Singer, "Is the 'Mom Job' Really Necessary?" *New York Times* (October 4, 2007), http://www.nytimes.com/2007/10/04/fashion/04skin.html?scp=1&sq=is%20the%20'mom%20job'%20really%20necessary&st=cse (accessed March 28, 2008).

278   *It goes without*   See Singer, ibid., for a slightly different discussion of this topic.

279   *[As a society]*   Hellmich, "Do Thin Models Warp Girls' Body Image?"

Chapter 21: Toxic Males and Tarty Females

281   *Show us your*   David Picker, "A Halftime Ritual of Harassment," *New York Times* (November 20, 2007), D1.

282   *All men must*   "Bush's Basket: Why the President Had to Show His Balls," in Laura Flanders, ed., *The W Effect* (New York: Feminist Press, 2004), 176.

282   *The worst insult*   Author interview with Robert Jensen, 2007.

282   *Men are defined*   Robert Jensen, "The High Cost of Manliness," AlterNet (September 8, 2006), http://www.alternet.org/sex/41356/the high cost of _manliness/ (accessed March 28, 2007).

283 *No one would call*   Lisa Bennett, "'Hunting Bambi': Violence Against Women for Profit and Fun?" *NOW Newsletter* (July 24, 2003), http://www .now.org/issues/violence/072403violence.html (accessed December 8, 2008); Hunting for Bambi Web site, http://www.huntingforbambi.com/ (accessed May 1, 2008).

283 *In covering*   Kristen Kidder, "Free Publicity for Misogyny," AlterNet (August 28, 2003), http://www.alternet.org/module/printversion/16681 (accessed April 28, 2008); John E. Glass, Ph.D., "Hunting for Bambi. Hoax? Reality? Does It Matter?" CommonDreams.org (August 1, 2003), http:// www.commondreams.org/views03/0801-05.htm (accessed April 28, 2008).

283 *Images of men*   "Love Your Body: Offensive Ads," NOW Foundation, http://loveyourbody.nowfoundation.org/offensiveads/html (accessed April 2, 2008).

285 *Hip-hop began*   Ayanna, "The Exploitation of Women in Hip-Hop Culture," www.mysistahs.org/features/hiphop.htm (accessed April 2, 2008).

285 *If a man*   Ayanna, "The Exploitation of Women in Hip-Hop Culture"; Edward Armstrong, "Gangsta Misogyny: A Content Analysis," http://www. albany.edu/scj/jcjpc/vol8is2/armstrong.html.

285 *Their lyrics turn*   "Analysis of the Portrayals of Violence Against Women in Rap Music," *Journal of Criminal Justice and Popular Culture* 8 (2002): 96–126.

285 *He's reflecting what's*   Quoted in "Madonna Mauls Eminem's Critics," BBC News (February 20, 2001), http://news.bbc.co.uk/1/hi/entertainment/ 1180471.stm (accessed April 4, 2008).

286 *In our new gender*   "T. Denean Sharpley-Whiting Discusses Hip Hop's Attitude Toward Women," *California Literary Review* (June 15, 2007), http:// calitreview.com/225.

286 *Not all rap*   Jensen, "The High Cost of Manliness."

286 *The exploitation of*   Erik Eckholm, "Rap Fan Asks Hard Questions About the Music He Loves," *New York Times* (December 24, 2006), B14.

287 *Nikki, a thirty-year old*   Quoted in Ayanna, "The Exploitation of Women in Hip-Hop Culture."

287 *And while numerous*   Michael Cobb and Bill Bosettcher, "Ambivalent Sexism and Misogynistic Rap Musics: Does Exposure to Eminem Increase Sexism?" *Journal of Applied Social Pyschology* 37 (December 2007): 3025.

287 *It's awesome," said*   Quoted in Stephen A. Crockett Jr., "For Young Fans, the Name of the Video Game Is Gore," *Washington Post* (August 24, 2002), A01.

288 *And instead of* Kim Gregson, "Seduced: Sexism and Sex Appeal in Electronic Gaming" (October 2, 2007), http://www.kimgregson.com/pmwiki/pmwiki.php?n=WimerAndrewS.WimerAndrewS (accessed October 2, 2007).

288 *The level of* Crockett, "For Young Fans, the Name of the Video Game Is Gore."

288 *One way is* Daphne White, "A Look At..." *Washington Post* (August 13, 2000), B03.

288 *[E]very day millions* "MediaWise Video Game Report Card," National Institute on Media and the Family (December 19, 2002), http://www.mediafamily.org/research/vgrc_index.shtml (accessed November 27, 2006).

289 *One reviewer, defending* Quoted in Tracy Clark-Flory, "Grand Theft Misogyny," Salon.com (May 3, 2008), http://www.salon.com/mwt/broadsheet/2008/05/03/gta/index.html (accessed May 27, 2008).

289 *Video games also may* "APA Calls for Reduction of Violence in Interactive Media Used by Children and Adolescents," APAOnline (August 17, 2005), http://www.apa.org/releases/videoviolence05.html (accessed April 7, 2008); Jonathan D. Glater, "Lawyers See a Pay Day in Game's Hidden Sex Scenes," *New York Times* (June 24, 2008), A1; Eric Uhlmann and Jane Swanson, "Exposure to Violent Video Games Increases Automatic Aggressiveness," *Journal of Adolescence* 27 (2004): 41–52.

289 *Maintaining hegemony over* John Stoltenberg, *What Makes Pornography Sexy?* (New York: Milkweed, 1993), 7.

289 *Although the word* Karen A. Sherry, "Tales from the Vault: Searching for Early American Erotica," Common, place 4 (April 2004), http://www.common-place.org/vol-04/no-03/tales/ (accessed April 9, 2008).

290 *During the 1980s* Frank Rich, "Naked Capitalists," *New York Times* (May 20, 2001), http://query.nytimes.com/gst/fullpage.html?res=9D04E0DD173AF933A15756C0A9679C8B63&scp=1&sq=naked%20capitalists&st=cse (accessed April 1, 2008).

290 *Porn doesn't have* Quoted in Rich, "Naked Capitalists."

290 *My favorite movie* Quoted in George E. Curry, "A New Book on Clarence 'The Lawn Jockey' Thomas," *ChickenBones: A Journal of Literary and Artistic African-American Themes*, http://www.nathanielturner.com/dividedsoulofclarencethomas.htm (accessed December 19, 2008).

291 *The panelists at* Video of the "National Feminist Conference on Pornography and Popular Culture," Wheelock College (March 24, 2007).

291 *As one member* Ibid.

291 *The distorted message* Ibid.

292　*Other research posits*　　Author interview with Robert Jensen; James Check and Ted Guloein, "Reported Proclivity for Coercive Sex Following Repeated Exposure to Sexually Violent Pornography," in Dof Zillman (ed.), *Pornography: Recent Research, Interpretations and Policy Considerations* (Hillside, NJ: Lawrence Erlbaum), 159–184.

292　*First, many women*　　Neil Malamuth et al., "Pornography and Sexual Aggression: Are There Reliable Effects and Can We Understand Them?" *Annual Review of Sex Research* II (2000): 26–94.

293　*They go around*　　Quoted in Anna Quindlen, "Public & Private; And Now, Babe Feminism," *New York Times* (January 19, 1994), A22, http://query.nytimes.com/gst/fullpage.html?res=9804E6DE1430F93AA25752C0A962958260 (accessed April 11, 2006).

293　*Being sex-positive*　　Quoted in D. Parvaz, "Be 'Sex Positive' and Fear No Pleasure," *Seattle Post-Intelligencer* (November 21, 2003), http://www.seattlepi.com/lifestyle/149186_sexpositive.html (accessed April 10, 2008).

293　*[m]asturbation is a*　　*The New Our Bodies, Ourselves* (New York: Simon & Schuster, 1984), 166.

294　*I think of*　　Quoted in Jennifer Baumgardner and Amy Richards, *Manifesta* (New York: Farrar, Straus & Giroux, 2000), 66.

294　*You don't have to support*　　Jennifer Pozner in *Ms.* magazine, http://www.msmagazine.com/arts/chat/2004-12-03-pozner.asp (accessed October 24, 2006).

294　*We should try*　　National Feminist Conference (March 24, 2007).

295　*You're supporting an*　　Robert Jensen, in interview with the author.

295　*It's her choice*　　Speaking on *Anderson Cooper 360*, CNN (March 10, 2008).

295　*Don't prostitutes own*　　John Stossel, "Defending the D.C. Madam," ABC News (May 1, 2007), http://abcnews.go.com/print?id=3105239 (accessed April 13, 2008).

296　*And girls are*　　"Teen Girls' Stories of Sex Trafficking in U.S.," ABC News (February 9, 2006), http://abcnews.go.com/print?id=1596778 (accessed April 14, 2008).

296　*It's the men*　　Melissa Farley and Victor Malarek, "The Myth of the Victimless Crime," *New York Times* (March 12, 2008), A27.

296　*In one study*　　John J. Potterat et al., "Mortality in a Long-Term Open Cohort of Prostitute Women," *American Journal of Epidemiology* 159 (2004): 778–785; Melissa Farley, "Prostitution of Five Countries: Violence and Post Traumatic Stress Disorder," *Feminism and Psychology* 8 (1998): 405–426.

297   *Because most prostitutes*   Nicholas D. Kristof, "The Pimps' Slaves," *New York Times* (March 16, 2008), A15.

297   *Not one of the 250*   Ibid.

298   *Bad Girl*   Clark Hoyt, "So Much Sex, but What's Fit to Print?" *New York Times* (March 23, 2008), http://www.nytimes.com/2008/03/23/opinion/23pubed.html?scp=1&sq=so%20much%20sex,%20but%20what's%20fit%20to%20print&st=cse (accessed April 14, 2008); Andrea Peyser, "Boo-Hoo! Don't Shed Any Tears for This Busty Brat," *New York Post* (March 14, 2008), 1.

298   *[M]en are pretty dumb*   Quoted in Tom Head, "The Trouble with Prostitution," About.com: Civil Liberties, http://civilliberty.about.com/b/2008/03/17/the-trouble-with-prostitution.htm (accessed April 13, 2008).

298   *It's a lesson many*   *Reasonable Reasons to Wait* (student workbook) 6, quoted in "Common Characteristics of Fear-Based, Abstinence-Only Until Marriage Curricula," http://www.communityactionkit.org/index.cfm?pageId=895 (accessed April 16, 2008).

298   *Deep down, you*   Ibid.

298   *Evangelical Mike Mathews*   Mike Mathews, "Finding True Love, Is He Mr. Right? Is She the One?" LoveMatters.com, http://www.prolife.com/SexyFashions.htm (accessed April 25, 2008).

299   *I love sex*   Sharon Waxman, "The Graying of Naughty," *New York Times* (December 31, 2006), Sect. 9, 1, 5.

299   *And* Tech Digest   "Peekaboo Pole Dancing Concept Game," *Tech Digest* (April 14, 2008), http://www.techdigest.tv/2008/04/peekaboo_poll_d.html (accessed April 21, 2008); Tina Kelly, "Pole Dancing Parties Catch On in Book Club Country," *New York Times* (February 24, 2007), http://www.nytimes.com/2007/02/24/nyregion/24pole.html?pagewanted=print (accessed April 15, 2008).

300   *A striking example*   Stephenie Meyer, *Twilight* (New York: Little, Brown, 2005), 272.

300   *Many young women*   Caroline Heldman, "Out of Body Image," *Ms.* magazine (Spring 2008), 52–55.

301   *It's empowering, it's*   Claire Hoffman, "Joe Francis: 'Baby Give Me a Kiss,'" LATimes.com (August 6, 2006), http://www.latimes.com/features/magazine/west/la-tm-gonewild32aug06,0,2664370.story (accessed February 21, 2007).

301   *In reality we're*   Jennifer L. Pozner, "Forum: Post Feminism, the Market and the Media," *Media and Gender Monitor* (October 2003).

302   *Anybody enjoys the*   Hoffman, "Joe Francis: 'Baby Give Me a Kiss.'" For a further discussion of this theme, see Ariel Levy, *Female Chauvinist Pigs* (New York: Free Press, 2005).

302   *I want everyone*   Hoffman, "Joe Francis: 'Baby Give Me a Kiss.'" *It isn't a question*. A similar point is made by Heldman, "Out of Body Image," 54.

Chapter 22: Desperately Seeking Self

303   *We may not*   Ariel Levy, "Life's A Bitch," *Conde Nast Archive* (February 2007), 287.

303   *My parents' generation*   Sandra Kobrin, "Teens Call Hypersexualized Media Images 'Normal,'" Women's eNews (October 2007), http://www .womensenews.org/article.cfm?aid=2940.

303   *Larger-than-life*   Susan Douglas, "Enough with the Celebutantes!" *In These Times* (August 1, 2006), http://www.inthesetimes.com/article/2734 (accessed April 26, 2008).

303   *Graydon Carter, editor*   "US Obsessed by 'Celeb' Culture," BBC News, http://news.bbc.co.uk/2/hi/entertainment/3708420.stm (accessed February 14, 2009).

304   *We want to live*   Hannah Thibodeaux, "Obsessed with Celebrities," *North Star News* (March 20, 2007), http://media.www.northstarnewsonline .com/media/storage/paper398/news/2007/03/20/Entertainment/Obsessed .With.Celebrities-2789667.shtml; Jonathan Yardley, "Why So Many Americans Desperately Want to Be Celebrities," WashingtonPost.com, http://www .washingtonpost.com/wp-dyn/cotent/article/2008/08/14AR2008081402576 .html (accessed April 26, 2008).

304   *And given the*   Jake Halpern, interviewed on National Public Radio by Tom Ashbrook (July 7, 2007).

304   *Back in 2004*   Jake Halpern, "Britney Spears and Breaking News," *Wall Street Journal* (October 8, 2007).

304   *In the first half*   Douglas, "Enough with the Celebutantes!"; Lynda Richardson, "Celebrity Weekly Shocker: Editor Is No Diva," *New York Times* (February 25, 2004), http://www.nytimes.com/2004/02/25/nyregion/ 25profile.html?ex=1237435200&en=42c033e565c729f0&ei=5070 (accessed April 25, 2008).

304   *VH1, formerly a*   Douglas, "Enough with the Celebutantes!"

305   *Typing in celebrity*   Computer search conducted by author on April 18, 2008.

305   *As the number*   Yardley, "Why So Many Americans Desperately Want to Be Celebrities."

305   *Hair stylists have*   Camille Sweeney, "A Girl's Life with Highlights," *New York Times* (April 3, 2008), C3.

305   *We feel we*   Calin Flora, "Seeing by Starlight: Celebrity Obsession," *Psychology Today,* http://www.psychologytoday.com/articles/pto-20040715-000004.html (accessed February 7, 2007).

306   *These anecdotal findings*   Shankar Vedantam, "Social Isolation Growing in U.S., Study Says," *Washington Post,* http://www.mitpressjournals.org/doi/abs/10.1162/dmal.9780262693646.229 (accessed April 28, 2008).

307   *We're pulled into*   Halpern quoted in Yardley. "Why So Many Americans Desperately Want to Be Celebrities" makes a similar point.

307   *Some commentators have*   Alex Williams, "Boys Will Be Boys, Girls Will Be Hounded," *New York Times* (February 17, 2008), Styles, 1.

307   *Jess is jealous*   OK Weekly (April 28, 2008), 52.

307   *Kate Hudson and*   Ibid., 9.

307   *Paris Hilton is*   US Weekly (May 5, 2008), 60.

307   *Camille Paglia loves*   National Public Radio show with Tom Ashbrook (July 17, 2007).

307   *Not since the*   "Celebrity Babies Becoming Big Business," *Cleveland Leader* (March 27, 2008), http://www.clevelandleader.com/node/5285 (accessed April 26, 2008).

308   *The one thing*   Gabriel Sherman, "US Editor Janice Min Dictates," *New York Observer* (July 2, 2006), 6.

308   *Halle Berry is*   Star (May 5, 2008), 60.

308   *Nicole Richie never*   Ibid.

308   *Gwen Stefani's baby*   Ibid.

308   *The tabloid goes*   Ibid.

308   *My passion is*   Us Weekly (May 5, 2008), 47.

308   *I can't imagine*   Karen Valby, "The Lady Vanishes," EW.com (September 17, 2004), http://www.ew.com/ew/articles/0.695237.00.html (accessed April 30, 2008); *In Touch Weekly* (May 5, 2008), 15.

309   *The seductive, picturesque*   For a longer discussion on this topic, see Susan Douglas and Meredith W. Michaels, *The Mommy Myth* (New York: Free Press, 2004).

Chapter 23: More Than a Few Good Women

311   *I had to read*   "The Mother of Feminism," Emily Brazelton, *New York Times Magazine* (December 31, 2006), 8–9.

312   *It wasn't her*   Ibid.

313   *Sexist media content*   Jennifer Pozner, "Media on the Feminist Agenda," TomPaine.com (November 13, 2006), http://www.tompaine.com/articles/ 2006/11/13/media_on_the_feminist_agenda.php (accessed November 15, 2006).

313   *Women own less*   S. Derek Turner, *Out of the Picture: Minority and Female TV Station Ownership in the United States* (New York: Free Press, 2006), 2.

313   *Even though I*   Author interview with Marlene Sanders.

313   *But the enthusiasm*   Sheila Gibbons, "Media Women at Standstill? More Waiting Won't Work," Women's eNews, http://www.womensenews.org/ article.cfm/dyn/aid/2927 (accessed May 2, 2008).

313   *Women currently make*   "Industry Statistics," Media Report to Women, http://www.mediareporttowomen.com/statistics.htm (accessed January 1, 2007).

314   *A simple count*   Ruth Davis Konigsberg, "3 to 1—Male Writers Dominate 'Thought Leader' Magazines," Women's Media Center (October 3, 2006), http://www.womensmediacenter.com/ex/100306.html (accessed February 22, 2008).

314   *Another counting project*   Hannah Seligson, "One by One, Women Count Bylines," Women's eNews (December 26, 2005), http://www.womensenews .org/article.cfm/dyn/aid/2581/context/archive (accessed February 5, 2007).

315   *And the bad*   "50 Best Journalists," Washingtonian.com, http://www .washingtonian.com/articles/businssscareers/1743.html (accessed February 15, 2009).

315   *Those who tell*   Pozner, "Media on the Feminist Agenda"; see also Pozner, "Power Shortage for Media Women," Fairness and Accuracy in Reporting (July/August 2001), http://www.fair.org/index.php?page=1074 (accessed May 2, 2008).

315   *With few women*   Glory E. Dharmaraj, "Global Media Monitoring Evaluated Role and Images of Women" (February 16, 2006).

315   *A Farewell Wish*   Jennifer L. Pozner, "What Happened to the Gender Gap?" in Laura Flanders (ed.), *The W Effect* (New York: Feminist Press, 2004), 202.

316 *For certain people* Quoted in Joe Hagan, "Alas, Poor Couric," *New York* magazine (July 16, 2007), 87.

316 *Why aren't we* Bob Herbert, "Why Aren't We Shocked?" *New York Times* (October 16, 2006), A22.

317 *And she was* Maureen Dowd, "A Flawed Feminist Test," *New York Times* (February 13, 2008), A23.

318 *We must refuse* Quoted in Nicholas D. Kristof, "Who Is More Electable?" *New York Times* (February 7, 2008), A31.

318 *We can make* Nicholas D. Kristof, "Our Racist, Sexist Selves," *New York Times* (April 6, 2008), A14.

318 *A strange facet* Eric Boehlert, "For Chris Matthews, Misogyny Pays Handsomely," AlterNet (April 17, 2008), http://www.alternet.org/story/82744/for_chris_matthews,_misogyny_pays_handsomely/.

319 *Nancy Shrew* Deborah Orin-Eilbeck, "Call Her 'Nancy Shrew,'" *New York Post*, http://www.nycivic.org/artilces/061117.html (accessed November 20, 2006).

319 *Wicked Witch of* Fox News *Special Report*, http://mediamatters.org/items/200611180002?f=s_search (accessed November 20, 2006).

319 *When Condoleezza Rice* Robin Givhan, "Condoleezza Rice's Commanding Clothes," *Washington Post* (February 25, 2005), C01.

320 *Her hair—clipped* Robin Givhan, "A Troubling Decision by Harriet Miers," *Washington Post* (October 28, 2005), C02.

Conclusion: The Change We Need

324 *In discussing her* John Heilemann, "2012? You Betcha!" *New York* magazine (November 10, 2008), 26.

326 *And she seemed* Mark Leibovich, "Among Rock-Ribbed Fans of Palin, Dudes Rule," *New York Times* (October 19, 2008), A25.

329 *Money for school* Paul Krugman, "The Destructive Center," *New York Times* (February 9, 2009), A23.

330 Man Caves, *a* "Guys Gone Wild: 'Man Caves' Craze Takes Off," *Home and Garden*, MSNBC.com, http://www.msnbc.msn.com/id/28885927/ (accessed February 5, 2009).

330 *I had to have* Quoted in Charles Memminger, "Cave Men," *Star Bulletin* 12 (November 18, 2007), http://archives.starbulletin.com/2007/11/18/features/memminger.html (accessed February 18, 2009).

330   *And what about*   "Ninety Percent of Adolescent Girls Experience Sexual Harassment," Feminist Majority Foundation (May 20, 2008), http://www.feminist.org/news/newsbyte/uswirestory, asp?id=11031.

Resources

I'm grateful to Jennifer Baumgardner and Amy Richards, *Grassroots* (New York: Farrar, Straus & Giroux, 2005), and to Lis Wiehl, *The 51% Minority* (New York: Ballantine Books, 2007), for their lists of Web sites, some of them included here.

BIBLIOGRAPHY

Allyn, David. *Make Love Not War: The Sexual Revolution: An Unfettered History.* New York: Routledge, 2002.

Asbell, Bernard. *The Pill.* New York: Random House, 1995.

Badinter, Elisabeth. *The Unopposite Sex: The End of the Gender Battle.* New York: Harper & Row, Inc., 1989.

Bank, Barbara J., and Peter M. Hall. *Gender, Equity and Schooling: Policy and Practice.* New York: Garland Publishing, 1997.

Barnes, Annie S. *Single Parents in Black America.* Lima: Wyndham Hall Press, 1987.

Barnett, Rosalind, and Carly Rivers. *Same Difference: How Gender Myths Are Hurting Our Relationships, Our Children, and Our Jobs.* New York: Basic Books, 2004.

Baumgardner, Jennifer, and Amy Richards. *Manifesta: Young Women, Feminism and the Future.* New York: Farrar, Straus & Giroux, 2000.

———. *Grassroots: A Field Guide for Feminist Activism.* New York: Farrar, Straus & Giroux, 2005.

Beauvior, Simone de. *The Second Sex.* New York: Alfred A. Knopf, 1971.

Belkin, Lisa. *Life's Work: Confessions of an Unbalanced Mom.* New York: Simon & Schuster, 2002.

Berg, Barbara J. *The Remembered Gate: Origins of American Feminism.* New York: Oxford University Press, 1978.

———. *The Crisis of the Working Mother: Resolving the Conflict Between Family and Work.* New York: Summit Books, 1986.

———. *Nothing to Cry About.* New York: Seaview Books, 1981.

———. *The Women's Movement and Young Women Today.* Englewood Cliffs, NJ: Enslow Press, 2000.

Bergmann, Barbara R., and Suzanne W. Helburn. *America's Childcare Problem: The Way Out.* New York: Palgrave, 2001.

Bernard, Jessie. *Academic Women.* New York: New American Library, 1964.

Boston Women's Health Book Collective. *The New Our Bodies, Ourselves.* New York: Simon & Schuster, 1975.

Boushey, Heather, et al. *Hardships in America: The Real Story of Working Families.* Washington, DC: Economic Policy Institute, 2001.

Boyle, Karen. *Media and Violence.* London: Sage Publications, 2005.

Brazelton, T. Berry. *Infants and Mothers.* New York: Dell Publishing, 1969.

Bright, Susie. *On Sex, Motherhood, Porn and Cherry Pie.* New York: Thunder's Mouth Press, 2003.

Brizendine, Louann, M.D. *The Female Brain.* New York: Morgan Road Books, 2005.

Brock, David. *Blinded by the Right.* New York: Three Rivers Press, 2005.

Brooks, Andree Aelion. *Children of Fast-Track Parents.* New York: Viking, 1989.

Brumberg, Joan Jacobs. *Fasting Girls: History of Anorexia Nervosa.* New York: New American Library, 1989.

Burkett, Larry. *Women Leaving the Workplace.* Chicago: Moody Press, 1995.

Carlson, Dale. *Girls Are Equal Too.* Canada: McClelland & Steward, Ltd., 1973.

Carter, Jimmy. *Our Endangered Values.* New York: Simon & Schuster, 2005.

Coalition for Women Prisoners. *My Sister's Keeper.* New York: Correctional Association of New York, 2008.

Cobble, Dorothy Sue. *The Other Women's Movement: Workplace Justice and Social Rights in Modern America.* Princeton, NJ: Princeton University Press, 2005.

Coles, Robert. *The Moral Life of Children.* Boston: Houghton Mifflin, 1986.

Conason, Joe. *Big Lies.* New York: Thomas Dunne Books, 2003.

Coontz, Stephanie. *The Way We Never Were.* New York: Basic Books, 2000.

Cott, Nancy. *The Grounding of Modern Feminism.* New Haven: Yale University Press, 1989.

Davis, Flora. *Moving the Mountain: The Women's Movement in America Since 1960.* New York: Simon & Schuster, 1991.

Deak, JoAnn. *How Girls Thrive.* Washington, DC: NAIS, 1998.

Deutsch, Helene. *The Psychology of Women.* New York: Grunner & Stratton, 1944.

Dixon, Wheeler Winston, ed. *Film and Television After 9/11.* Carbondale: Southern Illinois University, 2004.

Djerassi, Carl. *The Pill, Pygmy Chimps, and Degas' Horse.* New York: Basic Books, 1992.

Douglas, Susan. *Where the Girls Are: Growing Up Female with the Mass Media.* New York: Penguin, 1994.

Douglas, Susan, and Meredith W. Michaels. *The Mommy Myth.* New York: Free Press, 2004.

DuBois, Ellen Carol, and Lynn Dumenil. *Through Women's Eyes*. New York: St. Martin's Press, 2005.

Epstein, Cynthia Fuchs. *Woman's Place: Options and Limits in Professional Careers*. Berkeley: University of California Press, 1998.

Erikson, Kai T. *Wayward Puritans: A Study in the Sociology of Deviance*. New York: Macmillan, 1966.

Evans, Sara. *Born for Liberty: A History of Women in America*. New York: Free Press, 1989.

Faludi, Susan. *Backlash: The Undeclared War Against American Women*. New York: Crown, 1991.

Farrell, Amy Erdman. *Yours in Sisterhood: Ms. Magazine and the Promise of Popular Feminism*. Chapel Hill: University of North Carolina Press, 1998.

Feagin, Joe R. *Subordinating the Poor: Welfare and American Beliefs*. Englewood Cliffs, NJ: Prentice Hall, 1975.

Feldman, S., and Glen Elliott. *At the Threshold: The Developing Adolescent*. Cambridge: Harvard University Press, 1993.

Fels, Anna. *Necessary Dreams: Ambition in Women's Changing Lives*. New York: Anchor, 2004.

Firestone, Shulamith. *The Dialectic of Sex*. New York: William Morrow and Co., 1970.

Flanders, Laura, ed. *The W Effect: Bush's War on Women*. New York: Feminist Press, 2004.

Flippin, Royce, ed. *The Best American Political Writing*. New York: Thunder's Mouth Press, 2006.

Freedman, Estelle B., et al., eds. *The Lesbian Issue: Essays from* Signs. Chicago: University of Chicago Press, 1983.

Friedan, Betty. *The Feminine Mystique*. New York: Laurel, 1983.

Galician, Mary-Lou, and Debra L. Merskin, eds. *Critical Thinking About Sex, Love, and Romance in the Mass Media*. New York: Lawrence Erlbaum Associations, Inc., 2007.

Galinsky, Ellen. *Between Generations: The Stages of Parenthood*. New York: Times Books, 1981.

Goode, Erich, and Ben-Yehuda Nachman. *Moral Panics: The Social Construction of Deviance*. Cambridge: Blackwell Publishers, 1995.

Gordon, Linda. *Woman's Body, Woman's Right: Birth Control in America*. New York: Penguin Books, 1990.

Greenberg, Judith, ed. *Trauma at Home After 9/11*. Lincoln: University of Nebraska, 2003.

Greer, Germaine. *The Female Eunuch*. New York: McGraw-Hill, 1971.

Gregory, Raymond F. *Women and Workplace Discrimination*. New Brunswick, NJ: Rutgers University Press, 2003.

Gross, Michael. *The More Things Change: Why the Baby Boom Won't Fade Away*. New York: Cliff Street Books, 2002.

Hagen, Susan, and Mary Carouba. *Women at Ground Zero: Stories of Courage and Compassion*. Indianapolis: Alpha Books, 2002.

Hewlett, Sylvia Ann. *A Lesser Life: The Myth of Women's Liberation in America*. New York: William Morrow & Co., 1986.

Heywood, Leslie, and Jennifer Drake, eds. *Third Wave Agenda*. Minneapolis: University of Minnesota Press, 1997.

Hochschold, Arlie Russsel. *The Commercialization of Intimate Life: Notes from Home and Work*. Los Angeles: University of California Press, 2003.

Hollows, Joanne. *Feminism, Femininity and Popular Culture*. Manchester: Manchester University Press, 2000.

Jones, Gerard. *Honey I'm Home! Sitcoms: Selling the American Dream*. New York: St. Martin's Press, 1992.

Kanowitz, Leo. *Women and the Law*. Albuquerque: University of New Mexico Press, 1968.

Kennedy, David M. *Birth Control in America*. New Haven: Yale University Press, 1973.

Kilbourne, Jean. *Can't Buy My Love: How Advertising Changes the Way We Think and Feel*. New York: Simon & Schuster, 1999.

Kitch, Carolyn. *The Girl on the Magazine Cover: The Origins of Visual Stereotypes in American Mass Media*. Chapel Hill: University of North Carolina Press, 2001.

Konopka, Gisela. *The Adolescent Girl in Conflict*. Englewood Cliffs, NJ: Prentice-Hall, 1977.

Krugman, Paul. *The Great Unraveling*. New York: Norton, 2004.

Lakoff, George. *Don't Think of an Elephant*. White River Junction, VT: Chelsea Green Publishing, 2004.

Lamb, Sharon, and Lyn Mikel Brown. *Packaging Girlhood: Rescuing Our Daughters from Marketers' Schemes*. New York: St. Martin's, 2006.

Lasch, Christopher. *The Culture of Narcissism*. New York: Warner Books, 1979.

Leach, Penelope. *Children First: What Our Society Must Do—And Is Not Doing—for Children Today*. New York: Knopf, 1994.

Lerner, Gerda. *The Female Experience*. New York: Oxford University Press, 1977.

Levin, Diane E., and Jean Kilbourne. *So Sexy So Soon: The New Sexualized Childhood and What Parents Can Do to Protect Their Kids*. New York: Ballantine Books, 2008.

Lopata, Helena Z. *Occupation Housewife*. New York: Oxford University Press, 1971.

Love, Barbara J. *Feminists Who Changed America, 1963–1975*. Carbondale: University of Illinois Press, 2006.

Lundberg, Ferdinand, and Marynia F. Farnham. *Modern Woman: The Lost Sex*. New York: Harper & Bros., 1947.

Mainiero, Lisa A., and Sherry E. Sullivan. *The Opt-Out Revolt*. Mountain View, CA: Davies-Black, 2006.

Marks, Lara V. *Sexual Chemistry: A History of the Contraceptive Pill*. New Haven, CT: Yale University Press, 2001.

May, Elaine Tyler. *Homeward Bound: American Families in the Cold War Era*. New York: Basic Books, 1989.

Melich, Tanya. *The Republican War Against Women*. New York: Bantam Books, 1992.

Micklethwait, John, and Adrian Wooldridge. *The Right Nation: Conservative Power in America*. New York: Penguin, 2004.

Miller, Alice. *The Drama of the Gifted Child*. New York: Basic Books, 1990.

Miller, Mark Crispin. *Cruel and Unusual*. New York: Norton, 2004.

Mohr, James C. *Abortion in America: The Origins and Evolution of National Policy*. New York: Oxford University Press, 1978.

Nye, F. Ivan, and Lois Wadis Hoffman. *The Employed Mother in America*. Chicago: Rand McNally, 1963.

Oakley, Ann. *Woman's Work*. New York: Vintage House, 1979.

Olds, Sally Wendkos. *The Working Parents' Survival Guide*. New York: Bantam, 1983.

Olsen, Tillie. *Silences*. New York: Delta, 1979.

Orbach, Susie. *Hunger Strike*. New York: Penguin, 1993.

Orenstein, Peggy. *School Girls: Young Women and Self-Esteem and the Confidence Gap*. New York: Doubleday, 1994.

Peskowitz, Miriam. *The Truth Behind the Mommy Wars: Who Decides What Makes a Good Mother*. Emeryville, CA: Seal Press, 2005.

Reverby, Susan, and David Rosner, eds. *Health Care in America*. Philadelphia: Temple University Press, 1979.

Rice, David G. *Dual Career Marriage*. New York: Free Press, 1979.

Rich, Adrienne. *Of Women Born: Motherhood as Experience and Institution*. New York: Norton, 1976.

Richardson, Laurel, et al., eds. *Feminist Frontiers*. New York: McGraw-Hill, 2004.

Roberts, Sam. *Who We Are Now: The Changing Face of America in the Twenty-First Century*. New York: Times Books, 2004.

Rosenberg, Carroll Smith. *Disorderly Conduct*. New York: Alfred A. Knopf, 1986.

Rosenberg, Rosalind. *Beyond Separate Spheres: Intellectual Roots of Modern Feminism*. New Haven, CT: Yale University Press, 1982.

Sadker, Myra, and David Sadker. *Failing at Fairness: How America's Schools Cheat Girls*. New York: Charles Scribner's Sons, 1994.

Sanders, Darcie, and Martha M. Bullen. *Staying Home: From Full-Time Professional to Full-Time Parent*. Boulder: Spencer & Waters, 2001.

Schoen, Johanna. *Choice and Coercion: Birth Control, Sterilization and Abortion in Public Health and Welfare*. Chapel Hill: University of North Carolina Press, 2006.

Seifer, Nancy. *Nobody Speaks for Me: Self-Portraits of American Working Class Women*. New York: Simon & Schuster, 1979.

Shaevitz, Marjorie Hansen. *The Superwoman Syndrome*. New York: Warner Books, 1984.

Smith, John M. *Women and Doctors*. New York: Atlantic Monthly Press, 1992.

Solinger, Rickie. *Pregnancy and Power*. New York: New York University Press, 2007.

Sommers, Christina Hoff. *Who Stole Feminism?* New York: Touchstone, 1994.

Spigel, Lynn. *Make Room for TV: Television and the Family Ideal in Postwar America*. Chicago: University of Chicago Press, 1992.

Stacey, Judith, ed. *And Jill Came Tumbling After: Sexism in American Education*. New York: Dell, 1974.

Steinem, Gloria. *Moving Beyond Words*. New York: Simon & Schuster, 1994.

Steiner, Leslie Morgan, ed. *Mommy Wars*. New York: Random House, 2006.

Stone, Geoffrey R. *The Bill of Rights in the Modern State*. Chicago: University of Chicago Press, 1992.

Straight, Benjamin A. *The Two Finger Diet: How the Media Has Duped Women into Hating Themselves*. iUniverse Books, 2004.

Taylor, Ella. *Prime Time Families*. Berkeley: University of California Press, 1989.

Watkins, Elizabeth Siegal. *On The Pill. A Social History of Oral Contraceptives, 1950–1970*. Baltimore: Johns Hopkins University Press, 1998.

Wertz, Dorothy, and Richard Wertz. *Lying-In: A History of Childbirth in America*. New York: Schocken Books, 1979.

Whelehan, Imelda. *Overloaded: Popular Culture and the Future of Feminism*. London: Women's Press Ltd., 2000.

Wilson, Marie C. *Closing the Leadership Gap: Why Women Can and Must Help Run the World*. New York: Penguin Books, 2004.

Wolf, Naomi. *The Beauty Myth*. New York: Anchor, 1992.

Wykes, Maggie, and Barrie Gunter. *The Media and Body Image*. London: Sage Publications, 2005.

INDEX